Price Guide to
FLEA MARKET TREASURES

Price Guide to
FLEA MARKET
TREASURES

Harry L. Rinker, Jr.

Wallace-Homestead Book Company · Radnor, Pennsylvania

Published in Radnor, Pennsylvania 19089, by Wallace-Homestead,
a division of Chilton Book Company

Designed by Arlene Putterman
Manufactured in the United States of America

Library of Congress Cataloging in Publication Data
Rinker. Harry L., Jr.
Price guide to flea market treasures / Harry L. Rinker, Jr.
p.   cm.
Includes bibliographical references and index.
ISBN 0-87069-636-X (pbk.)
1. Flea markets—Prices—United States.   2. Americana—Catalogs.
I. Title.
HF5482.M54   1991
381″.192″0296—dc20   91—50431
CIP

1 2 3 4 5 6 7 8 9 0   0 9 8 7 6 5 4 3 2 1

Contents

Foreword

The Rinker-Prosser gene pool from which Harry Junior descends includes a "saver" gene and an "accumulator" gene. The "collector" gene is totally absent. Within our family, one either saves for the sake of saving (it's too good to throw out; I will never know when I will need it) with value not a factor, or accumulates by paying more attention to quantitiy (he who has the biggest pile when he dies wins) than to value.

Savers differ from collectors in that saving is a natural and neutral instinct while collecting is learned and aggressive. Harry Junior and I are not savers. Collectors differ from accumulators because they discriminate and limit. Accumulators see no limit to the amount or type of things to be accumulated. This is how Harry Junior and I think.

Frankly, I am surprised by this. Family history supports the argument that the accumulator gene skips a generation. There is little question in anyone's mind, including my own, that I am an accumulator. Harry Junior should have been a saver, but actually he is as much of an accumulator as I am. The lyrics of a popular country song say it best: "Where did I go wrong; where did he go right?"

An early indication of Harry Junior's accumulation tendencies occurred on Christmas Day 1980. Connie, Harry's stepmother, had waited in line for hours to buy a Star Wars wristwatch as one of Harry's Christmas presents. Christmas morning arrived. Harry Junior opened the package, was surprised and elated, and quickly carried his treasure off to his room. As we gathered around the dining room table to partake of Christmas dinner, Connie noticed that Harry Junior was not wearing his watch.

"Where's your new Star Wars watch, Harry?"

"It's in my room."

"What's wrong with it? Why aren't you wearing it?"

"Dad told me that the minute you remove something from its original packaging, you ruin its value. That watch is going to be worth money some day. I am not going to touch it."

Harry Junior was thirteen at the time. His room already was cluttered with objects that he had accumulated—things people gave him because it seemed the thing to do to the original packaging for most of his toys. A safety inspector would have declared his room a fire hazard.

Things got worse as Harry Junior became older. What was I to do? Lead by example? Do not do as I do, do as I say? I just sat back, watched, and repeated over and over again to myself, *This kid has a future.*

Never once did I suggest to Harry Junior that he should accumulate what I accumulate. Heaven forbid. I hardly needed a rival in my own house.

My advise was simple: Accumulate whatever *you* like. The joy comes from the act of doing. For once in his life, Harry Junior listened.

While the size of some of his piles rivals the size of some of my piles, our piles are quite different. His piles reflect his concerns and those of his generation just as mine do the same for me and my generation. What more can I ask? Things from his piles have appeared as illustrations in *Warman's Americana & Collectibles* and things from my piles appear as illustrations in this book. This is as it should be.

Harry Junior is a son that you could learn to hate—driven, independent, opinionated, stubborn, given to occasional excesses, and single-minded. He is a hustler of the first order. He can be charming when he wants, but deep within resides a mean streak of no small consequence. I do not know from whom he learned these characteristics. Certainly he did not learn them from me.

Although there is no doubt that Harry Junior is an accumulator, he has not yet developed a full-blown love affair with objects. This *Price Guide to Flea Market Treasures* is an attempt on my part to initiate a courtship between Harry Junior and objects. On more than one occasion when Harry Junior complained "This category does not turn me on," I replied, "Tough, do it anyway. It will eventually."

The lesson that Harry Junior must learn is to put aside his accumulating likes and prejudices. It is a rare accumulator, auctioneer, collector, or dealer who can do this. I want Harry Junior to recognize and accept the potential joy and enthusiasm that is inherent in every object, to feel as excited about an Avon bottle as he does about a *Star Wars* comic book. "Trust the Force, Harry Junior."

Those who see this book as Harry Junior following in my footsteps will be making a big mistake. First, the kid will never be good enough to fill my shoes. Second, he has no desire to wear "used" goods.

Harry Junior is Harry Junior. He is not a chip off the old block. He is a block unto himself. *Price Guide to Flea Market Treasures* is his book. If you like it, praise him. If you find fault, blame him. However, it is only fair to warn you that you will see much in Harry Junior's book that smacks of me. Harry Junior denies it is there. But I see it, my staff sees it, and others who have read the manuscript who know the both of us have seen it. This will not come as welcome news to some in the antiques and collectibles field. *Yes! There is another.*

I admit I kept a watchful eye and exercised my editorial prerogative from time to time. What father wouldn't? I have a strong sense of pride in this book that you are about to read and use.

Harry Junior prepared this book while working on his undergraduate degree in commercial and fine arts at Millersville University in Millersville, Pennsylvania. Whether or not it paves the way for Harry Junior and me to work together in the future remains an open question.

Harry Junior got a taste of the commitment and work involved in compiling price guides. It wasn't a bitter taste. However, this book did not challenge Harry Junior's design and artistic skills, areas where he feels strong, comfortable, and wants to develop further. Hopefully, we can find projects within the antiques and collectibles field that allow him to use these talents. I suspect we can.

I hope this is the first of many forewords that I will write for Harry Junior's books. I look forward to the day when his reputation is such that he will write a foreword for one of mine.

Harry L. Rinker
Vera Cruz, PA
May 1991

Acknowledgments

I want to thank Dad for never saying no to my accumulating. He turned his back on more than one occasion when he could and should have said, "Get rid of that junk." More than anyone, he taught me that treasure as well as beauty is in the eye of the beholder.

This book would not have been possible without the full support of the Rinker Enterprise staff, known affectionately in-house and throughout the trade as the Rinkettes. Ellen Schroy, Terese Oswald, Dana Morykan, Diane Sterner, and Jocelyn Butterer all contributed. Their presence is everywhere. Thanks for being so understanding.

My sincere thanks to all the promoters, managers, workers, dealers, collectors, and others at flea markets across the United States that took time to share their knowledge and their objects with me. The list is so large that one big thank you must suffice for everyone.

Finally, thank you for buying and using this book. It is my first effort. Hopefully, subsequent editions will appear. Your suggestions on ways to make the book better will be most appreciated. Are there flea markets that I left out of my top-twenty list that should be included? Are there categories that you would like to see covered, but were not? Do you have survival tips of which I have not thought? Send your comments to Harry L. Rinker, Jr., *Price Guide to Flea Market Treasures*, 5093 Vera Cruz Road, Emmaus, PA 18049.

Harry L. Rinker, Jr.
Millersville, PA
May 1991

Price Guide to
FLEA MARKET TREASURES

Introduction

As I was preparing the book proposal for this *Price Guide to Flea Market Treasures*, Harry L. Rinker, my dad, told me the following story.

When Dad was first approached to edit *Warman's Antiques and Their Prices*, the publisher gave him copies of several rival price guides and said, "Look them over and incorporate their best features in our guide. We have the second-best-selling guide in most markets, and I would like to retain that position." The owner obviously did not know Dad very well. *Second-best* is not a word in Dad's vocabulary except when referring to something or someone else.

"I prefer to set my own standards," my Dad replied to his publisher. "I will study the market, see what is needed, and do it. When it is done, it will be the best."

Dad immediately recognized that antiques and collectibles price guides were stuck in a rut. It was time for a major change, and he made it. The Warman format transformed the general price guide into a user's guide, in which you found information on history, books, periodicals, collector's clubs, reproductions, and more—in addition to price listings. His Warman guides are where you start but rarely where you end.

His story was a challenge. Just as general price guides were stuck in a rut in the early 1980's, flea market price guides had achieved the same status in the early 1990's. Dad's instructions were simple: "Do an overhaul. Create the flea market price guide that is needed in today's market."

As you will quickly discover, *Price Guide to Flea Market Treasures* is much more than just a list of objects and prices. It is a new concept.

The first section is an educational guide for flea marketeers. It helps you identify a "true" flea market, tells you how to find and evaluate flea markets, compiles a list of the top twenty flea markets nationwide, gives tips for surviving the flea market scene and honing your shopping skills, and provides some in-depth analysis of the flea market scene in the early 1990s.

Readers who have attended flea markets for several years will be tempted to skip this first section. If you do, you are making a mistake. The smart person in the antiques and collectibles field knows there is always something more to be learned. You may be surprised at what you do not know.

The second section is devoted to price listings by category. At first glance, it may appear similar to a standard antiques and collectibles price guide. Look again.

You will find many categories that are not in the general guides, e.g., "Dearly Departed." This book was prepared on the assumption that everything imaginable is going to turn up at a flea market. In some cases, imaginations ran wild.

In a few categories you will not find specific priced items. Instead you are provided with information that enables you to understand and deal with the category on a broad plain. In a few cases, you are referred to specialized books on the subject.

One of the wonderful aspects of the modern collecting market is the high level of organization. There are a wealth of collectors' clubs, newsletters, and periodicals designed to serve specific collecting interests. You will find these listed in their appropriate categories before the price listings.

Finally, you will find that the category introductions range from serious to humorous to sublime. If the key to a great flea market is that it evokes these emotions and more within you, why should this book do any less?

First, last, and foremost, flea markets are places of fun. The joy is in the collecting. Go and collect.

Part One
A FLEA MARKET
EDUCATION

What Is a Flea Market?

1

It is difficult to explain the sense of excitement and anticipation felt by collectors and dealers as they get ready to shop a flea market. They are about to undertake a grand adventure, a journey into the unknown. Flea markets turn the average individual into an explorer in search of buried treasure. The search is not without adversity, ranging from a hostile climate to intense competition as one waits with other collectors and dealers for the gates to open. Victory is measured in "steals" and bargains and in stories that can be shared at the end of the day over dinner with friendly rivals.

Flea markets provide the opportunity for prospective collectors to get their feet wet in the exciting world of antiques and collectibles and for novice dealers to test their merchandise and selling skills at minimal expense. Many "first" contacts, some of which last a lifetime, are made between and among collectors and dealers. More than any other aspect of the antiques and collectibles trade, the flea market is the one forum where everyone is on equal footing.

Before discussing how to find, evaluate, and survive flea markets, it is important to understand *exactly* what a flea market is, how it fits into the antiques and collectibles market, and the many variations that exist. This is the first step to identifying the flea markets that are most likely to provide the greatest opportunities for you.

Defining a Flea Market

Few terms in the antiques and collectibles field are as difficult to define as *flea market*. If you visit the Rose Bowl Flea Market in Pasadena, California, you will find discontinued and knockoff merchandise, handmade crafts, clothing (from tube socks to dresses), home care items, plants of all types, and specialty foods more in evidence than antiques and collectibles. On the other hand, if you visit the Ann Arbor Antiques Market in Michigan, you will find primarily middle- and upper-level antiques and collectibles. Both are flea markets, yet they are light years apart.

The flea market concept is generations old. As it spread throughout the world, each country changed and adapted the form to meet its own particular needs. Regional differences developed. In New England, the Mid-Atlantic states, and throughout the Midwest, the term generally is used to describe a place where antiques and collectibles are sold. In the South and Southwest the term is more loosely interpreted, with emphasis on secondhand and discounted goods.

It is not hard to see where the confusion originates. Check the dictionary definition for *flea market*. *Webster's Ninth New Collegiate Dictionary* (Springfield, MA: Merriam-Webster, Inc., 1984) defines a flea market as "a usually open-air market for secondhand articles and antiques." Individuals involved with antiques and collectibles make a big distinction between secondhand, (recycled or reusable goods) and antiques and collectibles. Although the dictionary may lump them together, collectors and dealers clearly differentiate one from the other. The flea markets described in this book fit a much more narrow definition.

When collectors use the term flea market, they mean *a regularly scheduled market,*

either indoors or outdoors, in which the primary goods offered for sale are those defined by the trade as antiques or collectibles . Occasionally, you will find some handcrafted products and "used" goods among the offerings, especially in the seasonal and roadside flea markets where professional flea market dealers mix with individuals doing them on a one-shot basis.

The problem with trying to define flea market, even when limited to the antiques and collectibles sector, is that a multiplicity of flea market types exist. There are the great seasonal flea markets such as Renninger's Extravaganza (Kutztown, Pennsylvania) and Brimfield's (Brimfield, Massachusetts), the monthlies such as the Metrolina Expo (Charlotte, North Carolina), and numerous weeklies scattered across the country. Personally, I feel that the Atlantique City market held in March each year is really a flea market rather than the "show" it purports to be.

One of the best ways to understand what an antiques and collectibles flea market encompasses is to discuss how it differs from three other closely related institutions in the antiques and collectibles trade: the mall, garage sale, and show. On the surface the differences may appear subtle. However, they are significant to collectors and dealers.

Prior to the arrival of the mall, there was a clearly defined ladder of quality within the antiques and collectibles community which progressed from garage sale or country auction to flea market to small show to major show or shop. This is how most goods moved through the market. This is the route many dealers used to establish themselves in the trade. Two things changed the equation: (a) the recognition on the part of collectors of the role flea markets played as the initial source of goods and their active participation in order to eliminate the middleman, and (b) the development of the antiques and collectibles mall.

The 1980s was the decade of the antiques-and-collectibles mall. Malls resulted because many flea market and weekend dealers wanted a means of doing business on a daily basis without the overhead of their own shop. They also needed an indoor environment free from the vagaries of weather. Additionally, the buying public wanted to find as many sellers as possible in one location when shopping for antiques and collectibles.

5

Antiques and collectibles malls bring together a number of dealers—from ten to hundreds—in one location. Malls differ from flea markets in that they are open for business on a daily basis (a minimum of five and often seven days a week), the display and sales process is often handled by a manager or other representative of the owner of the items, a more formal business procedure is used, and the quality of material is somewhat higher than that found at flea markets. The main drawbacks are that the buyer generally has no contact with the owner of the merchandise and price negotiation is difficult.

Garage sales are usually one-time events, often conducted by an individual with no pretensions of being an antiques or collectibles dealer, but who is attempting to get rid of used or damaged goods that are no longer useful to him. While it is true that some antiques and collectibles enter the market through this source, most individuals conducting garage sales have enough good sense to realize that this is the worst way to sell these items. Emphasis in a garage sale is on secondhand merchandise, often in heavily used and partially damaged condition.

A recent development in the garage sale area is the annual or semiannual community garage sale. A promoter rents a large hall or auditorium and sells space to any individual wishing to set up. Usually there is a rule that no established antiques and collectibles dealers are allowed to take part. However, many dealers sneak in with friends or simply use a different name to rent a space in order to "pick" the merchandise during the setup period. Although community garage sales fit the dictionary definition of a flea market, the large volume of secondhand merchandise distinguishes them from the flea markets discussed in this book.

An antiques or collectibles show consists of a number of professional dealers (weekend, full-time, or a combination of both) who meet in a fixed location on a regular basis, usually two to three times each year, to offer quality antiques and collectibles primarily to collectors, interior decorators, and others. Once an antique or collectible reaches the show circuit, the general assumption is that it is priced close to book value. Flea markets thrive on the concept that merchandise priced for sale is significantly below book value. While this concept is more myth than reality in the 1990s, it still prevails.

Confusion arises because a number of monthly flea markets have dropped the term "flea market" from their titles. They call themselves *show* or *market*. They do not use *flea* because of a growing list of problems, ranging from unscrupulous dealers to an abundance of unmarked reproductions, that plague flea markets in the 1990s. Calling yourself something else does not change what you really are. Most monthly markets and shows are nothing more than flea markets in disguise.

Seasonal Flea Markets

Seasonal flea markets are those held a maximum of three times a year. Theoretically, they are held outdoors. However, many sites now provide either indoor or pavilion shelters for participants, especially those whose merchandise is expensive or susceptible to damage by weather. Most have clearly established dates. For example, Renninger's Extravaganza is held the last weekend in April, June, and September.

If there is a Mecca in the flea market world, it is Brimfield. The name is magic. You are not an accomplished flea marketeer until you have been there. Actually, Brimfield is not a flea market, it is an event. For the first full week in May, July, and September over fifteen separate flea markets open and close. On Fridays the dealer count exceeds 1,500. Area motel rooms are booked over a year in advance. Traffic jams last hours.

For the past several years Renninger's has been promoting seasonal markets during the winter months at its Mount Dora, Florida, location. They are an important stop on the Southern winter circuit. Although there are a few seasonal markets in the Mid-west, none are on a par with the Renninger's Extravaganzas and the Brimfield weeks.

Monthly Flea Markets

The monthly flea market's strength rests on a steady dealer clientele supplemented by other dealers passing through the area, a frequency that allows dealers enough time to find new merchandise, and a setting that is usually superior to the seasonal and weekly flea markets. The monthlies range from the upscale Ann Arbor Antiques Market to the mid-range antiques-and-collectibles show copycat (for example, The Arizona State Fairgrounds Antique Market in Phoenix, Arizona) to the something-for-everybody flea market, (like the Kane County Flea Market in St. Charles, Illinois).

Most of the monthly flea markets have some outdoor spaces. The Kentucky Flea Market in Louisville, Kentucky, and the Arizona State Antique Fairgrounds Market are two exceptions. Flea markets with outdoor space operate only during warm weather months, generally April through November. A few of the larger operations, e.g., the Springfield Antiques Show and Flea Market in Springfield, Ohio, operate year-round. Double-check a flea market's schedule, unless it is located in the Deep South or Southwest, if you plan a visit between November 1 and April 30.

Another strength of the monthly flea markets rests in the fact that they attract a large number of dealers who appear on a regular basis, hence collectors and dealers have time to cultivate good working relationships. A level of buying trust is created because the collector knows that he will be able to find the seller again if questions develop.

Weekly Flea Markets

The weekly flea markets break down into two types: those held on a weekday and those held on a weekend. The weekday markets are primarily for dealers in the trade. Monday flea markets at Perkiomenville, Pennsylvania, and Wednesday flea markets at Shipshewana, Indiana, are legends. These markets begin in the predawn hours. The best buys are found by flashlight as participants check merchandise as it is being unpacked.

7

Most selling ends by 9:00 A.M. These markets are designed primarily for individuals actively involved in the resale of antiques and collectibles. Most collectors prefer something a bit more civilized.

Renninger's #1 in Adamstown, Pennsylvania, shows the staying power of the weekend flea market. Within driving distance of several major population centers, yet far enough in the country to make the day an "outing," Renninger's combines an ever-changing outdoor section with an indoor facility featuring primarily permanent dealers. Renninger's #1 has survived for years by opening only on Sundays, except for Extravaganza weekends. However, because buyers like to shop for antiques and collectibles on Saturdays as well, Renninger's Promotions created Renninger's #2 in Kutztown, Pennsylvania.

Weekend flea markets are now a fixture across the country and constitute the largest segment of the flea market community. It is not unusual to find several in one location as each tries to capitalize on the success of the other. However, their quality varies tremendously.

The biggest problem with weekend flea markets is merchandise staleness. Many dealers add only a few new items each week. Most collectors shop them on a four- to eight-week cycle. The way to avoid missing a shot at a major new piece is to maintain a close working relationship with the dealers at the flea markets who specialize in the category of items that you collect. Most weekend flea market dealers do get to shop the market. They can be your eyes when you are not there.

As with the monthly flea markets, you can buy from indoor dealers knowing that you are likely to find them if a problem develops later. You must be much more careful when purchasing from the transient outside dealers. The key is to get a valid name, address, and phone number from anyone from whom you make a purchase at a flea market.

One of the things I like best about large weekend flea markets is that they feature one or more book dealers who specialize in antiques and collectibles books. I always stop at their booths to check on the latest titles. They carry a large stock of privately published titles. In some cases, I never saw the book advertised in a trade paper. Some of the dealers offer search services for out-of-print titles. Spending time getting to know these book dealers is something that I never regret.

Roadside Flea Markets

I have ignored roadside flea markets up to this point because the merchandise they offer for sale is more often than not secondhand, and of garage sale quality. This is not to say that I have not experienced some great finds at roadside markets at which I have stopped. However, when I consider the amount of time that I spend finding these few precious jewels, I quickly realize that I can do much better at one of the more traditional flea markets.

Chances are that you collect one or two specific categories. If so, not every type of flea market is right for you. How do you find the best markets? What type of evaluation can you do in advance to save the frustration of coming home empty-handed? These questions and more are answered in the next chapter.

Finding and Evaluating Flea Markets

2

In order to attend a flea market, you have to locate one. It is not as easy as it sounds. In order to thoroughly research the available markets in any given area, you will have to consult a variety of sources. Even when you have finished, you are still likely to spot a flea market that you missed in your research along the way. I told you there was a strong sense of adventure in flea marketeering.

Flea Market Guides

There are three national guides to United States flea markets: *Clark's Flea Market U.S.A.* (Clark's Publications, 2156 Cotton Patch Lane, Milton, FL 32570), *The Great American Flea Market Directory* (Cranbrook House, Saginaw, MI 48608), and *The Official Directory to U.S. Flea Markets* (House of Collectibles, Division of Ballantine Books, New York, NY). Buy them all.

Clark's lists approximately 2,300 flea markets. The guide is organized alphabetically by state. The secondary organization is city or town closest to the flea market within the state. You will find information on name, address, days open (but no times), and phone numbers. Information provided about each market varies greatly. Completely missing are directions for hard-to-find markets.

The Great American guide, which is updated twice a year, lists approximately 2,500 markets using the same format as Clark's. Much of the information is vague—a Minnesota listing reads "Pine City, Wednesdays, Flea Market, downtown." The lack of a detailed location is particularly unhelpful.

The *Official Directory* guide covers fewer markets—approximately 475. (They list a few annual markets, which technically are not flea markets in our working definition, which raises the number of listings to over 550.) However, it provides quality information about the ones that are covered by devoting a full page to each market. Detailed comments about merchandise and operating practices are extremely helpful.

I am not quite certain how to classify *Swap Meet USA* (Swap Meet USA, P. O. Box 200, Grover City, CA 93433). Some of the listings are flea markets; others are community garage sales. This seventy-two-page publication covers 1,800 markets in approximately forty pages (the balance of the pages are devoted to advertising), using small type and a triple-column format. Of special interest to flea marketeers are the advertisements for market merchandise and equipment.

Antiques and collectibles flea markets are not unique to the United States. In fact, the modern antiques and collectibles flea market originated in Paris. Flea markets play a vital role throughout Europe, especially in France, Great Britain, and Germany. Accordingly, Travel Keys (P. O. Box 16091, Sacramento, CA 95816) has published a separate flea market price guide for each country. Peter B. Manston is editor of *Manston's Flea Markets of Britain*, *Manston's Flea Markets of France*, and *Manston's Flea Markets of Germany*. The introductory material, especially the section on export laws and regulations, is something that should be read carefully.

Regional Shop Guides

A number of specialized regional guides for locating antiques and collectibles flea markets, malls, and shops exist. Most are published by trade papers. A few are done privately. None focus solely on the flea market scene.

The *Antique Week Mid-Central Antique Shop Guide* (Antique Week, P. O. Box 90, Knightstown, IN 46148) is typical. Organization is by state, region, and alphabetically by city and town within a region. Brief listings for each business are supplemented by display advertising. The Mid-Central Edition (there is also an Eastern Edition) covers more than 3,000 flea markets, malls, shops, and shows. One of the features I like most about the guide is that it designates businesses selling new gift and reproduction items. The principal problem with the guide is that you have to pay a fee in order to be listed. As a result coverage is limited to those willing to do so. It is a great starting point for the region it covers, but it is not all-encompassing.

When planning to visit a new area, contact some of the trade papers that serve the region and ask if they publish a regional guide or know of such a guide. Regional guides are inexpensive, ranging from $4.00 to $10.00. Many of the businesses listed in the guide sell it across the counter. I always pick up a copy. The floor behind the front seat of my car is littered with road maps and regional guides, most of which show signs of heavy use.

Trade Newspapers

The best source of flea market information is advertisements in trade newspapers. Some papers put all the flea market advertisements in one location, while others place them in their appropriate regional section. Most trade papers' events calendars include flea markets with the show listings.

Once again, the problem rests with the fact that all advertising is paid advertising. Not all flea markets advertise in every issue of a trade paper. Some advertise in papers outside their home area because the locals know where and when to find them. Flea markets that operate between April and September usually do not advertise in December and January. The only way to conduct a complete search is to obtain a four- to six-month run of a regional paper and carefully scan each issue. When doing this, keep your eyes open for reports or features about flea markets. As advertisers, flea markets expect to get written up at least once a year.

The following is a list of national and regional trade papers that I recommend you consult for flea market information. You will find their full addresses and phone numbers (when known) in Appendix II.

NATIONAL TRADE PAPERS

Antique Monthly, Atlanta, GA
Antique Trader Weekly, Dubuque, IA
Antique Week, Knightstown, IN
Antiques & The Arts Weekly, Newtown, CT
Collector News, Grundy Center, IA
Maine Antiques Digest, Waldoboro, ME

REGIONAL TRADE PAPERS

New England
MassBay Antiques, Danvers, MA
New England Antiques Journal, Ware, MA

Middle Atlantic States
Antiques & Auction News, Mount Joy, PA
New York-Pennsylvania Collector, Fishers, NY
Renninger's Antique Guide, Lafayette Hill, PA
Treasure Chest, New York, NY

South
The Antique Press, Tampa, FL
Cotton & Quail Antique Trail, Monticello, FL
MidAtlantic Antiques Magazine, Henderson, NC
The Old News Is Good News Antiques Gazette, Baton Rouge, LA
Southern Antiques, Decatur, GA

Midwest
Antique Gazette, Nashville, TN
Antique Review, Worthington, OH
Collectors Journal, Vinton, IA
Yesteryear, Princeton, WI

Southwest
Arizona Antique News and Southwest Antiques Journal, Phoenix, AZ

Rocky Mountain States
Mountain States Collector, Evergreen, CO

West Coast
Antique & Collectables, El Cajon, CA
Antiques Today, Sonora, CA
West Coast Peddler, Whittier, CA

This list is by no means complete. These are the papers with which I am familiar or of which my dad has sample copies in the Rinker Enterprises's files. Appendix II contains an expanded listing of papers.

Which Flea Market Is Right for You?

The best flea market is the one at which you find plenty to buy at good to great prices. This means that most flea markets are not right for you. Is it necessary to attend each one to make your determination? I do not think so.

I am a great believer in using the telephone. If long distance rates jump dramatically as a result of the publication of this book, I plan to approach AT&T and ask for a piece of the action. It is a lot cheaper to call than to pay for transportation, lodging, and meals—not to mention the value of your time. Do not hesitate to call promoters and ask them about their flea markets.

What type of information should you request? First, check the number of dealers. If the number falls below one hundred, think twice. Ask for a ratio of local dealers to transient dealers. A good mix is seventy-five percent local and twenty-five percent transient for monthly and weekly markets. Second, inquire about the type of merchandise being offered for sale. Make a point not to tell the promoter what you collect. If you do, you can be certain that the flea market has a number of dealers who offer the material. Do not forget to ask about the quality of the merchandise. Third, ask about the facilities. The more indoor space available, the higher the level of merchandise is likely to be. What happens if it rains? Finally, ask yourself this question: *Do you trust what the promoter has told you?*

When you are done talking to the promoter, call the editor of one of the regional trade papers and ask his opinion about the market. If they have published an article or review of the market recently, request that a copy be sent to you. If you know someone who has attended, talk to him. If you still have not made up your mind, try the local daily newspaper or chamber of commerce.

Do not be swayed by the size of a flea market's advertisement in a trade paper. The Kane County advertisement is often less than a sixteenth of a page. A recent full-page advertisement for Brimfield flea markets failed to include J & J Promotions or May's Antique Market, two of the major players on the scene. This points out the strong regional competition between flea markets. Never rely on what one promoter tells you about another promoter's market unless it is a balanced presentation.

Evaluating a Flea Market

After you have attended a flea market, it is time to decide if you will attend it again, and if so, how frequently. Answer the following nineteen questions yes or no. In this test, *no* is the right answer. If more than half the questions are yes, forget about going back. There are plenty of flea markets from which to choose. If six or fewer are answered yes, give it another chance in a few months. If seventeen or more answers are no, plan another visit soon. What are you doing next week?

YES	NO	
_____	_____	Was the flea market hard to find?
_____	_____	Did you have a difficult time moving between the flea market and your car in the parking area?
_____	_____	Did you have to pay a parking fee in addition to an admission fee?
_____	_____	Did the manager fail to provide a map of the market?
_____	_____	Was a majority of the market in an open, outdoor environment?
_____	_____	Were indoor facilities poorly lighted and ventilated?
_____	_____	Was there a problem with enough toilet facilities or their cleanliness?
_____	_____	Was your overall impression of the market one of chaos?
_____	_____	Did collectibles outnumber antiques?
_____	_____	Did secondhand goods and new merchandise outnumber collectibles?
_____	_____	Were reproductions, copycats, fantasy items, and fakes in abundance?
_____	_____	Was there a large representation of home crafts and/or discontinued merchandise?
_____	_____	Were the vast majority of antiques and collectibles that you saw in fair condition or worse?
_____	_____	Were individuals that you expected to encounter at the market absent?
_____	_____	Did you pass out less than five wants lists?
_____	_____	Did you buy fewer than five new items for your collection?
_____	_____	Were more than half the items that you bought priced near or at book value?
_____	_____	Was there a lack of good restaurants and/or lodging within easy access of the flea market?
_____	_____	Would you tell a friend never to attend the market?

There are some flea markets that scored well for me, and I would like to share them with you. They are listed in the next chapter.

Top Twenty U.S. Flea Markets

3

Selecting twenty flea markets from the thousands of flea markets throughout the United States was not an easy task. Everyone will have regional favorites that do not appear on this list. I wish I could list them all, but that is not the purpose of this price guide.

In making my choices, I have used the following criteria. First, I wanted to provide a representation for the major flea market groups—seasonal, monthly, and weekly. Since this price guide is designed for the national market, I made certain that the selections covered the entire United States. Finally, I selected flea markets that I feel will "turn on" a prospective or novice collector. Nothing is more fun than getting off to a great start.

This list is only a starting point. Almost every flea market has a table containing promotional literature for other flea markets in the area. Follow up on the ones of interest. Continue to check trade paper listings. There are always new flea markets being started.

Finally, not every flea market is able to maintain its past glories. Are there flea markets that you think should be on this list? Have you visited some of the listed flea markets and found them to be unsatisfactory? As each edition of this guide is prepared, this list will be evaluated. Send any thoughts and comments that you may have to: Harry L. Rinker, Jr., Rinker Enterprises, Inc., P. O. Box 248, Zionsville, PA 18092.

NAME OF FLEA MARKET

Location
Frequency and general admission times
Type of goods sold and general comments
Number of dealers, indoor and/or outdoor, and special features
1991 Admission Fee
Address and phone number (if known) of manager or promoter

Seasonal Flea Markets

BRIMFIELD

Route 20, Brimfield, MA 01010
Ten days, starting on Thursday before the first full weekend in May, July, and September, and ending on the second Saturday of the month.
Antiques, collectibles, and secondhand goods
Over 3,000 dealers. Outdoor and indoor.
1991 Admission: Varies according to field, ranging from free admission to $3.00. Average parking fee: $3.00.

More than ten different promoters: Brimfield Acres North/ The Last Hurrah, P. O. Box 397, Holden, MA 01520, (508) 754-4185; Central Park Antiques Shows, P. O. Box 224, Brimfield, MA 01010, (413) 596-9257; The Dealers Choice, P. O. Box 28, Fiskdale, MA 01518, (508) 347-3929; Faxon's Treasure Chest/Midway Shows, P. O. Box 28, Fiskdale, MA 01518, (508) 347-3929; Heart-O-The-Mart, P. O. Box 26, Brimfield, MA 01010, (413) 245-9556; J & J Promotions, Route 20, Brimfield, MA 01010, (413) 245-3436 or (508) 597-8155; May's Antique Market, P. O. Box 416, Brimfield, MA 01010, (413) 245-9271; New England Motel Antiques Market, Inc., P. O. Box 139, Sturbridge, MA 01010, (413) 245-9427; Shelton Antique Shows, P. O. Box 124, Brimfield, MA 01010, (413) 245-3591.

You can subscribe to the *Brimfield Antique Guide* at Brimfield Publications, Route 20, Brimfield, MA 01010. Phone (413) 245-9329. Three issues for $7.95.

RENNINGER'S EXTRAVAGANZA

Noble Street, Kutztown, PA 19530
Thursday, Friday, and Saturday of last full weekend of April, June, and September. Thursday opens 10:00 A.M. pre-admission only ($40.00 per car, includes one to four people). Friday and Saturday, 7:00 A.M. to 5:00 P.M.
Antiques and collectibles.
Over 1,200 dealers. Indoor and outdoor.
1991 Admission: $3.00 on Friday, $2.00 on Saturday
Renninger's Promotions, 27 Bensinger Drive, Schuylkill Haven, PA 17972. Monday through Friday, (717) 385-0104; Saturday, (215) 683-6843; and Sunday, (215) 267-2177.

Monthly Flea Markets

ANN ARBOR ANTIQUES MARKET

5055 Ann Arbor-Saline Road, Ann Arbor, MI 48103
Third Sunday of the Month, April through October, 5:00 A.M. to 4:00 P.M. November market usually occurs second Sunday of month.
Antiques and select collectibles. The most upscale flea market in the trade.
Over 350 dealers. All under cover. Locator service for specialties and dealers.
1991 Admission: $3.00
M. Brusher, Manager, P. O. Box 1512, Ann Arbor, MI 48106

ALLEGAN ANTIQUES MARKET

Allegan Fairgrounds, Allegan, MI 49010
Last Sunday of the month, April through September, 7:30 A.M. to 4:30 P.M.
Antiques and collectibles
Over 170 dealers indoors, 200 dealers outdoors
1991 Admission: $2.00
Larry L. Wood and Morie Faulkerson, 2030 Blueberry Drive N.W., Grand Rapids, MI 49504, (616) 453-8780 or (616) 887-7677.

15

ARIZONA STATE FAIRGROUNDS ANTIQUES & COLLECTIBLES SHOW & SALE

Arizona State Fairgrounds, 19th Avenue & McDowell, Phoenix, AZ 85009
Third weekend of the month, year around, except March (fourth weekend) and December
(first weekend). Saturday, 9:00 A.M. to 5:00 P.M. and Sunday 10:00 A.M. to 4:00 P.M.
Antiques, collectibles, and crafts. Antique glass and clock repairs.
Approximately 200 dealers. All indoors.
1991 Admission: Free
Jack Black Shows, P. O. Box 61172, Phoenix, AZ 85082-1172, (800) 678-9987 or (602)
247-1004.

BURLINGTON ANTIQUES SHOW

Boone County Fairgrounds, Burlington, KY 41005
Third Sunday of the month, April through October, 8:00 A.M. to 3:00 P.M.
Antiques and collectibles
Outdoor
1991 Admission: $2.00
Paul Kohls, P. O. Box 58367, Cincinnati, OH 45258, (513) 922-5265.

CARAVAN ANTIQUES MARKET

The Fairgrounds, State Route 86, Centreville, MI 49032
One Sunday per month, May through October, excluding September, 7:00 A.M. to 4:30
P.M.
Antiques and collectibles. All merchandise guaranteed.

16

Over 600 dealers
1991 Admission: $3.00
Humberstone Management, 1510 N. Hoyne, Chicago, IL 60622, (312) 227-4464.

DON SCOTT ANTIQUES MARKET

Ohio State Fairgrounds, Columbus, OH
Saturday 9:00 A.M. to 6:00 P.M. and Sunday 9:00 A.M. to 5:00 P.M., March, April, May,
   June, November, and December
Antiques and collectibles
1,500 booths. Indoor and outdoor.
1991 Admission: Free
Don Scott, P. O. Box 60, Bremen, OH 43107, (614) 569-4912
Note: Don Scott conducts a second monthly flea market: The Don Scott Antique Market,
   Atlanta Exposition Center (I-285 to Exit 40 at Jonesboro Road, two miles east of
   Atlanta airport), second weekend of every month.

GORDYVILLE USA FLEA MARKET & AUCTION

Rantoul, Illinois 61866. On Route 136 or 7 1/2 miles east of I-57 on Route 136.
Second weekend (Friday, Saturday, Sunday) of each month. Friday 4:00 P.M. to 9:00 P.M.;
   Saturday 9:00 A.M. to 6:00 P.M.; and Sunday, 9:00 A.M. to 4:30 P.M.
Antiques, collectibles, vintage items, arts, crafts, and other unique items.
Outdoor and indoor.
1991 Admission: Free
Gordon Hannagan Auction Company, P. O. Box 490, Gillford, IL 61847, (217) 568-7117.

(KANE COUNTY) ANTIQUES FLEA MARKETS

Kane County Fairgrounds, Randall Road, St. Charles, IL 60175
First Sunday of every month and preceding Saturday. Year around. Saturday, 1:00 P.M. to
   5:00 P.M.; Sunday, 7:00 A.M. to 4:00 P.M..
Antiques, collectibles, and some crafts. A favorite in the Midwest, especially with the
   Chicago crowd.
Combination indoor and outdoor. Country breakfast served.
1991 Admission: $3.00
Mrs. J. L. Robinson, Mgr., P. O. Box 549, St. Charles, IL 60174, (708) 377-2252.

KENTUCKY FLEA MARKET

Kentucky Fair and Exposition Center (take Exit 12B off Interstate 264), Louisville, KY
Three or four day show first weekend of most months. Fridays from noon until 8:00 P.M.,
   Saturdays 10:00 A.M. to 8:00 P.M., and Sundays from 11:00 A.M. to 5:00 P.M..
Antiques, collectibles, arts and crafts, and new merchandise
Approximately 1,000 booths. Indoors, climate controlled.
1991 Admission: Free
Stewart Promotions, 2950 Breckinridge Lane, Suite 4A, Louisville, KY 40220, (502) 456-
   2244.

LONG BEACH OUTDOOR ANTIQUES & COLLECTIBLES MARKET

Veterans Stadium, Long Beach, CA
Third Sunday of each month, 8:00 A.M. to 3:00 P.M.
Antiques and collectibles including: vintage clothing, pottery, quilts, primitives, advertising, etc.
Over 700 dealers
1991 Admission: $3.50
Americana, P. O. Box 69219, Los Angeles, CA 90069, (213) 655-5703.

METROLINA EXPO

Charlotte, NC 18221
First weekend of every month, year-round. Friday, Saturday, and Sunday, 8:00 A.M. to 5:00 P.M.
Antiques and collectibles
Indoor and outdoor, over 1,250 dealers.
Metrolina hosts two Spectaculars yearly—April and November—which feature more than 2,000 dealers.
1991 Admission: $3.00/day, $6.00 for a three-day pass.
Metrolina EXPO Center, P. O. Box 26652, Charlotte, NC 18221, (704) 596-4643.

SANDWICH ANTIQUES MARKET

The Fairgrounds, State Route 34, Sandwich, IL 60548
One Sunday per month, May through October, 8:00 A.M. to 4:00 P.M.
Antiques and collectibles

Over 600 dealers
1991 Admission: $3.00
Humberstone Management, 1510 N. Hoyne, Chicago, IL 60622, (312) 227-4464.

SPRINGFIELD ANTIQUES SHOW & FLEA MARKET

Clark County Fairgrounds, Springfield, OH
Third weekend of the month, year around, excluding July. December market is held the
second weekend of the month. Saturday, 8:00 A.M. to 5:00 P.M., Sunday 9:00 A.M. to
4:00 P.M.. Extravaganzas are held in May and September.
More than half the market is antiques and collectibles
Over 400 dealers inside, 900 dealers outside
1991 Admission: $1.00
Bruce Knight, P. O. Box 2429, Springfield, OH 45501, (513) 325-0053.

Weekly Flea Markets

ADAMSTOWN

Route 272, Adamstown, PA 19501
Sundays
Antiques, collectibles, secondhand material, and junk
1991 Admission: Free
Three major markets

> **Black Angus,** 8:00 A.M. to 5:00 P.M., year around, indoors and outdoors; Carl
> Barto, 2717 Long Farm Lane, Lancaster, PA 17601, (717) 569-3536 or (215)
> 484-4385.
> **Renninger's No. 1,** 7:30 A.M. to 5:00 P.M., year around, indoors and outdoors;
> Renninger's Promotions, 27 Bensinger Drive, Schuylkill Haven, PA 17972.
> Phone on Sunday: (215) 267-2177.
> **Shupp's Grove,** 8:00 A.M. to 5:00 P.M., April through September, indoors and
> outdoors; Shupp's Grove, 1686 Dry Tavern Road, Denver, PA 17517. Informa-
> tion: (215) 484-4115; dealer reservations: (717) 949-3656.

ATLANTA FLEA MARKET

5360 Peachtree Industrial Boulevard, Chamblee, GA 30341
Friday and Saturday, 12:00 P.M. to 8:00 P.M., Sunday, 12:00 P.M. to 7:00 P.M.
Antiques, collectibles, and gift items
150 dealers. Indoors.
1991 Admission: Free
Atlanta Flea Market, 5360 Peachtree Industrial Blvd, Chamblee, GA 30341, (404) 458-
0456.

LAMBERTVILLE ANTIQUES FLEA MARKET

Route 29, 1 1/2 miles south of Lambertville, NJ 08530
Saturday, and Sunday, 6:00 A.M. to 4:00 P.M.

Antiques and collectibles
150 dealers. Indoor and outdoor.
1991 Admission: Free
Mr. & Mrs. Errhalt, 324 S. Main St., Pennington, NJ 08534, (609) 397-0456.

RENNINGER'S ANTIQUES CENTER

Mount Dora, FL 32757
Saturdays and Sundays, 8:00 A.M. to 5:00 P.M.
Antiques and collectibles
Over 500 dealers. Indoor and outdoor.
1991 Admission: Free
Florida Twin Markets, P. O. Box 939, Zellwood, FL 32798 (904) 383-8393.

SHIPSHEWANA AUCTION AND FLEA MARKET

On State Route 5 near the southern edge of Shipshewana, IN 46565
Wednesdays, 6:00 A.M. to dusk from May through October, 7:30 A.M. to dusk from
    November through April.
Antiques, collectibles, new merchandise, and produce. In fact, you name it, they sell it.
Can accommodate up to 800 dealers. Indoor and outdoor.
1991 Admission: Free
Shipshewana Auction, Inc., P. O. Box 185, Shipshewana, IN 46565.

Thus far you have learned to identify the various types of flea markets, how to locate them, the keys to evaluating whether or not they are right for you, and my recommendations for getting started. Next you need to develop the skills necessary for flea market survival.

Your state of exhaustion at the end of the day is the best gauge that I know to judge the value of a flea market—the greater your exhaustion, the better the flea market. A great flea market keeps you on the go from early morning, in some cases 5:00 A.M., to early evening, often 6:00 P.M. The key to survival is to do advance homework, have proper equipment, develop and follow a carefully thought out shopping strategy, and do your follow-up chores as soon as you return home.

If you are a Type-A personality, your survival plan is essentially a battle plan. Your goal is to cover the flea market as thoroughly as possible and secure the objectives (bargains and hard-to-find objects) ahead of your rivals. You do not stop until total victory is achieved. Does not sound like you? No matter, you also need a survival plan if you want to maximize fun and enjoyment.

Advance Homework

Consult the flea market's advertisement or brochure. Make certain that you understand the dates and time. You never know when special circumstances may cause a change in dates and even location. Check the admission policy. It may be possible to buy a ticket in advance to avoid the wait in line at the ticket booth.

Determine if there is an early admission fee and what times are involved. It is a growing practice at flea markets to admit collectors and others to the flea market through the use of an early admission fee. In most cases the fee is the cost of renting a space. The management simply does not insist that you setup. Actually, this practice had been going on for some time before management formalized it. Friends of individuals renting space often tag along as helpers or assistants. Once inside, the urge to shop supersedes their desire to help their friend.

Review the directions. Are they detailed enough to allow you to find the flea market easily? Remember, it still may be dark when you arrive. If you are not certain, call the manager and ask for specific directions. Also, make certain of parking provisions, especially when a flea market takes place within a city or town. Local residents who are not enamored with a flea market in their neighborhood take great pleasure in informing police of illegally parked cars and watching them be towed away. In some cases, I have found locating parking to be more of a problem than locating the flea market. Avoid frustration; and plan ahead.

Decide if you are going to stay overnight, either the evening before the flea market opens or during the days of operation. In many cases local motel accommodations are minimal. It is not uncommon for dealers as well as collectors to commute fifty miles each way to attend Brimfield. The general attitude of most flea market managers is that accommodations are your problem, not their problem. If you are lucky, you can get a list of accommodations from a local chamber of commerce. The American Automobile Association regional guidebooks provide some help. However, if you attend a flea market expecting to find nearby overnight accommodations without a reservation, you are the world's biggest optimist.

If possible, obtain a map of the flea market grounds. Become familiar with how the spaces are laid out. If you know some of your favorite dealers are going to setup, call and ask them for their space number. Mark the location of all toilet facilities and refreshment stands. You may not have time for the latter, but sooner or later you are going to need the former.

Finally, try to convince one or more friends, ideally someone who collects in a totally different area, to attend the flea market with you. Each becomes another set of eyes for the other. Convenient meeting at predesignated spots makes exchanging information easy. It never hurts to share the driving and expenses. Best of all, war stories can be told and savored immediately.

Flea Market Checklist

In order to have an enjoyable and productive day at the flea market, you need the right equipment ranging from clothing to packing material for your purchases. What you do not wear can be stored in your car trunk. Make certain that everything is in order the day before your flea market adventure.

CLOTHING CHECKLIST

_____ Hat
_____ Sunglasses
_____ Light jacket or sweatshirt
_____ Poncho or raincoat
_____ Waterproof work boots or galoshes

FIELD GEAR CHECKLIST

_____ Canvas bag(s)
_____ Cash, checkbook, and credit cards
_____ Wants lists
_____ Address cards
_____ Magnifying glass
_____ Swiss Army pocket knife
_____ Toilet paper
_____ Sales receipts
_____ Mechanical pencil or ball point pen
_____ _Warman's Antiques And Their Prices_, _Warman's Americana & Collectibles_, and this price guide

CAR TRUNK CHECKLIST

_____ Three to six cardboard boxes
_____ Newspaper, bubble wrap, diapers, and other appropriate packing material
_____ Sun block
_____ First aid kit
_____ Cooler with cold beverages

The vast majority of flea markets that you attend will either be outdoors or have an outdoor section. If you are lucky, the sun will be shining. Beware of sunburn. Select a hat with a broad rim. I prefer a hat with an outside hat band as well. First, it provides a place to stick notes, business cards, or other small pieces of paper I would most likely lose otherwise. Second, it provides a place to stick a feather or some other distinguishing item that allows my friends to spot me in the crowd. Some flea marketeers use the band as a holder for a card expounding their collecting wants. Make certain that your hat fits snugly. Some flea market sites are quite windy. An experienced flea market attendee's hat will look as though it has been through the wars. It has.

I carry sunglasses, but I confess that I rarely use them. I find that taking them on and off is more trouble than they are worth. Further, they distort colors. However, I have found them valuable at windswept and outdoor markets located in large fields. Since I usually misplace a pair a year, I generally buy inexpensive glasses.

The dress key to flea markets is a layered, comfortable approach. The early morning and late evening hours are often cool. A light jacket or sweatshirt is suggested. I found a great light jacket that is loaded with pockets. Properly outfitted, it holds all the material I would normally put in my carrying bag.

You must assume that it is going to rain. I have never been to Brimfield when it was not raining. Rain, especially at an outdoor flea market, is a disaster. What is astonishing is how much activity continues in spite of the rain. I prefer a poncho over a raincoat because it covers my purchases as well as my clothing.

Most flea markets offer ponchos for sale when rain starts. They are lightweight and come with a storage bag. Of course, you have to be a genius to fold them small enough to get them back into their original storage bag. The one I purchased at Kane County has lasted for years. Mrs. Robinson, being a shrewd promoter, just happened to have them imprinted with information about her flea market. I had a great time there so I have never objected to being a walking bulletin board on her behalf.

The ideal footwear for a flea market is a well-broken-in pair of running or walking shoes. However, in the early morning when the ground is wet with dew, a pair of waterproof work boots is a much better choice. I keep my running shoes in the car trunk and usually change into them by 9:00 A.M. at most flea markets.

Rain at outdoor flea markets equals mud. The only defense is a good pair of galoshes. I have been at Brimfield where the rain was coming down so fiercely that dealers set up in tents were using tools to dig water diversion ditches. Cars, which were packed in the nearby fields, sank into the ground. In several cases, local farmers with tractors handsomely supplemented their income.

I always go to a flea market planning to buy something. Since most flea market sellers provide the minimum packaging possible, I carry my own. My preference is a double handled canvas bag with a flat bottom. It is not as easy an item to find as it sounds. I use one to carry my field gear along with two extra bags that start out folded. I find that I can carry three filled bags comfortably. This avoids the necessity of running back to the car each time a bag is filled.

If you are going to buy something, you have to pay for it. Cash is always preferred by the sellers. I carry my cash in a small white envelope with the amount with which I started marked at the top. I note and deduct each purchase as I go along. If you carry cash, be careful how you display it. Pickpockets and sticky-fingered individuals who cannot resist temptation do attend flea markets.

Since I want a record of my purchases, I pay by check whenever I can. I have tried to control my spending by only taking a few checks. Forget it. I can always borrow money on Monday to cover my weekend purchases. I make certain that I have a minimum of ten checks.

Most flea market sellers will accept checks with proper identification. For this reason, I put my driver's license and a major credit card in the front of my checkbook before entering the flea market. This saves me the trouble of taking out my wallet each time I make a purchase.

A surprising number of flea market sellers are willing to take credit cards. I am amazed at this practice since the only means they have of checking a card's validity is the canceled card booklet they receive each week. They wait until later to get telephone authorization, a potentially dangerous practice.

I buy as much material through the mail as I do at flea markets. One of the principal reasons I attend flea markets is to make contact with dealers. Since flea markets attract many dealers from other parts of the country, I expand my supplier sources at each flea market I attend. The key is to have a wants list ready to give to any flea market seller that admits to doing business by mail. My wants list fills an 8 1/2" × 11" sheet of writing paper. In addition to my wants, it includes my name, post office box address, UPS address, and office and home telephone number. I also make it a point to get the full name and address of any dealer to whom I give my list. I believe in follow-up.

Not every dealer is willing to take a full page wants list. For this reason, I have an address (business) card available with my name, street address, phone numbers, and a brief list of my wants. Most take it as a courtesy. However, I have received quotes on a few great items as a result of my efforts.

I carry a simple variety-store ten-power magnifying glass. It is helpful to see marks clearly and to spot cracks in china and glass. Ninety-nine percent of the time I use it merely to confirm something that I saw with the naked eye. Jewelers loupes are overkill unless you are buying jewelry.

Years ago I purchased a good Swiss Army pocket knife, one which contains a scissors as part of the blade package. It was one of the smartest investments that I made. No flea market goes by that I do not use the knife for one reason or another. If you do not want to carry a pocket knife, invest in a pair of operating room surgical scissors. They will cut through most anything.

I am a buyer. Why do I carry a book of sales receipts? Alas, many flea market sellers operate in a nontraditional business manner. They are not interested in paper trails, especially when you pay cash. You need a receipt to protect yourself. More on this subject later.

I keep a roll of toilet paper in the car and enough for two sittings in my carrying bag. Do not laugh. I am serious. Most outdoor flea markets have portable toilets. After a few days, the toilet paper supply is exhausted. Even some indoor facilities give out. If I had five dollars from all the people to whom I supplied toilet paper at flea markets, I would be writing this book in Hawaii instead of Pennsylvania.

I carry a mechanical pencil. When I pick up someone's business card, I note why on the back of the card. Use the pencil to mark dealer locations on the flea market map. I do not always buy something when I first spot it. The map helps me relocate items when I wish to go back for a second look. I have wasted hours at flea markets backtracking to find an item that was not located where I thought it was. A ball point pen works just as well. The mechanical pencil is a personal preference.

Anyone who tells you they know everything about antiques and collectibles and their prices is a liar. I know the areas in which I collect quite well. But there are many categories where a quick source check never hurts. *Warman's Antiques And Their Prices* and *Warman's Americana & Collectibles* are part of my field gear. I could tell you that I carry them out of loyalty to my dad who edits them. The truth is that I carry them because I have found them more helpful and accurate than other general price guides. I have also scored some major points with dealers and others when I offered to share some of the information found in the category introductions with them.

My car trunk contains a number of cardboard boxes, several of which are archival file boxes with hand inserts on the side. I have them because I want to see that my purchases make it home safe and sound. One of the boxes is filled with newspaper, diapers, and some bubble wrap. It supplements the field wrapping so that I can stack objects on top of each other. I check the trunk seals on a regular basis. A leaking car trunk once ruined several key purchases I made on an antiquing adventure.

A wide-brim hat may protect the face and neck from the sun, but it leaves the arms exposed. I admire those individuals who can wear a long-sleeved shirt year around. I am not one of them. In the summer, I wear short-sleeved shirts. For this reason, I keep a bottle of sun block in the trunk.

I also have a first aid kit that includes aspirin. The most used object is a Band-Aid for unexpected cuts and scratches. The aspirin comes in handy when I have spent eight or more hours in the sun. My first aid kit also contains packaged cleaning towelettes. I always use one before heading for home.

It does not take much for me to get a flea market high. When I do, I can go the entire day without eating. The same does not hold true for liquid intake. Just as toilet paper is a precious commodity at flea markets, so is ice. I carry a small cooler in my trunk with six to a dozen cans of my favorite beverage of the moment. The fastest way to seal a friendship with a flea market dealer is offer him a cold drink at the end of a hot day.

How to Shop a Flea Market

After attending flea markets for a number of years, I would like to share some of the things that I do to bag the treasures found in the flea market jungle. Much of what I am about to tell you is no more than common sense, but we all know that this is probably one of the most ignored of all the senses.

Most likely you will drive to the flea market. Parking is often a problem. It does not have to be. The general rule is to park as close to the main gate as possible. However, most flea markets have a number of gates. I usually try to park near a secondary gate. First, I get

closer. Second, I have long recognized that whatever gate I use is "my" main gate and can serve well as home base for my buying operations.

As soon as I arrive at the flea market, I check three things before allowing my buying adrenalin to kick into high gear—the location of toilets and refreshment stands and the relationship between outdoor and indoor facilities. The latter is very important. Dealers who regularly do the flea market are most likely to be indoors. If I miss them this time around, I can catch them the next. Dealers who are just passing through are most likely setup outdoors. If I miss them, I may never see them again.

I spend the first half hour at any flea market doing a quick tour in order to (a) understand how the flea market is organized, (b) spot those dealers that I would like to visit later, and (c) develop a general sense of what is happening. I prefer to start at the point farthest from my car and work my way front, just the opposite of most flea market shoppers. It makes trips back to the car shorter each time and reduces the weight of purchases that I am carrying over an extended period of time.

Whenever I go to a flea market to buy, I try to have one to four specific categories in mind. If one tries to look at everything, one develops "antiques and collectibles" shock. Collectors' minds short circuit if they try to absorb too much. They never get past the first aisle. With specific goals, a quick look at a booth will tell me whether or not it is likely to feature merchandise of interest. If not, I pass it by.

Since time is always at a premium, I make it a practice to ask every dealer, "Do you have any ————?" If they say "no," I usually go to the next booth. However, I have learned that dealers do not always remember what they have. When I am in a booth that should have the type of merchandise that I am seeking, I take a minute or two to do a quick scan to see if the dealer is right. In about twenty-five percent of the cases, I have found at least one example of the type of material for which I am looking.

I eat on the run, if I eat at all. A good breakfast before the market opens carries me

26

until the evening hours when dusk shuts down the market. I am at the flea market to stuff my bag and car trunk, not my face.

When I find a flea market that I like, I try to visit it at least once in the spring and once in the late summer or early fall. In many flea markets the same dealers are located in the same spot each time. This is extremely helpful to a buyer. I note their location on my sketch map of the market. When I return the next time, I ask these dealers if they have brought anything that fills my needs. If they say "yes," I ask them to hold it until I return. In most cases, a dealer will agree to hold a piece for one to two hours. Do not abuse the privilege, but do not hesitate to take advantage of it either.

There is an adage among antiques and collectibles collectors that "if you bought something at a flea market, you own it." I do my best to prove this adage wrong if I am not happy with a purchase. I am successful most of the time.

I try to get a receipt for every purchase that I make. Since many individuals who sell at outdoor flea markets are part-time dealers, they often are unprepared to give a receipt. No problem. I carry a pad of blank receipts and ask them to fill one out.

In every case, I ask the dealer to include his name, shop name (if any), mailing address, and phone number on the receipt. If I do not think he is telling me the truth, I ask him for identification. If they give me any flack, I go to their vehicle (usually located in their booth) or just outside their indoor stand and make note of the license plate number. Flea market dealers, especially the outdoor group, are highly mobile. If a problem develops with the merchandise that I bought, I want to reach the dealer in order to solve the problem.

Whenever possible, the receipt should contain a full description of the merchandise along with a completeness and condition statement. I also ask the dealer to write "money back guaranteed, no questions asked" on the receipt. This is the only valid guarantee that I know. Phrases such as "guaranteed as represented" and "money back" are open to interpretation and become relatively meaningless if a dispute develops.

I always shop around. At a good flea market, I expect to see the same merchandise in several booths. Prices will vary, often by hundreds if not thousands of percent. I make a purchase immediately only when a piece is a "real" bargain, priced way below current market value. If a piece is near current market value, I often inspect it, note its location on my sketch map, and walk away. If I do not find another in as good condition, at a cheaper price, or both, I go back and negotiate with the dealer.

I take the time to inspect carefully any piece that I buy in natural sunlight. First, I check for defects such as cracks, nicks, scratches, and signs of normal wear. Second, if the object involves parts, I make certain that it is complete. I have been known to take the time to carefully count parts. The last two times that I did not do this, the objects that I bought turned out to be incomplete when I got them home.

I frequently find myself asking a dealer to clean an object for my inspection. Outdoor flea markets are often quite dusty, especially in July and August. The insides of most indoor markets are generally not much better. Dirt can easily hide flaws. It also can discolor objects. Make certain you know exactly what you are buying.

I force myself to slow down and get to know those dealers from whom I hope to make future purchases. Even though it may mean that I do not visit the entire flea market, I have found that the long-term benefits from this type of contact far outweigh the short-term gain of seeing every booth.

Flea Market Food

Flea market food is best described as overcooked, greasy, and heartburn-inducing. I think I forgot to mention that my first aid kit contains a roll of antacid pills. Gourmet eating facilities are usually nonexistent. Is it any wonder that I often go without eating?

Several flea markets take place on sites that also house a farmer's market. When this is the case, I take time to shop the market and eat at one of its food counters or buy something that I can eat while sitting in my car. I make a point to spot any fast food restaurants in the vicinity of the flea market. If I get desperate, I get in the car and drive to one of them.

I do make it a point to inquire among the dealers where they go to have their evening meals. Their concerns generally focus on good food, plenty of it, and at an inexpensive cost. At the end of the day I am hungry. I do not feel like driving home, cleaning up, and then eating. I want to eat where the clientele can stand the appearance and smell of a flea marketeer. I have rarely been disappointed when I followed a flea market dealer's recommendation.

The best survival tactic is probably to bring your own food. I simply find this too much trouble. I get heartburn just thinking about a lunch sitting for several hours inside a car on a hot summer day. No thanks, I will buy what I need.

Follow-Up

Immediately upon returning home, at worst the next day, unpack and record all your purchases. If you wait, you are going to forget important details. This is not the fun part of collecting. It is easy to ignore. Discipline yourself to do it. Get in the habit. You know it is the right thing to do, so do it.

Review the business cards that you picked up and notes that you made. If letters are required, write them. If telephone calls are necessary, make them. Never lose sight of the fact that one of your principal reasons for going to the flea market is to establish long-term dealer contacts.

Finally, if your experiences at the flea market were positive or if you saw ways to improve the market, write a letter to the manager. He will be delighted in both instances. Competition among flea markets for dealers and customers is increasing. A good manager wants to make his market better than his competitors'. Your comments and suggestions will be welcomed.

Honing Your Shopping Skills

$$5$$

Earlier I mentioned that most buyers view flea markets as places where bargains and steals can be found. I have found plenty. However, the truth is that you have to hunt long and hard to find them and in some cases they evolve only after intense bargaining. Shopping a flea market properly requires skills. This chapter will help shape and hone those shopping skills and alert you to some of the pitfalls involved with buying at a flea market.

With What Type of Dealer Are You Dealing?

There are essentially three types of dealers found at flea markets—(a) the professional dealer, (b) the weekend dealer, and (c) the once-and-done dealer. Each brings a different level of expertise and merchandise to the flea market. Each offers pluses and minuses. Knowing with which type you are dealing is advantageous.

So many flea markets developed in the 1980s and 1990s that there are now professional flea market dealers who practice their craft on a full-time basis. Within any given week, you may find them at three or four different flea markets. They are the modern American gypsies; their living accommodations and merchandise are usually found within the truck, van, or station wagon in which they are traveling. These individuals survive on shrewdness and hustle. They want to turn their merchandise as quickly as possible for the best gain possible and are willing to do whatever is necessary to achieve this end.

Deal with the professional flea market dealer with a "questioning" mind, i.e., question everything they tell you about an object from what it is to what they want for it.

Their knowledge of the market comes from hands-on experience. It is not as great as they think in most cases. They are so busy setting up, buying, selling, and breaking down that they have little time for research or to follow trade literature. More than any other group of dealers in the trade, they are weavers of tales and sellers of dreams.

A professional flea market dealer's circuit can stretch from New England to California, from Michigan to Florida. He is constantly on the move. If you have a problem with something he sold you, finding him can prove difficult. Do not buy anything from him unless you are absolutely certain about it.

Judge the credibility and integrity of the professional flea market dealer by the quality of the merchandise he displays. He should have middle- and high-quality material in better condition than you normally expect to find. If his offerings are heavily damaged and appear poorly maintained, walk away.

Do not interpret what I have said to imply that all professional flea market dealers are dishonest. The vast majority are fine individuals. However, this group has the largest share of rotten apples in its barrel, more than any other group of dealers in the flea market field. Since there is no professional organization to police the trade and promoters do not care as long as their space rent is paid, it is up to you to protect yourself.

The antiques and collectibles field works on the principle of *caveat emptor*, "let the buyer beware." Just remember that the key is to beware of the seller as well as the merchandise. It pays to know with whom you are doing business.

Weekend flea market dealers are individuals who have a full-time job elsewhere and are dealing on the weekends to supplement their income. In most cases, their weekday job is outside the antiques and collectibles field. However, with the growth of the antiques mall, some of these weekend dealers are really full-time antiques and collectibles dealers. They spend their weekdays shopping and maintaining their mall locations, while selling on the weekend at their traditional flea market location.

In many cases, these dealers specialize, especially if they are in a large flea market environment. As a result, they are usually familiar with the literature relating to their areas of expertise. They also tend to live within a few hours drive of the flea market in which they set up. This means that they can be found if the need arises.

Once-and-done dealers range from an individual who is using the flea market to dispose of some inherited family heirlooms or portions of an estate to a collector who has culled his collection and is offering his duplicates and discards for sale. Bargains can often be found in both cases. In the first instance, bargains result from lack of pricing knowledge. However, unless you are an early arrival, chances are that the table will be picked clean by the regular dealers and pickers long before you show up. Bargains originate from the collector because he knows the price levels in his field. He realizes that in order to sell his discards and duplicates, he will have to create prices that are tempting to dealer and collector alike.

The once-and-done dealer is the least prepared to conduct sales on a business basis. Most likely they will not have a receipt book or a business card featuring their address and phone number. They almost never attempt to collect applicable sales tax.

There is little long-term gain in spending time getting to know the individual who is selling off a few family treasures. However, do not leave without asking, "Is there anything else you have at home that you are planning to sell?" Do spend time talking with the collector. If you have mutual collecting interests, invite him to visit and view your collection. What you are really fishing for is an invitation to view his holdings. You will be surprised how often it is given if you show genuine interest.

What Is It?

You need to be concerned about two things when looking at an object—what is it and how much is it worth? In order to answer the second question, you need a correct answer to the first. Information provided about objects for sale at flea markets is minimal and often nonexistent. In a great many cases, it is false. The only state of mind that protects you is a defensive one.

There are several reasons for the amount of misidentification of objects at flea markets. The foremost is dealer ignorance. They simply do not take the time to do proper research. I also suspect that they are quite comfortable with the adage that "ignorance is bliss." As long as an object comes close, they give it the most prestigious label they can.

When questioning a dealer about an object, beware of phrases such as "I think it is an. . . .," "As best as I can tell," "It looks exactly like," and "I trust your judgment." Push the dealer until you pin him down. The more he vacillates, the more suspicious you should become. Insist that the sales receipt carry his full claim about the object.

In many cases misidentification is passed along from person to person because the dealer who bought the object trusted what the dealer who sold him the object told him. I am always amazed how convinced dealers are that they are right. I have found there is little point in arguing with them in most cases. The only way to preserve both individuals' sanity is for me to walk away.

If you do not know what something is, do not buy it. The Warman guides that you have in your carrying bag can point you in the right direction, but they are not the final

answer. If you simply must persist in finding out right at that minute, consult the reference listings in the Warman guides and then check with the antiques and collectibles book dealer to see if the specific book you need is in stock.

Stories, Stories, and More Stories

A flea market is a place where one's creative imagination and believability level is constantly tested. The number of cleverly crafted stories to explain the origin of pieces and why the condition is not exactly what one expects are endless. The problem is that they all sound plausible. Once again, I come back to the concept that flea market survival hinges on a questioning mind.

I often ask a dealer to explain the circumstances by which he acquired a piece and what he knows about it. Note what I said. I am not asking him to reveal his source. No one should be expected to do that. I am testing the openness and believability of the dealer. If the dealer claims there is something special about an object, i.e., it belonged to a famous person or was illustrated in a book, I ask to see proof. Word-of-mouth stories have no validity in the long run.

Again, there are certain phrases that serve as tip-offs that something may be amiss. "It is the first one I have ever seen," "You will never find another one like it," "I saw one a few aisles over for more money," "One sold at auction a few weeks ago for double what I am asking," and "I am selling it to you for exactly what I paid for it" are just a few examples. If what you are hearing sounds too good to be true, it probably is.

Your best defense is to spend time studying and research the area in which you want to collect before going to flea markets. Emphasis should be placed equally on object identification and an understanding of the pricing structure within that collecting category. You will not be a happy person if you find that the object you bought is what you thought it should be but you paid far more than it is worth.

Period Reproduction, Copycat, Fantasy, or Fake

The number of reproductions, copycats, fantasy, and fake items at flea markets is larger than in any other segment of the field. Antiques and collectibles malls run a close second. In fact, it is not uncommon to find several stands at a flea market selling reproductions, copycats, and fantasy items. When you recognize them, take time to study their merchandise. Commit the material to memory. In ten years when the material has begun to age, you will be glad that you did.

Although the above terms are familiar to those who are active in the antiques and collectibles field, they may not be understood by some. A period piece is an example made during the initial period of production. The commonly used term is *real*. However, if you think about it, all objects are real, whether period or not. *Real* is one of those terms that should set your mind to questioning.

A reproduction is an exact copy of a period piece. There may be subtle changes in areas not visible to the naked eye, but essentially it is identical to its period counterpart. A copycat is an object that is similar, but different than the period piece it is emulating. It may vary in size, form, or design elements. In some cases, it is very close. In auction terms, copycats are known as "in the style of." A fantasy item is a form that was not issued during the initial period of production. An object licensed after Elvis's death would be an Elvis fantasy item. A Chippendale-style coffee table, a form which did not exist during the first Chippendale period, is another example.

The thing to remember is that reproductions, copycats, and fantasy items are generally mass-produced and start out life honestly. The wholesalers who sell them to dealers in the trade make it clear exactly what they are. Alas, some of the dealers do not do so when they resell them.

Because reproductions, copycats, and fantasy items are mass produced, they appear in the market in quantity. When you spot a piece in your collecting area that you have never seen before, quickly check through the rest of the market. If the piece is mint, double-check. Handle the piece. Is it the right weight? Does it have the right color? Is it the quality that you expect? If you answer "no" to any of these questions, put it back.

The vast majority of items sold at any flea market are mass-produced, twentieth century items. Encountering a new influx of never-seen-before items does not necessarily mean reproduction, copycat, or fantasy item. Someone may have uncovered a hoard. The trade term is *warehouse find*. A hoard can seriously affect the value of any antique or collectible. All of a sudden the number of available examples rises dramatically. So usually does the condition level. Unless the owner of a hoard is careful, this sudden release of material can drive prices downward.

A fake is an item deliberately meant to deceive. They are usually one-of-a-kind items, with many of them originating in shops of revivalist craftspersons. The folk art and furniture market is flooded with them. Do not assume that because an object is inexpensive, it is all right. You would be surprised how cheaply goods can be made in Third World countries.

It is a common assumption that reproductions, copycats, fantasy items, and fakes are of poor quality and can be easily spotted. If you subscribe to this theory, you are a fool. There are some excellent reproductions, copycats, fantasy items, and fakes. You probably have read on more than one occasion how a museum was fooled by an object in its collection. If museum curators can be fooled, so can you.

This is not the place for a lengthy dissertation on how to identify and differentiate period objects, reproductions, copycats, fantasies, or fakes. There are books on the subject. Get them and read them. What follows are a few quick tips to put you on the alert:

1. If it looks new, assume it is new.
2. Examine each object carefully looking for signs of age and repair that should be there.

3. Use all appropriate senses—sight, touch, smell, and hearing—to check an object.
4. Be doubly alert when something appears to be a steal.
5. Make a copy of any articles from trade papers or other sources that you find about period, reproduction, copycat, fantasy, and fake items and keep them on file.
6. Finally, handle as many correct objects as possible. The more you do, the easier the bad objects will be to spot.

What's a Fair Price?

I have imposed on my dad for permission to excerpt portions of "What's a Fair Price?" from *Rinker on Collectibles* (Wallace-Homestead Book Company: 1989), a compilation of some of his early weekly columns. The information he presents is worth considering.

Using price guides is fraught with dangers. They make people greedy. Novices turn to them for guidance without knowing how to evaluate the prices. . . .

Price guides should be viewed in the same context as a retail catalog from a department store. Admittedly, the prices are not as fixed and the exact items are not actually for sale.

However, any seller must understand that the prices in a price guide represent what a *serious* collector will pay. As such, they reflect the highest potential value for an object to a very select, very small group of people.

An Elvis Presley guitar in its original box has a book value of $400 to $600. But it has that value only to an Elvis Presley collector and only to an Elvis collector who does not already own one. Someone who collects Avon bottles might not be willing to pay $10 for the Elvis guitar. . . .

The biggest component of any collectible's value is the buyer. Without the buyer, the collectible is worth very little. Knowing to whom to sell a collectible is worth between fifty and sixty-five percent of its value. . . .Dealers and others have spent years learning who the "top buyers" are in each specialized collectibles category. . . .

Dealers have a right to make a profit and deserve the profit that they make. The expenses are considerable for a dealer with an open shop or who works the show circuit regularly. Overhead must be paid before they can pay themselves a salary. Selling collectibles is one of the hardest ways of making a living.

Selling collectibles is labor- and capital-intensive. When a dealer buys a collection it must be sorted, prepared for sale, researched, stored, displayed, and merchandised. This takes time, and time is money. . . .

A good price is a price at which both the buyer and seller are happy. [In most cases, this price is determined at a flea market through negotiation.]

Flea Market Haggling

Few prices at a flea market are firm prices. No matter what anyone tells you, it is standard practice to haggle. You may not be comfortable doing it, but you might as well learn how. The money that you save will be your own.

In my mind there are only three prices—a bargain price, a negotiable price, and a ridiculous price. If the price on an object is already a bargain, I pay it. I do this because I like to see the shocked look on a seller's face when I do not haggle. I also do it because I want that dealer to find similar material for me. Nothing encourages this more than paying the price asked.

If the price is ridiculous, marked several times above what it is worth, I simply walk

away. No amount of haggling will ever get the price to where I think it belongs. All that will happen is that the dealer and I will become frustrated. Who needs it? Let the dealer sit with his pieces. Sooner or later, the message will become clear.

I firmly believe it is the responsibility of the seller to set the asking price. When an object is not marked with a price, I become suspicious that the dealer is going to set his asking price based on what he thinks I can pay. I have tested this theory on more than one occasion by sending several individuals to inquire about the value of an unmarked item. In every case, a variety of prices were reported back to me. Since most of the material that I collect is mass-produced, I walk away from all unpriced merchandise. I will find another example somewhere else. This type of dealer does not deserve my business.

I have too much to do at a flea market to waste time haggling. If I find a piece that is close to what I am willing to pay, I make a counteroffer. I am very clear in what I tell the seller. "I am willing to pay 'x' amount. This is my best offer. Will you take it?" Most dealers are accustomed to responding with "Let's half the difference." Hard though it is at times, I never agree. I tell the dealer that I made him my best offer to save time haggling, and I intend to stick by it.

If the flea market that I am attending is a monthly or weekly, I may follow the object for several months. At the end of four to five months, I speak with the dealer and call his attention to the fact that he has been unsuccessful in selling the object for the amount he was asking. I make my counteroffer, which sometimes can be as low as half the value marked on the piece. While he may not be totally happy selling the object at that price, the prospect of any sale is often far better than keeping the object in inventory for several more months.

In Summary

If you are gullible, flea markets may not be for you. While not a Darwinian jungle, the flea market has pitfalls and traps which must be avoided in order for you to be successful. The key is to know that these pitfalls and traps exist.

Further, successful flea marketeering comes from practice. There is no school or seminar where you can learn the skills you need. You fly by the seat of your pants, learn as you go, wing it. The tuition that you pay will be the mistakes that you make along the way. Never get discouraged. Everyone else you see at the flea market has experienced or is experiencing exactly what is happening to you. When you become a seasoned veteran, you will look back upon the learning period and laugh. In the interim, at least try to smile.

The Flea Market Scene Today

6

This is an extremely difficult analysis for me to write. Thus far, my approach has been positive, and, I hope, occasionally humorous. Now, I must get serious—deadly serious. Flea markets face a myriad of problems in the 1990s. I think you should be aware of them. I do not believe in the adage: "If you cannot say something nice about something, do not say anything at all." Nothing is achieved by sweeping the problems under the carpet. On the other hand, bad news and good news often go hand in hand. This holds true for the 1990s flea market scene. Since I want to end this introduction to flea markets on an upbeat note, I address the negative aspects first.

Even though flea markets lost a great deal of their luster in the 1980s, they remain a major selling route in the antiques and collectibles field. As the 1990s begin, antiques and collectibles flea markets are at a crossroads. If they continue in their traditional mode, they will move farther and farther away from the main stream. They need to change. The critical questions are how and who will take the lead?

In the late 1980s new flea markets were created and existing flea markets enlarged their size to accommodate the ever increasing number of individuals who wanted to be antiques and collectibles dealers. The number of Brimfield sites doubled. The market expanded from a four-day event to a ten day event.

Collectors became confused. What market should they attend? In any given weekend, especially in the East, their choices may range over half a dozen sites. If you have only two weeks of vacation a year, how can you attend three ten-day sessions at Brimfield? What is the best day to attend? Many flea markets now open on a weekday. The collector is forced to take off from work. If he does not, he fears that he will miss the bargains. No one wants the leavings or to find a piece after it has passed through several dealers' hands with the corresponding price increases.

While the cost to rent space at most flea markets remains modest, the secondary costs of doing a flea market have began to cut heavily into the profit margin of most flea market dealers. Motel costs have doubled and often tripled. The price of food and gasoline spirals upward. These same costs also affected collectors who were accustomed to spending a weekend at a flea market and now must stretch their stay if they hope to cover the entire event.

The number of dealers is increasing faster than the availability of quality antiques and collectibles, especially pre-1940 objects. In the mid-1980s this resulted in an across-the-board rise in value for most categories of antiques and collectibles. The availability of reasonably priced merchandise dried up in late 1989. By mid-1990 many flea market dealers were not replacing stock that they sold, especially in the antiques sector.

Rentals at many flea markets dropped by twenty-five to thirty-five percent. The economic recession of 1990 is a blessing in disguise. As dealers drop out and weak flea markets fail, the resulting consolidation of quality dealers in a few strong markets will result in more stable prices than those seen during the speculative boom of the late 1980s.

Much of the flea market activity is moving indoors. As the value of antiques and collectibles rise, fewer and fewer dealers are willing to risk their stock to the elements. In a way, I miss the tables of Mount Washington and cameo glass outdoors at Brimfield and Renninger's. Seeing the good stuff in natural sunlight was part of the charm. Even

Renninger's gave into the trend and built several pavilions for their Kutztown Extravaganza.

Although I know flea market managers do not want to hear this and will argue strenuously against it, the quality and condition of material offered for sale at flea markets in the 1980s took a serious downward turn. Many of the offerings were nothing more than junk. It would be more proper for them to reside in a landfill than in a collector's home. Based on my observations, one-quarter to one-third of all the so-called antiques and collectibles dealers at most flea markets should not be allowed to setup.

As new antiques and collectibles flea markets were created and established markets expanded, not all the available spaces were filled. Managers began renting space to sellers of crafts, reproduction and copycat wholesalers, discontinued merchandise, new merchandise, clothing, plants, produce, and food. Collectors who traveled for several hours or days expecting to find a field or building filled with recognizable antiques and collectibles were understandably disappointed. Word of their disappointment spread. The Rose Bowl Flea Market in Pasadena, California, fell from legend to "avoid" status. Antiques and collectibles flea market managers have to realize that their customers are going to become even more selective in the future. A housecleaning is long overdue.

Many new dealers were unwilling to spend years learning the trade and building a viable inventory. Instead, they turned to the reproduction and copycat wholesalers for merchandise. Entire booths can be found at many flea markets filled with new "old" things. More often than not, no effort is made to mark them as reproductions. Things are getting so bad that I suspect that upwards of ten to fifteen percent of the material at flea markets is questionable. Actually, I am being conservative. I have heard discussions in which the figure approached forty and fifty percent. The public is growing increasingly aware of the problem. Managers can no longer look the other way. If they do, they put their market at risk.

Perhaps the hardest thing for old-time antiques and collectibles flea market dealers to accept is the changing chronological period for flea market merchandise. The "hot" material at a 1990s flea market dates after 1945. The vast majority of today's young collectors focus on this period. It is far easier to sell a Hopalong Cassidy lunch box than it is a copper luster creamer. Flea market goers, more than any other group, tend to collect what they remember from their childhood. Flea market dealers who stock this merchandise at reasonable prices are doing well.

There is a growing knowledge gap between many flea market dealers and their customers. Collectors are becoming much more educated and sophisticated. In many cases, their knowledge is now greater than that of the flea market dealer. No longer can flea market dealers rely simply on the prestige of their being a dealer to add credibility to what they say and what they sell.

Collector sophistication is best documented by the increasing demand for objects in very good or better condition. Flea market merchandise was mass-produced. This means that items were made in tens and hundreds of thousands. Collectors know that they do not have to settle for a damaged or incomplete example. One in very good condition or better will come along.

Flea market customers, accepting the fact that there is likely to be more than one example of any given object for sale in the marketplace, began to do comparison shopping. The urge to buy the minute an object was spotted was tempered. I think it has been lost. Further, I am not certain it can ever be recaptured.

Finally, antiques and collectibles flea markets have to address the competition created by the antiques and collectibles mall. The mall environment provides dealers with a freedom that is unavailable at weekly and monthly flea markets. In general malls are cleaner and brighter, feature attractive displays and display units, have a higher degree of professional management, and, in many instances, provide computer search services.

In order to survive, flea markets must go on the offensive. First, they have to match these operating practices. Second, they need to introduce innovative marketing tools that provide services that malls do not.

As I said earlier, the flea market scene has problems. It also has positive features as well.

Flea markets still remain one of the best initial sources for goods entering the market. You have to hunt longer and harder for the bargains and the steals, but there is not a flea market in existence that does not have plenty.

Flea market dealers were the first group to respond to the recent economic recession by reexamining their pricing structure. Many lowered prices, especially in middle- and low-level merchandise. There is an increased willingness to negotiate. Objects above average in quality and condition retain high prices. These objects sell no matter what the nation's economy.

Flea market dealers have accepted the fact that one of the keys to survival is customer service. The arrogance, and I believe some of the greed, of the 1980s is gone. The chaotic tenor of the 1980s has given way to a more relaxed, easy-going pace. Some of this has to do with the fact that the number of attendees is down. Flea markets are simply not as crowded as they used to be. Dealers and managers may not be happy with this turn of events. However, the individuals who are attending are the serious buyers. It is the "lookers" who are gone, a group about which dealers have been complaining for years.

Actually, this is a great time to shop a flea market if you are willing to accept the challenge of the hunt. It is a buyer's market. More and more flea market dealers are supplementing their flea market sales by quoting merchandise through the mail. In the 1980s, the collector cultivated the dealer. Now the situation is reversed. The wants lists that you hand out will bear more fruit than ever.

A number of managers have begun to correct some of the problems listed above. Renninger's Twin Markets in Mount Dora, Florida, is light years ahead of its Adamstown and Kutztown, Pennsylvania, parents. It is housed in a new, well lighted, spacious

building that is properly maintained. It still has a major problem with the amount of reproductions and copycats being offered for sale. But, at least you have room to spot them and adequate light to see them.

Some promoters are policing their markets. They are demanding that reproductions or copycats be properly marked or removed from sale. They become involved in resolving problems that develop between one of their dealers and a customer. When a dealer shows up with poor quality merchandise, they refuse to allow him to setup.

Several years ago, the antiques and collectibles show promoters organized. It is time for the antiques and collectibles flea market managers to do the same. Many flea market managers have aggressive, competitive, and somewhat brusque personalities. This is why they survive. Putting ten of them in a room and trying to get them to agree on anything may require an act of God. I hope He acts soon.

Permit me one final thought. The key to having an enjoyable experience at a flea market does not rest with the manager, the dealers, the physical setting, or the merchandise. The key is you. Attend with reasonable expectations in mind. Go to have fun, to make a pleasant day of it. Even if you come home with nothing, savor the contacts that you made and the fact that you spent a few hours or longer among the goodies.

As a smart flea marketeer, you know the value of customers to keep a flea market alive and functioning. When you find a good flea market, do not keep the information to yourself. Write or call the regional trade papers and ask them to do more stories about the market. Share your news with friends and others. Encourage them to attend. There is plenty for everyone.

Happy Hunting from my dad, the Rinkettes, and me.

Part Two
FLEA MARKET
TREASURES

Price Notes

Flea market prices for antiques and collectibles are not as firmly established as those at malls, shops, and shows. As a result, it is imperative that you treat the prices found in this book as *guides*, not *absolutes*.

Prices given are based on the national retail price for an object that is complete and in fine condition. *Please Note: These are retail prices.* They are what you would expect to pay to purchase the objects. They do not reflect what you might realize if you were selling objects. A "fair" selling price to a dealer or private collector ranges from 20 to 40 percent of the book price depending on how commonly found the object is that you are trying to sell.

Prices quoted are for objects that show a minimum of wear and no major blemishes to the display surface. The vast majority of flea market objects are mass produced. As such, they survive in quantity. Do not buy damaged or imcomplete objects. It also pays to avoid objects that show signs of heavy use.

Regional pricing is a factor within the flea market arena, expecially when objects are being sold close to their place of manufacture. When faced with strong regional pricing, I have chosen to use the price an object would bring in a neighboring state or geographic area. In truth, regional pricing has all but disappeared due to the large number of nationally-oriented antiques and collectibles price guides, magazines, newspapers, and collectors' clubs.

Finally, *you* determine price; it is what *you* are willing to pay. Flea market treasures have no fixed prices. What has value to one person may be totally worthless to another.

Is it possible to make sense out of this chaos? Yes, but in order to do so, you have to jump in feet first, attend flea markets, and buy.

Happy Hunting! May all your purchases turn out to be treasures.

Abbreviations

These are standard abbreviations used in the listings in *Price Guide to Flea Market Treasures.*

adv	advertising	mfg	manufactured
C	century	MIB	mint in box
c	circa	mkd	marked
circ	circular	MOP	mother of pearl
d	diameter or depth	No.	number
dec	decorated	orig	original
dj	dust jacket	oz	ounces
emb	embossed	pcs	pieces
ext.	exterior	pgs	pages
ftd	footed	pkg	package
h	height	pr	pair
hp	hand painted	qt	quart
illus	illustration	rect	rectangular
imp	impressed	sgd	signed
int.	interior	SS	sterling silver
j	jewels	sq	square
K	karat	vol	volume
l	length	w	width
lb	pound	yg	yellow gold
litho	lithograph		

Categories and Prices

ABINGDON POTTERY

Over the years, Roseville and Weller pottery, favorites of old–time traditionalist collectors of mass–produced pottery wares, have become more and more expensive. In the 1970s and 1980s collectors with limited budgets began concentrating on firms such as Gonder, Hall, Hull, McCoy, Stangl, and Vernon Kiln. Now this material is going up in value. Stretch your dollar by concentrating on some of the firms that still have limited collector appeal. Abingdon Potteries, Inc., J. A. Bauer Pottery Company, Haeger Potteries, Metlox Potteries, and Pfaltzgraff Pottery Company are a few suggestions. I'll bet you can think of many more.

The Abingdon Sanitary Manufacturing Company began manufacturing bathroom fixtures in 1908 in Abingdon, IL. In 1938, they began production of art pottery made with a vitreous body. This line continued until 1970 and included over 1,000 shapes and pieces. Almost 150 colors were used to decorate these wares. Given these numbers, forget about collecting an example of every form in every color ever made. Find a few forms that you like and concentrate on them. There are some great ones.

Bookends, pr
   Cactus, 6" h 60.00
   Sea Gull, 6" h 40.00
Bowl, 13½" d, white, oval 6.00
Cookie Jar
   Daisy, 8" h 30.00
   Humpty Dumpty, gold trim 115.00
   Little Girl, 9½" h 40.00
   Pineapple, 10½" h 70.00
Planter
   Cactus, 7" l, bookend type, pr 55.00
   Scroll and Leaf pattern, 9" × 3½", yellow 6.50
String Holder, mouse, 8½" d 80.00
Vase
   Cactus, #669 . . . . 15.00
   Scroll, soft green, flared, 9" h 5.00
   Sea Horse 18.00

Wall Pocket
   Book 40.00
   Calla 20.00
   V–shape 35.00

ACTION FIGURES

Action, action, action is the key to action figures. Action figures show action. You can recognize them because they can be manipulated into an action pose or are modeled into an action pose.

There are a wealth of supporting accessories for most action figures, ranging from clothing to vehicles, that are as collectible as the figures themselves. A good rule is the more pizzazz, the better the piece.

This is a relatively new collecting field. Emphasis is placed on pieces in mint or near–mint condition. The best way to find them is with their original packaging. Better yet, buy some new and stick them away.

Periodical: *Action Figure News & Review, 39 N. Hillside Lane, Monroe, CT 06468.*

NONPOSABLE FIGURES

Batman and Robin, Ideal, c1967, 3" h, plastic, painted to match figure's costume 39.00
James Bond 007, replica figures, A.C. Gilbert, c1965, 3½" h, molded base, each painted to the character's costume, ext. Bond in black dinner jacket, Goldfinger in yellow suit etc 5.00
101 Dalmatians, Disney, Marx, 2½" white, soft plastic, 10 figures, set 75.00
World of Tomorrow, spacemen figures, Archer, 4" h, hard plastic, metallic green 12.00

POSABLE ACTION FIGURES

Green Hornet, Lakeside Inc, 6" h, green, gray, and black, fleshtone face and hands, 1966 20th Century Fox copyright 35.00

Aquaman, Mego, 8" h, hard plastic, yellow, green, and black outfit, gloves, "A" sticker on belt, National Periodical Publications Inc 1972 copyright on box. . . . **75.00**
Indiana Jones, Kenner c1982, 3¾" h, plastic, painted to match character's costume **6.00**

ADVENTURE GAMES

Adventure games have been played for hundreds of years. In an adventure game, each player is asked to assume the role of a character. The character's fate is determined by choices that he and other players make. The rules are often very complex; games can last for days, even months.

There are many different game scenarios, ranging from sports and entertainment, war and conflict, to finance and fortune. The principal marketing source for current games is the comic book shop. Some comic book shops are also starting to handle discontinued games.

Collectors fall into two groups: those who buy discontinued games to play them and those who buy them solely for the purpose of collecting them. Both groups place strong emphasis on completeness. Many of the games contain more than one hundred different playing pieces. Few take the time to count all the parts. This is why adventure games tend to be relatively inexpensive when found at garage sales and flea markets.

A small group of individuals have begun to collect playing pieces, many of which are hand painted. However, rarely does the price paid exceed the initial cost of the figure.

Avalon Hill, Management, copyright 1960. . . . . **15.00**
Avalon Hill, Gettysburg, copyright 1958. . . . . **30.00**
Psychology Today Games, Woman & Man: The Classic Confrontation, copyright 1971 . . . . **12.50**
3M (Minnesota Mining and Manufacturing Company), High-Bid: The Auction Game, copyright 1965. . . . . **7.50**

ADVERTISING ITEMS

Break advertising items into two groups: items used to merchandise a product and items used to promote a product. Merchandising advertising is a favorite with interior decorators and others who want it for its mood–setting ability. It is often big, splashy, and showy. Promotional advertising (giveaways) are primarily collector–driven.

The thing to remember is that almost every piece of advertising is going to appeal to more than one collector. As a result, prices for the same piece will often differ significantly depending on who the seller views as the final purchaser.

Almost all advertising is bought for the purpose of display. As a result, emphasize theme and condition. The vast majority of advertising collectibles are two–dimensional. Place a premium on large three–dimensional objects.

Avalon Hill, Management, copyright ©1960, $15.00.

Sign, Little Mommie Brand Sox, metal, white, red, and black lettering, 14" × 7", $35.00.

Clubs: Antique Advertising Association, P.O. Box 1121, Morton Grove, IL 60053, 708/446-0904; The Ephemera Society of

America, P. O. Box 37, Schoharie, NY 12157; Tin Container Collectors Association, P. O. Box 440101, Aurora, CA 80014.

Trade card, G. W. Fairchild, Diamonds, Watches, and Jewelry, Bridgeport, CT, blank back, 2⅝" × 4¹/₁₆", $3.00.

Newspapers: *National Association of Paper and Advertising Collectibles*, P. O. Box 500, Mount Joy, PA 17552; *Paper Collectors' Marketplace* (PCM), P. O. Box 128, Scandinavia, WI 54917.

Anvil, Anvil Overalls, Hard to Beat, High Point, NC 35.00
Ashtray, GE Transformers 18.00
Ball, Poll Parrot Shoes, rubber, 1930s 20.00
Billhook, Ceresota Flour 45.00
Blotter
Brown & Bigelow, 9", signed "Paul Webb" 7.00
Webster Flour 4.00
Booklet, Western Ammo, 1930s 15.00
Brochure, Max Factor Make-up, includes Lana Turner, Loretta Young 10.00
Change Receiver, Teaberry Gum 75.00
Checkerboard, Mueller's Spaghetti, 1940s 25.00
Counter Display, box type
Aunt Lydia's Button & Carpet Thread, black letters, natural oak finish, dovetailed wood case, 11" × 9½" × 4½" 70.00
Dennison Xmas Seals, 48 boxes of seals, c1930 . . . . 75.00
Jar, Kiss Me Gum 85.00
Lunch Pail, Union Leader Tobacco 32.50
Pencil Clip
Keller's Butter/Eggs,⅞", red, white, and

blue celluloid, silvered tin clip, c1940 . . . . 15.00
Viking Snuff,⅞", blue and white celluloid, silvered tin clip, 1930s 20.00
Pinback Button
Atlantic Lawn Grass Seed, 1¼" d, green, red, and white, c1930s 10.00
Aunt Jemima Breakfast Club, 1½" × 2¼", tin, litho, diecut, portrait, red and white lettering 15.00
Blue Valley Creamery Co,¾" × 1½", celluloid, diecut, milk can shape, silver, early 1900s 20.00
Dandee Bread, 1¼" d, tan, black, and white, early 1900s 20.00
Guernsey Products, 1" d, blue lettering, yellow ground, c1930s 10.00
Huber Steamer, multicolored 70.00
Nuttall Gear, 1½", celluloid, oval, diecut, black and white gear wheel, red inscription "Every Nuttall Gear is Registered, Nuttall, Pittsburgh," c1920s 10.00
Red, White and Blue Coffee, 1" d, red, white, and blue, 1930s–1940s 12.50
Ridgways Tea,⅞" d, green and white, red lettering, c1920s 15.00
Saginaw Silo, multicolored 25.00
Sunbeam Bread, 1⅛" d, litho, Sunbeam Girl, red, white, and blue, 1930s–1940s 15.00
Tennent Shoe Co, multicolored 25.00
Tonic Moka Java Coffee,½" × ¾", celluloid, diecut, coffee cup and saucer, light blue, red, and white, early 1900s 15.00
Playing Cards, Brown & Bigelow, 50th anniversary, 1946 . . . . 20.00
Poster
Cocomalt, 10" × 16", full color, features premium book "Walt Disney's Pinocchio," 1939 . . . . 150.00
Lux Radio Theater, 15" × 23", full color, adv Broadway hits broadcast through Columbia network, sponsored by Lux Toilet Soap, c1930 . . . . 40.00
Weatherbird Shoes, free standing, multicolored, rooster weather vane 75.00
Winchester, squirrel, 1955 . . . . 50.00
Shoe Horn, Queen Quality, 2" × 6", celluloid, curled handle, color portrait of lady, one ivory, one beige, early 1900s, pr 35.00
Sign
Harley Davidson Cigarettes, tin 45.00
Spoon, Iron Monarch Range 45.00
Stickpin, Burk Pork Packers, pig, c1900 . . . . 35.00
Store Display, Butterfly Barrettes, holds 12, c1930 . . . . 30.00
Tin
CD Kinney Coffee 30.00
Du Pont, powder, 1924 . . . . 40.00

46

Grandma Moses Coffee	**18.00**
Lucky Strike, domed	**15.00**
Mick McQuaid Tobacco	**10.00**
Winchester Bullets, 1960s	**45.00**
Trade Card	
Johnson Shoes, mechanical, Santa	**35.00**
Wilbur's Chocolate & Cocoa, boy and	
girl, multicolored front and back,	
diecut, c1890	**20.00**
Tray, Teaberry Gum, glass, yellow	**125.00**
Tumbler, Klee–Klo Eskimo	**24.00**
Watch Fob, Old Reliable Coffee	**85.00**
Whistle, Butter–Nut Bread, c1920s	**17.00**

AFRICANA

The bulk of what you see out there is junk—either souvenirs brought home by tourists or decorative pieces sold by discount or department stores. The problem is twofold. First, modern–day African craftsman continue to work in centuries–old traditions, making pieces with the same tools and in the same form as did their ancestors. Second, telling the difference between a piece made a century ago and a piece made a few months ago requires years of study. The only safe assumption is that most flea market dealers do not have the slightest idea which is which.

When buying African art at flea markets, be cheap about it. Never pay more than you can afford to lose. Buy primarily for decoration. When you think that you have found the real thing, have it checked by a museum curator.

Many pieces of African art involve the use of animal hides and tusks. Be extremely cautious about buying any object made from animals that are on the endangered species list.

Quality African art does show up at flea markets. The listings show some possibilities if you spot the real thing.

Bowl, 29" h, cov, carved woman sitting on
  top, geometric edges, three legs, flat
  base, c1920 . . . . **350.00**
Door Lock, 19" × 19", carved man, cross
  bar handle, dark brown stain, Mali,
  20th C **270.00**
Figure
  Ibiji, 12" h, male effigy, punch hole eyes,
    Nigeria, late 19th C **125.00**
  Senufo, 39" h, female, relief facial dec,
    brown and black paint, Ivory Coast,
    1940s **350.00**
Grain Scoop, 16¼" l, dark wood, handle tip
  carved with Dan style face, Liberia,
  1930s **175.00**

Helmet, 15" l, wood, engraved geometric
  triangular, Bobo, 1920s **170.00**
Knife, 22½", iron blade, wood handle,
  engraved snakeskin pattern, late 19th to
  early 20th C **145.00**
Mask, wood, carved
  Dan, oval–shaped face, dark brown
    paint, Liberia Border **300.00**
  Guro Bird, 13½", bird atop head, Ivory
    Coast **120.00**
  Horned Guro, 16", curved horns, Ivory
    Coast **175.00**
Staff, 15" l, wood, head–shaped finial,
  varnished, Zaire, Yaka Tribe, 1940s **125.00**
Stool, 12" h, 17" l, wood, U–shaped seat,
  brown, openwork dec, 1930–1940 . . . **425.00**

AKRO AGATE GLASS

When the Akro Agate Company was founded in 1911, its principal product was marbles. The company was forced to diversify during the 1930s, developing floral ware lines and children's dishes. Some collectors specialize in containers made by Akro Agate Company for the cosmetic industry.

Akro Agate merchandised a great many of its products as sets. Full sets that retain their original packaging command a premium price. Learn what pieces and colors constitute a set. Some dealers will mix and match pieces into a false set, hoping to get a better price.

Most Akro Agate pieces are marked "Made in USA" and have a mold number. Some, but not all, have a small crow flying through an "A" as a mark.

Flower pot, Westite, brown streaks, 5¼" h,
$15.00.

47

Club: Akro Agate Art Association, P. O. Box 758, Salem, NH 03079.

Ashtray

Ellipsoid, dark jade	5.00
Westite, gray and brown marble, rect playing card, recessed spade	10.00

Basket, orange and white marbleized, two handles ... 28.50

Bowl

5", orange and white marbleized, emb leaves	35.00
6", Westite, brown and white marbleized.	18.00

Children's Dishes

Saucer, Interior Panel, opaque, green	3.00
Set, Concentric Rib, 12 pcs, opaque, green plate and cup, tan saucer	32.00

Teapot

Concentric Ring, opaque, cobalt, white lid	30.00
Interior Panel, opaque, green	9.00
Octagonal, 2¾", opaque, blue, white lid	13.00
Water Set, Stack Disc, opaque, green pitcher, six white tumblers, orig box	90.00

Cigarette Box, Mexicali ... 28.00

Demitasse Cup and Saucer, orange and white ... 12.50

Flower-pot

1¾", yellow, ribbed top	9.50
4", Stacked Disc, blue and white marbleized	15.00
5¼", Westite, brown and white marbleized.	15.00

Jardiniere, 4½", Westite, green and white marbleized. ... 17.50

Match Holder, 3", gun shape, marbleized ... 10.00

Nasturtium Bowl, 6" d Graduated Darts, pumpkin, ftd ... 15.00

Planter, 4½ × 2½" Hexagon, opaque, green ... 15.00

Powder Box, 3½" d Spun, green marble, cov, ftd ... 30.00

Powder Jar, Scottie, blue ... 48.00

Tumbler, 2⅝", octagonal, green and white ... 6.00

Urn, 3¼", orange and white, ftd ... 6.50

Vase

6¼" h, Westite, gray and brown marble, tab handles.	30.00
8", Ribs and Flutes, cobalt	38.00

ALADDIN

The Mantle Lamp Company of America, founded in 1908 in Chicago, is best known for its lamps. However, in the late 1950s through the 1970s, it also was one of the leading producers of character lunch boxes.

Aladdin deserves a separate category because of the large number of lamp collectors who concentrate almost exclusively on this one company. There is almost as big a market for parts and accessories as for the lamps themselves. Collectors are constantly looking for parts to restore a lamp in their possession.

Club: The Mystic Light of the Aladdin Knights, R. D. #1, Simpson, IL 62985.

Bracket, Model B	75.00
Caboose, Model 23, shade.	45.00
Floor, Model 1250, 60" h.	325.00

Hanging

Model B, parchment shade	125.00
Model 4, opal shade.	275.00
Model 9	225.00

Kerosene

Model C, table, aluminum font	45.00
Model 14, table, brass font, England	75.00
Model 23, table, aluminum font	35.00
Style B-62, Short Lincoln Drape, ruby crystal.	425.00
Style B-82D, Beehive, amber, dark crystal.	100.00
Style B-122, Majestic, green moonstone.	150.00
Style B-133, Orientale, silver.	100.00
Style B-137, Treasure, bronze	75.00

Practicus

Parlor.	350.00
Table	175.00

Table

Style 100, Venetian, white	50.00
Style 106, Colonial, amber crystal.	125.00
Style 108, Cathedral, green crystal	70.00
Style B-104, Corinthian, clear font, black foot	60.00
Style B-116, Corinthian, rose moonstone.	150.00

ALBUMS

The Victorian craze has drawn attention to the Victorian photograph album that enjoyed an honored place in the parlor. The more common examples had velvet or leather covers. However, the ones most eagerly sought by collectors are those featuring a celluloid cover with motifs ranging from floral to Spanish American War battleships.

Most albums housed "family" photographs, the vast majority of which are unidentified. If the photographs are head and shoulders or baby shots, chances are they have little value unless the individuals are famous. Photographs of military figures, actors and actresses, and freaks are worth checking out further.

Cardboard albums still have not found favor with collectors. However, check the interior contents. In many cases, they contain postcards, clippings, match covers, or photographs that are worth far more than the album.

Daguerreotype, gutta percha, baroque motif cover.	**45.00**
Victorian family photograph album	
Celluloid cover	
Beautiful woman.	**150.00**
Floral motif	**75.00**
Spanish–American War battleship	**200.00**
Leather cover.	**30.00**
Velvet cover	
Fancy with raised design and gold highlights.	**45.00**
Plain.	**25.00**

ALUMINUM, HANDWROUGHT

With increasing emphasis on post-World War II collectibles, especially those from the 1950s, handwrought aluminum is enjoying a collecting revival. The bulk of the pieces were sold on the giftware market as decorative accessories.

Do not be confused by the term *handwrought.* The vast majority of the pieces were mass produced. The two collecting keys appear to be manufacturer and unusualness of form.

There is an enormous difference between flea market prices and prices at a major show within driving distance of New York City. Handwrought aluminum is quite trendy at the moment among the "arty" community.

Newsletter: *The Alumist,* P. O. Box 1346, Weatherford, TX 76086.

Ashtray, Wendell August Forge, Quaker State Motor Oil adv	**7.50**
Basket, Milcraft, 13", Intaglio Wheat pattern	**10.00**
Bowl, Continental Silverlook, 11¼", Chrysanthemum pattern.	**14.00**
Candleholder, Everlast Forged Aluminum, lily	**5.00**
Compote, Continental Handwrought, Silverlook, 5" h, wild rose	**12.00**

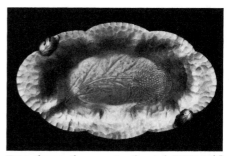

Tray, chrysanthemum, Continental, #572, 13¼" × 7¾", $15.00.

Creamer and Sugar, World Hand Forged, cupped shape.	**8.00**
Gravy Boat, Hand Forged/Everlast Metal, 7".	**10.00**
Ladle, Argental Cellini Craft, 14½"	**18.00**
Matchbox Holder, Wendell August Forge	**8.00**
Pitcher, Buenilum, ovoid, twisted handle	**24.00**
Serving Dish, Continental Hand Wrought, Silverlook, 7¾", wild rose pattern	**10.00**
Silent Butler, Henry & Miller, 6" × 8", oval, floral bouquet	**8.00**
Tray	
Buenilum, 12" × 18", leaf and flower dec	**18.00**
National Silver Co, 11" × 16", bird on flowering limb dec	**15.00**
Rodney Kent, 14" × 20", tulip dec.	**25.00**

AMERICAN CHINA DINNERWARE

There is a growing appreciation for the thousands of dinnerware patterns that graced the tables of low–, middle–, and some upper–income families during the first three-quarters of the twentieth century. Some of America's leading industrial designers were responsible for forms and decorative motifs.

Collectors fall into three groups: those who collect the wares of a specific factory or factories, often with a strong regional emphasis; individuals who are reassembling the set they grew up with; and those who are fascinated by certain forms and motifs. The bulk of the books on the subject appeared in the early 1980s. Prices stabilized in the mid-1980s and remain so today.

Several of the companies have become established collecting categories in their own right. This is why you will find companies such as Blue Ridge and Hall elsewhere in this book.

COORS
Coors Pottery was manufactured in Golden, CO, from 1920 to 1939.

Purinton, Apple, plate, 6⅞", $5.00.

Rosebud
Baking Pan, 12¼" × 8¾"	**20.00**
Bean Pot, cov, yellow	**22.00**
Cake Plate	**18.00**
Cereal Bowl, 6"d, yellow...........	**12.00**
Custard Cup, blue	**12.00**
Mixing Bowl, handle, orange	**25.00**
Plate	
6"d, bread and butter............	**10.00**
9"d, dinner....................	**12.00**
Teapot, rose...................	**50.00**
Utility Jar, cov, yellow.............	**25.00**

CROOKSVILLE
The Crooksville China Company, Crooksville, OH, was founded in 1902 for the manufacture of artware "such as vases, flowerpots, and novelties." Dinnerware soon became its stock and trade. Manufacture continued until 1959.

Euclid, 1935
Casserole, 8"d	**18.00**
Creamer......................	**5.00**
Cup and Saucer.................	**6.50**
Syrup Jug.....................	**15.00**
Platter, 11½"l, rect...............	**5.00**
Sugar........................	**8.00**

Pantry Bak–In Ware, 1931
Bean Pot	**20.00**
Cake Plate	**6.00**
Custard Cup...................	**2.50**
Leftover, 6"d, round	**7.50**
Pie Baker	**7.50**
Tray, 9"sq.....................	**5.00**

EDWIN M. KNOWLES CHINA COMPANY
Dinnerware was produced by this company in East Liverpool, OH, from 1900 to 1963.

Deanna, 1938
Butter........................	**10.00**
Coaster.......................	**8.00**
Creamer......................	**5.00**
Cup and Saucer.................	**5.00**
Eggcup.......................	**5.00**
Pickle Dish....................	**3.00**
Plate, 9"d.....................	**4.50**
Soup, lug handle	**4.00**
Sugar........................	**8.50**

Yorktown, 1936
Bowl, 5½"d, yellow...............	**3.75**
Casserole, cov	**15.00**
Creamer, rust..................	**4.50**
Cup and Saucer.................	**4.50**
Plate, 10"d....................	**4.00**
Sugar........................	**6.00**

FRANCISCAN
Produced by Gladding McBean and Co, CA, 1934 to the present.

Apple
Bowl, 8½"d	**20.00**
Butter Dish, cov................	**17.50**
Creamer......................	**8.50**
Cup and Saucer.................	**14.00**
Eggcup.......................	**12.50**
Pitcher, 9"h	**40.00**
Plate	
6"d, bread and butter............	**4.00**
10½"d, dinner	**17.50**
Relish........................	**20.00**
Spoon Rest....................	**12.00**
Sugar, cov	**12.00**

Duet Rose
Creamer......................	**6.00**
Cup, green rim..................	**2.00**
Party Platter...................	**18.00**
Plate	
6"d, bread and butter............	**2.00**
9"d, dinner....................	**8.00**
Platter, 15"l...................	**16.00**
Saucer	**1.50**
Sugar, cov	**8.00**

El Patio
Cereal Bowl, yellow gloss	**5.00**
Creamer, Redwood Brown	**8.00**
Cup, Redwood Brown.............	**5.00**
Gravy, yellow gloss	**20.00**
Vegetable Bowl, divided, green gloss........................	**15.00**

METLOX
Metlox Potteries was founded in Manhattan Beach, CA in 1927 and is currently still producing art ware, novelties, and Poppytrail dinnerware.

California Ivy
Coaster	5.00
Creamer	6.50
Cup and Saucer	6.50
Gravy	12.00
Mug	8.00
Plate, 8" d	6.00
Salad Bowl, 11¼" d	12.00
Vegetable, 11" d, divided	17.50

Homestead Prov
Ashtray, sq	12.00
Bread Plate	20.00
Cup	6.00
Dish, 6" l	6.00
Lazy Susan, 7 pcs	125.00
Mug, tankard	17.50
Plate	
7½" d, luncheon	7.50
10" d, dinner	8.50
Saucer	2.00
Tumbler, 11 oz	20.00

PURINTON

Purinton Pottery was founded by Bernard Purinton in Wellsville, OH, in 1936. The pottery ceased operations around 1959.

Apple
Berry Bowl	6.50
Cookie Jar, cov	35.00
Creamer	10.00
Cup and Saucer	6.00
Honey Pot, 7" d	10.00
Plate, 9" d, dinner	6.00
Relish, divided	20.00
Salt and Pepper Shakers, pr	15.00
Sugar, cov	18.00
Esmond, canister set, red	30.00
Intaglio, plate, 9½" d	8.00
Plaid, salad bowl, 11½" d	12.00

ROYAL CHINA COMPANY

Royal China Company began production of dinnerware in Sebring, OH, in 1934 and continues to the present.

Colonial Homestead
Bowl, 6" d	2.00
Cup and Saucer	3.00
Plate	
6¼" d	2.00
10" d	3.00
Soup, flat	3.00

Currier & Ives, blue and white
Cake Plate, 10½" d	6.50
Creamer	4.00
Cup and Saucer	3.50
Plate	
9" d	2.50
10" d	3.00
Soup, flat	4.00
Sugar, cov	5.00

Memory Lane, pink and white
Berry Bowl	4.00
Cake Plate, tab handle	12.00
Creamer	4.00
Cup and Saucer	3.50
Plate	
6" d, bread and butter	2.00
10" d, dinner	4.00
Soup, flat	4.00
Sugar, cov	5.00
Tumbler	
Old fashioned glass	4.00
Water, 5½" h	4.00

WATTS POTTERY

Watts Pottery was founded in 1922 for the manufacture of stoneware. In 1935 production of kitchenware began. The Crooksville, OH, plant was destroyed by fire in 1965 and not rebuilt.

Apple
Bean Pot	75.00
Cereal Bowl	24.00
Mug	65.00
Pie Plate	65.00
Salad Bowl	40.00
Vegetable, cov	48.00

Rooster
Bowl, adv	50.00
Pitcher, adv	48.00
Salt Shaker, adv	50.00

AMUSEMENT PARKS

From the park at the end of the trolley line to today's gigantic theme parks, such as Six Flags, amusement parks have served many generations. No trip to an amusement park was complete without a souvenir, many of which are now collectible.

Prices are still modest in this new collecting field. When an item is returned to the area where the park was located, it often brings a twenty– to fifty–percent premium.

Asbury Park, pinback button, 1¼" d, black and white, bathing beach scene, c1900 . . . . 10.00

Disneyland

Ashtray, 7½" d, ceramic, brown, green marbleized center recessed section, raised images of Haunted Mansion, Monorail, Sleeping Beauty Castle, Jungle Cruise, Mark Twain, c1960 . . . . 25.00

Book, *Walt Disney's Guide to Disneyland*, 8" × 11 ½", 28 pgs, 1960, full color 30.00

Game, Disneyland Riverboat Game, Parker Bros, 8" × 16" × 1½" box, minor use wear, c1955 . . . . **50.00**
Lunch Box, Ludwig Von Drake in Disneyland, emb steel, orig thermos, Aladdin, 1961 copyright, slight use wear. **100.00**
Hat, Mouseketeers, stiff black felt, large black plastic ears, white, blue, and orange "Disneyland/Mickey Mouse" patch, c1960 . . . . **25.00**
Magazine, "Disneyland Vacationland Summer 1970," 8½" × 11", 20 pgs, light general wear **18.50**
Salt and Pepper Shakers, pr, 1" × 3" × 2½", orig 2" × 4" tray with raised "Disneyland" name, white metal, silver and gold metallic finish, fit together to form castle, orig cork and "Japan" sticker, c1950 . . . . **35.00**
Sweater Guard, cardboard case, clear plastic slipcover, bright brass chain, two brass star shaped charms with pink glass stones, "Disneyland" spelled out in brass, c1960 . . . . **40.00**
Ticket, 2½" × 5½", paper, black and purple illus, $4.75 adult admission ticket, checklist of attractions on back, c1960 . . . . **15.00**
Viewmaster Reel
　　Disneyland/Fantasyland, 4½" sq color envelope, three reels, sealed package, Sawyer, c1960 . . . . **30.00**
　　Mickey Mouse Club Circus Visits Disneyland, color envelope, three reels, #856−A−B−C, 1956 Disney copyright **35.00**
Disney World, lunch box, orig Aladdin cardboard tag, thermos, c1972 . . . . **40.00**
Hershey Park
　　Pennant, felt, brown ground, white letters, c1950. . . . . **25.00**
　　Pinback Button, multicolored, child emerging from cocoa bean, c1905. . . **35.00**

ANIMAL DISHES, COVERED

Covered animal dishes were a favorite of housewives during the first half of the twentieth century. Grandmother Rinker and her sisters had numerous hens on nests scattered throughout their homes. They liked the form. It did not make any difference how old or new they were. Reproductions and copycats abound. You have to be alert for these late examples.

Look for unusual animals and forms. Many early examples were enhanced through hand−painted decorations. Pieces

with painting in excellent condition command a premium.

Hen on nest, milk glass, red glass eyes, 6⅞" × 6½" h, $50.00.

Camel, 6¼" l, two humped, "Humphrey," Westmoreland trademark on inside of lid, frosted amber glass, late 1970s **50.00**
Chick and Eggs, 11" h, emerging chick, Atterbury, white milk glass **185.00**
Dog, patterned quilt top, white milk glass, sgd "Vallerystahl". **175.00**
Duck, 6" l, "Mama Quack," Jeannette Glass Co, crystal, hp eyes and bill, 1941−early 1950s **11.00**
Eagle, on nest, banner reads "The American Hen," white milk glass **85.00**
Elephant
　　6" × 13", "Jumbo," Co−Operative Flint Glass Co, natural back cov, ruby glass, 1920s−1930s. **200.00**
　　4" × 7", "Jumbo", reissue, Indiana Glass Co, crystal, 1981 . . . . **19.00**
Fish, 8¾" l, walking, detailed scales, red glass eyes, white milk glass **175.00**
Frog, sitting, "Kermit," Co−Operative Flint Glass Co, green glass, 1920s−1930s . . . **85.00**
Hen
　　6½" l, blue, frosted, quilted base **75.00**
　　7½" l, Atterbury, white and deep blue marbleized glass, lacy base. **165.00**
Rabbit
　　4½" l, rect, narrow stylized head, emb features, footed, underside emb "Dermay−Fifth Avenue−New York−970," pink frosted glass **225.00**
　　6" l, white frosted glass. **70.00**

ANIMAL FIGURINES

Animal collectors are a breed apart. Collecting is a love affair. As long as their favorite animal is pictured or modeled, they willingly buy the item. In many cases, they own a real life counterpart to go with their objects. I hope I never get invited to visit a person who collects snake things.

Clubs: Cat Collectors, 31311 Blair Drive, Warren, MI 48092; Equine Collectors Club, Box 4764 New River Stage II, Phoenix, AZ 85027; The Frog Pond, P. O. Box 193, Beech Grove, IN 46107; The National Elephant Collectors Society, 380 Medford Street, Somerville, MA 02145; Russell's Owl Collector Club, P. O. Box 1292, Bandon, OR 97411.

Dog, Airdale, porcelain, white, black collar, marked "Made In Japan," $2.50.

Bambi with Butterfly, Japan	**35.00**
Bluejay, 6½" h, on stump, natural colors, Midwest Potteries Inc, 1940–1944	**15.00**
Cat	
5¼" h, 6½" l, two attached tabby cats, playing, striped, red bows, Japan paper label, marked "Deebee"	**30.00**
7" h, blue bow, marked "Made in Spain" and "Vista Allegra D'Art"	**32.00**
Dog	
Boxer, marked "Morton Studios"	**35.00**
Cocker Spaniel, marked "Goldscheider"	**65.00**
Hound Dog, paw over eye, Morton Pottery Co, #576	**10.00**
Elephant, 6" h, 5" l, blue–gray glaze, carrying boxes on sides, Cliftwood Art Potteries, Inc	**60.00**
Horse, Dale Evans on horse, Buttermilk, Hartland	**15.00**
Lioness, 12" h, 7" l, green glaze, Cliftwood Art Potteries, Inc	**25.00**
Pig	
Jumping over Green Fence, black, bisque	**55.00**
Poking Head Out of Potty, 2½ h"	**48.00**
Rabbit, Thumper, 1¾", Goebel	**35.00**
Skunk, Flower, American Potteries	**45.00**
Turtle, 5½" h, Weller, Coppertone	**85.00**

APPLIANCES, ELECTRICAL

Nothing shows our ability to take a relatively simple task, e.g., toast a piece of bread, and create a wealth of different forms to achieve it better than electrical appliances, one of the best documents of stylistic design in utilitarian form.

Collectors tend to concentrate on one form. Toasters are the most commonly collected, largely because several books have been written about them. Electric fans have a strong following. Waffle irons are pressing toasters for popularity. Modernistic collectors seek bar drink blenders from the 1930s through the 1950s.

Clubs: American Fan Collector's Association, P. O. Box 804, South Bend, IN 46624; Electric Breakfast Club, P. O. Box 306, White Mills, PA 18473.

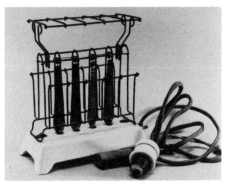

Toaster, G. E., model D-12, patent 1908, removable warming rack, $125.00.

Coffee Grinder, Kitchen Aide	**65.00**
Coffee Percolator, Royal Rochester, 10" h, nickel body over copper, black wooden handles, #366 B–29, 1920s	**15.00**
Fan, GE, 6" d, brass blades	**55.00**
Flour Sifter, Miracle Electric Co, ivory metal body, push button above blue wooden handle, decal label, unused, 1930s	**35.00**
Iron, Sunbeam, "Iron Master," 2¾ lb chrome body, steam attachment, orig box, unused, #52, 1940s	**40.00**
Mixer, Handy Hannah, natural wooden handle, single shaft, quart jar base, Cat #495, late 1930s	**22.00**
Popcorn Popper, Knapp–Monarch, oil type, aluminum body, wire base, domed glass lid with vented sides, walnut handles, measuring cup, Cat #12A–500B, 1930–1940	**20.00**
Toaster, Manning Bowman, nickel body,	

53

double wire mechanical turnover doors, Bakelite knobs, #1225, 1926 . . . **35.00**

Waffle Iron, Universal, horizontal type, 8″ × 4½″ rect top, nickel, black wooden handles, two-headed cord **75.00**

ASHTRAYS

Most price guides include ashtrays under advertising. The problem is that there are a number of terrific ashtrays in shapes that have absolutely nothing to do with advertising. Ashtrays get a separate category in this book.

With the nonsmoking movement gaining strength, the ashtray is an endangered species. The time to collect them is now.

Advertising, Westinghouse, 6⅞″ × 5¾″, $27.50.

Airplane, chrome 35.00
Bird, chrome, Art Deco, figural 18.00
Cloisonne, 5″ d, blue, covered match
  holder 70.00
Cowboy Hat, lusterware 15.00
Devil Head, bronze, open mouth. 75.00
Playboy, 1960 . . . . 15.00
Saddle on Fence, copper 15.00
Scottish Terrier, 4½″ h, 5¾″ w, figural, glass
  insert 25.00
Tire
  Amber Insert, cigarette rests 35.00
  BF Goodrich Silvertone, green in-
    sert 30.00
  Kelly Springfield, green insert, heavy
    duty 30.00
Vargas Girl, tin, 1950s 10.00

AUTOGRAPHS

Collecting autographs is a centuries-old hobby. A good rule to follow is the more recognizable the person, the more likely the authograph is to have value. Content is

a big factor in valuing autograph material. A clipped signature is worth far less than a lengthy handwritten document by the same person.

Before spending big money for an autograph, have it authenticated. Many movie and sports stars had secretaries and other individuals sign their material, especially photographs. An autopen is a machine that can sign up to a dozen documents at one time. The best proof that a signature is authentic is to get it from the person who stood there and watched the person sign it.

Clubs: Manuscript Society, 350 Niagara Street, Burbank, CA 95105; Universal Autograph Collectors Club, P. O. Box 6181, Washington, DC 20044.

Dwight D. Eisenhower, framed and matted picture with autograph, $100.00.

Alda, Allen **15.00**
Clark, Arthur C, author **30.00**
Crabbe, Buster. **75.00**
Crosby, Bing **125.00**
Dangerfield, Rodney **10.00**
Esposito, Phil, hockey **20.00**
Evert, Chris, tennis **17.00**
Fontaine, Joan. **30.00**
Foreman, George, boxer **25.00**
Goldberg, Whoopi, entertainer **35.00**
Gretzky, Wayne, hockey **35.00**
Hamilton, Margaret **50.00**
Jackson, Jesse **55.00**
Keel, Howard **10.00**
Lancaster, Burt **15.00**
Lawford, Peter, entertainer **65.00**

Montana, Joe	25.00
Murray, Ken, entertainer	25.00
Parker, Frank, singer	25.00
Peck, Gregory	35.00
Reynolds, Debbie	15.00
Rutherford, Ann, entertainer	35.00
Shatner, William	25.00
Staubach, Roger	20.00
Wahlberg, Donnie, singer	60.00
Williams, Esther	15.00

AUTOMOBILES

The automobiles that we remember most fondly are those that we first owned. They had class and bright colors. My dad refers to them as "dudemobiles." Cars from my youth are still traded on the secondary market. The cars from my dad's youth have changed from classy to classic, although a 1957 Chevy can still turn a young girl's head.

Clubs: Antique Automobile Club of America, 501 W. Governor Road, Hershey, PA 17033; Classic Car Club of America, P. O. Box 443, Madison, NJ 07940; Milestone Car Society, P. O. Box 50850, Indianapolis, IN 46250.

Periodicals: *Hemmings Motor News*, Box 100, Bennington, VT 05201; *Old Cards Price Guide*, 700 E. State Street, Iola, WI 54990; *Old Cars Weekly*, 700 E. State Street, Iola, WI 54990.

AMX, 1968, hard top, $2,000.00.

Buick
1956, Century 66C, convertible, fine	9,800.00
1962, LeSabre Series 4400, four door hard top, fine	3,500.00

Cadillac
1955, Eldorado Biarritz, convertible, fine	20,300.00
1964, Fleetwood 60, sedan, fine	5,600.00
Checker, Marathon, sedan, fine	2,500.00

Chevrolet
1953, DeLuxe 210, station wagon, fine	4,900.00
1965, Malibu Super Sport, convertible, fine	7,700.00

Chrysler
1950, New Yorker, club coupe, fine	5,050.00
1960, 300F, convertible, fine	10,500.00
DeSoto, 1955, Firedome, Sportsman hard top, fine	5,600.00

Ford
1956, Country Squire, station wagon, fine	4,550.00
1957, Thunderbird, convertible, hard top, fine	22,400.00
1965, Mustang, convertible, fine	7,700.00
Hudson, 1954, Jet Liner, sedan, fine	3,850.00
Kaiser, 1955, Manhattan, club sedan, fine	6,050.00
Lincoln, 1957, Capri, coupe, hard top, fine	4,900.00
Mercury, 1963, Monterey, four door hard top, fine	2,800.00
Nash, 1956, Ambassador, custom hard top, fine	4,500.00
Oldsmobile, 1962, Starfire, convertible, fine	7,000.00
Packard, 1954, Clipper, Panama hard top coupe, fine	5,900.00
Plymouth, 1965, Valiant Signet, Barracuda, fastback coupe, fine	4,200.00
Pontiac, 1954, Chieftain Deluxe, two door hard top, fine	6,400.00
Studebaker, 1951, Champion Regal, Starlight Coupe, fine	4,000.00

AUTO PARTS AND ACCESSORIES

An automobile swap meet is twenty-five percent cars and seventy-five percent car parts. Restoration and rebuilding of virtually all car models is never ending. The key is to find the exact part needed.

All too often, auto parts at flea markets are not priced. The seller is going to judge how badly he thinks you want the part before setting the price. You have to keep your cool.

Two areas that are attracting outside collector interest are promotional toy models and hood ornaments. The former have been caught up in the craze for 1950s and 1960s Japanese tin. The latter have been discovered by the art community, who view them as wonderful examples of modern streamlined design.

Ashtray, Buick, dash type	20.00
Carburetor, Buick, 1924–25	25.00

THE FAMOUS AUTOMOBILE CARD GAME

TOURING

REG. U.S PATENT OFFICE
IMPROVED EDITION
PARKER BROTHERS INC SALEM, MASS., NEW YORK, LONDON

Game, Touring, Parker Bros, card game, 99 cards, black, red, and white litho, copyright 1926, $25.00.

Clock, Motor, "Luna," 8 day, luminous dial, brass and bronze, 1914 .... **120.00**
Engine
  Maxwell, 1914, complete **200.00**
  Packard, 1935 .... **800.00**
Gearshift Knob, glass swirl, blue and white **15.00**
Grill, Packard, 1941. .... **125.00**
Headlamp, bull's eye, Marchal, 12" d, orig. **700.00**
Hood Ornament
  Dodge Ram, 8"l. **35.00**
  Lion, dated 1924 .... **30.00**
Horn, Pierce Arrow, 1915–20, cowl mounted, correct bracket **175.00**
Hubcaps, Plymouth, 1939–40, set of 4 ... **250.00**
License Plate, 1933, North Dakota, orig wrapper, pr **7.50**
Match Holder, Exide Battery & Goodyear Tire, orig box **35.00**
Ornament, radiator
  Buick, front grill emblem, 1934. ...... **30.00**
  Hubmobile Nash **25.00**
  Plymouth, 1933. .... **45.00**
  Pontiac, feather headdress, 1958. ..... **15.00**
  Reo, colorful **30.00**
  Willy's Knight **25.00**
Owner's Manual, Ford, 1914, Model T... **15.00**
Radio, Cadillac, 1937 .... **250.00**
Reference Guide, 1931 Buick **15.00**
Trunk, Packard, pre WWII, metal, 18 × 36" **450.00**
Shop and Parts Manual
  Cadillac, 1941, ... **110.00**
  DeSoto, 1936, master **45.00**
Tube Patcher, Cameo **10.00**
Visor, 1932 Ford, full length **125.00**

SALES AND PROMOTIONAL ITEMS

Ashtray, Goodyear, tire, amber glass wheel center **30.00**
Blotter
  Goodyear Tires **5.00**
  Kelly Tires, 1910s **28.00**

"Smooth as a '47 Ford," nude baby, bottom up **20.00**
Booklet, Chevy, 1939, Soap Box Derby Rules, illus **20.00**
Brochure, dealer, fold out
Buick
  1933, Series 90, orig photos, 8 × 10", black and white **7.00**
  1957. .... **24.00**
Chevrolet
  1937, prices shown for several models **40.00**
  1949. .... **25.00**
Chrysler, Town & Country, 1946 ..... **26.00**
Ford, color pictures, nine different models, prices, 1929 .... **85.00**
Franklin Car, 1921 .... **45.00**
Studebaker **35.00**
Catalog
  Auburn, 1935, part color, 9 × 16", 16 pgs **35.00**
  Kissel Kar, 10 × 13", 36 pgs. **125.00**
Magazine Advertisement, Wayne Cut 278, 1912. .... **85.00**
Pinback Button, Buick, "Looking Fine For 39". **45.00**
Pocket Mirror, Studebaker Vehicle Works, South Bend, IN, 1910, 2¼" oval **125.00**
Post Card, DeSoto, 1939, full color, one with four door Sedan, other with two door Sedan, pr **8.00**
Poster, Buick, "Kansas City," 1921–22, 25 × 38", black and white **85.00**
Program, Indy 500, 1953. .... **40.00**
Shoulder Patch, Oldsmobile Service, emblem, c1940. .... **23.00**
Sign, dealer's
  Ford, neon **750.00**
  United Motor, neon outline of early auto **1,250.00**

AUTUMN LEAF

The Hall China Company developed Autumn Leaf china as a china dinnerware premium for the Jewel Tea Company in 1933. The giveaway was extremely successful. The term "Autumn Leaf" did not originate until 1960. Previously, the pattern was simply known as "Jewel" or "Autumn." Autumn leaf remained in production until 1978.

Pieces were added and dropped from the line over the years. Limited production pieces are most desirable. Look for matching accessories in glass, metal, and plastic made by other companies. They also made Jewel Tea toy trucks.

Club: National Autumn Leaf Collector's Society, 120 West Dowell Road, McHenry, IL 60050.

Salt and pepper shakers, range size, $17.50.

Bowl
6½", cereal	....	**8.50**
8½", soup	....	**10.00**
Cake Plate	....	**14.00**
Canister Set, sq, 4 pcs.	....	**125.00**
Casserole Dish	....	**25.00**
Coffeepot, electrical.	....	**240.00**
Cookie Jar	....	**90.00**
Creamer.	....	**8.00**
Cup	....	**7.00**
Custard Cup	....	**5.00**
Fruitcake Tin	....	**5.00**
Gravy Boat.	....	**18.00**
Mixing Bowl, nested set of 3	....	**40.00**
Mug, ftd.	....	**75.00**
Pie Baker	....	**19.00**
Pitcher, ball shape	....	**25.00**
Plate
6", bread and butter	....	**4.00**
8", salad	....	**8.50**
10", dinner.	....	**9.00**
Platter, 11½", oval	....	**15.00**
Salad Bowl	....	**14.00**
Salt and Pepper Shakers, pr, small.	......	**14.00**
Saucer	....	**4.00**
Sugar, vertical lines	....	**20.00**
Tea Towel	....	**20.00**
Tidbit Tray, three tiers	....	**40.00**
Toaster Cover, plastic	....	**20.00**
Tray, metal, oval	....	**50.00**
Vase, bud.	....	**150.00**
Vegetable Dish, divided.	....	**55.00**

AVIATION COLLECTIBLES

Now is the time to get into aviation collectibles. The airline mergers and bankruptcies have produced a wealth of obsolete material. There were enormous crowds when Eastern held its liquidation sale in spring 1991. I have a bunch of stuff from Piedmont and Peoples, two airlines that flew off into the sunset in the 1980s.

The wonderful thing about airline collectibles is that most of them initially

were free. I try to make a point to pickup several items, from bathroom soap to playing cards, each time I fly. Save the things most likely to be thrown out.

Club: The World Airline Historical Society, 3381 Apple Tree Lane, Erlanger, KY 41018.

Sheet music, Wait Till You Get Them Up In The Air Boys, *words by Lew Brown, music by Albert Von Tilzer, Broadway Music Corp publisher, $10.00.*

Book
Principals American Technical Society	....	**15.00**
Heroes of Aviation, Laurence LaTourette Driggs, dj, 1927	....	**20.00**
Calendar Plate, 6½" d, biplane, 1912	.....	**35.00**
Pen, Allegheny Airlines.	....	**5.00**
Propeller, 32" l, wood, marked "Kroehler"	....	**50.00**
Puzzle, American Airlines, 707 jet in flight, frame tray, Milton Bradley, 1960 copyright	....	**15.00**
Toy, adv, Eastern Whisper Jet, 7" l, Aero.	....	**18.00**
Tray, beverage, Pan–Am.	....	**15.00**
Umbrella, Capital Airlines.	....	**100.00**
Watch Fob, 1¼ × 1½", silvered white metal, raised illus of single wing passenger plane, c1920	....	**18.00**

AVON BOTTLES

Back in the late 1960s, my mother worked briefly as an Avon Lady. If only she had saved one example of every product that she sold, I am not certain that she would be rich, but she would have one heck of a collection.

Avon products, with the exception of

California Perfume Company material, are not found that much at flea markets any longer. The 1970s were the golden age of Avon collectibles. There are still a large number of dedicated collectors, but the legion that fueled the pricing fires of the 1970s has been hard hit by desertions. Avon material today is more likely to be found at garage sales rather than flea markets.

Clubs: Bud Hatin's National Avon Collector's Club, P. O. Box 9868, Kansas City, MO 64134; Western World Avon Collectors Club, Box 23785, Pleasant Hills, CA 93535.

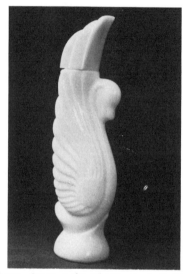

Cologne, Swan Lake Charisma, 3 fluid oz, $5.00.

Betsy Ross, white, 1976.	**12.00**
Cable Car, green, 1975	**7.50**
Calculator, black, 1979	**5.00**
Church Mouse Bride, milk glass base, 1978.	**5.00**
Eight Ball, black and white	**2.50**
Flower Maiden, yellow paint, 1974	**7.50**
Golf Cart, green, 1973	**4.50**
Library Lamp, gold plated base, 1976	**5.00**
Looking Glass, hand mirror shape, 1970.	**3.00**
Pheasant, brown, green plastic head, 1972.	**7.50**
Rainbow Trout, 1973	**5.00**
Santa, MIB	**35.00**
Spirit of St Louis, silver paint, 1970	**12.00**
Stage Coach, brown	**7.50**
Swan Lake Charisma, 8"h, 1972–76	**5.00**

BADGES

Have you ever tried to save a name tag or badge that attaches directly to your clothing or fits into a plastic holder? We are victims of a throwaway society. This is one case where progress has not been a boon for collectors.

Fortunately, our grandparents and great–grandparents loved to save the membership, convention, parade, and other badges that they acquired. The badge's colorful silk and cotton fabric often contained elaborate calligraphic lettering and lithographed scenes in combination with celluloid and/or metal pinbacks and pins. They were badges of honor, often having an almost military quality about them.

Look for badges with attached three–dimensional miniatures. Regional value is a factor. I found a great Emmaus, Pennsylvania, badge priced at $2.00 at a flea market in Florida; back home, its value is $20.00 plus.

Penn Central RR, brass, lacquered, $75.00.

Bicycling
  Century Wheelman of Camden, NJ, 1897, 1½" × 2½" darkened bronze type, link badge, hanger bar with small bike lantern and inscribed "Camden to Atlantic City & Return Aug 29, '97"; "Survivor" inscribed on center bar, bottom disk with potted tropical plant, victory wreath, and club name **60.00**
  Thistle Cycling Club, 1895, 1¼" × 2¾", link badge, engraved diecut hanger with thistle bloom surrounded by wreath of leaves, gold plated con-

necting bar inscribed "Sept 15-95," 1″ d enameled diecut brass disk inscribed "2nd Annual Century/ Elgin–Aurora–Chicago," second bar inscribed "Aug 2-96" **85.00**
Convention, BPOE, Moline, 1923, 1¼″ celluloid button, 2 ½″ w diecut celluloid hanger with purple plow, white ground........................ **35.00**
Military
    Confed Veterans Reunion, 1¼″ diecut brass, aluminum insert with 1898 date of Atlanta reunion **30.00**
    GAR Commander Staff Aide, bronzed metal, raised portrait of IN Walker, Commander In Chief GAR, inscribed "Walker National Staff, St Paul 1896," unmarked gold fabric ribbon **15.00**
    GAR Veteran, 1¾″ diecut brass pendant, red, white, and blue flag ribbon, brass hanger bar of eagle, crossed cannons, cannonballs, and saber, GAR symbol on pendant and serial number, c1890 .... **20.00**
Occupational, chauffeur's, 1936, Missouri......................... **15.00**
Political, "Robert A La Follette/Burton K Wheeler," bronze, 1924 Progressive Campaign **20.00**
Prohibition
    Award, silverplated, engraved "Demorest Prohibition Prize," and "Awarded to Blanche V Fegley Oct 1st '91," pin missing **30.00**
    Pledge, eagle dec on hanger, darkened brass color, red, white, and blue ribbon, aluminum token inscribed "Beautiful Water My Beverage Shall Be," reverse inscribed "Tis Here We Pledge Perpetual Hate, To All That Can Intoxicate," early 1900s **40.00**
Union, Chairman of Committee, 5″ l, brass hanger with celluloid insert, red, white, and blue ribbon with gold lettering "Annual Ball Jan 27th, 1940," white metal medallion with celluloid insert inscribed "Bakery Workers Union, Local 50 AF of L"...................... **25.00**

BAKELITE

This is a great example of a collecting category gone price-mad. Bakelite is a trademark used for a variety of synthetic resins and plastics used to manufacture colorful, inexpensive utilitarian objects. The key word is inexpensive, which can also be interpreted as cheap.

There is nothing cheap about Bakelite collectibles in today's market. Collectors, especially those from large metropolitan areas who consider themselves design–conscious, want Bakelite in whatever form they can find it—from jewelry to radio cases.

Buy a Bakelite piece because you love it. The market has already started to collapse for commonly found material. Can the high end pieces be far behind?

Dresser set, amber, imitation mother of pearl, black and green Art Nouveau design, $35.00.

Bookends, pr, geometric Art Deco style, green and yellow................. **65.00**
Cake Server, green handle............ **5.00**
Cigarette Case, hand-shaped closure, French........................175.00
Cocktail Set, Bakelite and chrome shaker, six cocktails, chrome tray **45.00**
Dominoes **25.00**
Flatware, service for six, red handles, 26 pcs **85.00**
Food Chopper, red handle............ **10.00**
Inkwell, black, streamlined........... **24.00**
Jewelry
    Beads, amber, ovals, 14″ l **60.00**
    Bracelet, bangle, bright yellow, red, black, and green enamel dec **25.00**
    Pendant, rose, yellow flower, green leaves....................... **25.00**
    Pin, figural
        Bambi **18.00**
        Cherries, cluster of three **20.00**
Mortar and Pestle, yellow and orange swirl.......................... **25.00**
Napkin Ring, figural
    Dog **25.00**
    Rabbit, orange.................. **40.00**
Pencil Sharpener, Scottie **35.00**
Salt and Pepper Shakers, pr, green and yellow half moons, matching tray..... **15.00**
Souvenir Pin, 1939 NY World's Fair, 1¼″ h, trefoil, Trylon, inscribed "New York World's Fair/Bakelite," pink **40.00**
Telephone, Kelloggs Series 1000, brown, Art Deco style, chrome dial **90.00**
View–Master, Model B, black, 4″ d, c1944, orig box **65.00**

59

BANDANNAS

Women associate bandannas with keeping their hair in place. Men visualize stage coach holdups or rags to wipe the sweat from their brow. Neither approach recognizes the colorful and decorative role played by the bandanna.

Some of the earliest bandannas are political. By the turn of the century, bandannas joined pillow cases as the leading souvenir textile found at sites ranging from the beach to museums. Hillary Weiss's *The American Bandanna: Culture on Cloth from George Washington to Elvis* (Chronicle Books: 1990) provides a visual feast for this highly neglected collecting area.

The bandanna plays an important role in the Scouting movement, serving as a neckerchief in Boy and Girl Scouts. Many special neckerchiefs were issued. There is also a close correlation between scarfs and the bandanna. Bandanna collectors tend to collect both.

Boy Scout, 1935 Jamboree, blue, white letters, $90.00.

Beatles, white ground, faces, records, and
  instruments design, 26″ sq **25.00**
Grover Cleveland and Allen G.
  Thurman, 1888 Democratic presidential and vice presidential candidates,
  jugate center portraits, white ground,
  red background, black lettering, "OUR
  CANDIDATES" in white banner, center with crossed brooms and rooster
  on perch **85.00**
Crockett, Davy, cotton, bright blue, yel-
  low, red, and white, Indian blankets,
  ranch symbols, spurs, boots, cowboy
  hat, center with Davy as bronc rider,
  13½″ × 14″ **40.00**

Lone Ranger, bright deep red, printed
  white and blue design, portrait, rail
  fence, crossed guns, coiled lasso, and
  horseshoe, 1949–1950 Cheerios pre-
  mium, 21″ × 23″ **65.00**
Mickey Mouse, cotton, black, white, and
  red figures of Mickey, Goofy, Minnie,
  and Donald, green border, 22″ sq,
  c1960 . . . . **35.00**
Mix, Tom, Tom on Tony, facsimile signa-
  ture, black and white, purple shirt,
  brown horse, red border with black and
  white illus, 16½″ × 17″ **60.00**
Rogers, Roy, King of the Cowboys, glossy
  fabric, bright yellow center, red, black,
  and white fence border, Ranch Gate on
  two corners, Roy, Trigger, and Bullet,
  25″ sq **80.00**

BANKS, STILL

Banks are classified into two types—mechanical (action) and still (nonaction). Chances are that any mechanical bank that you find at a flea market today is most likely a reproduction. If you find one that you think is real, check it out in one of the mechanical bank books before buying it.

The still or nonaction bank dominates the flea market scene. There is no limit to the ways that you can collect still banks. Some favor type (e.g., advertising), others composition (cast iron, tin, plastic, etc.), figural (shaped like something), or theme (Western). Dad collects banks that were used to solicit money. Says something about him, doesn't it?

Beware of still bank reproductions, just as you are with mechanical banks, especially in the cast iron sector. Most banks were used, so look for wear where you expect to find it. Save your money and do not buy if you are not certain that what you are buying is a period original.

Advertising
  Amoco 586 Oil **15.00**
  Automobile Club of Buffalo, pig, green,
    gold trim **15.00**
  Bokar Coffee **35.00**
  Briardale Food Stores, can **8.50**
  Electrolux, iron, refrigerator **28.00**
  Frigidaire, metal **23.00**
  Red Goose Shoes, celluloid **45.00**
  Rival Dog Food **10.00**
  Thompson Auto Products, Indian,
    teepee **50.00**
  Underwood Typewriter, 1½″ h, white
    metal, dark gold paint **35.00**
  Wolf's Head Oil, can shape **16.00**

Globe, tin, marked "J. Chein," c1930, $25.00.

World Book Encyclopedia, figural
  book, slide top 10.00
Cast Iron
  Mail Box, blue and red, made in US,
    marked "Iron Art" 46.00
  Pig, sgd "Decker's" 85.00
Ceramic
  Batman 40.00
  Pinocchio. 75.00
Chalkware, buffalo 15.00
China
  Cat, red sneakers, Kliban. 40.00
  Miss Piggy, Sigma 45.00
Copper, Davy Crockett, figural 40.00
Glass, figural
  Pig 10.00
  Snoopy 15.00
  Lucky Joe. 30.00
Metal
  Jackpot Dime, 6" × 3½" 20.00
  Mail Box, 9", olive green, schedule on
    front 35.00
  Roy Rogers and Trigger Savings Bank,
    plastic horseshoe, wall mount 85.00
Plastic, Fred Flintstone, 1971 . . . . 20.00
Porcelain, Batman, figural 45.00
Pottery
  Pig, spongeware 85.00
  Uncle Sam, red, three coin, Western
    Stamping Co 25.00
Tin
  Television, figural 10.00
  Watch Me Grow Tall, 3" × 6", grows to
    10" 45.00

BARBED WIRE

Barbed wire is a farm, Western, and military collectible. It is usually collected in eighteen-inch lengths and displayed mounted on boards. While there are a few rare examples that sell in the hundreds of dollars for a piece, the vast majority of what is found are common types that sell between $2.00 to $5.00 for an example.

Club: International Barb Wire Collectors Historical Society, Sunset, TX 76270.

BARBERSHOP AND BEAUTY PARLOR COLLECTIBLES

Let's not discriminate. This is the age of the unisex hair salon. This category has been male-oriented for far too long. Haven't you wondered where a woman had her hair done in the nineteenth century?

Don't forget drug store products. Not everyone had the funds or luxury to spend time each day at the barbershop or beauty salon.

Sign, emb cardboard, blue letters, 11" × 8⅜", $20.00.

After Shave Talc, Palmolive. 7.50
Antiseptic Container, 8"h, plated brass. . . 40.00
Blade Bank, J B Williams, tin litho 23.00
Blade Tin, Yankee, c1900 . . . . 55.00
Bobby Pins, orig card
  Gayla Hold, illus of woman on front . . . 2.75
  Sta–Rite. 1.50
Business Card, 6 × 3¼", man cutting hair,
  "The Newest and Most Sanitary Shop in
  Providence". 10.00
Chair, pedestal base, Theo Kochs Manu-
  facturer 350.00
Clippers, Andis, c1940 . . . . 20.00
Cologne, stick
  Morning Glory. 4.25
  Zia 4.00
Hair Groom, Brylcreem. 6.00
Hair Net
  Cameo, c1930 . . . . 3.00
  Doloris. 4.75
  Gainsborough 4.25

Jal–Net	5.50
Hair Tonic	
Lan–Tox	12.00
Nowland's Lanford Oil	7.50
Hair Treatment	
Marchand's Hair Rinse	4.25
Nestle	
Baby's	7.00
Curling Lotion	.75
Egyptian, hair tent	11.00
Hair Wax, Lucky Tiger, large jar	10.00
Postcard, Unsafe Safety Razor, c1910	12.00
Razor Blade	
Broadway Double Edge.	5.00
Gold Tone	1.50
Pal Double Edge.	1.50
Treet.	1.50
Shaving Brush, aluminum handle, emb	
design, c1910.	8.50
Shaving Cream	
Brisk, tin and display box.	8.00
Krank's Brush Lather Shave	8.00
Palmolive.	5.00
Prep Brushless Shave.	8.00
Sign, neon, "Beauty Shop," pink, orig	
transformer	200.00
Strop, Ingersoll, razor blade stropping kit,	
MIB	12.00
Thermometer, Schick adv, 1950s	75.00
Towel Steamer, nickel-plated copper, por-	
celain over steel base	300.00

Barbie #2, brown ponytail, pearl earrings, orig stand, 1960, $350.00.

BARBIE DOLLS

As a doll, Barbie is unique. She burst upon the scene in the late 1950s and remains a major factor in the doll market over forty years later. No other doll has enjoyed this longevity.

Every aspect of Barbie is collectible, from the doll to her clothing to her play accessories. Although collectors place the greatest emphasis on Barbie material from the 1950s and 1960s, there is some great stuff from the 1970s and 1980s that should not be overlooked. Whenever possible, try to get original packaging. This is especially important for Barbie material from the 1980s forward.

Accessories	
Baseball Cap, Ken, ball, mitt, plastic . . .	3.00
Hunting Cap, Ken, red plastic	2.00
Roller Skates, Ken	2.50
Beauty Kit, 1961, MIB.	25.00
Clothing Outfit	
American Airlines Stewardess, #984,	
1961.	27.50
Ballerina, #989, 1961.	20.00
Evening Gala, #1660, 1965	45.00

Graduation, Ken, black gown and	
mortar board	12.50
Orange Blossom, #987, 1962	25.00
Rally Day, Ken, all weather coat and	
hat, #795.	8.00
Colorforms Set	7.50
Doll	
Barbie	
American Girl	75.00
Bubble Cut Fashion, 1962 copyright,	
MIB	90.00
Happy Holidays, MIB	75.00
Julia, Twist 'n' Turn, 2 pc uniform,	
1969.	40.00
Ken, 12" h, molded hard plastic, mova-	
ble head, arms, and legs, flocked	
blonde hair, orig "Sport Shorts" out-	
fit #783, orig wire pedestal and box,	
1961.	150.00
Doll Carrying Case, vinyl cov cardboard	
Barbie and Midge, 14 × 18 × 4", light	
blue, metal snap closure, pink, tan,	
and black and white illus, 1963 Mat-	
tel copyright, heavy play wear	25.00
Ken, 11 × 13 × 4", olive–yellow, blue,	
yellow, white, and black illus of Ken,	
Barbie, and sports car, black plastic	
handle, 1962 copyright, heavy play	
wear.	30.00
Dream House, 1962, minor wear	75.00
Game, Queen of the Prom	30.00
Horse, Dallas, MIB	30.00
Magazine, *Mattel Barbie Magazine*,	
Jan–Feb 1969, 22 pgs	15.00
Record Case, 1961, MIB	20.00

Soap, Jergens, Barbie Doll Soap Circles,
  MIB **30.00**
Suitcase, featuring 1962 Ken and
  Barbie **17.00**
Thermos, 8½" h, litho metal, red plastic
  cap, full color illus, black ground, 1962
  Mattel copyright **35.00**
Wrist Watch, 1963 . . . . **48.00**

BASEBALL CARDS

Collecting baseball cards is not for kids any
longer. It is an adult game. Recent trends
include buying and stashing away complete boxed sets of cards, placing special
emphasis on rookie and other types of
cards, and speculation on a few "rare"
cards that have a funny habit of turning up
in the market far more frequently than one
would expect if they were so rare.

Baseball cards date from the late 19th
century. The earliest series are tobacco
company issues dating between 1909 and
1915. During the 1920s American Caramel, National Caramel, and York Caramel
issued cards.

Goudey Gum Company (1933 to 1941)
and Gum, Inc., (1939) carried on the tradition in the 1930s. When World War II
ended, Bowman Gum of Philadelphia, the
successor to Gum, Inc., became the baseball giant. Topps, Inc., of Brooklyn, New
York, followed. Topps purchased Bowman
in 1956 and enjoyed almost a monopoly in
card production until 1981 when Fleer of
Philadelphia and Donruss of Memphis
challenged its leadership.

In addition to sets produced by these major companies, there were hundreds of
other sets issued by a variety of sources
ranging from product manufacturers, such
as Sunbeam Bread, to minor league teams.
There are so many secondary sets now issued annually that it is virtually impossible
for a collector to keep up with them.

The field is plagued with reissued sets
and cards as well as outright forgeries. The
color photocopier has been used to great
advantage by unscrupulous dealers. Never
buy cards from someone that you can't find
six months later should a problem develop.

The listing below is simply designed to
give you a rough idea of baseball card
prices and to show you how they change
depending on the decade of the cards that
you wish to collect. For detailed information about card prices consult the following

price guides: James Beckett, *Sports Americana Baseball Card Price Guide, No. 10*, Edgewater Book Co., 1988; Editors of Krause
Publications, Sports, *Baseball Card Price
Guide, Fourth Edition*, Krause Publications,
1990; Editors of Krause Publications,
Sports, *Standard Catalog of Baseball Cards,
Second Edition*, Krause Publications; and,
Gene Florence, *The Standard Baseball Card
Price Guide, Second Edition*, Collector Books,
1990. Although Beckett is the name most
often mentioned in connection with price
guides, I have found the Krause guides to
be much more helpful.

Periodicals: *Baseball Card News*, 700 East
State Street, Iola, WI 54990; *Beckett Baseball
Monthly*, 3410 Mid Court, Suite 110, Car-
rolto, TX 75006; *Current Card Prices*, P. O.
Box 480, East Islip, NY 11730; *Sports Collectors Digest*, 700 East State Street, Iola, WI
54990.

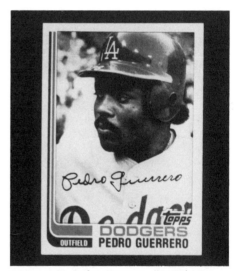

Topps, 1982, Pedro Guerrero, #247, $.25

American Caramels, 1922, common
  player. **5.00**
Bowman
  Complete set
    1948. . . . . **550.00**
    1951. . . . . **3,850.00**
  Common player
    1948, black and white **7.50**
    1949, black and white **6.00**
    1951, color. **5.00**
    1952, color. **2.00**
    1953, black and white **10.00**
    1955, color. **4.50**
Goudey and Gum, Inc, common player
  1933, color. **17.50**

1941, black and white	16.00

Topps
Complete set

1958.	975.00
1966.	750.00
1977.	110.00
1981.	60.00
1984.	60.00

Common player

1951, blue back	12.00
1953.	4.50
1955.	4.50
1957, cards 1–264 and 353–407 . . .	1.25
1959, cards 1–110	1.00
1961, cards 371–522	.75
1965, cards 199–446	.45
1973, cards 397-528	.25

BASEBALL MEMORABILLA

What a feast for the collector! Flea markets often contain caps, bats, gloves, autographed balls, and photos of your favorite all–stars, baseball statues, regular and world series game programs, and team manuals or rosters. Do not overlook secondary material such as magazine covers with a baseball theme. Condition and personal preference should always guide the eye.

Be careful of autograph forgeries. The general feeling among collectors is that over fifty percent of the autographed baseballs being offered for sale have faked signatures. But do not let this spoil your fun. There is plenty of great, good stuff out there.

Autographed Baseball

Boudreau, Lou, bold blue ink signature.	35.00
Hubbel, Carl, bold black marker signature.	30.00
Calendar, St Louis Cardinals, 1980	15.00
Coin, Salada Tea, 1$\frac{3}{8}$" d, plastic, Mickey Mantle, black rim, 1962	15.00
Dixie Lid, Joe Medwick/St Louis Cardinals, 2$\frac{1}{4}$", brown photo, c1937	50.00
Hartland, Hank Aaron, 7" h, bat missing, late 1950s.	80.00
Lapel Pin, Bert & Harry Fan Club.	25.00

Napkin, World Series, Los Angeles, 1959, 7" × 5", "Dodgers Win It," Snider and

Sherry pictured	10.00

Pennant, Philadelphia Athletics, 28", navy

blue felt, inscription in white	50.00

Photo Button, Indianapolis Champions 1897, 1$\frac{1}{2}$" d, sepia, 15 uniformed

players	200.00

Pinback Button
7/8" d, Miller/Pittsburgh Pirates, Sweet

Caporal Cigarettes	20.00

1$\frac{1}{4}$" d, Brooklyn Dodgers, blue and

white, c1945	15.00

Press Pin, World Series
1943, NY Yankees, $\frac{7}{8}$", sterling silver, crossed bats beneath baseball, Dieges

& Clust, threaded post fastener	300.00

1967, Chicago White Sox Phantom, 1$\frac{1}{8}$", enameled, gold batter, white stocking, deep red center, deep blue border, Balfour, needle post fas-

tener.	80.00

Record, Richie Ashburn, 1952, 7" ×

7$\frac{1}{2}$".	20.00

Tobacco Silk, Phillies, 2" × 3", brown portraits of John W Bates and John

Titus, c1911	25.00

BASKETBALL

As the price of baseball cards and baseball memorabilia continues to rise, collectors are turning to other sports categories based on the affordability of their material. Basketball and football are new "hot" sport collecting fields.

Collecting generally centers around one team, as it does in most other sport collecting categories. Items have greater value in their "hometown" than they do "on the road." You know a category is becoming strong when its secondary material is starting to bring strong prices. Check the prices for the games in the list below.

Game
APBA Pro Basketball Game, APBA

Game Co, Lancaster, PA c1960	30.00

Hartland statue, Mickey Mantle, $185.00.

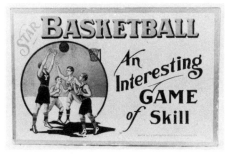

Game, Star Basketball, Star Paper Box Co, Chicago, bagatelle, copyright 1926, $40.00.

Bas–Ket, Cadaco, 1973 . . . . 25.00
NBA All–Star Basketball Game, Tudor Metal Products, metal playing board, plastic basketball figures, basketball net, and styrofoam ball, 1968 . . . . 45.00
Mug, 3″, Milwaukee Bucks, china, cartoon illus, black inscription, 1969–1970 . . . . 15.00
Nodder, 7″ h, composition, holding brown basketball, gold base, inscribed "Millersville," 1960s. 30.00
Palm Puzzle Game, 3″ d, styrene plastic case, cardboard center with basketball design, metallic ball, 1950s 12.00
Pen, 6″, New York Knicks, plastic, orange, clear cylinder with spectator image 15.00

BAUER POTTERY

J. A. Bauer established the Bauer Pottery in Los Angeles, CA, in 1909. Flowerpots were among the first items manufactured, followed by utilitarian items. Dinnerware was introduced in 1930. Artware came a decade later. The firm closed in 1962.

La Linda, 1939–1959
Chop Plate, 13″ d 25.00
Creamer. 8.00
Cup and Saucer 15.00
Plate, 9″ d, dinner. 8.00
Sugar 15.00
Vegetable, 10″ l, oval 25.00
Teapot, olive green, glossy pastel, Aladdin 35.00
Monterey, 1936–45
Butter Dish. 50.00
Casserole, cov, 2 qt, chartreuse, metal frame, crazed lid. 35.00
Creamer. 12.00
Cup, olive green. 12.00
Gravy. 35.00
Plate, 9½″ d, chartreuse 9.00
Soup Bowl, 7″ d 18.00
Sugar 20.00
Tumbler, 8 oz. 15.00

Ring, c1931
Baking Dish, cov, orange–red, 4″ d 25.00
Candlestick, spool 35.00
Coffee Server, wood handle, 6 cup 28.00
Creamer. 15.00
Mixing Bowl
Olive Green, #12. . . . . 28.00
Yellow, #24. . . . . 15.00
Plate, bread and butter, yellow 8.00
Ramekin, 4″ d 7.50
Refrigerator Set, 4 pcs 80.00
Shaker, green. 12.00
Souffle Dish 25.00
Vase, 8″ h 20.00
Vegetable, oval, divided 50.00

BEATLES

Ahhh! Look, it's the Fab Four! The collector will never need *Help* to find Beatle memorabilia at a flea market. Place mats, dishes, records, posters, and much more. The list is a *Magical Mystery Tour*. John, Paul, George, and Ringo will be found in a variety of shapes and sizes. They are likely to be heavily played with, so they will vary from poor to good. Take a good look. You may see *Strawberry Fields Forever.*

Club: Beatles Fan Club of Great Britain, Superstore Publications, 123 Marina, St. Leonards on Sea, East Sussex, England TN 38 OBN.

Periodicals: *Beatlefan*, P. O. Box 33515, Decatur, GA 30033; *Good Day Sunshine*, Liverpool Productions, 397 Edgewood Avenue, New Haven, CT 06511.

Bank, 8″ h, papier mache, rubber plug, mfg by Pride Creations 100.00
Belt Buckle, 2″ × 3″, metal, gold, black, and white group picture 25.00
Cake Set, blue, four figures 37.50
Comb, 3¼″ × 15″, plastic, Beatles and signature label, Lido Toys, 1964 . . . . . 90.00
Fan Club Pin 15.00
Flasher Ring, set 40.00
Head Band, orig package. 40.00
Locket Set 35.00
Pencil Case, 8″ l, vinyl, blue, group picture and autographs, zipper top, Standard Plastic Products 35.00
Photo Album, Sgt Pepper 30.00
Photograph
Movie Still, *A Hard Day's Night,* John with uncle 30.00
Promo, 1960s
John Lennon, Memory of a Rock Superstar 12.00
Ringo 10.00

Stoney's Pilsner Beer, Jones Brewing Co, Smithton, PA, $40.00.

Notebook, white ground, black letters, sepia figures, NEMS Enterprises, $35.00.

Playing Cards, single deck, orig box **50.00**
Puzzle, Yellow Submarine, 650 pgs,
  unopened, Jaymar, 1968 copyright . . . **75.00**
Sheet Music, She Loves You, red tone and
  white photo, 1963 copyright **18.00**
Tie Tac, Ringo, orig card **35.00**
Wallet, girl's, 1964, unused. **70.00**

BEER CANS

Beer can collecting was very popular in the 1970s. Times have changed. The field is now dominated by the serious collector and most trading and selling goes on at specialized beer canventions.

The list below contains a number of highly sought-after cans. Do not assume these prices are typical. Most cans fall in the quarter to fifty cent range. Do not pay more unless you are certain of the resale market.

There is no extra value to be gained by having a full beer can. In fact, selling a full can of beer without a license, if only to a collector, violates the liquor law in a large number of states. Most collectors punch a hole in the bottom of the can and drain out the beer.

Finally, before you ask! Billy Beer, either in individual cans, six packs, or cases, is not worth hundreds or thousands of dollars. The going price for a can among collectors is between fifty cents and $1.00. Billy Beer has lost its fizz.

Club: Beer Can Collectors of America, 747 Merus Court, Fenton, MO 63026.

Ace Hi M.L., Ace, Chicago, IL, 7 oz, flat
  top **100.00**
Altes, National, Detroit, MI, 12 oz, flat
  top **35.00**
Bantam, Goebel, Detroit, MI, 8 oz, flat
  top **25.00**
Budweiser, Anheuser–Busch, 7 cities, 10
  oz, pull top **5.00**
Colt 45 M.L., National, 4 cities, 8 oz, pull
  top **1.25**
Dawson, Lager, Dawson, Hammonton,
  NJ, 11 oz, pull top **1.50**
Eastside Old Tap, Pabst, Los Angeles, CA,
  12 oz, flat top **10.00**
Fehr's Draft, Fehr, Louisville, KY, 11 oz,
  pull top. **15.00**
Great Falls Select, Great Falls, Great Falls,
  MT, 12 oz, flat top **15.00**
Haas Pilsner, Haas, Houghton, MI, 12 oz,
  cone top **70.00**
Hamm's, Hamm's, St Paul, MN, 12 oz, pull
  top **2.50**
Krueger Ale, Krueger, Cranston, RI, 16 oz,
  pull top. **12.00**
Lite, Miller, 3 cities, 10 oz, pull top **1.00**
Lucky Lager, Lucky Lager, San Francisco,
  CA, 7 oz, flat top. **10.00**
Milwaukee's Best, Miller, Milwaukee,
  WI, 12 oz, pull top **5.00**
Neuweiler, Neuweiler's, Allentown, PA, 8
  oz, flat top **20.00**
North Star, Associated, 3 cities, 11 oz, pull
  top **2.00**
Old Crown Ale, Centlivre, Ft Wayne, IN,
  12 oz, flat top **42.50**
Rahr's, Rahr's Green Bay, Green Bay, WI,
  12 oz, Crowntainer cone top **45.00**
Spur Spout, M.L., Sick's Rainier, Seattle,
  WA, 15 oz, pull top **40.00**
Stag Premium Dry, Griesedieck–Western,
  2 cities, 12 oz, cone top **25.00**

Tavern Pale, Atlantic, Chicago, IL, 12 oz,
flat top 25.00
Whale's White Ale, National, 4 cities, 15
oz, pull top 25.00

BELLS

Bell collectors are fanatics. They tend to want every bell they can find. Admittedly, most confine themselves to bells that will fit on a shelf, but there are those who derive great pleasure from an old school bell sitting out in their front lawn.

Be alert for wine glasses that have been converted into bells. They are worth much less than bells that began life as bells. Also, collect limited edition bells because you like them, rather than with the hope they will rise in value. Many limited edition bells do not ring true on the resale market.

Club: American Bell Association, Rt. 1, Box 286, Natronia Heights, PA 15065.

School, wooden handle, brass, 4⅝" d, 8" h, $50.00.

Boxing, 10" d, trip hammer 75.00
China, 4", Limoges, cow shape, pale blue,
pink roses, gilded handle 40.00
Commemorative, 4½" h, Queen Elizabeth
II Silver Jubilee, marked "Aynsley" . . . 25.00
Desk, bronze, white marble base, side tap,
c1875 . . . . 45.00
Farm, cast iron, yoke 85.00
Fire, 12", brass 75.00

Glass
Carnival, figural, Southern Belle, white
imperial 38.00
Cranberry, gold edge, acid leaves 30.00
Milk, smocking, marked "Akeo, Made
in USA" 22.00
Hand, brass, figural
Lady, 3⅝", bust, quilted pattern on
bell 35.00
Turtle, bell bracket and striker on
shell 30.00
Horse, 3", brass 15.00
School, 7½" h, brass, wood handle 45.00
Sleigh, four, graduated sizes, shaft type,
iron strap 45.00
Yacht, 5¾", brass 40.00

BELT BUCKLES

This is a category loaded with reproductions and fakes. Beware of any cast buckle signed Tiffany. Surprisingly, many collectors do not mind the fakes. They like the designs and collect them for what they are.

A great specialized collection can be built around military buckles. These can be quite expensive. Once again, beware of recasts and fakes, especially Nazi buckles.

Arizona Downs 8.00
C B'ers 2.00
The Fonz 4.00
Hire's Rootbeer, Tiffany. 30.00
Jefferson Starship 4.00
Nazi, World War II, white metal 50.00
Panama Red 25.00
Schlitz Beer 25.00
Wells Butterfield 65.00
Wells Fargo 25.00

BIBLES

The general rule to follow is that any Bible less than two hundred years old has little or no value in the collectibles market. For a number of reasons, individuals are reluctant to buy religious items. Bibles are proof positive that nothing is worth anything without a buyer.

Many have trouble accepting this argument. They see a large late nineteenth century family Bible filled with engravings of religious scenes and several pages containing information about the family. It is old and impressive. It has to be worth money. Alas, it was mass-produced and survived in large quantities. The most valuable thing about it is the family data, and this can be saved simply by copying the few pages involved on a photocopier.

An average price for a large family Bible from the turn of the century is between $25.00 and $50.00. Of course, there are Bibles that sell for a lot more than this. I have listed a few of the heavy hitters. Most date from the seventeenth and eighteenth centuries. Bibles such as these do remain in private hands. Never speculate when buying a Bible, God would not like it.

Arabic, 1616, *Novum Testamentum Arabice*, Leiden edition by Thomas Erpenius, 8″ × 10″, early vellum boards **1,000.00**
Dutch, 1657, Amsterdam, *Biblia Sacra, dat is de Geheele Heylighe Schrifture*, Christoffel Van Sichem, 2 vol, 12″ × 5″, engraved title, woodcuts, old suede and calf **500.00**
English
1668, Cambridge, *Holy Bible*, John Field, engraved title with fine architectural border by John Chantry, Van Hove copperplates, 8″ × 10″, 18th C mottled calf, neatly rebacked, gilt edges **350.00**
1810, London, *The Christian's New and Complete British Family Bible*, A Hogg, 12″ × 5″, morocco gilt **195.00**
1908, London, *Bible*, Groiler Society, 14 vols, orig pigskin, soiled, fitted wooden bookcase **325.00**
German, 1702, Nuremberg, *Bible*, JL Buggel, two engraved titles, over 250 plates, 8″ × 10″, contemporary calf gilt over wooden boards, loose, lacking clasps **350.00**
Latin, 1629, Antwerp, *Biblia Sacra*, six parts, five volumes, early morocco gilt, rubbed **175.00**

BICENTENNIAL

America's 200th birthday in 1976 was PARTY TIME for the nation. Everyone and everything in the counrty had something stamped, painted, printed, molded, casted, and pressed with the commemortive dates 1776–1976. The America spirit of "overdo" and "outdo" always puts our nation in a great mood. We certainly overdid it during the Bicentennial.

The average flea market will have a wide variety of Bicentennial goodies. Prices have come down in recent years as the patriotic spirit waned and the only buyers left in the market were the collectors. Remember the Bicentennial was only sixteen years ago. This is one category where you only want to buy in fine or better condition.

Whiskey Bottle, Spirit of '76 Special, Wheaton Glass Co, $7.50.

Drinking Glasses, set of four
Burger King, 1776–1976 Have It Your Way Collector Series, 5 ½″ h, feature symbols of the American Revolution. **6.00**
Coca–Cola, Heritage Collector Series, Revolutionary War heroes **4.00**
Pin, ¼″ × ½″ red, white, and blue enamel on brass flag, orig 1½″ sq card inscribed "Official Pin, Quick Chek" **12.00**
Pinback Button, 2⅜″ oval, white Statue of Liberty, brown accents, yellow ground, red and white dates "1776" and "1976," white lettered "Bicentennial" **10.00**
U.S. Federal Reserves Two Dollar Bill, Series 1976 Neff–Simon, fr#1935-b*, New York, picture of the signing of the Declaration of Independence printed on back **5.00**
U.S. minted one dollar coin, 1976D copper–nickle clad variety I, representation of the Liberty Bell superimposed against the moon **14.00**

BICYCLES

Bicycles are divided into two groups— antique and classic. Chances of finding an antique bicycle, e.g., a high wheeler, at a flea market are slim. Spotting a great balloon tire classic are much greater.

Do not pay much for a bicycle that is incomplete, rusted, or repaired with nonoriginal parts. Replacement of parts that deteriorate, e.g., leather seats, is acceptable. It is not uncommon to heavily restore a bicycle, i.e., to make it look like new. If the amount of original parts is less than fifty percent, question an extremely high price.

There is a great market in secondary material from accessories to paper ephemera in bicycle collectibles. Since most bicycle fanatics haunt the automobile flea markets, you might just get lucky and find a great bicycle item at a low cost at an antiques and collectibles flea market.

Club: Wheelmen, Henry Ford Museum, Dearborn, MI 48121.

Periodicals: *Antique/Classic Bicycle News*, P. O. Box 1049, Ann Arbor, MI 48106; *Bicycle Trader*, P. O. Box 5600, Pittsburgh, PA 15207.

Game, Game of Bicycle Race, McLoughlin Bros, boxed board game, six pieces, multicolored litho, wooden box, copyright 1895, $250.00.

Advertising Trade Card, Clark Bicycle Co, Christmas, Santa on high wheeler, c1880. . . . . **20.00**
Badge, 1¼" × 2" link type, marked "Solid Silver" on back, enameled center front disk, hanger bar inscribed "Queens Co Course June 19–1898," pendant rim inscription "Century Medal/Survivor" and "Royal Arcanum Wheelman/New York City" **60.00**
Bicycle
BF Goodrich, boy's, 26" tires, new paint, orig light, carrier, locking fork, bendix auto 2–speed **150.00**
Comet, men's, worn orig paint, coaster brake, aluminum fenders **85.00**
Higgins, lady's, worn orig paint, carrier, skirt guard, truss rod, rusty rims. **85.00**

Roadmaster, girl's, cream and blue, red pinstripe, horn tank, headlight, carrier, chrome rims, orig condition. . . . **140.00**
Walton, tandem, wood rim, block chain fixed drive, rat trap pedals, new cork grips, new polymer tires. **450.00**
Chain, Diamond **10.00**
Horn, Yoder, c1950 . . . . **7.00**
Lapel Stud, Corbin Bells, The Best, metal, copper finish, handlebar bell, late 1890s. **30.00**
Light, Schwinn Phantom, chrome, battery operated. **60.00**
Pedals, Schwinn, girl's, glass reflectors . . . **50.00**
Pinback Button
Damascus Bicycle,⅞" d, multicolored, green and yellow gold Sword of Damascus, blue rim inscribed "Terre Haute Mfg Co, Dixon, IL," c1896, small tear in orig back paper **35.00**
Topeka Wheelmen Track Association, 1¼" d, lightly tinted black and white illus, four female cyclists approaching head on, light blue center ground blending to white edges, blue rim inscription, red serial number, c1890 . . . . **60.00**
Tried and True Pierce, 1¼" d, black and white logo, plum red ground, logo border inscribed "The Geo H Pierce Co/Makers/Buffalo, NY, USA," 1890s. **50.00**
Saddle Pin, replica of bicycle seat, short stickpin soldered on back, late 1890s Mesinger,¾" × ⅞", diecut tin **30.00**
Richards Bicycle,⅞" × 1½", silvered brass, inscription at top "Richards/Buchanan, Mich" **40.00**
Stickpin, replica of nameplate, diecut Cleveland, brightly silvered, mounted on brass backing, late 1890s **35.00**
Tribune, slightly rolled silvered brass, inscription "The Black Mfg Co, Erie, PA," late 1890s **40.00**
Tire, Schwinn, wide, white sidewalls, knobbys. **15.00**

BINOCULARS

Looking for field glasses or through them is an eye–opening experience. The binocular has been in use for more than two hundred years, continuing to improve our view of things. Though their greatest use has been by the military, civilian demand has given binocular production and versatility quite a push.

A flea market stand may not have that Bausch and Lomb super-deluxe, see-the-planet-like-it's-next-to-you model, but they might have an old pair of WWII spotter's glasses. Take care when going through a selection of binoculars. If they are still in the original case, they are more valuable than if they are just sitting on a seller's table. Look closely at the optics to check for cracks and loose lenses. Happy spotting.

French opera glasses, mother–of–pearl
exterior, dated 1902, Hmed "Lemaire
Fi., Paris"....................... **35.00**
German
North Africa Corps tan camouflage
trench binoculars, original tripod and
dual sun shades, lenses swing to different widths, 15" h, base marked
"S.F.14z.Gi,H/6400", orig lens
covers....................**350.00**
"Voightlander" binoculars, leather
neck strap and black leatherette
carrying case, 8" × 36" high power,
Hmed Braunschweig address, long
range glasses **150.00**
World War I, French Officer's, binoculars,
leather carrying case, Hmed, Paris, 8" ×
32".......................... **30.00**
World War II, German, binoculars, tropical canvas, neck strap, optics, calibrated
range finders on the lenses, Hmed "EK,
J.E.S., 6 × 9".................... **30.00**

BISQUE

Every time I look at a bisque figure, I think of grandmothers. There are just some types of antiques and collectibles that do this. I keep wondering why I never see a flea market table labeled "ONLY THINGS A GRANDMOTHER WOULD LOVE."

Bisque is pottery ware that has only been fired once and not glazed. It is a technique that is centuries old and is still being practiced today. Unfortunately, some of today's figures are exact copies of those made hundreds of years ago. Be especially aware of bisque piano babies.

Collectors differentiate between Continental (mostly German) and Japanese bisque with premiums generally paid for Continental pieces. However, the Japanese made some great bisque. Do not confuse the cheap five-and-dime "Occupied Japan" bisque with the better pieces.

Ashtray, 2¼", heart shape, hp floral spray,
white ground, Occupied Japan **12.00**
Basket, 8", barefoot boy with wide brim
hat seated on rim, marked "Germany"......................... **50.00**
Box, egg shape, relief windmill scene,
ftd........................... **45.00**

Salt, girl, pink jacket, white skirt, blue dots, tan and black bucket, 3¼" × 1½" × 2¾", $50.00.

Creamer, figural, cow, Occupied Ja-
pan......................... **20.00**
Figure
Baby, painted, Occupied Japan....... **17.00**
Bonnie Prince Charlie, 8", French **30.00**
Frog, 3½", Occupied Japan **15.00**
Match Holder, figural, Dutch girl, copper
and gold trim, includes striker........ **35.00**
Nodder, 2½" × 3½", jester, seated hold-
ing pipe, pastel peach and white, gold
trim **75.00**
Pitcher, miniature, multicolored applied
floral spray, pink ground, Occupied Ja-
pan......................... **8.00**
Planter
Girl with Water Jug, sitting by well,
coral and green **48.00**
Peasant Girl, 6", figural, standing beside leaf covered planter, Occupied
Japan........................ **35.00**
Salt, 3" d, figural, walnut, cream, branch
base, matching spoon **70.00**
Shelf Sitter, 4¾", Oriental girl, green, Occupied Japan **12.00**
Toothpick Holder, lady with flower **35.00**
Vase, 7", ftd, emb floral dec, Occupied Ja-
pan.......................... **18.00**
Wall Pocket, 5", cuckoo clock, orange
luster, pine cone weights, Occupied Japan.......................... **12.00**

BLACK GLASS

This glass gets its name from the fact that when it is sitting on a table, it looks black. When you hold it up to the light, it is a deep purple color. It was extremely popular in the period between World War I and II.

Some forms were decorative, but most were meant for everyday use. As a result, you should expect to find signs of use on most pieces.

Animal Cov Dish
  Hen on Nest, 5⅛″ l basketweave base, turned white opalescent head, red painted comb, Westmoreland, c1900...................... **100.00**
  Swan, Westmoreland, c1950 .... **115.00**
Bookends, pr, Rearing Horses, LE Smith, c1930.......................... **20.00**
Candlesticks, pr
  6½″ h, swan, Fenton, c1938.......... **50.00**
  9″ h, black stem and foot, clear lusters, Fostoria, c1931 .... **40.00**
Candy Dish, cov, 6″ d, gold rose dec, Cambridge, c1930.................... **45.00**
Centerpiece Bowl, 11″ d, cupped, Fostoria, c1930 .... **30.00**
Creamer, Pillar Flute, Imperial, c1930 ... **3.50**
Figure
  Dog, bridge, Cambridge, c1930....... **12.00**
  Elephant, Co−Op Flint Glass, c1920... **70.00**
  Monkey, metal collar, rhinestone eyes **20.00**
Pickle Dish, Pillar Flute, Imperial, c1930.......................... **3.00**
Plate
  Do−Si−Do pattern, silver painted dec, L E Smith, c1930................. **10.00**
  Three Owls, marked "Westmoreland"................ **25.00**
Sherbet, Floral Sterling, Hazel−Atlas, c1930.......................... **3.50**
Sugar Shaker, Windermere's Fan, hp floral dec, Hobb's Glass, c1890 .... **120.00**
Tom and Jerry Set, bowl, ten matching mugs, marked "McKee," c1930 ...... **80.00**
Vase, 10″ h, Peacock and Rose, Paden City, c1928.......................... **50.00**
Window Box, 8″ l, dancing ladies dec, L E Smith, c1930.................... **15.00**

BLACK MEMORABILIA

Black memorabilia is enjoying its second renaissance. It is one of the "hot" areas in the present market. The category is viewed quite broadly, ranging from slavery era items to objects showing ethnic stereotypes. Prices range all over the place. It pays to shop around.

Because black memorabilia ranges over a wide variety of forms, the Black memorabilia collector is constantly competing with collectors from other areas, e.g., cookie jar, kitchen, and salt and pepper shaker collectors. Surprisingly enough, it is the collectors of Black memorabilia who realize the vast amount of material available and tend to resist high prices.

Reproductions, from advertising signs (Bull Durham Tobacco) to mechanical banks (Jolly Nigger), are an increasing problem. Remember—if it looks new, chances are that it is new.

Periodical: *Black Ethnic Collectibles*, 1401 Asbury Court, Hyattsville, MD 20782.

Advertising trade card, Higgins Soap, Black family dressed to go to church, Forbes, Boston, $7.50.

Bank, Jolly Nigger, cast iron, mechanical **195.00**
Book, *Little Black Sambo*, large, colorful, 1939............................. **75.00**
Bottle, molasses, Aunt Dinah **55.00**
Cook Book, mammy, 1939............ **52.00**
Cookie Jar
  Aunt Jemima, soft plastic **295.00**
  McCoy, mammy **145.00**
  Mosaic Tile, mammy, one yellow, one blue, pr....................... **975.00**
  National, mammy, silver............ **295.00**
Creamer and Sugar, Aunt Jemima and Uncle Mose, green, F&F **250.00**
Doll
  Horsman, 15″ h, sleeper............. **135.00**
  Negro, cloth, 1930s **95.00**
  Topsy−turvy **25.00**
  Uncle Mose, oilcloth, mint in orig envelope with order blank, 1949........ **85.00**
Flour Sack, 5 lb, Aunt Jemima **5.00**
Hat, Aunt Jemima Breakfast Club....... **45.00**
Memo Holder, chalk, mammy **50.00**

Memo Pad Refill, #123, mammy	12.50
Pancake Cutter, Aunt Jemima	250.00
Pancake Mold, Aunt Jemima	125.00
Pancake Shaker, Aunt Jemima	
Blue	48.00
Yellow	68.00
Paper Plate, Aunt Jemima	38.00
Piebird	
Chef, yellow clothes	50.00
Mammy, pink, white, and blue clothes	68.00
Pinback Button, Aunt Jemima Breadfast Club	
Drummer	32.00
Face	18.00
Program, Amos & Andy, "Amos Wedding," Dec 25, 1935, six pgs.	38.00
Salt and Pepper Shakers, Luzanne mammy, green apron, orig box, F&F, pr	198.00
Spice Set, mammy, plastic, F&F	295.00
Syrup, mammy, plastic, F&F	48.00
Vase, lady head, Blackamoor, Royal Copley	35.00
Watch, Little Rascals "Buckwheat," Lewco	25.00

BLUE RIDGE

Southern Potteries of Erwin, TN, produced Blue Ridge dinnerware from the late 1930s until 1956. Four hundred patterns graced eight basic shapes.

Newsletter: *National Blue Ridge Newsletter*, P. O. Box 298, Blountville, IN 37617.

Periodical: *The Daze*, Box 57 , Otisville, MI 48463.

Arlington Apple, Skyline	
Cup, rope handle	3.00
Plate, 9½" d	5.00
Cherry Tree Glen	
Bowl	
5½" d	5.00
6¼" d	6.00
9½" d	12.00
Creamer	7.00
Plate	
6" d	3.00
7½" sq	15.00
9½" d	8.00
Vegetable Bowl, 9¼" l, oval	15.00
Mardi Gras	
Creamer	2.50
Cup	5.00
Fruit Bowl	3.25
Gravy Boat, underplate	18.00
Plate	
6½" d, bread and butter	1.25
7" d, luncheon	2.25
9½" d, dinner	3.25
Saucer	.75
Vegetable Bowl, 9" l	8.00
Mountain Ivy, vegetable bowl, oval	20.00
Poinsettia	
Creamer	8.00
Cup	6.00
Plate	
6¼" d	3.00
9¼" d	8.00
Rustic Plaid	
Creamer	3.50
Cup	2.00
Plate	
6" d, bread and butter	1.50
9" d, dinner	3.75
Saucer	1.00
Sugar	3.50

Pom Pom Variation, 9¼" d plate, blue and pink flowers, $5.00.

BOOKENDS

Prices listed below are for pairs. Woe to the dealer who splits pairs apart!

Sailing ships, metal, 5" × 5", $35.00.

72

Brass, 7½" h, sentries on orb mounted
base, Bakelite trim, imp mark, Chase
Chrome and Brass Co **165.00**
Bronze, anchors **35.00**
Cast Iron
Flowers in basket, painted **50.00**
Nudes, 5" × 7", bronze finish, full fig-
ured, kneeling, Art Deco **70.00**
Chrome Plated, 4¼" h, terrier dogs, round
back and base, c1920 . . . . **100.00**
Copper, 10 × 5", fleur–de–lis, Roycroft
orb mark **100.00**
Glass
Cornucopia, 5¾" h, New Mar-
tinsville **50.00**
Daddy Bear, 4½" h, New Mar-
tinsville **100.00**
Fish, Heisey **150.00**
Ivory, elephants, teakwood base **165.00**
Leather, 6" × 6", tooled design, wood
base, Roycroft orb mark **150.00**
Plaster, Lincoln Memorial, bronze finish,
detailed **25.00**
Soapstone, urn and flowers **85.00**
White Metal, race horse and jockey,
bronze finish, Art Deco **75.00**

BOOKS

There are millions of books out there. Some
are worth a fortune. Most are hardly worth
the paper they are printed on. Listing specific titles serves little purpose here. By following ten guidelines below, you can
quickly determine if the books that you
have uncovered have value potential.

1. Check your book titles in *American
Book Prices Current*, published annually by
Bancroft–Parkman, Inc., and available at
most libraries and *The Old Book Value Guide,
Second Edition* (Collector Books: 1990).
When listing your books in preparation for
doing research include the full name of the
author, expanded title, publisher, copyright
date, and edition and/or printing number.

2. Examine bindings. Decorators buy
handsomely bound books by the foot at
prices ranging from $40.00 to $75.00 per
foot.

3. Carefully research any children's
book. Illustration quality is an important
value key. Little Golden Books are one of
the hottest book areas in the market today.
In the late 1970s and early 1980s Big Little
Books were hot.

4. Buy all hardcover books about antiques and collectibles that you find that are
cheaply priced, i.e., less than five dollars.
There is a growing demand for out-of-print
antiques and collectibles books.

5. Check the edition number. Value, in
most cases, rests with the first edition.
However, not every first edition is valuable.
Consult Blank's *Bibliography of American
First Editions* or Tannen's *How to Identify and
Collect American First Editions*.

6. Look at the multifaceted aspects of the
book and the subject that it covers. Books
are collected by type, e.g., mysteries, westerns, etc. Many collectors buy books as
supplements to their main collection. A
Hopalong Cassidy collector, although focusing on the objects licensed by Bill Boyd,
will want to own the Mulford novels in
which Hopalong Cassidy originated.

7. Local histories and atlases always have
a good market, particularly those printed
between 1880 and 1930. Add to this centennial and other celebration volumes.

8. Generally an author's signature increases the value of the book. However, it
was common practice to put engraved signatures of authors in front of books during
the last part of the nineteenth century. The
Grant signature in the first volume of his
two-volume memoir set is not original, but
printed.

9. Book club editions have little or no
value except for books done by George and
Helen Macy's Limited Editions Club.

10. Accept the fact that the value of most
books falls in the 50¢ to $2.00 range and
that after all the searching that you have
done, this is probably what you have
found.

BOOTJACKS

Unless you are into horseback riding, a
bootjack is one of the most useless devices
that you can have around the house. Why
do so many individuals own one? The answer in our area is "just for nice." Actually,
they are seen as a major accessory in trying
to capture the country look.

Cast-iron reproductions are a major
problem, especially for "Naughty Nellie"
and "Beetle" designs.

Advertising
Clown Cigarettes, 8" l, iron, orig
paint **245.00**
Musselman's Plug Tobacco, cast iron,
ornate **150.00**
Brass, beetle, 10" l **90.00**
Cast Iron
Cricket, 11¾" l, emb lacy design **25.00**
Mule's head **40.00**

Cast iron, lyre base reads "Try Me," 12" l, $48.00.

Wood
    Fish shape, 19" l, relief carving, red
        stain **30.00**
    Maple, 13" l, hand hewn **15.00**
    Pine, 25 "l, oval ends, sq nails. **28.00**

BOTTLE OPENERS, FIGURAL

Although this listing focuses on cast iron figural bottle openers, the most sought after type of bottle openers, do not forget the tin advertising openers, also known to some as church keys. The bulk still sell between $2.00 and $10.00, a very affordable price range.

Clubs: Figural Bottle Opener Collectors, 13018 Clarion Road, Fort Washington, MD 20744; Just For Openers, 63 October Lane, Trumbull, CT 06611.

All are cast iron unless otherwise specified.

Drunk, painted white metal, 4" h, $25.00.

Black Boy, 3" h, hand in air, green alligator
    and base, John Wright Co **165.00**
Clown, 4" h, brass, wall mount, white
    bowtie, red polka dots, bald head, sgd
    "495" on back, John Wright Co **70.00**
Cowboy, 4⅞" h, "San Antonio, Texas" . . . **225.00**
Drunk
    4" h
        At lamppost, polychrome paint,
            worn. **25.00**
        With palm tree, polychrome paint,
            some wear **65.00**
    At signpost, polychrome paint, "Balti-
        more, MD" **10.00**
Girl
    3⅞" h, with buck teeth, polychrome
        paint, marked "Wilton Prod" **50.00**
    4½" h, at sign post, polychrome paint,
        minor wear **35.00**
Pelican, 3¾" h, cream, orange beak and
    feet, green base, John Wright Co **140.00**
Rooster, 3¼" h, polychrome paint,
    worn **50.00**
Seagull, 3¼" h, on stump, polychrome
    paint, minor wear **175.00**
Steel worker, 3¼" h, polychrome paint,
    minor wear **175.00**
Teeth, 3⅜" l, polychrome paint, very
    worn **95.00**
Toucan on perch, 5" h, polychrome paint,
    some wear **55.00**

BOTTLES

Bottle collecting is such a broad topic that the only way one can hope to survive is by specialization. It is for this reason that several bottle topics are found elsewhere in this book.

Bottles have a bad habit of multiplying. Do not start collecting them until you have plenty of room. I know one person whose entire basement is filled with Coca-Cola bottles bearing the imprint of different cities.

There are many bottle categories that are still relatively inexpensive to collect. In many cases, you can find a free source of supply in old dumps. Before getting too deeply involved, it pays to talk with other bottle collectors and to visit one or more specialized bottle collectors show.

Club: Federation of Historical Bottle Collectors, 14521 Atlantic, Riverdale, IL 60627.

Periodical: *Antique Bottle And Glass Collector,* P. O. Box 187, East Greenville, PA 18041.

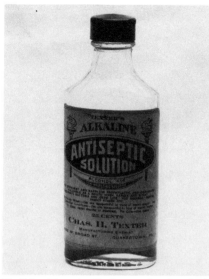

Medicine, Texter's Alkaline Antiseptic Solution, blue letters, orig paper label, 5½" h, $3.50.

BEVERAGES

Bubble Up Pop	4.75
Buster Brown Rye, swirled, enameled	55.00
Double Line Soda, Kokomo, IN	6.00
Fruitbowl Grapefruit Wine	12.00
Glicquot Soda, paper label	5.00
Grapette Pop	8.00
Klassy Tops In Taste Pop	8.00
Korker The OK Refresher Pop	5.50
Mountain Valley Mineral Water	13.00
Schlitz Beer, ruby red, label	15.00

FLAVORINGS

A & S, lemon extract, c1905	24.00
Bob White Golden Syrup, Louisville, KY	11.00
Colgate, vanilla extract, c1910	20.00
Duncan's Exone Cough Syrup	8.50
Herberlings, banana flavoring, 8" h, paper label	8.00
HICO Imitation Lemon Flavoring, clear, 8 oz	6.00
Highland Maple Sap Syrup	9.00
James Chaskel & Co Extract	35.00
Louis & Co, lemon extract	10.00
McCormick Imitation Pineapple	5.50

FOOD

Cross & Blackwell Mint Sauce	3.00
Frank's BBQ Sauce	6.50
L & S Sweet Dill Strips	8.50
Marvel Sweet Pickles	12.00
Spears Vinegar	8.00

HEALTH AND BEAUTY

Anticipitic Talcum Powder	5.00
Hostetter's Bitters	15.00
Lydia E Pinkham's Vegetable Compound, green	8.00

HOUSEHOLD

Alma Polish, aqua, name emb on shoulder, 5" h, marked "M & Co" on base	5.00
Mexican Imperial Bluing, clear, gold cap, 10 oz	7.50
Snow Bird Liquid Wax, brown bottle, red cap, blue and white label, 6 oz	7.50

BOXES

We have reached the point with some twentieth century collectibles where the original box may be more valuable than the object that came in it. If the box is colorful and contains a picture of the product, it has value.

Boxes have always been a favorite among advertising collectors. They are three-dimensional and often fairly large in size. The artwork reflects changing period tastes. Decorators like the pizazz that boxes offer. The wooden box with a lithographed printed label is a fixture in the country household.

Candy box, Payday, Salted Nut Roll, Hollywood Brands, Inc., yellow ground, black, red, and blue lettering, 24 bar box, 8" × 10" × 2", $15.00.

Advertising

Big Time OH–Gee Candy	**8.00**
Blanar Banana.	**55.00**
Bossie's Best Brand Butter, pound	**2.00**
Boston Wafers Candy, children and wafers illus.	**20.00**
Donald Duck Straws, 1950s	**22.00**
Dr Johnson's Educator Crackers	**35.00**
Forbes Co, St Louis, allspice, Buster Brown illus	**40.00**
Regal Underware, cardboard	**15.00**
Empty, original	
Marx Toy, police siren motorcycle	**170.00**
Tootsietoy, furniture	**85.00**
Walt Disney, Mickey Mouse wrist watch.	**110.00**
Sample, National Lead Co, paint chip samples.	**15.00**
Shipping	
Armour's Washing Powder.	**5.00**
Baker's Chocolate, 12 lbs, wooden	**15.00**
Pickney Spice, wooden, store size	**80.00**
Royal Baking Powder, wood,	

Sheet music, March of the Boy Scouts, G. A. Grant–Schaefer, music, Oliver Ditson Co publisher, 1913–1915, $10.00

BOY SCOUTS

This is another collecting area in which adults dominate where you would normally expect to find kids. When my dad was a Boy Scout, emphasis was on swapping material with little concern for value. One for one was the common rule.

Today old Scouting material is viewed in monetary terms. My dad's Eagle badge books at over seventy-five dollars. The key is to find material that was officially licensed. Unlicensed material is generally snubbed by collectors.

Boy Scout collecting is so sophisticated that it has its own shows or swap meets. Strong retail value for Boy Scout material occurs at these shows. Flea market prices tend to be much lower.

Badge, Scouting Around the World, metal, attached red, white, and blue fabric ribbon, inscribed "Fort Indian Town Gap 1978".	**15.00**
Bank, orig paint.	**95.00**
Book, *Troop Committee*, 5½ × 8″, 42 pgs, 1931 Boy Scouts of America copyright	**25.00**
Canteen, aluminum, hip type, red canvas cov	**8.00**
Handbook, Norman Rockwell cover, c1950.	**8.00**
Membership Card, 2½″ × 3¾″, typed name and October 31, 1941, includes 2¾″ × 4″ brown manila envelope.	**12.00**
Mirror	**7.50**

Notepad, 2½″ × 4″, Boy Scout signaling illus on front, 1914 copyright	**25.00**
Pennant, 30″ l, felt, blue, white inscription, c1940.	**20.00**
Plaque	
Art, 11¾″, hardwood, Norman Rockwell illus of three young scouts, Berton Braley poem "The Scouting Trail"	**50.00**
Award, 6½″ × 9½″, masonite, full color portrait picture, awarded by National Council of Boy Scouts for participation in Onward For God And My Country Program, 1958.	**45.00**
Signal Set, Fleran, double	**65.00**
Wall Plaque, Cub Scouts, plaster molded bear, wolf, and lion	**18.00**

BOYD CRYSTAL ART GLASS

The Boyds, Bernard and his son, purchased the Degenhart Glass Factory in 1978. Since that time they have reissued a number of the Degenhart forms. Their productions can be distinguished by the color of the glass and the "D" in a diamond mark. The Boyd family continues to make contemporary collectible glass at its factory in Cambridge, Ohio.

Balloon Bear, Patrick, Alexandrite	**6.00**
Basket, 4½″, Milk White, hp	**20.00**

76

Bell
  Owl, Violet Slate **15.00**
  Santa, Carnival **20.00**
  Bunny on Nest, White Opal. **9.00**
  Candleholder, sleigh, White **22.00**
  Colonial Doll, Sunflower Yellow **20.00**
  Debbie Duck, White **5.00**
  Dog, Skippy, Light Rose **8.50**
  Ducklings, Crown Tuscan. **2.75**
  Hobo Clown, Freddie, Cobalt Blue **9.00**
  Joey, Chocolate. **30.00**
  Lamb, salt, Grape Parfait **10.00**
  Louise, doll
    Apricot. **20.00**
    Mother's Day, 1991, red shawl, red
    purse, red and blue hearts on dress,
    American flag on lower left side. **17.00**
  Rooster, Orange Calico **10.00**
  Suee Pig, Autumn Beige **7.50**
  Tractor, Spinnaker Blue, 2" h **10.00**
  Willie, mouse, 2" h, Lime Carnival **10.00**

BRASS

Brass is a durable, malleable, and ductile
metal alloy consisting mainly of copper and
zinc. It appears in this guide because of the
wide variety of objects made from it. I have
never met a brass collector whose interest
spans all forms, but I have met baggage
check and key collectors.

Pot, American, 12" d, $175.00.

Baggage Check, Texas Central RR, local,
  1⅝" × 2", strap, Poole Bros, Chicago . . . **35.00**
Bowl, handles, Dutch **50.00**
Box, 6¼" l, hanging, emb floral dec **25.00**
Call Bell, 6¼" h, red granite base **25.00**
Door Handles, pr, 16" l, sq elongated form,
  cast floral dec **10.00**
Fireplace Fan, 38" w, 25" h, folding, griffin
  detail **65.00**
Jardiniere, 6" h, globular form, incised
  geometric and floral motif, 19th C **20.00**

Key
  Door, 5", standard bow and bit **8.00**
  Watch, 1", plain, swivel. **2.00**
Knife, Golden Wedding Whiskey **20.00**
Letter Opener, Pittsburg Coal Co, Indian
  head on handle **15.00**
Matchsafe, International Tailoring, nickel
  plated, emb Indians and lion **55.00**
Mortar and Pestle, 2½" h **40.00**
Padlock
  Combination, 2½" h, Sesamee, dials on
    bottom. **15.00**
  Lever Push Key, 2¼" d, Champion Six
    Lever, emb **5.00**
Plant Stand, gilded, white onyx shelf and
  top **50.00**
Suppository Mold **80.00**
Switch Lock, Adlake, Penn Central. **20.00**

BREAD BOXES

Bread boxes are too much fun to be hidden
in a Kitchen Collectibles category. There
are plenty of great examples both in form
and decoration. They have disappeared
from the modern kitchen. I miss them.

Chrome, rect, black wood handle **10.00**
Graniteware, sq, gray, raised red handles
  and letters "Bread" **25.00**
Metal
  Painted, yellow, fruit decal **15.00**
  Red Poppy pattern. **17.00**
  Tin, 12" l, white, red enameled top **12.00**
  Wood, carved "Give Us This Day," 12½"
    h. **80.00**

BREAD PLATES

Bread, the staff of life, has been served on
ornate plates of all types, ranging from colored glass of the Victorian era to the
handwrought aluminum of the 1950s.
Some bread plates included mottos or com-
memorated historical events.

Avoid plain examples. A great bread
plate should add class to the table.

Aluminum, hand wrought, flying geese
  dec **15.00**
China, 14" × 7", hp, spring scene, pas-
  tel colors, gold band, artist sgd, Ba-
  varian. **90.00**
Cut Glass, 13½" l, brilliant cut, sgd "Lib-
  bey". **175.00**
Pattern Glass
  Actress, HMS Pinafore, 7" × 12" **90.00**
  Aurora, ruby stained, 10" d, center
    star. **35.00**

Glass, "Be Industrious," clear, 12" × 8¼", $45.00.

Beaded Ovals	50.00
California, emerald green	45.00
Egyptian, Cleopatra	65.00
Kansas, emb "Our Daily Bread"	45.00
New Jersey, ruby stained	100.00
US Coin, clear coins	175.00
Silverplated, grape clusters on self handles	65.00
Wooden, Flemish Art, hp florals, motto, sgd	50.00

BREWERIANA

Beer is liquid bread, or so I was told growing up in Pennsylvania German country. It is hard to deny German linkage with the brewing industry when your home community contained the Horlacher, Neuweiler, and Uhl breweries.

Brewery signs and trays, especially from the late nineteenth and early twentieth century, contain some of the finest advertising lithography of the period. The three-dimensional advertising figures from the 1930s through the 1970s are no slouches either.

Brewery advertising has become expensive. Never fear. You can build a great breweriana collection concentrating on barroom accessories such as foam scrappers, coasters, and tap tops.

Clubs: American Breweriana Association, P. O. Box 6082, Colorado Springs, CO 80934; National Association Breweriana Advertising, 2343 Met-To-Wee Lane, Wauwatosa, WI 53226.

Ashtray, Canadian Club **20.00**
Blotter, 7½" × 3", Bergdoll Brewing Co, black and white portrait of Louis Bergdoll, holly dec, 60th anniversary, 1909, unused **50.00**

Mirror, green ground, red, yellow, and white letters, 1¹³⁄₁₆" × 2¾", $35.00.

Bottle
  Beckers Beer, Evanston, WY **10.00**
  Calgary Ale **10.00**
Clock, Old Milwaukee, bar display, ship's bell time **60.00**
Coaster, Simon Pure Beer, metal **5.00**
Corkscrew, Anheuser–Busch, encased **75.00**
Fishing Lure, Schlitz, bottle shape **10.00**
Foam Scraper, Meister Brau, celluloid ... **20.00**
Ice Pick, Empire Lager, Black Horse Ale **25.00**
Lapel Pin, Pabst Breweries, enameled 14K gold **25.00**
Lamp
  Budweiser, wall, pr **22.00**
  Seagrams Whiskey, oil **20.00**
Match Safe, Pabst Beer, pocket **48.00**
Pinback Button
  Emil Sick's Select Beer, 1½" d, red number "6" logo, yellow ground, black letters, gold rim and accents, c1930 .... **20.00**
  Poth's Beer, 1" d, white letters, khaki ground, c1900 .... **12.00**
  Schlitz Beer, 1¼" d, white ground, red letters, crossed key center, early 1900s **20.00**
Sign, Piels Beer, Sammy Davis Jr, bus **100.00**
Shot Glass, etched, Peoria Co Club Whiskey, Peoria, IL **25.00**
Stein
  Budweiser, Ceramarte **22.00**
  Hamm's, Octoberfest, 1973, McCoy ... **25.00**
  Miller High Life, 1984 .... **25.00**
  Old Milwaukee **18.00**
  Schlitz **18.00**
Tap Knob, Hamm's Beer, metal **15.00**

Thermometer, Rueter & Co, Highland Spring Brewery, Boston, patented 1885, brass **175.00**
Tip Tray, Budweiser **8.00**
Tray
Hamm's, bear **20.00**
Miller Beer, girl sitting on moon **40.00**
Watch Fob
Anheuser–Busch, diecut, silvered brass, enameled red, white, and blue trademark **50.00**
Brown Gin and Liquors, brass, raised moose head, reverse "Sold by H Obernauer & Co, Pittsburgh, PA" . . . **40.00**

BRITISH ROYALTY COMMEMORATIVES

This is one of those categories where you can get in on the ground floor. Every king and queen, potential king and queen, and their spouses is collectible. Buy some of the stuff when it is new. I have a few Prince Harry items. We may not have royal blood in common, but. . . .

Most individuals collect by monarch, prince, or princess. Take a different approach—collect by form, e.g., mugs, playing cards, etc. British royalty commemoratives were made at all quality levels. Stick to high-quality examples.

It is fun to find recent issues at flea markets for much less than their original selling price. Picking is competitive. There are a lot of British royalty commemorative collectors.

Mug, Prince Andrew and Miss Sarah Ferguson, color portrait, 3³⁄₄" h, Coronet, $25.00.

Bell, Queen Elizabeth II, Silver Jubilee, 1977, 5¹⁄₂", applied roses, silver trim, Crown Staffordshire **30.00**

Bowl, Prince William of Wales, 1982, 6", color portraits and nursery scenes **35.00**
Candy Tin, 7" × 10" × 1¹⁄₂", Queen Elizabeth II, Coronation, pink border, full color portrait, paper adv sticker, Sharps Toffee **40.00**
Cup and Saucer, Queen Elizabeth II, Coronation, gold trim, Washington Pottery Ltd **20.00**
Dish, Prince Charles, Investiture as Prince of Wales, July 1, 1969, 5¹⁄₂", multicolored coat of arms, ftd, Aynsley **50.00**
Mug
3¹⁄₄", Queen Elizabeth II, Silver Jubilee, 1977, red portrait, red and blue dec, Adams **25.00**
3¹⁄₂", Prince Charles and Lady Diana Spencer, Royal Wedding, July 29, 1981, sepia portraits, color dec, Pall Mall Ware **35.00**
3⁵⁄₈", King Edward VII, Coronation, ceramic, white, full color picture, inscription, 1937 . . . . **50.00**
Plate
8³⁄₄" d, Queen Elizabeth II, Coronation, color portrait and dec, gold trim, Royal Winton **20.00**
10¹⁄₂" d, Prince Charles and Lady Diana Spencer, Royal Wedding, July 29, 1981, black and white portraits, color and gold dec **40.00**
Playing Cards, Prince Charles and Lady Diana Spencer, Royal Wedding, July 29, 1981, double deck, British Monarchs, color portraits, Grimaud **30.00**
Pocket Watch, Queen Elizabeth II, Coronation, 2" d, brightly silvered metal pocket watch, back engraved with royal family crest **250.00**
Stamp Packet, Queen Elizabeth II, Coronation, 4" × 6" envelope, unseparated block of sixty different stamps, 1953, pr **20.00**
Tea Towel, Prince Charles and Lady Diana Spencer, wedding, Irish linen, color portraits **15.00**

BROWNIES, PALMER COX

Palmer Cox created *The Brownies*, comical elflike creatures, for *St. Nicholas* magazine. Each Brownie had a distinct personality and name. Thirteen books were published about them.

Beware of imitation Brownies. The Brownies' success led other illustrators to utilize elf figures in their cartoons. The only way to tell the copies from the originals is to carefully study and memorize the Cox illustrations.

Game, Brownie Kick–In Top, M. H. Miller Co, c1910, $50.00

Advertising Trade Card, American Machine Co, ice cream freezers 15.00
Basket, desk type, brass, 2″ × 4″, Brownie at base 75.00
Book, *Brownie Primer*, Palmer Cox, Century Co 45.00
Box, Little Buster Popcorn 12.00
Charm, 1″, white metal, black finish, vest and cap, c1900 . . . . 35.00
Needle Book, Columbian Expo, Brownie Policeman illus, 1893 . . . . 50.00
Plate, marked "Cook & Hancock, Trenton" 60.00
Ruler, adv, Mrs Winslow's Soothing Syrup 25.00
Stickpin, Brownie Policeman 20.00

BUBBLE GUM CARDS

Based on the publicity received by baseball cards, you would think that they were the only bubble gum cards sold. Wrong, wrong, wrong! There are a wealth of non-sport bubble gum cards.

Prices for many of these card sets are rather modest. Individual cards often sell for less than $1.00. The classic cards were issued in the 1950s, but I bought a pack of the recent Desert Storm cards just to be on the safe side.

Periodical: *The Wrapper*, 1903 Ronzheimer Avenue, St. Charles, IL 60174.

Bowman
1948, Movie Stars, 2 1/16″ × 1½″, 36-card set 75.00
1953, Antique Autos, 2½ × 3¾″, 48-card set 50.00

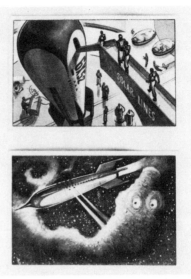

Jets, Rockets, Spaceman (R701), Bowman Gum Inc., Philadelphia, 1951, 108 cards in set, top: Card 4, Final Check Before Blast Off, $2.50; bottom: Card 33, Battling Space Cell, $2.50.

1954, US Navy Victories, 2½ × 3¾″, 48 card set 50.00
Donruss
1964, Combat, Series I, 66 cards 55.00
1966, Monkees, 44 cards 38.00
1973, Osmonds, 66 cards 30.00
1979, Rock Stars, 66 cards 2.50
1980, Dukes of Hazzard, 66 cards 3.50
Fleer
1965, Gomer Pyle, 66 cards 10.00
1968, My Kookie Klassmates, 20 cards, 9 autograph stamp sheets 15.00
1979, Gong Show, 66 cards, 10 stickers 5.00
1983, Mad, 128 stickers 15.00
Leaf, 1967, Star Trek, 72 cards 550.00
Philadelphia Chewing Gum Co
1965, James Bond, 66 cards 55.00
1966, Tarzan, 66 cards 40.00
1969, Dark Shadows, Series II, 66 cards, green 80.00
Topps
1962, Civil War News, 88 cards 175.00
1965, Daniel Boone, 55 cards 25.00
1965, King Kong, 55 cards 20.00
1970, Brady Bunch, 88 cards 150.00
1980, Empire Strikes Back, Series I 5.00

BUSTER BROWN

R. F. Outcault could have rested on his Yellow Kid laurels. Fortunately, he did not and created a second great cartoon character - Buster Brown. The strip first appeared in the Sunday, May 4, 1902, *New York Herald*. Buster's fame was closely linked to Tige, his toothily grinning evil-looking bulldog.

Most of us remember Buster Brown and Tige because of Buster Brown Shoes. The shoe advertisements were popular on radio and television shows of the 1950s. "Look for me in there too."

Pinback button, Buster Brown Bread, multicolored, 1½" d, $12.50.

Advertising Sign **45.00**
Bandana **50.00**
Bike, merry–go–round horse, Buster and
   Tige advertisement, Hollywood Jr. **295.00**
Book, *Book of Travels*, 1912 . . . . **45.00**
Box, stockings, graphics **39.00**
Calendar Plate, 7", Buster and Tige,
   1909. . . . . **48.00**
Cigar **10.00**
Clicker, Buster Brown Hosiery, red, white,
   and blue, 1930–1940 . . . . **22.00**
Coat Hook **28.00**
Compact, 2" d, brass, emb logo "Buster
   Brown Shoes, First Because Of The
   Last," Buster holding shoe along Tige,
   reverse with hinged door and small mir-
   ror, c1930 . . . . **65.00**
Cup and Saucer, Buster and Tige, sgd **45.00**
Fan, framed **85.00**
Kite **35.00**
Lapel Stud, 1¼", white metal, silver finish,
   Buster with hand on Tige's head,
   c1900. . . . . **40.00**
Mirror, pocket, 1946. . . . . **22.00**
Periscope, Secret Agent, unused **21.00**
Pinback Button
   7/8"
      Buster Brown Hose Supporter,
      multicolor **20.00**
      Buster Brown Gang, multicolor, li-
      tho, c1920 . . . . **20.00**
   1", Buster Brown Blue Ribbon Shoes,
   sepia, photo–like portrait of Buster

and Tige, paper text on back,
   c1902–10 . . . . **18.00**
Pitcher, 3¼" **30.00**
Plate, Buster and Tige, china **55.00**
Postcard, Buster and Tige, colorful, Tuck,
   1906. . . . . **25.00**
Shoe Box, Buster Brown Shoes. **15.00**
Shoehorn **40.00**
Spice Box, Forbes Co, St Louis, allspice. . . **40.00**
Stickpin, diecut, emb, name on hat,
   c1900. . . . . **50.00**
Wallet, 1946 . . . . **22.00**
Whistle, 1" × 2⅝", litho tin,
   multicolored, brown ground, Buster
   and Tige, c1920. . . . . **35.00**

BUTTONS, PINBACK

Around 1893 the Whitehead & Hoad Company filed the first patents for celluloid pinback buttons. By the turn of the century, the celluloid pinback button was used as a promotional tool covering a wide spectrum, ranging from presidential candidates to amusement parks, not that there is much difference between the two.

This category covers advertising pinback buttons. Presidential pinbacks can be found in the Political category. To discover the full range of non-political pinbacks consult Ted Hake and Russ King's *Price Guide To Collectible Pin–back Buttons 1896–1986* (Hake's Americana & Collectibles Press: 1986).

Convention, Chicago, celluloid, multicolored, 2⅛" d, $25.00.

American Express Money Orders, 1¾" d,
   red, white, and blue, global logo center,
   c1930–40 . . . . **18.00**
Comfort Soap, 1¾" d, multicolored, por-
   trait of red headed child, toothy grin,
   blue ground, yellow letters,
   c1901–10 . . . . **300.00**

Diamond C Hams, 1½" d, multicolored, packaged ham from Cudahy Packing Co, dark green ground, white rim inscription, 1900–12 . . . . **35.00**
Frigidaire, 1¼" d, blue and white, Frigidaire delivery man, refrigeration unit on shoulder, c1930. . . . . **15.00**
Golden Glow Butter, 1¾" d, multicolored, butter package on blue center, blue lettering on soft yellow border, early 1900s. **40.00**
Homepathic Hospital, ⅞" d, black and white, homepathic nurse, c1920. . . . . . **15.00**
IGA Booster Club, 1933, 1" d, red, white, and blue, pink eagle logo **15.00**
Lion Coffee, 1¼" d, multicolored, white rim with black lettering, 1903 Indianapolis celebration **20.00**
McDonald's Merry Widow Chocolates, 1¼" d, black and white, light blue accents, lady wearing exaggerated feather hat between pair of suitors, 1900–12 . . . . **25.00**
Royal Typewriter Contest, 1½" d, red, white, and blue, Dawson Co, Cleveland, mid 1950s **15.00**
Sweet Clover Brand Condensed Milk, 1¾" d, multicolored, canned milk container with round clover design label, pale yellow and green sun rays, early 1900s . . . **65.00**
Turkey From Henry Ballard's Flock, 1½" d, multicolored, Puritan hunter displaying large turkey to wife and daughter, yellow rim lettering, c1925 . . . . **50.00**
Zig Zag Modern Confection, 1¼" d, multicolored, black lettering, orig back paper with name and PA candy dealer. **65.00**

CAKE

Dad's a pie man; I love cake, the more icing the better. At the moment cake collectors are concentrating on baking implements and wedding cake statues. It's a much broader category than that. Opportunity awaits.

Cake Cutters, Jr Card Party, card shape, four suits, orig box **12.00**
Cake Decoration, wedding **1.50**
Cake Decorator, aluminum, tube, six tips, MIB **10.00**
Cake Plate, Wild Rose, Harker. **18.00**
Cake Server, china, hp, tined, English registry marks **18.00**
Cake Tin, 11" × 12" × 6", multicolored litho scenes of Manhattan Island, c1915. . . . . **25.00**
Pan
    Angel Food Tube, small **12.00**
    Round, metal. **5.00**

Santa Shape–a–Cake, instructions, MIB **8.00**
Square, metal. **6.00**
Upside Down, metal **7.00**
Wilton Pattern Book, 1986 . . . . **.50**

CALCULATORS

The Texas Instruments TI–2500, Datamath, entered the market in the early 1970s. This electronic calculator, the marvel of its era, performed four functions—addition, subtraction, multiplication, and division. This is all it did. It retailed for over $100.00. Within less than a decade, calculators selling for less than $20.00 were capable of doing five times as many functions.

Early electronic calculators are dinosaurs. They deserve to be preserved. When collecting them, make certain to buy examples that retain their power transformer, instruction booklet, and original box. Make certain any calculator that you buy works. There are few around who know how to repair one.

It is a little too early for a category on home computers. But a few smart collectors are starting to stash away the early Texas Instrument and Commodore models.

Calculator, four functions **10.00**
Calculator, five or more functions **5.00**
Calculator, thirty or more functions **20.00**
Calculator, solar-powered **3.00**
Calculator, not working **0.00**

CALENDAR PLATES

Calendar plates are one of the traditional, affordable collecting categories. A few years ago, they sold in the $10.00 to $20.00 range; now that figure has jumped to $35.00 to $50.00.

Value rests with the decorative motif and the place for which it was issued. A fun collection would be to collect the same plate and see how many different merchants and other advertisers utilized it.

1908, 9½", two monks drinking wine **65.00**
1909, 8¼", flowers **18.00**
1910, Betsy Ross, Dresden **30.00**
1911, deer in meadow, scenic panels between months **35.00**
1911, Moose Lake, Minn **30.00**
1913, 9", roses and holly **25.00**
1915, 7", Panama Canal **25.00**

1909, John Kemper, Harness Maker, Butler, PA, 9" d, $25.00.

1916, 8¼", eagle with shield and american flag............................ **32.00**
1922, dog watching rabbit............. **30.00**
1929, 6¼", flowers, Valentine, NE....... **25.00**

1908, A. J. Russlow, Livery & Feed Stable, Randolph, VT, 14¼ x 10", $15.00.

1916, Putnam Dyes.................. **37.50**
1919, Woodrow Wilson.............. **10.00**
1929, Clothesline **60.00**
1940, Columbian Rope.............. **40.00**
1944, Sinclair Gasoline, twelve color wildlife pictures.................. **20.00**
1961, TWA, 16" × 24", six sheet........ **15.00**
1975, Kewpie **18.00**

CALENDARS

The primary reason calendars are collected is for the calendar art. Prices hinge on quality of printing and the pizazz of the subject. A strong advertising aspect adds to the value.

A highly overlooked calendar collecting area is the modern art and photographic calendar. For whatever reason, there is little interest in calendars dating after 1940. Collectors are making a major mistake. There are some great calendars from this later time period selling for less than $2.00.

'''Gentlemen's'' calendars did not grace the kitchen wall, but they are very collectible. Illustrations range from the pinup beauties of Elvgren and Moran and the *Esquire* Vargas ladies in the 1930s to the Playboy Playmates of the 1960s. Early Playboy calendars sell in the $50.00 plus range.

But, what's the fun of having something you cannot display openly? The following list will clear corporate censors with no problems.

1894, Hoyt's, lady's, perfumed **10.00**
1896, Singer Sewing Machines......... **37.50**
1900, Hood's, full pad, two girls **45.00**
1903, Franco American, miniature...... **15.00**
1909, Bank of Waupun, emb lady....... **30.00**
1915, Hoosier **18.00**

CAMBRIDGE GLASS

The Cambridge Glass Company of Cambridge, Ohio, began in 1901. Its first products were clear tablewares. Later color, etched, and engraved pieces were added to the line. Production continued until 1954. The Imperial Glass Company, Bellaire, Ohio, bought some of the Cambridge molds and continued production of these pieces.

Club: National Cambridge Collectors, Inc., P. O. Box 416, Cambridge, OH 43725.

Caprice, creamer and sugar, blue, $45.00.

Bonbon, Rosepoint, 6", handle, gold
trim **36.00**
Bookends, Scotty, pr **60.00**
Bowl
10"d, Caprice, crystal, ftd **30.00**
10½" d, Martha Washington,
heatherbloom **55.00**
Candlesticks, pr, Caprice, blue, prisms,
7" **75.00**
Coaster, Caprice, crystal **9.00**
Cocktail
Cascade, 3¾" **12.50**
Wildflower **22.00**
Cocktail Shaker, Farberware. **30.00**
Compote
Caprice, 7"d, ftd. **60.00**
Farberware, amethyst, 7½", Farberware
stem **45.00**
Cornucopia, yellow, 10" **70.00**
Creamer, Caprice, blue, 4½" **16.00**
Cup and Saucer, Caprice, crystal. **15.00**
Decanter, Mosaic gold and ebony, orig
handle and stopper **165.00**
Dresser Compact, amethyst. **60.00**
Fruit Bowl, Caprice, blue, 5" **55.00**
Goblet, water
Caprice, blue **40.00**
Cascade, 5½" **15.00**
Elaine. **20.00**
Martha Washington, heatherbloom . . . **55.00**
Iced Tea, Portia **24.00**
Mayonnaise, Caprice, blue, 2 pcs **60.00**
Plate, 8½", Caprice, blue **38.00**
Platter, Decagon, light blue **40.00**
Salt and Pepper Shakers, pr, Diane **42.50**
Sherbet
Caprice, blue, 3¼" **30.00**
Diane, amber, tall **20.00**
Elaine. **17.50**
Sugar
Caprice, blue **18.00**
Rosepoint **22.00**
Swan, Crown Tuscan, 3½". **35.00**
Tray, Diane, 11 × 12½" **55.00**
Tumbler, Cascade, 3⅞" **8.50**
Vanity Tray, pink, four parts **30.00**
Wine
Apple Blossom, yellow **25.00**
Portia. **24.50**
Wildflower **24.00**

CAMEOS

Cameos are one form of jewelry that has
never lost its popularity. They have been
made basically the same way for centuries.
Most cameos are dated by their settings,
although this is risky since historic settings
can be duplicated very easily.

Normally one thinks of a cameo as
carved from a piece of conch shell. However, the term cameo means a gem carved
in relief. You can find cameos carved from
gemstones and lava. Lava cameos are especially desirable.

Beware of plastic and other forms of
copycat and fake cameos. Look carefully at
the side. If you spot layers, shy away. A real
cameo is carved from a single piece.

Your best defense when buying a cameo
is to buy from a dealer that you can find
later and then have the authenticity of the
cameo checked by a local retail jeweler. Do
not use another antiques jewelry dealer.
They have a bad habit of backing up each
other even when they know the piece is
bad.

*Ring, Wedgwood cameo of Atlas, silver mount-
ing, $210.00.*

Bracelet, carved lava, various color panels,
Victorian 14K yg mounting **1,300.00**
Brooch
Triple portrait, carved shell, 14K yg set-
ting. **100.00**
Woman, head and shoulders
Flowers in hair, Victorian carved agate, gold knife edge and beadwork
frame, 18K yg setting **800.00**
Grapevine and leaves entwined in
hair, 14K yg setting **300.00**
Compact, onyx cameo, marcasite ring,
yellow guilloche enamel **400.00**
Pendant, full figure, dancing, flowing
gown, Victorian agate, framed by
pearls, 14K yg setting. **700.00**
Ring, portrait of Caesar, hardstone, plat-
inum swivel mount, rose cut dia-
monds **1,400.00**
Stickpin, carved opal, planished gold
frame, rubies and diamonds highlights, 14K yg setting, marked "Tiffany
& Co" **650.00**
Suite, brooch and pr cuff buttons,

hardstone, colored floral highlights, gold frame with twisted wire and beadwork, 14K yg setting **1,000.00**

CAMERAS

Just because a camera is old does not mean that it is valuable. Rather, assume that the more examples of a camera that were made the less likely it is to be valuable. Collectors are after unusual cameras or examples from companies that failed quickly.

A portion of a camera's value rests on how it works. Check all bellow cameras by shining a strong light over the outside surface while looking at the inside. Check the seating on removable lenses.

It is only recently that collectors have begun to focus in on the 35mm camera. You can still build a collection of early models at a modest cost per camera.

There is a growing market in camera accessories and ephemera. A camera has minimum value if you do not know how it works. Whenever possible, insist on the original instruction booklet as part of the purchase.

Clubs: National Stereoscopic Association, P. O. Box 14801, Columbus, OH 43214; Photographic Historical Society, P. O. Box 9563, Rochester, NY 14606.

Perfex, One–O–One Camera Corp of America, 1947–50, $30.00.

Blair Camera Co, Baby Hawk Eye, box, c1896......................... **125.00**
Character
   Dick Tracy, 3" × 5", plastic, black, Seymore Products, Chicago....... **45.00**
   Hopalong Cassidy **125.00**
   Mickey Mouse, 3 × 3 × 5", plastic, black, red plastic straps, uses 127 film, early 1960s.................... **50.00**
   Roy Rogers and Trigger, 3 × 3¼ × 3¼",

plastic, black, metal flash attachment, vinyl carrying strap, Herbert George Co, Chicago, 1940–1950 .... **100.00**
Conley Camera Co, Kewpie No 2A, box........................... **15.00**
Eastman Kodak Co
   Brownie, No 2, box **12.00**
   Bullet Camera, plastic, 127 film....... **10.00**
   Kodak 35, Rangefinder, 35 mm **20.00**
Minolta, SR–1S, 1964............... **80.00**
Olympic Camera Works, Super Olympic, bakelite, 35 mm, c1935 .... **85.00**
Polaroid 95, orig model.............. **20.00**
Spartus Press Flash, box, built–in flash reflector........................ **12.00**
Zeiss, Nettar, 6 × 6 cm, folding **35.00**

CANDLEWICK

Imperial Glass Corporation issued its No. 400 pattern, Candlewick, in 1936 and continued to produce it until 1982. In 1985 the Candlewick models were dispersed to a number of sources, e.g., Boyd Crystal Art Glass, through sale.

Over 650 items and sets are known. Shapes include round, oval, oblong, heart, and square. The largest assortment of pieces and sets were made during the late 1940s and early 1950s.

For a list of reproduction Candlewick pieces check the Candlewick category in *Warman's Americana & Collectibles.*

Newsletter: The National Candlewick Collector Newsletter, 275 Milledge Terrace, Athens, GA 30606.

Nappy, sweetheart shape, $17.50.

Basket, 11", applied handle, 400/73/0.... **75.00**
Bowl
   6", sq, 400/232 .... **35.00**
   10", two handles, 400/145B **20.00**
Butter Dish, beaded edge, 6¾" l, 4" w, 400/276.......................... **45.00**
Candleholder, 6", urn, rolled over, beaded top, one bead stem, 400/129R **35.00**

Celery Tray, 13½", oval, curved handles,
400/105 . . . . **25.00**
Creamer and Sugar, light blue **50.00**
Cup and Saucer, beaded handle cup, 5½"
saucer, 400/37 . . . . **8.50**
Pitcher, beaded handle, ice lip, 400/24 . . . **75.00**
Plate, beaded edge
8", salad, 400/5D **8.00**
9", luncheon, 400/7D **12.00**
10½" dinner, 400/10D **19.50**
12", crimped, handles, 400/145C **27.50**
Relish Dish, 8", divided, beaded edge, two
tab handles, 400/268 . . . . **15.00**
Salt and Pepper Shaker, pr, round, beaded
foot, chrome top, 400/96 . . . . **10.00**
Stemware
Champagne, flared bell tops, four grad-
uated beads, 3400 line **12.50**
Goblet, bell stems, beaded, trumpet
shaped bowl. **15.00**
Wine, flared bell tops, four graduated
beads **17.50**
Tumbler, juice, beaded base, 400/19 . . . . . **8.00**
Vase
8", fan, graduated beads, 400/87F **22.50**

feather hat, pr of well dressed suitors,
black and white, light blue accents,
1900–1912 . . . . **30.00**
Sommer–Richardson's Candies, 1", red
"Red Cross" logo, white ground, blue
letters, early 1900s **15.00**
Zig Zag Modern Confection, 1¼" d,
multicolored, 1903–1905 . . . . **50.00**
Ruler, Clark Bars, wood **6.00**
Sign
Kibber's Candies, 9" × 8", brass **50.00**
Ox Heart Chocolate, tin **75.00**
Sweet Maris Gum, diecut **45.00**
Tape Dispenser, Baby Ruth **25.00**
Tin
Bunte Candy, gold, 5 lb **25.00**
Fireside Gems Candy, 8", round, girl sit-
ting on bench **10.00**
Orange Mellowmints **15.00**
Trade Card
Monarch Teenie Weenie Toffies **15.00**
Wilbur's Chocolate & Cocoa, diecut,
boy and girl, multicolored front and
back, c1890 . . . . **20.00**

CANDY COLLECTIBLES

Who doesn't love some form of candy? Forget the chocoholics. I'm a Juicy Fruit man.

Once you start looking for candy–related material, you are quickly overwhelmed by how much is available. Do not forget the boxes. They are usually discarded. Ask your local drugstore or candy shop to save the more decorative ones for you. What is free today may be worth money tomorrow.

Advertising Giveaway, Zatek Chocolate,
Indian girl, cutout, multicolored, 1918,
uncut **20.00**
Bonbon Tongs, candy store, tin **4.00**
Box, Hershey Nougat–Almond **10.00**
Candy Bar Mold, Clark Bar, multiple
openings **15.00**
Candy Container
George Washington, composition **95.00**
Pelican, papier mache **58.00**
Rabbit, seated, white, carrot in mouth,
Germany **40.00**
Display Rack, Beech–Nut Beechies,
metal, two shelves **20.00**
Eraser, Hershey's miniature candy wrap-
per, mint **10.00**
Gum Wrapper, Wrigley's, yellow, purple,
and gold **10.00**
Hammer, 3½", Seeds Candies adv **20.00**
Pinback Button
Baker's Chocolate, oval, pretty lady . . . **30.00**
McDonald's Merry Widow Chocolates,
1¼" d, lady wearing exaggerated

CAP PISTOLS

Classic collectors collect the one–shot, cast–iron pistols manufactured during the first third of the twentieth century. Kids of the 1950s collect roll cap pistols. Children of the 1990s do not know what they are missing.

Prices for roll cap pistols are sky-

*Sign, Oh Boy Gum, Gouday Gum Co, Bos-
ton–Chicago, 15½" × 7³⁄₈", $90.00.*

rocketing. Buy them only if they are in working order. Ideally, acquire them with their appropriate accessories, e.g., holsters, fake bullets, etc.

Club: Toy Gun Purveyors, Box 243, Burke, VA 22015.

Sharpshooter, white plastic handles, horse and brand mark on both sides, $18.50.

American West, orig card	8.00
Hubley Remington 36	75.00
Kilgore	
Ranger, cast iron, maroon plastic grips, 1950s	75.00
Six–Shooter, cast iron, black finish	100.00
McCloud, MIB	35.00
Mustang 500, MIB	155.00
Safety Trooper, cast iron	65.00
U.N.C.L.E. 7.63mm Automatic, metal, black, Lone Star, 1960s	75.00
Yacht, repeating, cowboy graphics	12.00

CARNIVAL CHALKWARE

Carnival chalkware is my candidate for the kitsch collectible of the 1980s. No one uses *quality* to describe these inexpensive prizes given out by games of chance at carnivals, amusement parks, and ocean boardwalks.

The best pieces are those depicting a specific individual or character. Since most were bootlegged (made without permission), they often appear with a fictious name, e.g., "Smile Doll" is really supposed to be Shirley Temple. The other strong collecting subcategory is the animal figure. As long as the object comes close to capturing the appearance of a pet, they buy.

Cat, 10", bank, c1940	10.00
Circus Horse, 10", c1930	18.00
Dog	
Collie, 12"	8.00
Terrier, 8", black and white, rhinestone eyes, c1940	10.00
Dopey, 6", c1937	42.00
Elephant, bank, c1930	12.00
Ferdinand the Bull, 8½", c1940	20.00

Gigolo, string holder	28.00
Lady and Dog, 11¼", full ruffled skirt, floral trim, c1935	12.00
Lamb, 7", flat back, marked "Rosemead Novelty Co," c1940	5.00
Miss America, 15", bathing suit, c1940	20.00
Sailor Girl, 9", c1940	10.00
Ship, 10", flat back, c1940	5.00
Soldier Boy, 9", c1940	10.00
Squirrel, 12", eating corn, c1940	7.50
Wimpy, 18", c1940	32.00

CARTOON COLLECTIBLES

This is a category with something for each generation. The characters represented here enjoyed a life in comic books and newspaper pages. Many also had a second career on movie screens and television.

Every collector has a favorite. Buy examples that bring back the only pleasant memories. "That's All Folks."

Game, Dick Tracy Detective Game, Whitman Publishing Co, boxed board game, Chester Gould, licensed by Famous Artist Syndicate, 18 pcs, copyright 1937, $50.00.

Bank	
Casper, glow in the dark, 1967	75.00
Krazy Kat, graduation outfit	55.00
Barrette, Li'l Abner, 2⅛", oval, brass, diecut, 1940s	18.00
Book, *Woody Woodpecker's Peck of Trouble*, Whitman, 1951	5.00
Candy Bar Wrapper, Dick Tracy, color picture, premium offer, 1950s	10.00
Charm, Popeye, 1¼", celluloid, brass loop, orange, pink, black, and green, Japanese, 1930s	20.00
Clicker, Felix the Cat, tin litho, Germany, 1929	25.00
Clock, alarm, Betty Boop, animated, boxed	45.00
Coloring book, 8½" × 11", Blondie, 1954, Dell Publishing, unused	20.00
Cookie Jar, Yogi Bear, felt tongue	195.00
Doll	
Barney Google, Snuffy Smith, 17", stuf-	

fed, felt, movable head, amber and
black eyes, 1930s **150.00**
Little Lulu, 15″ h, stuffed cloth, black
felt and yarn hair, western outfit,
1940s **80.00**
Figure
Daffy Duck, Dakin, 1968, orig tag **28.00**
Speedy Gonzales, 1970 . . . . **22.00**
Sylvester The Cat, Dakin, orig tag,
1960s **18.00**
Tweety Bird **14.00**
Game
Harold Teen, spinner and orig tokens,
boxed, 1930s **15.00**
Huckleberry Hound Bumps **38.00**
Quick Draw McGraw Private Eye, Mil-
ton Bradley, 1960 . . . . **40.00**
Ice Cream Mold, Yellow Kid, 4¾″, full fig-
ure, hinged **185.00**
Key Chain, Winnie Winkle, characters on
each side, 1940s **15.00**
Lunch Box
Bullwinkle and Rocky, steel, Jay Ward
Productions copyright, Universal,
c1962 . . . . **200.00**
Joe Palooka, tin, litho, 1948 . . . . **45.00**
Underdog **300.00**
Marionette, Flintstone, 1960s **75.00**
Necktie, 10½″ l, Bugs Bunny, clip–on,
c1940 . . . . **50.00**
Nodder
Moon Mullins, 3⅞″, bisque, Ger-
many **60.00**
Smitty, bisque **85.00**
Pen Holder, Snoopy **65.00**
Pinback Button
Dan Dunn, 1¼″, litho, Philadelphia Eve-
ning Ledger, "I'm Operative 48," orig
back paper, 1930s **65.00**
Gasoline Alley, 13/16″, Uncle Walt, li-
tho **12.00**
Plaque, 7″, Andy Panda, ceramic, figural,
marked "Napco Ceramics," 1958 . . . . . **55.00**
Playsuit, Popeye **85.00**
Salt and Pepper Shakers, pr, 2½″, figural,
Maggie and Jiggs, marked "Made In Ja-
pan," 1930s **65.00**
Toy, Porky Pig, 5½″, rubber, marked "Sun
Rubber Co" **45.00**
Tumbler, 5″, glass, Li'l Abner running with
two Shmoos, 1949 . . . . **8.50**
Vase, 7½″ h, china, Bugs Bunny resting
against tree stump, Warner Bros Copy-
right, c1940 . . . . **100.00**
Whistle, Foxy Grandpa, clay, figural **40.00**

CASH REGISTERS

If you want to buy a cash register, you had
better be prepared to put plenty of money
in the till. Most are bought for decorative
purposes. Serious collectors would go
broke in a big hurry if they had to pay the
prices listed below for every machine they
buy.

Beware of modern reproductions. Cash
registers were meant to be used. Signs of
use should be present. There is also a tendency to restore machines to their original
appearance through replating and
rebuilding. Well and good. But, when all is
said and done, how do you tell the
refurbished machine from a modern reproduction? When you cannot, it is hard to
sustain long–term value.

American, copper plated, fifty key **900.00**
McCaskey, 23″ × 23″ × 27″, oak, orig
decal, metal account files, two drawers,
refinished **150.00**
Michigan #1, twenty–two key **200.00**
National
Model 312, dolphin pattern,
1902–16 . . . . **700.00**
Model 349, two drawers, 1910 . . . . **800.00**
Model 421, crank operated, oak cash
drawer, receipt machine on side,
23″ **650.00**
Model 542, brass, crank operated,
drawer, 24″ h **600.00**
Peninsula, Muren, nickel plated,
c1912 . . . . **200.00**

CASSETTE TAPES

Flea markets thrive on two types of
goods—those that are collectible and those
that serve a second–hand function. Cas-
sette tapes fall into this latter group. Buy
them for the purpose of playing them.

The one exception is when the promotional pamphlet covering the tape shows a
famous singer or group. In this case, you
are really buying the piece of paper ephemera more than the tape, but you might as
well have the whole shooting match.

Several times within recent years there
have been a number of articles in the trade
papers about collecting eight–tracks. When
was the last time you saw an eight–track
machine? They are going to be as popular
in thirty years as the wire tape recorder is
today. Interesting idea—too bad it
bombed.

Average price . . . . **50¢ to $2.00**

CAST IRON

This is a category where you should be suspicious that virtually everything you see is a reproduction or copycat. More often than not, the object will not be original. They are even reproducing cast iron frying pans.

One of the keys to spotting the newer material is by the rust. If it is orange in color and consists of small pinpoint flakes, forget it. Also check paint patina. It should have a mellow tone from years of exposure to air. Bright paint should be suspect.

Cast iron is a favorite of the country collector. It evokes memories of the great open kitchen fireplaces and wood/coal burning stoves of our ancestors. Unfortunately, few discover what a great cooking utensil cast iron can really be.

Trivet, Trafford Foundry, Family Day, 1953, 4¾" × 8½", $12.50.

Bottle Opener
   Donkey, 3⅝" h, polychrome traces **65.00**
   Drunk, 4⅛" h, lamp post. **25.00**
Cigarette Dispenser, 8½" l, elephant, bronze repaint **30.00**
Door Knocker, basket of flowers, 3¾" l, orig polychrome paint **30.00**
Fence, 43" × 70" l, four section, old green paint **240.00**
Hitching Post, 62½" h, tree form, branch stubs, marked "Patent" **100.00**
Lawn Ornament, jockey, polychrome repaint **100.00**
Mortar and Pestle, 5½" h **20.00**
Nut Cracker, 11" l, figural, dog, nickel fin-

ish, marked "The LA Althoff Mfg Co, Chicago" **40.00**
Pretzel, souvenir, Reading, PA **30.00**
Skillet, 9¾" d, three short feet, 9¼" handle **35.00**
Tea Kettle, 8" h, brass lid, decorative finial, wrought handle **45.00**
Waffle Iron, 24" l, wrought handles, pitted **65.00**

CAT COLLECTIBLES

It is hard to think of a collecting category that does not have one or more cat-related items in it. Chessie the Cat is railroad-oriented; Felix is a cartoon, comic, and toy collectible. There rests the problem. The poor cat collector is always competing with an outside collector for a favorite cat item.

Cat collectors are apparently as stubborn as their pets because I have never seen a small cat collectibles collection. One additional thing that I have noticed is that, unlike most dog collectibles collectors, cat collectors are more willing to collect objects portraying other breeds of cats than the one that they own.

Club: Cat Collectors, 31311 Blair Drive, Warren, MI 48092.

Game, Game of Authors, J Ottmann Litho Co, card game, 41 pcs, c1900, $35.00.

Advertising Trade Card
   Carter's Little Liver Pills, four striped cats playing with yarn, Mayer, Merkell & Ottmann Litho **5.00**

Choose Black Cat Reinforced Hosiery, 6″, multicolored diecut **15.00**

Clarks Mile End Spool Cotton, cat walking over spool, calendar on back, 1881 . . . . **10.00**

Ashtray, 5″ l, ceramic, brown crouching cat, front paws extended, marked "Made in China" **20.00**

Calendar, wall, three parts, several peeking cat faces, titled "Little Mischief," Tuck, 1903 . . . . **25.00**

Match Holder, cat scene, ftd, marked "Wavecrest" **225.00**

Mirror, pocket, White Cat Union Suits, 2¾″ l, black and white, celluloid, cartoon illus, early 1900s **65.00**

Pinback Button

- 7/8″ d, Cat's Paw Heels, yellow and black, early 1900s **15.00**
- 1¼″ d, tinted, multicolored, kitten in high top shoe **12.00**
- 1⅜″ d
  - Chessie, full color, sleeping kitten, Chesapeake & Ohio Railway, compliments text on reverse, c1940 . . . **30.00**
  - Hep Cat, red, white, and blue, c1940 . . . . **10.00**
- 2¼″, Morris For President, multicolored photo portrait, bright red, white, and blue border, Nine Lives Cat Food, 1988 . . . . **10.00**

Planter, 6¾″ h, kitten with basket, Hull pottery **15.00**

Print, 14″ × 11″, two cats in hat, titled "A Love Song," J Ottmann Litho, 1894 . . . **25.00**

Salt and Pepper Shakers, pr, 4″ h, comical Siamese, paper label marked "Norcrest Japan" **10.00**

Top, spinning, litho tin, yellow prowling cats, blue ground, red trim, red wood handle, marked "Ohio Art Co" **20.00**

CAUSE COLLECTIBLES

Social cause collectibles are just now coming into their own as a collecting category. Perhaps this is because the social activists of the 1960s have mortgages, children, and money in their pocket to buy back the representations of their youth. In doing so, they are looking back past their own protest movements to all forms of social protest that took place in the twentieth century.

Great collections can be built around a single cause, e.g., women's suffrage or the right to vote. Much of the surviving material tends to be two-dimensional. Stress three-dimensional items the moment you begin to collect. As years pass, these are the objects most likely to rise in value.

Autograph

- Barton, Clara, black and white sgd photo, 5″ × 7″ pamphlet titled "The National First Aid Association of America" **250.00**
- Dickinson, Anna E, suffrage leader, autographed quotation sgd, 4″ × 3″ . . . **25.00**
- North, Oliver, autographed first day cover of Virginia Statehood Bicentennial, 1988 . . . . **20.00**

Medal, 1¾″ d, Peace, emb brass, Angel of Peace waving palm branch, text on back with dates of opening and ending of World War I **15.00**

Pinback Button

- Humane Society, 1¼″ d, tinted light blue and yellow scene, angel rescuing horse, c1900 . . . . **25.00**
- King Memorial, 3″ d, litho, black and white portrait, red, white, and blue circles and lettering, c1968 . . . . **30.00**
- Laundry Workers Union No. 22, ⅞″ d, black and white shirt, shaking hands, red ground, c1900 . . . . **15.00**
- Make Jobs, Return Musicians to Theaters, red, white, and blue, c1930 . . . **10.00**
- Peace and Freedom Party, 1¼″ d, black and day glow red, 1968 . . . . **10.00**
- Supporting Labor's Cause, 13/16″ d, litho, gold letters, light purple ground, c1930 . . . . **12.00**
- Sweet Daddy Grace, 1¼″ d, black evangelist, c1950 . . . . **20.00**
- Votes for Women, ½″ d, gold letters, purple ground **60.00**

Post Card, prohibition, "I'm On The Water Wagon Now," 3½″ × 5½″, black, white, red, and yellow illus, 1906 . . . . **25.00**

Poster

- Give–Welfare Federation, 14 × 22″, Jessie Wilcox Smith, c1920, little girl and two babies, green and yellow ground **165.00**
- Lend Your Strength To The Red Triangle, 20″ × 30″, Gil Spear, man lifting YMCA stone **50.00**
- Vietnam, Anti–War, 23″ × 27″, anonymous, c1967, black and white montage **85.00**

Sign, Bring Back Prosperity, tin, 4½″ × 8″, diecut and emb, beer glass shape, letter "B" shaped like twisted pretzel, made by De Vo Novelty Co, Asbury Park, NJ, c1932 . . . . **80.00**

CELLULOID

Celluloid is the trade name for a thin, tough, flammable material made of cellulose nitrate and camphor. Originally used for toilet articles, it quickly found a use as inexpensive jewelry, figurines, vases, and other household items. In the 1920s and 1930s, it was used heavily by the toy industry.

Be on the lookout for dealers who break apart sets and sell the pieces individually as a way of getting more money. Also check any ivory or tortoise shell piece that is offered to you. Both were well imitated by quality celluloid.

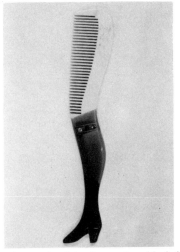

Mustache comb, stained gray leg, black high button boot, 5¾" l, $50.00.

Animal
Pig, 2" l.......................... **6.00**
Reindeer, Occupied Japan........... **22.00**
Swan, white..................... **5.00**
Bookmark, adv, Poole Piano........... **15.00**
Bracelet, bangle, mottled brown, tortoise shell imitation, rhinestones......... **25.00**
Bride and Groom, 1920s, pr........... **60.00**
Cigar Bowl, football player, Tampa, FL, Occupied Japan.................. **25.00**
Doll, cowboy, 7½" h, Japan, c1940–50... **24.00**
Dresser Set
3 pcs, blue, rosebuds.............. **22.00**
5 pcs, amberoid, Art Deco design...... **35.00**
Figure, Baby, 4" h, movable arms and legs............................ **4.00**
Flip–it, novelty, adv, Golden Orangeade, mechanical, diecut, pin–on, orange, 1910s.......................... **25.00**
Kewpies, bride and groom, 2½" h, pr..... **45.00**
Manicure Set, leather roll–up case, eight pcs............................ **9.00**
Matchbook Cover, adv, Evansville Hat Works, celluloid on metal........... **15.00**
Pencil Clip, Diamond Edge,⅞", black, white, and red, silvered tin clip, early 1900s.......................... **10.00**
Pencil Sharpener, clock, amber, Ger-

man.......................... **20.00**
Place Card Holder, snowman, angels, and elves, set of eight, MIB.............. **17.50**
Program, sorority dance............. **10.00**
Rattle, 4½", cupid in wreath........... **15.00**
Sewing Kit, red stripes............... **8.00**
Stamp Case, adv, Tom Moore Cigar..... **35.00**
Tape Measure, fish.................. **25.00**
Toothbrush Holder, young girl, 1920s... **40.00**
Toy, Roly Poly, cat, 1½", waving hello.... **8.50**

CEREAL BOXES

There is no better example of a collectible category gone mad than cereal boxes. Cereal boxes from the first half of the twentieth century sell in the $15.00 to $50.00 range. Cereal boxes from the 1950s through the 1970s sell in the $50.00 range and up. Where's the sense?

The answer rests in the fact that the post-World War II cereal box market is being manipulated by a shrewd speculator who is drawing upon his past experience with the lunch box market. Eventually, the bubble will burst. Don't get involved unless you have money to burn.

Cheerios, individual, 1940s........... **14.00**
Crystal Oats, Quaker, round........... **18.00**
George Washington Corn Flakes, unopened...................... **60.00**
Highland Oats..................... **30.00**
Kellogg's Corn Flakes, sample size, c1920......................... **15.00**
Mother Hubbard Wheat Cereal........ **22.00**
Mother's Oats..................... **20.00**
Quaker Muffets Shredded Wheat, 3" × 6" × 7", side panel adv "Authentic Model Civil War Cannon," 1960s.......... **37.50**
Quaker Puffed Rice, 5 oz, 1919......... **20.00**
Scotch Brand Oats.................. **30.00**
Superior Rolled Oats, Sioux City, IA..... **16.50**
White Swan, oatmeal, 4 oz............ **27.50**

CEREAL PREMIUMS

Forget cereal boxes. The fun rests with the goodies inside the box that you got for buying the cereal in the first place. Cereal premiums have changed a great deal over the past decade. No self-respecting manufacturer in the 1950s would have included as their premium a tube of toothpaste. Yuck!

Collectors make a distinction between premiums that came with the box and those for which you had to send away. The latter group is valued more highly because the items are often more elaborate and better made. My dad keeps telling me about all the neat things he received through the mail as a kid. I think my generation has missed something.

Wheaties premium, 1953, Western Pacific, black, red, and white, 3" sq, $2.00.

Badge, Post Raisin Brand, tin, General
Custer **12.00**
Booklet, The Frolie Grasshopper Circus, adv, multicolored, grasshoppers and clowns, whimsical scenes, American Cereal Co, Quaker Oats, 1895 . . . . **65.00**
Card, pop out, Dale Evans, Post Cereals, unused, mint **15.00**
Comic Book, Cap'n Crunch, miniature, 1963. . . . . **20.00**
Creamer, Kellogg's Correct Cereal **18.00**
Figure, Kellogg's, 7" h, rubber, Snap, Crackle, and Pop, set of 3 . . . . **50.00**
Flasher Card, Post Corn Flakes, Danny Thomas winks eye, 1950s **24.00**
Glass, cartoon, Toucan Sam, Kellogg's, 1977. . . . . **6.50**
Hike—o—meter, Wheaties, orig mailer . . . **40.00**
Model, punch out, C–54 Skymaster war plane, Kellogg's Pep, WWII. **24.00**
Plate, Kellogg's, 1985 . . . . **25.00**
Ring, Post Toasties, "Fritz," orig cellophane wrapper, 1949 . . . . **25.00**
Watch, Sugar Bear Cereal, shifting eyes **65.00**

CHILDREN'S COLLECTIBLES

Mothers of the world unite. This category is for you. The children who used it hardly remember it. It's the kind of stuff that keeps your children forever young in your mind.

There is virtually nothing written about this collecting category so what to collect is wide open. One collector I know has hundreds of baby planters. To each their own.

*Book, **Puss In Boots**, Pantomine Toy Books, McLoughlin Bros, NY, 7½" × 10⅛", $50.00.*

Baby Record Book, C Burd illus on each page. **32.00**
Baby Christening Outfit, cotton, white, gown, slip, and matching cap, c1920. . . . . **85.00**
Book
A Merry Coasting Party, Burgess, Cady. **18.00**
Adventures of Humpty Dumpty, 1877, baking soda giveaway **28.00**
Little Red Riding Hood, litho, Star Soap giveaway **28.00**
Little Tots ABC Book, c1900, linen **18.00**
Mickey Mouse Alphabet Book, 1936 . . . . . **75.00**
The Three Bears, Platt & Munk **15.00**
Busy Box, 14" × 20", twelve movable gadgets, Gabriel. **15.00**
Carriage, wicker, serpentine edges, natural finish, orig velvet upholstery, c1890. . . . . **450.00**
Clock Radio, three mice, Fisher Price **20.00**
Dish, 8", baby's, divided, three sections, Patriot China **50.00**
Toy
Dippee Bug, pull, rubber, multicolor, MIB **40.00**
Player Piano, eight muppets, Fisher Price. **45.00**
Toot Toot Train, pull, Fisher Price **15.00**
Toy Dishes
Coffeepot, aluminum, red metal handle **7.50**

Cookware Set, aluminum, 8 pcs,
boxed **110.00**
Flour Sifter, aluminum, red metal han-
dle, Bromwell **10.50**
Tea Kettle, aluminum, red metal han-
dle, whistle spout **6.00**
Toy Tea Set
Akro Agate, transparent green, 21
pcs **155.00**
German, maroon luster, 13 pcs **210.00**
Hazel Atlas Little Hostess, 16 pcs **140.00**
Wawky Tawky String Phone, 1940s **10.00**

CHINA CABINETS

If you are going to collect something, you
need a place to display it. This is why china
cabinets are included in this book. If you
are going to use one, try to find one that
matches the historical period of your
collectible. Plastic toys in an oak china cabinet simply does not work well.

Beware of modern oak reproduction
cabinets. Unscrupulous dealers will tell you
that they are refinished old cabinets. However, when you look inside, you see absolutely no signs of wear.

If you find a great old cabinet that is
cheap because the glass is broken, buy it.
Curved and other types of replacement
glass are readily available.

Burl olive wood, veneered, ebonized trim,
glass door, two drawers, refinished, 32"
× 52" × 58" **600.00**
Mahogany
Colonial style, carved columns, adjustable shelves, hairy paw feet, 48¾" ×
17" × 65¼" **325.00**
Hepplewhite style, inlaid, leaded
glass, velvet lined int., 63" × 21"
× 75½" **650.00**
Oak
Bow Front, leaded glass door panels,
37½" × 14½" × 61¾" **400.00**
Serpentine Front, carved details, glass
door and sides, 38 ½" × 16" × 62"
h. **600.00**
Victorian style, 30" × 64", hand carved,
beveled mirror, glass door and sides,
three shelves, splayed feet **450.00**
Walnut
Colonial, Chippendale style, veneered,
scrolled broken pediment, urn finial,
two glazed doors, two cupboard
doors, 44" x 15" × 76" **600.00**
Victorian style, 62" h **375.00**

CHINA DINNER SERVICES

How many dinner services do you own?
When was the last time that you used
yours? Who do you know who owns ten?
Dinner services are difficult to sell.

Actually, this works to the advantage of
the buyer. First, you can generally acquire
an old dinner service for less than half the
price of a new one. Second, the number of
serving pieces is often far greater than those
found with a modern service. Finally, you
have a pattern that you are not likely to
find in someone else's home.

Average price for an eight place setting
service of average quality china is $400.00
to $600.00. Twelve place settings raise the
figure to $500.00 to $750.00. If the maker
is well known, the pattern especially attractive, or the number of serving pieces large,
add another fifty percent.

*Homer Laughlin, Apple Blossom pattern, service
for six, $120.00.*

English China
15 pcs, dessert service for thirteen, 9"
plates, two compotes, ivy vine and
gilt design. **50.00**
18 pcs, dessert service for eight, two
compotes with openwork bases,
serving dishes and plates, flower border panels, flowing blue scrolls,
rococo scroll edge. **285.00**
Gaudy Dutch, seven plates, four soup
bowls, two side plates, two teabowls,
floral design, imp "Riley," c1830 . . **3,600.00**
Geisha Girl, service for six, luncheon set,
lithopane, teapot, creamer, sugar, cups
and saucers and luncheon plates **200.00**
Haviland China
55 pcs, service for eight, pink flowers,
marked "H and Co" **900.00**
77 pcs, service for twelve, gold band
trim, marked "Theo Haviland" . . . **1,200.00**

Limoges, 88 pcs, Saint–Saëns pattern, blue on white foliate motif, molded basketweave border **400.00**
Meissen, 18 pcs, dessert service for six, fighting cock center, dragon border, blue crossed swords mark **650.00**
Royal Crown Derby, 35 pcs, Japanese pattern, Imari palette, marked, c1870.. **1,400.00**
Royal Worcester, service for 12, numerous serving pcs with gilt elephant handles, blue floral calico pattern **500.00**

CHRISTMAS

Of all the holiday collectibles, Christmas is the most popular. It has grown so large as a category that many collectors specialize in only one area, e.g., Santa Claus figures or tree ornaments.

Anything Victorian is "hot." The Victorians popularized Christmas. Many collectors love to recapture that spirit. However, prices for Victorian items, from feather trees to ornaments, are quickly moving out of sight.

This is a field where knowledgeable individuals can find bargains. Learn to tell a late nineteenth/early twentieth century ornament from a modern example. A surprising number of dealers cannot. If a dealer thinks an historic ornament is modern and prices it accordingly, he is actually playing Santa Claus by giving you a present. Ho, Ho, Ho.!

Ornament, Santa Claus, multicolored, 3⅝" h, $75.00.

Newsletters: *Golden Glow of Christmas Past,* P. O. Box 14808, Chicago, IL 60614; *Hearts of Holly, The Holiday Collectors Newsletter,* P. O. Box 105, Amherst, NH 03031; *Ornament Collector,* R. R. #1, Canton, IL 61520.

Book, *A Northern Christmas,* Kent Rockwell, American Artists Group Inc, 1941......................... **7.00**
Card Book, flocked, 1950s **20.00**
Creche, paper, three–dimensional, USA, 1942......................... **15.00**
Figure, Santa, plastic, reindeer, Ertl, orig box........................... **35.00**
Greeting Card
"Christmas Blessing," leather type, S Hildersheimer & Co **5.00**
"Merry Christmas From Our House," USA, 1930s **2.50**
"Wishing You A Happy Christmas," sepia tones, Raphael Tuck & Sons, London......................... **3.00**
Light Bulb
Bubble, Noma, orig box............ **45.00**
Chinese Lantern, milk glass, Japan **10.00**
House, milk glass, pink and white, Japan........................... **10.00**
Set, bubblelights, orig box **35.00**
Ornament
Cat in Shoe, glass **38.00**
Clown, glass, painted face, German ... **38.00**
Flamingo, blue mercury glass **40.00**
Santa, honeycomb................. **8.00**
Snake............................ **32.00**
Pinback Button, 1¼", Santa Claus, celluloid, multicolor, steering auto, c1911......................... **40.00**
Postcard, hold to light type **35.00**
Putz Items
Animal
Cow, 3" h, celluloid, brown, USA ... **7.00**
Dog, 1" h, celluloid, brown, marked "Japan".................... **5.00**
Horse, 3½" h, brown and tan, rubber, USA **7.00**
Sheep, 1¾" h, composition, wool coat, wood legs............... **20.00**
Bank, 3", chalk, white, marked "Made in Japan"..................... **10.00**
Church, 6", cardboard, litho, frosted roof **8.00**
Fence, wood, eight 6" sections, 2½" h, red and green.................. **30.00**
House
2½", cardboard, frosted roof, marked "Japan".................... **4.50**
3", log type, frosted roof, marked "Germany" **10.00**
Wagon, wood, driver and horses, Germany **38.00**
Reflectors, copper foil, German, set of 10............................ **20.00**
Snowdome, chimney, red brick, water–filled fireplace, Santa, gifts, tree ... **20.00**

Spoon and Fork Sets, A Michelsen, large tablespoon size, sterling silver, heavy gold plate, Cloisonne handles
1925, filigreed poinsettia **90.00**
1946, Holly leaves and berries **85.00**
1949, Christmas wreath and candles **85.00**
1953, white angels, blue and gold **85.00**
1955, green and red spots **75.00**
1966, Madonna riding on donkey **75.00**
1967, gold sunburst pattern **80.00**
1968, modern Madonna and child **80.00**
Tree
Brush, 9" h, green, glass bead dec, red base **15.00**
Candle, matchless **38.00**
Cellophane, 15" **15.00**
Feather, 18" h, green, white base, 1920s, Germany **150.00**
Tree Top, angel, 4" h, plastic, white and silver, 1950s **5.00**

CHRISTMAS SEALS/ CHARITY STAMPS

Collecting Christmas Seals and Charity Stamps is one of the most inexpensive "stamp" hobbies. Sheets usually sell for between 50¢ and $1.00. Most collectors do not buy single stamps, except for the very earliest Christmas seals.

Club: Christmas Seal and Charity Stamp Society, 5825 Dorchester Avenue, Chicago, IL 60637.

CIGARETTE AND CIGAR

Cigarette products contain a warning that they might be hazardous to your health. Cigarette and cigar memorabilia should contain a warning that they may be hazardous to your pocketbook. With each passing year, the price for cigarette- and cigar-related material goes higher and higher. If it ever stabilizes and then drops, a number of collectors are going to see their collections go up in smoke.

The vast majority of cigarette and cigar material is two-dimensional, from advertising trade cards to posters. Seek out three dimensional pieces. There are some great cigarette and cigar tins.

Clubs: Cigarette Pack Collectors Association, 61 Searle Street, Georgetown, MA 01833; International Seal, Label & Cigar Band Society, 8915 East Bellevue Street, Tuscon, AZ 85715.

Sign, blue, yellow, and white letters, 13½" × 6", $50.00.

Ashtray, Fatima Cigarettes, matchbox holder, marked "Nippon" **100.00**
Chair, Piedmont Cigarettes, folding **225.00**
Cigar Holder, red, catalin, German **8.00**
Cigar Lighter, Art Deco, porcelain, counter top style **40.00**
Cigarette Card
Roses, Wills, c1912, set of 50 . . . . **95.00**
The King's Art Treasures, Wills, 1930s, set of 40 . . . . **48.00**
Cigarette Lighter, 6", figural, knight, armor, chrome **16.00**
Pinback Button
1", Phillip Morris, celluloid, Johnny, c1930 . . . . **18.00**
1¼", Union Made Cigars, red, white, blue, and black, light green cigar label, c1890 . . . . **20.00**
Poster, Kool Cigarettes, 12" × 18", smoking penguin points to pack, c1933 . . . . . **35.00**
Sign
A K Walch's Cigar, 8" × 14", tin, red and white **65.00**
Chesterfield/L&M, flange **95.00**
Hambone Cigar, 7" d, round, cardboard, two sided, hanging, caricature of black man wearing aviator goggles in tiny airplane **48.50**
Nickel King Cigars, 16" × 18", cardboard **35.00**
Pollocks Cigar, riverboats unloading and commercial buildings **175.00**
Red Dot Cigar, figural **52.00**
Smoking Jacket, cigar ribbons **250.00**
Tin
Chesterfield's, cat under celluloid **38.00**
Old Abe Cigars, round, paper label **60.00**
Reichard's Cadet Cigar **65.00**

CIRCUS

The only circus that I ever saw was at a theme park in Florida. Dad keeps telling me about traveling tent circuses and how exciting they really were. Based on the memorabilia that they left behind, I think he might be right.

Dad keeps threating to take me to see the

great annual circus parade in Milwaukee featuring the equipment from the Circus World Museum in Baraboo, Wisconsin. The reason that I get to be his traveling companion is that Connie, his wife, wants nothing to do with his circus fantasies. She says living with him is all the circus that she needs.

Clubs: Circus Fans of America, Four Center Drive, Camp Hill, PA 17011; The Circus Historical Society, 743 Beverly Park Place, Jackson, MI 49203; The Circus Model Builders International, 347 Lonsdae Avenue, Dayton, OH 45419.

Pinback button, Canada Dry advertising, c1950, 1½″ d, $20.00.

Book, *The Biggest, The Smallest, The Longest, The Shortest, A History of Wisconsin Circuses,* Dean Jensen, 230 pgs. **15.00**
Calendar, Circus World Museum, 1974. . . . . **5.00**
Lithograph, Ringling Bros, 12 × 16″, busts of five brothers and Barnum and Bailey. **125.00**
Menu, Greatest Show on Earth, Nov 12, 1898, full color. **100.00**
Postcard, Ringling Brothers, Freak Fisher family. **35.00**
Poster
  Barnum & Bailey, 1913, Lion and Tiger, reclining jungle cats, circus logo, Strobridge Litho. **275.00**
  Cole Bros, All The Marvels, animals in cages, Erie Litho. **210.00**
  Ringling Bros and Barnum & Bailey, 1938, The Greatest Wild Animal Display, presents Terrell Jacobs, World's Foremost Trainer, Strobridge Litho **625.00**
Program, Barnum & Bailey, 1953 . . . . . . **10.00**
Stereograph, Windsor & Whipple, Olean, NY, people with elephant **35.00**

Toy
  Acrobat, mechanical, celluloid, Banko **175.00**
  Hi Jinks at the Circus, clown with chimp. **295.00**
  Train, tin litho, clown's face and tiger illus, marked "Made In Japan," 1950s. **75.00**

CLICKERS

If you need a clicker, you would probably spend hours trying to locate a modern one. I am certain they exist. You can find a clicker at a flea market in a matter of minutes. As an experiment, I tried looking up the word in a dictionary. It was not there. Times change.

Clickers made noise, a slight sharp sound. I believe their principal purpose was to drive parents crazy. I understand they played a major role at parochial school, but cannot attest to the fact since I attended public school.

Tastykake, blue ground, white letters, $7.50.

Advertising
  Buster Brown **25.00**
  Calvert Whiskey, red and white, 1950s. **8.00**
  Humpty Dumpty Shoes, 2″ l, litho tin, c1930. . . . . **25.00**
  New and True Coffee, c1930 . . . . **15.00**
  Peters Weatherbird Shoes, ¾ × 1¾″, tin, litho, multicolor, c1930s **25.00**
  Real−Kill Bug Killer **18.00**
  Red Goose Shoes, ¾″ × 1¼″, tin, litho, red goose, yellow lettering and ground, 1930s **22.50**
  Clown, 1½″ × 2¼″, multicolored, Japan. **3.00**
  Felix, 1¾″ l, black and white, dark brown background, caption "Fancy You Fancying Me Felix!", 1930s **50.00**
  Halloween, witch and pumpkin, orange, black, and white **15.00**
  Mickey Mouse, playing drum **35.00**

CLOCKS

Look for clocks that are fun (have motion action) or that are terrific in a decorating scheme (a school house clock in a country setting). Clocks are bought to be seen and used.

Avoid buying any clock that does not work. You do not know whether it is going to cost $5.00, $50.00, or $500.00 to repair it. Are you prepared to risk the higher number? Likewise, avoid clocks that need extensive repair work to the case. There are plenty of clocks in fine condition awaiting sale.

Club: National Association of Watch and Clock Collectors, Inc. P. O. Box 33, Columbia, PA 17512.

Chef, electric, white, Sessions, 10½" h, $40.00.

Advertising
  Jacob Lucks Clothier, Watkins, NY, figural, dog, black man holding sign above **160.00**
  Peter's Shoes, alarm, Art Deco, New Haven Clock Co, c1930 . . . . **50.00**
  Purina Poultry Chows, electric, three dials, red, white, and blue checkerboard bag **40.00**
Alarm
  Baby Ben, round **28.00**
  Bradley, brass, double bells, Germany **35.00**
  Seth Thomas, 10¼", metal case, 1910–1920 . . . . **50.00**
Banjo, 17⅞", inlaid mahogany case, eagle finial, New Haven Clock Co, c1920 . . . . **150.00**
Beehive, 5¼", brass, porcelain dial, Chelsea, c1900 . . . . **50.00**

Box or Cottage, 13½", rosewood veneered case, orig glass and dial, Gilbert & Co, c1890 . . . . **120.00**
Character
  Bugs Bunny, 4" × 4½" × 1½", wind–up, alarm, hard plastic, animated, ivory enamel, Ingraham, c1951 . . . . **200.00**
  Cinderella, 2½" × 4½" × 4", alarm, windup, white metal case, orig box, Westclox **50.00**
  Donald Duck, 2" × 4½" × 4½", alarm, metal case, light blue, orig box, Bayard **250.00**
  Mickey Mouse, 2" × 4" × 4½", alarm, plastic case, Ingersoll, 1949 . . . . **250.00**
  Roy Rogers, wind–up, alarm, metal case, animated, Ingraham, c1951 . . . **300.00**
Cuckoo, 5" × 4" × 1¾", pressed log design, leaves, flowers, nest of birds, brass spring pendulum, Keebler Clock Co, Philadelphia, PA **90.00**
Kitchen, 11¾", white painted case, New Haven Clock Co, c1930 . . . . **60.00**
Mantel, 10½" h, rosewood veneered case, Seth Thomas, c1880 . . . . **75.00**
School House
  19½", oak case, orig label, Sessions Clock Co, 1915–1920 . . . . **300.00**
  24", mahogany veneered case, Waterbury Clock Co, c1890 . . . . **200.00**
Steeple, 20" h, refinished case, replaced door glass, Chauncey Boardman, c1840 . . . . **100.00**

CLOTHING AND ACCESSORIES

Decide from the beginning whether you are buying clothing and accessories for use or display. If you are buying for use, apply very strict standards with respect to condition and long term survival prospects if used. If you only want the items for display, you can be a little less fussy about condition.

Vintage clothing was a hot collectible craze in the 1980s. Things seemed to have cooled off a bit. Emphasis in the 1990s seems to be on accessories, with plastic purses from the 1950s leading the parade.

I love the wide ties from the late 1950s and early 1960s, but they have become so trendy and pricy that I find myself more often than not passing them by. Besides, Dad has a closet full at home that belonged to him as a young adult. He's come a long way in his tastes since then.

Club: The Costume Society of America, P. O. Box 761, Englishtown, NJ 08826.

Newsletter: *Vintage Clothing Newsletter*, P. O. Box 1422, Corvallis, OR 97339.

Child's dress, matching cape, white cotton, $85.00.

Apron, red and white calico	**25.00**
Bathing Suit, black, stretchy fabric, flared skirt, c1930	**45.00**
Bed Jacket, blue, satin, lace trim	**20.00**
Bloomers, crepe satin, peach, silk embroidery, lace	**20.00**
Blouse, white, cotton, Victorian cutwork	**20.00**

Change Purse
   Mesh

Art Nouveau head	**45.00**
Coins surrounding head	**40.00**
Mother of Pearl	**15.00**
Tin, small face opens mouth for change	**35.00**

Coat

Cashmere, silver fox collar, c1940	**45.00**
Muskrat, bell-shaped sleeves	**95.00**

Collar

Beaded, white	**15.00**
Linen, sq cutwork corners	**25.00**

Dress

Chiffon, blue, braid edge trim, 1925 . . .	**40.00**
Crepe, brown, evening, matching velvet caplet, feather trim, c1930	**45.00**
Silk, black, chiffon sleeves, embroidered, 1923	**50.00**
Dressing Gown, ruby red, satin, ruffled edges, 1930	**30.00**
Gloves, kid leather, opera length	**20.00**

Handbag

Alligator, suede lining	**20.00**
Beaded, pink and blue florals, gold frame	**45.00**
Plastic, lucite, pearlized, round lid, twisted handle, seashell dec.	**18.00**
Silk, clutch, black, cut steel beads, marked "France," c1930	**40.00**
Prom Gown, pink, net and taffeta, layered skirt, bow trim, c1950	**35.00**
Skirt, pink, felt, poodle dec	**25.00**
Spats, gray, wool, c1900	**25.00**

Sweater, cashmere, white pearl trim.	**35.00**
Tie, hand painted trout	**25.00**

COCA-COLA COLLECTIBLES

John Pemberton, a pharmacist from Atlanta, Georgia, is credited with creating the formula for Coca-Cola. Less than two years after his invention, he sold out to Asa G. Chandler. Chandler improved the formula and began advertising. By the 1890s America was Coca-Cola conscious.

Coke, a term first used in 1941, is now available worldwide. American collectors still focus primarily on Coca-Cola material designed for the American market. Although it would take a little effort to obtain, a collection of foreign Coke advertising would make a terrific display. What a perfect excuse to fly to the Orient.

Club: The Coca-Cola Collectors Club International, P. O. Box 546, Holmdel, NJ 07733.

Playing cards, 1943, $45.00.

Adv, pinback button

1⅛" d, red and white, "Drink Coca–Cola," c1950	**10.00**
1¼" d, red and white, "Coca–Cola Big Wheels Club," *Cleveland Press* newspaper, ship's wheel center, c1930s	**50.00**
Ashtray, different card suits, c1940	**40.00**
Beanie Hat, c1960	**7.00**

Blotter

1903.	**30.00**
1951.	**4.00**

Booklet, *The Truth About Coca–Cola,*

1912.	**30.00**
Bridge Score Pad	**5.00**
Can, bottle in diamond, c1960	**15.00**
Charm Bracelet, 6½" l, brass, NFL, four miniature charms, punter, football, NFL logo, Coke logo, enamel accents, c1970.	**20.00**

Check, canceled	**2.00**
Cigarette Lighter, 2½″ h, plastic, bottle shape, c1950	**18.50**
Cribbage Game, MIB.	**55.00**
Fly Swatter	**9.00**
Frisbee.	**20.00**
Key Chain, miniature bottle, c1950	**6.00**
Matchbook, c1930	**5.00**
Menu, girl serving tray, unused.	**30.00**
Pencil, bullet	**4.00**
Playing Cards, World War II airplane spotter series.	**30.00**
Pop Gun.	**4.00**
Post Card, showing c1940 Coke truck. . . .	**18.00**
Punch Board	
Large	**15.00**
Small	**8.00**
Soda Jerk Hat, Sprite boy.	**4.00**
Thermometer, 30″ h, tin, bottle shape, 1958.	**35.00**
Toy, truck, Buddy L, 1960s, MIB.	**200.00**
Tray, 1950s	**40.00**
Wallet, 1928	**18.50**

COIN-OPERATED MACHINES

This category covers any machine operated by inserting a coin, from arcade games to player pianos to vending machines. Since all these machines are mechanical, it is important to buy only machines in operating order. The techniques to repair them rest in the hands of a few enthusiasts. Many repair parts need to be made by hand.

Many museums, recognizing the long-term collectibility of coin-operated games, have already begun to acquire some of the early video games. Imagine Pacman in a museum. It doesn't seem that long ago that I was playing it in an arcade.

Newsletters: *Coin–Op Newsletter*, 909 26th Street, NW, Washington, DC 20037; *Jukebox Collector Newsletter*, 2545 SE 60th Street, Des Moines, IA 50317.

Game	
Challenger, target practice, ten shots for 1¢, ABT Mfg Corp, Chicago, USA . . .	**275.00**
Select–Em, dice game, Exhibit Supply Co, Chicago	**275.00**
Gum	
Adams, 1¢, 10″ × 4″ × 22½″, Art Deco lady on label.	**100.00**
Hawkeye, 1¢, cast metal, six-sided, red paint, c1931.	**120.00**
Jukebox	
AMI, model D	**400.00**
Mills, Empress Model	**950.00**
Seeburg, Model M100W	**650.00**
Wurlitzer, Model 1650, 48 selections, light up side columns, 55″ h, 1954 . . .	**500.00**
Peanut, Nut Jewel, 5¢, two columns, Lawrence Mfg Co	**100.00**
Slot Machine	
Bally Reserve, 5¢, award card and key.	**160.00**
Jubilee, blue wood sides, diamond dec on right side	**500.00**
Pace, 8 Star Bell, circular coin escalator, c1948	**1,000.00**

Arcade Game, pinball, Rocket Ship, Gottlieb, $500.00.

COINS, AMERICAN

Just because a coin is old does not mean that it is valuable. Value often rests more on condition than on age. Since this is the case, the first step to deciding if any of the coins that you have are valuable is to learn to grade them. Coins are graded on a scale of 70 with 70 being the best and 4 being good.

Start your research by acquiring Marc Hudgeons's *The Official 1991 Blackbook Price Guide To United States Coins, Twenty-Ninth Edition* (House of Collectibles: 1990). Resist the temptation to look up your coins immediately. Read the 100-page introduction, over half of which deals with the question of grading.

Do not overlook the melt (weight) value of silver content coins. In many cases, weight value will be far greater than collectible value. We would all be geniuses if we had sold when the industry was paying twenty times face in the midst of the silver craze in the early 1980s.

Club: American Numismatic Association, 818 North Cascade Avenue, Colorado Springs, CO 80903.

COINS, FOREIGN

The foreign coins that you are most likely to encounter at a flea market are the left-over change that someone brought back with them from their travels. Since the coins were in circulation, they are common and of a low grade. In some countries, they have been withdrawn from circulation and cannot even be redeemed for face value.

If you are a dreamer and think you have uncovered hidden wealth, use Chester L. Krause and Clifford Mishler's *1990 Edition Standard Catalog of World Coins* (Krause Publications: 1990). This book covers world coinage from 1801 through 1989.

Avoid any ancient coinage. There are excellent fakes in the market. You need to be an expert to tell the good from the bad. Coins are one of those categories where it pays to walk away when the deal is too good. Honest coin dealers work on very small margins. They cannot afford to give away anything. Good.

COLLEGE COLLECTIBLES

Rah, rah, sis-boom-bah! The Yuppies made a college education respectable again. They tout their old alma mater. They usually have a souvenir of their college days in their office at home or work.

You will not find a Harvard grad with a room full of Yale memorabilia and vice versa. Most of this stuff has value only to someone who attended the school. The expection is sport-related college memorabilia. This has much broader appeal, either to a conference collector or a general sports collector.

Periodical: *Sports Collectors Digest*, 700 East State Street, Iola, WI 54990.

Booklet, *The Freshman Herald, Princeton University, Class of 1941*, biographies, includes Malcolm Forbes **28.00**
Commemorative Glass, dinner **5.00**
Commemorative Spoon
  Cornell University, Art Nouveau woman **50.00**
  Iowa State College, Indian Chief, sterling silver **28.00**

Sheet music, College Yell, *JS Zamecnik, Sam Fox Publishing Co, 11" × 13¾", $5.00.*

Notre Dame **100.00**
State Normal School, Superior, Wisconsin **25.00**
Wellesley College, woman in cap and gown handle **50.00**
Magazine, Phi Gemma Delta, 1955 . . . . . . **10.00**
Plate, William and Mary, Wren building, 10" d, Jonroth **10.00**
Sheet Music
  Everybody Loves A College Girl, Kerry Mills, 1911 . . . . **3.00**
  Stein Song, Rudy Vallee **10.00**
Tie Clip, Yale, 2" l, key shape, bright gold colored plating, inscribed "The Yale & Towne Mfg Co" and "First For Ike," issued by Yale Ike Club, 1952 . . . . **75.00**
Tobacco Silk, Lehigh University, Richmond Straight Cut Cigarettes **15.00**
Yearbook, Princeton University
  Class of 1941, After 10 Years **12.00**
  Class of 1941, After 25 Years **10.00**
  Class of 1941, After 40 Years **8.00**
  Class of 1942 . . . . **28.00**

COLORING BOOKS

The key is to find these gems uncolored. Some collectors will accept a few pages colored, but the coloring had better be neat. If it is scribbled, forget it.

Most of the value rests on the outside cover. The closer the image is to the actual character or personality emphasized, the higher the value. The inside pages of most coloring books consist of cheap newsprint. It yellows and becomes brittle over time.

However, resist buying only the cover. Collectors prefer to have the entire book.

Batman and Robin, 8" × 11", Whitman, #1002, 1967, unused 15.00
Blondie, 8½" × 11", Dell Publishing, 1954, unused. 20.00
Blyth, Ann, 1952, unused. 35.00
Charlie Chaplin, 10" × 17", Donohue & Co, 1917 copyright 80.00
Dick Tracy, 8¼" × 11", Saalfield, #2536, 1946 copyright 25.00
Donald Duck, 7½" × 8½", Whitman, 1946, unused. 20.00
Eve Arden, 1953, unused 32.50
Hopalong Cassidy, 5¼" × 5¼", "William Boyd/Star of Hopalong Cassidy/On The Range," 48 pgs, Samuel Lowe Co, 1951 copyright 25.00
Lone Ranger, 8½" × 11", Whitman, 1956, 64 pgs, Cheerios premium. 75.00
Planet of the Apes, 8½" × 11", Saalfield, 1974 Apjac Productions copyright, unused. 15.00
Roy Rogers, 15" × 11", Roy Rogers and Dale Evans, 1952. . . . . 20.00
Shazam, 11" × 14", Whitman, 1975 National Periodical Publications copyright, pin–up poster on back cov 12.00
Spiderman, large size 18.00
Superman, 8" × 11", Whitman, 1966 National Periodical Publications copyright, unused. 25.00
Tom Mix, 11" × 14", Whitman, 1935, 96 pgs 50.00
Walt Disney's Disneyland, 8" × 11", Whitman, copyright 1965. . . . . 20.00

COMBS

The form is pretty basic. Value rests in how and in what material the comb is presented. Some hair combs are fairly elaborate and actually should be considered as jewelry accessories.

Beware of combs being sold separately that were originally part of larger dresser sets. Their value is less than combs that were meant to stand alone.

You can build an interesting collection inexpensively by collecting giveaway combs. You will be amazed to see how many individuals and businesses used this advertising media, from politicians to funeral parlors.

Bakelite, red top layer, yellow bottom layer, lunette parrots in flight design, c1900. . . . . 75.00
Ivory, Oriental, Victorian, c1860 . . . . 145.00

Bakelite, floral dec, 9" l, $4.00

Plastic, piercework, imitation blue stones, Art Nouveau 75.00
Pompadour, Art Nouveau, faux tortoise shell, gilt brass and turquoise glass accents. 37.50
Sterling Silver, flower and leaf motif, 1860–1870 . . . . 200.00
Tortoise Shell
Geometric   motif,   gold   inlay, 1920–1930 . . . . 120.00
Openwork scroll design, c1896. . . . . . . 125.00

COMIC BOOKS

Comic books come in all shapes and sizes. The number that have survived is almost endless. Although there were reprint books of cartoon strips in the 1910s, 1920s, and 1930s, the modern comic book had its origin in June 1938 when DC issued Action Comics No. 1, marking the first appearance of Superman.

Comics are divided into Golden Age, Silver Age, and Contemporary titles. Before you begin buying, read John Hegenberger's *Collector's Guide To Comic Books* (Wallace–Homestead: 1990) and D. W. Howard's *Investing In Comics* (The World of Yesterday: 1988).

The dominant price guide for comics is Robert Overstreet's *The Official Overstreet Comic Book Price Guide*. However, more and more you see obsolete comics being offered in shops and at conventions for ten to twenty-five percent less than Overstreet's prices. The comic book market may be facing a revaluation crisis similar to what happened in the stamp market several years ago when the editors of the Scott catalog lowered the value significantly for many stamps.

Periodicals: *Comic Buyers Guide*, 700 State Street, Iola, WI 54990; *Comics Values Monthly*, Attic Books, P. O. Box 38; South Salem, NY 10590.

Note: Most comics, due to condition, are not worth more than 50¢ to a couple of dollars. Very strict grading standards are applied to comics less than ten years old. The following list shows the potential in the market. You need to check each comic book separately.

Marvel Comics Group, 2001: A Space Odyssey, premiere issue #1, $3.50.

Amazing Adventures, #2 . . . . 18.00
Bewitched, 7" × 10", #7, Dec 1966,
Dell 10.00
Captain America, Marvel Comic Vol 1
#100, April 1968. . . . . 10.00
Captain Marvel, 6½" × 8¼", "Captain Marvel Adventure,' Wheaties adv and Bob Feller photo on back, 1964 copyright. 30.00
Cheyenne, #9, Nov–Jan, 1959, Dell 12.00
GI Joe, 7" × 10", vol 2, #18, Winter, 1952. . . . . 20.00
Hawkman, #5, Zatanna 6.00
Little Lulu, 5" × 7¼", 16 pgs, premium, Marjorie Henderson Buell 1964 copyright. 20.00
Rin Tin Tin and Rusty, #31, Aug–Oct, Dell 15.00
The Danny Thomas Show, 7½" × 10" #1249, Nov–Jan 1962 issue 12.00
Tom Mix, #23, Return of the Past, Tom Mix Western Comic, 1949. . . . . 12.00

COMIC PERSONALITY COLLECTIBLES

The great comedians, those individuals who have devoted their lives to making us laugh, deserve to be recognized. While most of the material that is available relates to their movie, radio, and television careers, do not overlook programs and other items from their stage and club appearances.

Pinback button, Ella Cinders, New York Evening Journal, red letters, black numbers, white ground, $10.00.

Autograph, "Sincerely Soupy Sales" on black and white picture post card of Sales. 20.00
Boxed Board Game, Jackie Gleason'a Awa-a-a-a-y We Go, Transogram, 1956. . . . . 125.00
Coloring Book
Jackie Gleason Coloring Book, cover depicts Gleason as Ralph Kramden driving his bus on Madison Avenue. 50.00
Pinky Lee's Health And Safety Cut–Out Coloring Book, Pocket Books, copyright 1955 . . . . 15.00
Fan, "I'm A Bilko Fan," quarter circle shape, black, white, and green stiff cardboard fan offered as a premium by Amana, the company that sponsored You'll Never Get Rich. 20.00
Lunch Box, Laugh–In, embossed steel, Aladdin 35.00
Mask, Groucho Goggles and Cigar, cart holding plastic cigar and diecut plastic face piece, small advertisement for NBC show sponsored by DeSoto Cars, copyright 1955 . . . . 40.00
Model Kit, Laurel & Hardy '25T Roadster, plastic, AMT, circa 1970 . . . . 30.00
Pencil Case, Soupy Sales, light blue vinyl, black illus of Sales, inscription "Soupy Sez Let's Do The Mouse," about 1960 . . . . 15.00
School Bag and Game Kit, Mr. Peppers, Pressman, copyright 1955 . . . . 40.00
Toy, lithographed tin, The Milton Berle Car, Marx, original box 300.00
TV Digest And Guide, March 20, 1953, cover features picture of Ethel and Fred

Mertz, neighbors of Lucy and Desi on the I Love Lucy show **100.00**

Club: Token and Medal Society, Inc., P. O. Box 951988, Lake Mary, FL 32795-1988.

COMMEMORATIVE GLASSES

Before the modern promotional drinking glass that you get from a fast food restaurant, garage, or by eating the contents of a glass food container, there were glasses that you bought (yes, you actually paid for them) as souvenirs. Most of the decoration and information on them is acid-etched. Although they are tough to find, they are not all that expensive. One collector I know specializes in advertising spirit glasses. Her collection numbers in the hundreds.

Goblet, G.A.R., 1887, 21st Encampment **100.00**
Mug, child's, World's Fair, 1893 . . . . **85.00**
Spirit Glasses, Advertising
  Compliments of Jos. Spand, 589 Atlantic Avenue, Boston, MA, 2⅜" h, circa 1910. . . . . **18.00**
  Green Mill Whiskey, S. M. Denison, Wholesale Liquor Dealer, Chillicothe, OH, 2¼" h, circa 1910 . . . . . . **15.00**
  Seattle Liquor Co., 1123 First Avenue, Seattle, WA, gold rim, 2 5/16" h, circa 1908. . . . . **20.00**
Tumblers
  McKinley, William and Theodore Roosevelt, prosperity and protection slogan **75.00**
  Spanish American War, five frosted busts. **75.00**

COMMEMORATIVE MEDALS

From the late nineteenth century through the 1930s, commemorative medals were highly prized possessions. The U. S. Mint and other mints still carry on the tradition today, but to a far lesser degree.

Distinguish between medals issued in mass and those struck for a limited purpose, in some cases in issues of one for presentation. An old medal should have a surface patina that has developed over the years causing it to have a very mellow appearance. Never, never clean a medal. Collectors like this patina look.

In most medals, the medal content has little value. However, medals were struck in both silver and gold. If you are not certain, have the metal tested.

Civil War, Dix Token, copper colored,³/₄" d.

American Red Cross, brass, emb Red Cross arm band, dark red enamel accents, c1930, 1" d. **20.00**
Anti–Slavery, brass, kneeling black woman, slogan "Am I Not A Woman & Sister/1838," wreath design on back with motto. **70.00**
Centennial, US, brass shell, New Mexico trading post, inscribed "J E Barrow & Co/Post Traders/Fort Union/New Mexico," reverse with Miss Liberty and 1776 date, 1⅜" d. **50.00**
Civil War, copper, Maj Gen Geo McClellan, USA, eagle, shield, and flag design, slogan on back "I Am Born To Defend My Country," 1¼" d. **35.00**
Exposition
  Alaska Yukon Pacific, 1909, emb "Virgin Utah Copper," Utah exhibit on front, rim inscribed, reverse with state seal, 1½" d. **20.00**
Columbian, 1893
  Bronze, raised scene of Columbus, reverse with trumpeting angels, ship, and commemorative text, 1½" d. **40.00**
  White Metal, raised bust portrait of Columbus, rim inscribed "Souvenir World's Columbian Exposition, Chicago, USA, 1892–1893," worn silver flashing, 2" d **25.00**
Cotton States, 1895, white metal, dark finish, Phoenix bird, center inscribed "Resurgens/Atlanta, Ga," out rim inscribed "Cotton States and International Exposition/Sept 18th to Dec 31st," 2" d. **30.00**
Sesquicentennial, Hamden, CT, brass, emb "Eli Whitney Arms Plant" and details, 1936, 1¼" d **15.00**

COMMEMORATIVE (SOUVENIR) SPOONS

Collecting commemorative spoons was extremely popular from the last decade of the nineteenth century through 1940. Actually, it has never gone completely out of fashion. You can still buy commemorative spoons at many historical and city tourist sites.

The first thing that you want to check is for metal content. Sterling silver was a popular medium for commemorative spoons. Fine enamel work adds to value.

Club: American Spoon Collectors, 4922 State Line, Westwood Hills, KS 66205.

Newsletter: *Spoony Scoop Newsletter*, 84 Oak Avenue, Shelton, CT 06484.

St Louis Cathedral, New Orleans, LA, sterling silver, Top: 5¹/₂" l, fleur–de–lis handle, $15.00; Bottom: 5" l, grape cluster handle, $15.00.

Art Palace, 1893 Columbian Expo	65.00
Battle Monument, Trenton, New Jersey	25.00
Ben Franklin, Philadelphia	40.00
Canada, SS	25.00
Chief Seattle, totem pole	22.00
Columbus, bust, plated	15.00
Duba, Morro castle	40.00
Denver, Columbine handle	16.50
Fort Dearborn, SS	12.00
Fredericton, New Brunswick, spiral handle, gold wash bowl	30.00
Golden Gate, San Francisco	30.00
Indianapolis, Soldier's & Sailor's Monument	18.00
Jamestown Expo	35.00
Lake Worth, Palm Beach, Florida	58.00
Madison, Wisconsin	10.00
Mt Vernon	10.00
New York Peace Monument, Lookout Mountain, Tennessee, picture bowl	25.00
Notre Dame	110.00
Old Hickory, Jackson Monument	55.00
Palm Springs Aerial Tramway, SP, John Brown, marked "Antico"	100.00
Pittsburgh, Ft Pitt	38.00

Quebec, openwork handle	15.00
Queen Elizabeth, 1953 Coronation	15.00
Rochester, New York	35.00
San Francisco, Mission Dolores 1776, bear on dec handle, gold bowl	35.00
Settle Memorial Church, Owensboro, Kentucky	25.00
Statue of Liberty, Tiffany	60.00
Teddy Roosevelt, riding horse, full figure handle	85.00
Washington DC, capitol	28.00
William Penn, Independence Hall	58.00

COMPACTS

The jewelry market is now so sophisticated that you have to look to its components to find out what is hot and what is not. Compacts are hot. They increased significantly in price in the 1980s. They are still rising in value.

Look for compacts that are major design statements or have gadget mechanisms. Many compacts came with elaborate boxes and pouches. These are necessary if the compact is going to be viewed as complete.

Club: The Compact Collectors Club, P. O. Box Letter S, Lynbrook, NY 11563.

Chrome, blue and white trim, Art Deco, 2¹/₄" sq, $20.00.

American Maid, heart shape, goldtone, engraved lid	30.00
Avon, oval, blue and green checkerboard lid	25.00
Columbian, applied flower in vase, 2⁵/₈" sq, rhinestone and enamel trim	40.00
Coro, halfmoon shape, satin and goldtone	45.00
Coty Chrome, 1³/₄" d	20.00

104

Plastic, hand mirror shape, powder puff
    dec on lid, lipstick handle **50.00**
Elgin, mother–of–pearl, American
    Beauty, MIB **45.00**
Elizabeth Arden, harlequin shape, light
    blue, c1940 . . . . **75.00**
Evening in Paris, wood, dec lid, c1940 . . . **45.00**
Gucci, goldtone, black enamel **60.00**
Houbigant, six-sided, goldtone, powder
    and rouge compartment **40.00**
Souvenir
    Empire State Building, enamel, painted
    green **40.00**
    New York World's Fair 1939, wood,
    tapestry design **80.00**
    Pennsylvania Turnpike scene **35.00**
Unknown Maker, faux tortoise shell, 3½″
    sq, mounted brass butterfly, loose mir-
    ror **12.00**
Yardley, rouge and powder, white, blue
    arcs **25.00**

CONEY ISLAND

I did not include Coney Island in the amusement park collectibles category because I think it deserves special honors. It was the "mother of all boardwalks," a legend that grows larger with each passing year. Each time I drive to JFK Airport in New York, I see the remains of the parachute ride. If the government wants to fund something historic, it would gain a lot more support for restoring the parachute ride than building a museum for Lawrence Welk.

Game, Excursion to Coney Island, Milton Bradley, card game, c1885, $25.00.

Baggage Tag, silvered brass, emb "Coney
    Island," numbered "1904," c1920 . . . . **25.00**
Medal, 1924, steeplechase face, orig rib-
    bon **90.00**

Pennant, 24″ l, maroon felt, white title,
    yellow, green, orange, and white scene
    of Steeplechase Pool, amusement
    rides, Luna Mill Sky Chaser building,
    c1930 . . . . **20.00**
Photograph, 8 × 10″ glossy, park scene,
    orig **50.00**
Pinback Button
    1¼″ d, multicolored, bathing beauty
    center, rim reads "Citizens Commit-
    tee of Coney Island," c1915 . . . . **35.00**
    1¾″ d, multicolored, Brooklyn, Coney
    Island, Arverne, center scene of ladies
    swimming, rim reads "Swimming
    Taught In Six Lessons By MacLevy
    Quick Trolley System," c1900 . . . . . . **150.00**
Post Card, 1920 scene of entrance gate . . . **10.00**
Poster, 1911 Mardi Gras, Coney Island . . . **450.00**
Sign, 36″ l, porcelain, arrow shape **350.00**
Ticket, Steeplechase **30.00**
Toy, 8½″ h, celluloid, traffic policeman,
    bright pink uniform, large white gloved
    hand, small silver badge, celluloid whis-
    tle, black visor on cap, upraised hand
    mounted on spring with word "Stop" in
    red letters on palm, marked "Japan,'
    c1930 . . . . **150.00**

CONSTRUCTION SETS

Children love to build things. Building block sets originated in the nineteenth century. They exist in modern form as Legos and Lego imitators.

Construction toys also are popular, especially with young boys who aspired to be engineers. The best known is the Erector Set, but it also had plenty of imitators. Alfred Carlton Gilbert, Jr. began his business by producing magic sets as the Mysto Manufacturing Company. With the help of his father, he bought out his partner and created the A. C. Gilbert Company located on Erector Square in New Haven, Connecticut.

A. C. Gilbert
    Chemistry Experiment Lab.,
    three–piece metal box **27.50**
    Erector Set
        No. 1, complete **30.00**
        No. 2, 1919, box, complete **75.00**
        No. 4, 1940, instructions, com-
        plete **275.00**
        No. 8½, instructions, complete, metal
        case **60.00**
        No. 10, giant deluxe set, makes
        zeppelin (fabric included), Hudson
        and Tender, White truck, etc., com-
        plete **1,500.00**
        No. 10181, Action Helicopter **75.00**

American National Building Box, The
White House, wooden pieces, complete
landscaping forms, wooden box **100.00**
Embossing Company
No. 408, Jonnyville Blocks, DeLuxe
Edition, blocks, trees, hook and lad-
der, and village plan **60.00**
No. 3105 Sky–Hy Building Blocks, con-
sist of four different size cubes and
caps, for constructing skyscraper
building **85.00**
Schoenhut's Little Village Builder, wood,
builds five buildings. **75.00**

COOKBOOKS

Hershey's Index Recipe Book, written by Mrs Christine Frederick, 1934 copyright, $10.00.

There are eighteenth and nineteenth century cookbooks. But, they are expensive,
very expensive. It pays to look through old
piles of books in hopes that a dealer has
overlooked one of these gems. But, in
truth, you are going to go unrewarded
ninety-nine percent or more of the time.

The cookbooks that you are most likely
to find date from the twentieth century.
Most were promotional giveaways. A fair
number came with appliances. Some were
associated with famous authors.

A couple of years ago, you could buy
them in the 50¢ to $1.00 range and had
piles from which to choose. No longer.
These later cookbooks have been discovered. Now you are going to pay between
$2.00 and $10.00 for most of them.

Cover art does effect price. Most are
bought for display purposes. Seek out the
ones that feature a recognizable personality
on the cover.

Club: Cookbook Collectors Club of America, Inc., P. O. Box 56, St. James, MO
65559.

All About Home Baking, General Foods
Corp, 144 pgs, yellow and black plaid
cov, 1935 . . . . **7.50**
Any One Can Bake, Royal Baking Pow-
der, 1929, 100 pgs **6.50**
Aunt Jemima, 1928. . . . . **8.50**
Benson–Hedges **8.00**
Better Homes and Gardens, 1953 . . . . **16.00**
Blondie's, 5½" × 8½", hard cover, 142 pgs,
1947 copyright, recipes selected and il-
lus by Chic Young **35.00**
Budget Watchers **8.00**
Campbell's Main Dishes **8.00**
Cook It Right **8.00**
Cutco. **8.00**
Dainty Junkets, little girl waitress on cov,
32 pgs, 1915. **15.00**

Economy Administration Cookbook,
1913, 696 pgs. **45.00**
Housekeeping in Old Virginia, slave reci-
pes by Mozis Addams, 1965 reprint. . . . **35.00**
Joys Jell–O **8.00**
Knox Gelatin, black child, 1915 . . . . **5.00**
Pennsylvania Dutch Cook Book of Fine
Old Recipes, Sunbonnet Girl on cov, 48
pgs, 1936 . . . . **15.00**
Pillsbury Family Cookbook, 1963. . . . . . . **10.00**
Shumway's Canning Recipes, booklet . . . **4.00**
Sourdough Jack's **8.00**
Spry **3.00**
Universal Cookbooks, Jeanie L Taylor,
185 pgs, 1888. . . . . **15.00**
Weight Watchers, first edition, 1978. . . . . **7.50**

COOKIE CUTTERS

When most individuals think of cookie cutters, they envision the metal cutters, often
mass-produced, that were popular during
the nineteenth century and first third of the
twentieth century. This is too narrow a
view. Do not overlook the plastic cutter of
recent years. Not only are they colorful, but
they come in a variety of shapes quite different from their metal counterparts.

If you want to build a great specialized
collection, look for cutters that were
giveaway premiums by flour and baking
related business. Most of these cutters are
in the $10.00 to $40.00 range.

Club: Cookie Cutters Club, 1167 Teal
Road, W. W., Dellroy, OH 44620.

Advertising
Egg Baking Powder Co, 1½" d, 1902 . . . **40.00**

Horse, aluminum, green painted handle, $3.00.

Swans Down Cake Flour, premium,
  aluminum **22.00**
Bear, 2½″ × 3″, handcrafted, irregular
  back, missing handle **10.00**
Bird, 4½″ l, spread wings, tin **15.00**
Cow, 4½″, l, tin, missing handle **5.00**
Dog, 4½″ l, tin **20.00**
Dutchman, 5¼″ h, tin **115.00**
Goblet, 4″, tin **100.00**
Man, 3″ × 5½″, handcrafted, hat and coat,
  handle removed **85.00**
Pitcher, 4¼″, tin **110.00**
Reindeer, 5″ × 6″, handcrafted, irregular
  back, four legs, grouped antlers **115.00**
Scissors, 5¼″, tin **100.00**
Whale, 3¾″, tin **20.00**
Woman with bustle, 5¼″ h, tin **110.00**

COOKIE JARS

Talk about categories that have gone nuts
over the past years. Thanks to the Andy
Warhol sale, cookie jars became the talk of
the town. Unfortunately, the prices reported for the Warhol cookie jars were so
far removed from reality that many individuals were deceived into believing their
cookie jars are far more valuable than they
really are.

The market seems to be having trouble
finding the right pricing structure. A recent
cookie jar price guide lowballed a large
number of jar prices. Big city dealers are
trying to sell cookie jars as art objects at
high prices instead of the kitcsh they really
are. You have to be the judge. Remember,
all you are buying is a place to store your
cookies.

Animal Cracker Clown **75.00**
Bagger, brown **50.00**
Basketball Trophy, 1929 . . . . **30.00**
Bobby Baker **38.00**
Bugs Bunny, McCoy **75.00**
Bunny, Brush–McCoy **160.00**

McCoy, coffee grinder, 6⅜ × 9¾″, $30.00.

Cat on basket, McCoy **60.00**
Chicken, iron lid, American Bisque **50.00**
Clown, bust, McCoy **38.00**
Coffeepot, American Bisque **25.00**
Elephant, Brush–McCoy **350.00**
Farmer Pig, Treasure Craft **45.00**
Fred Flintstone, Clay Arts **45.00**
Granny, McCoy **85.00**
Hobby Horse, Abingdon **175.00**
Jazz Singer, lady, Clay Arts **50.00**
Raggedy Ann **80.00**
Rooster, American Bisque **50.00**
Wizard, Clay Arts **45.00**
Woodsy Owl **150.00**

COPPER PAINTINGS

Copper paintings, actually pictures
stamped out of copper or copper foil, deserve a prize as one of the finest
"ticky–tacky" collectibles ever created. My
Dad remembers getting a four-picture set
from a bank as a premium in the late 1950s
or early 1960s. He takes great pride in
noting that these are one of the few things
that he has no regrets about throwing out.

However, to each his own–somewhere
out there are individuals who like this
unique form of mass-produced art. Their
treasures generally cost them in the $15.00
to $50.00 range depending on subject.

COSTUMES

Remember how much fun it was to play dress–up as a kid? Seems silly to only do it once a year around Halloween. Down South and in Europe, Mardis Gras provides an excuse; but, in my area, we eat doughnuts instead.

Collectors are beginning to discover children's Halloween costumes. I'll bet you are staggered by some of the prices listed below. Yet, I see costumes traded at these prices all the time.

There doesn't seem to be much market in adult costumes, those used in the theater and for theme parties. Costume rental shops are use to picking them up for a few dollars each.

Bat Masterson, orig box. **125.00**
Batman, display bag, vinyl cape, mask, cuffs, and badge, 1966 National Periodical Publications copyright **100.00**
Beatles, Paul, molded plastic mask, full length outfit, Nems copyright, 1964 . . . **175.00**
Captain Action, cloth outfit, mask, knife, two pistols, skull, brass knuckles, holster and belt, rifle, and boots, boxed, copyright 1966 Ideal Toy Corp **200.00**
Electronic Man, helmet and outfit, boxed, Fibre–Bilt Toys, 1950s **150.00**
Flash Gordon, space outfit, c1950. . . . . . **135.00**
Fred Flintstone, vinyl plastic mask and outfit, boxed Ben Cooper, 1973 Hanna–Barbera copyright **25.00**
Ken Maynard, bandanna, shirt and chaps, c1930. . . . . **100.00**
Kiss, Gene Simmons, molded and diecut plastic mask, vinyl and fabric costume, boxed, Collegeville Costumes, 1978 copyright **25.00**
Star Wars, R2D2, plastic mask, vinyl costume, boxed, Ben Cooper, 1977 copyright **25.00**
Superman, shirt, trousers, and cape, synthetic fabric, 1950s. **125.00**
The Shadow, fabric outfit, molded plastic mask, 1973 The Conde Nast Publications Inc **75.00**

COUNTRY AND WESTERN

If Country Western music is good enough for President Bush, it ought to be good enough for everybody. Country, Western, and Country and Western music have a tradition that dates back over one hundred years. Legendary performers are revered by its devotees.

Almost every price guide I know ignores country western collectibles. Maybe if I in-clude them here, others will get the hint that they deserve serious attention.

Watch Fob, banjo, white metal, mother of pearl trim, 1³⁄₈" l, $30.00.

Autograph
Ensemble, *Butch Cassidy & The Sundance Kid,* matted color photos of Newman, Ross, and Redford, signatures on white cards of Newman and Redford, 11" × 14" **75.00**
Photograph Signed
Harman, Fred, black and white inscription, cowboy riding horse, 5" × 3" **95.00**
Orbison, Roy, black and white glossy, scene from *The Fastest Gun Alive,* 10" × 8" **225.00**
Rogers, Kenny, Western attire, color, 8" × 10" **25.00**
Record
Aiken Country String Band, Carolina Stompdown, Okeh **8.00**
Allen Brothers, Glorious Night Blues, Victor **50.00**
Blue Ridge Mountain Girls, She Came Rolling Down The Mountain, Champion **10.00**
Carter Family, I'll Be Home Some Day, Bluebird **5.00**
Georgia Yellow Hammers, Peaches Down In Georgia, Victor **20.00**
Lone Star Rangers, Farm Relief Song, Paramount. **8.00**
Narmour & Smith, Sweet Milk And Peaches, Bluebird **15.00**
Uncle Dave Macon, Old Dan Tucker, Vocalion. **15.00**
Welling & McGhee, Ring The Bells Of Heaven, Champion **15.00**
Sheet Music
Cowboy Songs, 1935. . . . . **3.50**
El Rancho Grande, Bing Crosby cov . . . **15.00**
When A Lady Meets A Gentleman Down South, Oppenheim, 1936 . . . . **1.50**
Your Cheatin' Heart, Williams, 1952. . . . . **4.00**

COUNTRY STORE

There is something special about country stores. My favorite is Bergstresser's in Wassergasse, Pennsylvania. There is probably one near you that you feel as strongly about. Perhaps the appeal is that they continue to deny the present. I am always amazed at what a country store owner can dig out of the backroom, basement, or barn.

Country store collectibles focus heavily on front counter and back counter material from the last quarter of the nineteenth century and first quarter of the twentieth century. The look is tied in closely with Country. It also has a strong small town, rural emphasis.

Drop in and prop your feet up on the potbelly stove. Don't visit a country store if you are in a hurry.

Coffee Mill, Landers, Frary & Clark, New Britain, CT, cast iron, 12" h, $450.00.

Basket, produce, rect, small.	10.00
Box, Hershey Nougat Almond	10.00
Candy Jar, Primrose	10.00
Change Mat, Kool, rubber, green	3.50
Cigar Store Figure, 28" h, Indian maiden, pine, carved and painted, c1870.	3,575.00
Clock, regulator, Orange Crush adv . . .	1,095.00

Display Box

Flamemaster	15.00
Makepeace Evaporated Cranberry	10.00
Mexsana Skin Cream	6.00
Shoelace, cardboard	20.00
Receipt Holder, metal	3.00

Scale

Egg Grading, Acme, Jan 24, 1924	15.00
National, cast iron, brass pan and hardware, scarlet, red and gold pin striping, 10¼" × 12"	300.00

Seed Box, 8" × 25", stave construction, divided int.	125.00

Sign

Marvel Cigarette, cardboard	12.00
Sahara Coal, tin	18.00

COW COLLECTIBLES

Holy cow! This is a moovelous category, as entrenched collectors already know.

Book, *Blacky the Cow,* Thornton W Burgess, Harrison Day, illus, Grossett & Dunlap, 1922, 206 pgs.	8.00
Butter Stamp, 4¼" d, cow, turned handle	150.00
Cookie Jar, Cow jumping over moon, RRP Co, gold	80.00
Creamer, figural, Occupied Japan.	25.00
Doll, 12" h, Elsie the Cow, plush and vinyl, orig stitched tag, My-Toy Co, 1950–60	75.00
Milk Bottle, ½ pint, Hillcrest Farm, pictures cow	15.00
Mug, 3" h, white china, Elsie dancing through meadow of daisies, Continental Kilns signature, Borden Co copyright, late 1930s	50.00
Pin, Dominion Washing Sodas, enameled cow symbol, dark cherry red background, early 1900s.	15.00
Pinback Button, 1¾", cow's head with ring in nose, Aberdeen Angus adv, c1900.	25.00
Puppet, 10", Ferdinand the Bull, composition head, black and white fabric body, marked "Crown Toy Co," Enterprises copyright	50.00
Standup, cow, black and white tin, Holstein adv, 6"l	75.00
Stereograph, cows and sheep, Kilburn #739, 1870s	4.00

Advertising Box, Greer's "Moo Girl" Creamery Butter, 1 lb box, Sutherland Paper Co, Kalamazoo, MI, 1925 copyright, $3.50.

Stuffed Animal, 5½", felt, brown and white, galss eyes, wood wheels **65.00**
Toy, cow, Fisher Price, #132 . . . . **20.00**
Tray, 3½ × 5½", oval, cows in pasture, Carnation Milk adv **20.00**

Collectors tend to favor one cowboy hero. My Dad owns a few Roy Rogers and Gene Autry items, but he would never admit it publicly. As far as the world knows, he's a Hoppy man.

COWAN

R. Guy Cowan founded the Cowan Pottery in 1913 in Cleveland, Ohio. It remained in almost continuous operation until financial difficulties forced it to close in 1931. Initially utilitarian redware was produced. Cowan began experimenting with glazes, resulting in a unique lusterware glaze.

Children's boots, Hopalong Cassidy, black rubber, white trim, $95.00.

Candleholder, triple, ivory, 8½" w, $35.00.

Bowl, 9½", blue luster glaze, flared top, seahorse pedestal. **45.00**
Candlestick, pr, 4", pink **20.00**
Cigarette Holder, seahorse, ivory **30.00**
Flower Frog, nude, #686 . . . . **125.00**
Soap Dish, 4", seahorse, blue. **35.00**
Teapot, 7¼", white glaze **75.00**
Vase
   7¼", seahorse, standard, green glaze, imp mark **50.00**
   9", hp, dragonfly and cattails **80.00**

COWBOY HEROES

The cowboy heroes in this category rode the range in movies and on television. In a way, they were larger than their real life counterparts, shaping the image of how the west was won in the minds of several generations. Contemporary westerns may be historically correct, but they do not measure up where it counts.

The movie and television cowboy heroes were pioneers in merchandise licensing. If you were a child in the 1949 to 1951 period and did not own a Hopalong Cassidy item, you were deprived.

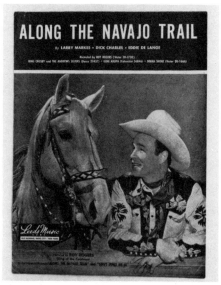

Sheet music, Roy Rogers, "Along The Navajo Trail," Larry Markes, Dick Charles, and Eddie de Lange, lyrics and music, 1942–1945, $15.00.

Gene Autry
   Comic Book, 1955. . . . . **16.00**
   Folio, sing–song **20.00**
   Pinback   Button,   photo, 1930s–early1940s. **25.00**
   Post card, Mile City, MT roundup **18.00**

110

Hopalong Cassidy
Blotter, promotional, pictures of Hoppy, Gabby Hayes, and Jimmy Ellison 25.00
Flashlight....................... 85.00
Mug 15.00
Pin, gun and holster 50.00
Pinback Button, Hopalong Cassidy Daily News 9.00
Ring, face 40.00
Wristwatch 50.00
Davy Crockett
Ascot 21.00
Baby Toy, rubber 20.00
Badge, Indian Scout, tin, pin–on, shield shape 18.00
Bowl 15.00
Decals, iron–on, complete, orig card 35.00
Doll, cloth, Hallmark 9.50
Wyatt Earp
Coloring Book, Hugh O'Brien cov, unused 35.00
Mug, milk glass 22.00
Puzzle, photo 15.00
Lone Ranger
Compass, silver bullet 35.00
Glass, water, 1938 .... 35.00
Hair Brush, orig card, 1939 .... 75.00
Jail Keys, orig card, 1950s 55.00
Paint Box, metal 45.00
Ring, atom bomb 45.00
Tom Mix
Arrow, lucite 85.00
Good Luck Spinner 30.00
Periscope, mailer 75.00
Ring, Look–A–Round 65.00
Telegraph, mailer 75.00
Annie Oakley
Board Game...................... 25.00
Shirt and Vest 45.00
Ranger Joe, bowl and mug, milk glass, red lettering and figures, set 27.00
Red Ryder
Mittens, unopened, orig pkg, pr 75.00
Target Game, orig box, complete 39.00
Rifleman
Comic Book, 1962 .... 14.00
Game, complete 40.00
Rin Tin Tin
Game, 1955 .... 20.00
Puzzle, photo 15.00
Roy Rogers
Belt, leather, buckle 35.00
Camera 50.00
Cigarette Lighter, Dale Evans, horse head 15.00
Guitar 45.00
Ring, branding iron 45.00
Wild Bill Hickock
Bunkhouse Kit, orig pkg 20.00
Lunchbox 45.00

CRACKER JACK COLLECTIBLES

You can still buy Cracker Jack with a prize in every box. The only problem is that when you compare today's prizes with those from decades ago, you feel robbed. Modern prizes simply do not compare. For this reason, collectors tend to focus on prizes put in the box prior to 1960.

Most Cracker Jack prizes were not marked. As a result, many dealers have Cracker Jack prizes without really knowing it. This allows an experienced collector to get some terrific bargains at flea markets. Alex Jaramillo's *Cracker Jack Prizes* (Abbeville Press: 1989) provides a wonderful survey of what prizes were available.

Bookmark, litho tin, brown dog, white ground, $15.00.

Baseball Card, Cracker Jack in baseball uniform, 1915 .... 17.50
Booklet, 4" × 6", "Angelus Recipes," black and white, 14 pgs 15.00
Bookmark, 2¾", diecut litho tin, c1930 . . . 15.00
Clicker, aluminum 15.00
Doll, stuffed cloth body, vinyl head, Vogue Dolls, 1980 copyright, unopened display card 25.00
Fortune Wheel, 1¾", tin, litho, red, white, and blue, alphabet letters, diecut opening 35.00
Hat, paper, "Me For Cracker Jack," red, white, and blue design, early 1900s. . . . 65.00
Mask, 8½" × 10", "Cracker Jack" on front, c1960 .... 15.00
Pencil, wood 15.00
Prize
Plate, 1¾" d, tin, silver, marked "Cracker Jack" in center 30.00
Top, 1½", tin, silver, wood peg 25.00
Puzzle Book, 2½" × 4", 4 pgs, Series one, 1917 copyright 75.00
Stationery, envelope, red and blue box . . . 6.00
Whistle, ¾" × 1½", plastic, red and white, Jack and dog one side, company name other side 10.00

111

CUPIDS

Be suspicious of naked infants bearing bows and arrows. It is not clear if their arrows are tipped with passion or poison.

Christmas ornament, white cupid, gold trim, gold hanger, plastic, 4" 5.00
Diecut, cupids with fan, folds in center ... 8.00
Dresser and tray scarves, linen, embroidered dec, matching pr 45.00
Garden statuette, sitting, legs crossed, wings folded around body, stone, antique finish, 12"h................. 28.00
Napkin ring, figural, sitting, legs crossed, candleholder and napkin ring combined, silver plated................. 175.00
Plaque, oval, red paint, gold braid trim, gold cupid in center, 11" x 7", pr...... 32.00
Postcard, Happy New Year, sgd "Rosie O'Neill"........................ 26.00
Print
  Cupid Awake and Cupid Asleep, photograph, oval, framed
    Small size..................... 15.00
    Medium size 25.00
    Large size..................... 50.00
  Cupid Awake and Cupid Asleep, stone lithographed, oval, framed
    Small size..................... 35.00
    Medium size 70.00
    Large size.................... 125.00
  Cupid with woman warming hands, Jean Aubert, 1882 .... 30.00
Woman in gauze dress with cupid on rock, 8" × 10" 30.00
Toothpick Holder, cupid holding flower basket, bisque 35.00
Valentine, heart, diecut
  Cupid soldier, 3¾", Winsch 10.00
  Cupid with birds, cut out violets, 6".... 20.00
  Two cupids on heart, crossed arrows... 12.00
Wall Hanging, three part, cupid on heart, flower, and butterfly 18.00

Stoneware, blue and white, 7½" d, $60.00.

Amberina Glass, 9" × 5", hourglass shape, ruffled rim, gold trim 375.00
Brass, Redskin Cut Plug Chewing Tobacco adv...................... 110.00
China, lady's hand, violets, turquoise beading, Nippon, green M in Wreath Mark 150.00
Pewter, 8" d, Gleason, Roswell, Dorchester, MA, c1850 .... 200.00
Pottery, 4½", pansies, marked "Loy–Nel Art"........................... 100.00
Redware, 8" × 4¼", tooled bands, brown and green running glaze with brown dashes 250.00
Salt Glazed, Red Wing Stoneware Company stamped on side 275.00
Spongeware, blue sponging, white ground, molded basketweave dec..... 150.00
Stoneware
  8", cobalt blue leaf and floral motif 175.00
  11" d, 6¾" h, cobalt blue dec ext., brown Albany slip int., marked "Livingston House"........................ 70.00
Yelloware, 5" × 7½", green, blue, and tan sponge glaze 60.00

CUSPIDORS

After examining the interiors of some of the cuspidors for sale at flea markets, I am glad that I was never in a bar where people "spit." Most collectors are enamored by the brass cuspidor. The form came in many other varieties as well. You could build a marvelous collection focusing on pottery cuspidors.

Within the past year a large number of fake cuspidors have entered the market. I have seen them at flea markets across the United States. Double-check any cuspidor with a railroad marking and totally discount any with a Wells Fargo marking.

CUT GLASS

Collectors have placed so much emphasis on American Brilliant Cut Glass (1880 to 1917) that they completely overlook some of the finer cut glass of the post-World War I period. Admittedly, much cut glass in this later period was mass-produced and rather ordinary. But, if you look closely, you will find some great pieces.

The big news in the cut glass market at the end of the 1980s was the revelation that many of the rare pieces that had been uncovered in the 1980s were of recent origin. Reproductions, copycats, fakes abound. This is one category where you had better read a great deal and look at hundreds of pieces before your start buying.

Remember, the antiques and collectibles market is governed by *caveat emptor* (let the buyer beware).

Club: American Cut Glass Association, 1603 SE 19th, Suite 112, Edmond Professional Building, Edmond, OK 73013.

Bowl, Swirled Primrose pattern, sgd "Tuthill," 8¼" d, $500.00.

Ashtray, hobstar	40.00
Bell, hobstars, fans, and strawberry diamond	265.00
Bowl, 8" d, cross–cut diamond and fans	75.00
Bread Tray, hobstars, sgd "Clark"	275.00
Candlestick, 9½" h, teardrop stem, hobstar cutting and base	225.00
Celery, 11½", hobstars, cross hatch, and notched prisms, figured blank	70.00
Cheese and Cracker Dish, sterling silver rim	150.00
Cheese Dish, cov	250.00
Cologne Bottle, strawberry diamond, fans, and hobstars	150.00
Compote, Ribbon Star, rayed foot	275.00
Cruet, Butterfly and Daisy, Pairpoint	85.00
Door Knob, facet cut	25.00
Finger Bowl, Glenwood pattern, Bergen	65.00
Goblet, Russian, facet cut teardrop stem, rayed base	125.00
Jar, Prism and Cane, rayed base, sterling silver repousse lid, marked "Unger Bros"	75.00
Mustard, cov, Renaissance pattern, matching underplate	140.00
Nappy, Harvard pattern, engraved "Good Wishes," handle	200.00

Pitcher, tankard, Brunswick pattern, sgd "Hawkes"	500.00
Plate, Hindoo pattern, Hoare	115.00
Punch Cup, ring handle, hobstars and fans	45.00
Punch Ladle, 11½" l, cut and notched prism handle, sterling silver emb shell dec	150.00
Sherbet, Chicago pattern, Fry	75.00
Spooner	80.00
Syrup, 6" h, brilliant cut	265.00
Tray, 12" d, pinwheels, hobstars, and florals	115.00
Tumbler, Harvard, rayed base	45.00
Wine, hobstars, fans, and strawberry diamond	30.00

CZECHOSLOVAKIAN

Czechoslovakia was created at the end of World War I out of the area of Bohemia, Moravia, and Austrian Silesia. Although best known for glass products, Czechoslovakia also produced a large number of pottery and porcelain wares for export.

Czechoslovakia objects do not enjoy a great reputation for quality, but I think they deserve a second look. They certainly reflect what was found in the average American's home from the 1920s through the 1950s.

Salt and pepper shakers, toby jugs, blue coats, red pants, 2¼" h, pr, $18.00.

Bookends, pr, Pouter Pigeon	45.00
Bowl, yellow int., black ext., polished pontil	45.00
Cologne Bottle, 4", blue, glossy, bow front	12.00
Container, head, fisherman, hat lid	75.00
Cup and Saucer, pheasant	32.50
Dish, frosted, cameo inset, filigree, ftd	45.00
Perfume Bottle	
Engraved design, amber frosted flowers, stopper, 5"	25.00

113

Cut, no stopper	**38.00**
Pitcher, 4" h, red black handle	**15.00**
Plate, 10" d, Art Deco, maiden, black and yellow, 1920s	**50.00**

DAIRY ITEMS

The dairy industry has been doing a good job for decades of encouraging us to drink our milk and eat only real butter. The objects used to get this message across as well as the packaging for dairy products has long been a favorite with collectors. Concentrate on the material associated with a single dairy, region, or national firm. If you try to collect one example of every milk bottle used, you simply will not succeed. The amount of dairy collectibles is enormous.

Periodical: *The Milk Route*, 4 Ox Bow Road, Westport, CT 06880.

Hot Pad Holder, Kriebel's Dairies, muslin, hemp backing, 4¼" sq, $1.50.

Bank, Rutter Bros Dairy Products, dairy truck, plastic, white, red decal, c1960	**40.00**
Booklet, Jones Milk Co, color lithos, giveaway, 1935	**18.00**
Box, Bing Crosby Ice Cream	**5.00**
Brochure, Eskimo Pie, premium, c1952	**15.00**
Bucket, Sunny Field Lard, 4 lbs	**28.00**
Clock	
Garst Bros Dairy, double globe	**125.00**
Sealtest Milk	**75.00**
Creamer	
Anthony's Cream	**13.00**
Rosebud Dairy	**9.00**
Doilies, Carver Ice Cream, linen–like, emb, Christmas, 1920s, pkg of 12	**10.00**

Milk Bottle	
Quart	
Borden Weiland, emb, round	**20.00**
VM&I Co, emb, amber	**50.00**
1½ Gallon, Gail Borden, amber	**22.00**
Milk Bottle Cap, Deerfoot Farms, Southborough, MA	**5.00**
Milk Can, plain	**10.00**
Mug, Elsie in daisy on outside, Elsie head on inside bottom	**35.00**
Punch Out Train, Borden, 1950s	**80.00**
Ruler, Breyer Ice Cream, colorful	**15.00**
Sign	
Borden, tin, red	**55.00**
Meiers Ice Cream, porcelain	**65.00**
Thermometer	
Primrose Dairy Products	**60.00**
Sealtest Milk, carton	**75.00**
Tie Clasp, Elsie medallion, c1930	**35.00**
Tip Tray, DeLaval	**85.00**

DEARLY DEPARTED

I know this category is a little morbid, but the stuff is collected. Several museums have staged special exhibitions devoted to mourning art and jewelry. Funeral parlors need to advertise for business.

I did not put one in the listings, but do you know what makes a great coffee table? A coffin carrier or coffin stand. Just put a piece of glass over the top. It's the right size, has leg room underneath, and makes one heck of a conversation piece.

Book, *Champion Expanding Encyclopedia of Embalming*, Champion Chemical Co, Springfield, OH, added to monthly, 9" x 12", approx 30 pgs each month, 1923–1928	**32.00**
Booklet, *Incineration*, by John B Beugless, United States Cremation Company, Ltd, 9¾" x 6", Portland vase pictured on front, 14 pgs and wraps	**18.00**
Bottle, poison	
Coffin, 3¼" h, cobalt blue, diamond design, emb "poison"	**6.00**
Triangle Poison, blue, label, skull and crossbones, Warner Co	**8.00**
Casket Plate, brass, "Rest in Pease," mounted	**27.00**
Catalog	
HS Eckels and Co, Philadelphia, PA, "Derma Surgery with Complete Catalog of Embalmer's Supplies," 9" x 12", 324 pgs, c1927	**35.00**
Springfield Metallic Casket Company, 6¼" x 9¼", folding casket carriages and pedestals, 24 pgs and wraps	**30.00**
Fan, adv	
Sisler Bros, Inc, Fine Monuments, 8½" x	

7½", cardboard, garden and mountain scene, multicolor, advertising on reverse, 11"l wooden handle....... **25.00**

Swallow Funeral Home, cardboard, four panel, folding, floral bouquet illustration, advertising on reverse...................... **30.00**

Jewelry, mourning

Ring, 18K gold, seed pearls, one diamond, locket on inside of shank, enamel "In Memory Of" on shank, English...................... **300.00**

Stickpin, gold, round, black enamel "In Memory Of," lock of hair under glass, c19th C..................... **165.00**

Memorial, 3⅜" x 4¼", abalone shell, watercolor, applied straw, paper willow, tomb, German inscription, black lacquered frame.................... **55.00**

Mortician's Basket, woven, adult size.... **125.00**

Mourning Picture, 8⅜" x 10⅜", watercolor, paper memorial, tomb, inscription, matted, gilt frame, dated 1810........ **65.00**

Pinback Button, adv

1¼" d, angel at cemetery plot, "Tag Day, Ninette Sanatorium," multicolor, 1910s...................... **8.00**

1¼" d, funeral wagon, "Pan–American, Pass Bearer One Way, Rock Falls Mfg Co, Sterling, IL," 1901–1910 ...... **12.50**

1¾" d, multicolor, man lying in coffin, two tall candlesticks, wheat, "This Man Died From Overwork, Trying To Beat The Parsons Feeder," 1896–1900 .... **85.00**

Post-Mortem Set, mahogany case, saws, scalpels, hooks.................. **485.00**

Remembrance Card, 4⅛" x 6⅜", cardboard, diecut, gold lettering and illus on black ground, 1888.................... **6.00**

Umbrella, black, "Beck & Fisher Funeral Home" on handle **35.00**

DEEDS

Deeds and copies of deeds are a common sale item at a country sale. Many eighteenth- and early nineteenth-century deeds are on parchment. In most cases, value is minimal, ranging from a few dollars to a high of $10.00.

First, most of the deeds are copies. The actual document is often on file in the courthouse. Second, check the signatures. Benjamin Franklin signed a number of Pennsylvania deeds. These are worth a great deal more then $10.00. Third, check the location of the deed. If it is a city deed, the current property owner may like to acquire it. If it is for a country farm, forget it.

Finally, a number of early deeds have an elaborate wax seal at the bottom. Framed, these make wonderful display pieces in attorney's offices. When this occurs, the price charged has little to do with the intrinsic worth of the deed. Sock it to the attorney— charge decorator prices.

DEGENHART GLASS

Degenhart pressed-glass novelties are collected by mold, by individual color, or by group of colors. Hundreds of colors, some rather close to one another in tone, were produced between 1947 and 1978. Prior to 1972 most pieces were unmarked. After that date a "D" or "D" in a heart was used.

Do not confuse Kanawha's bird salt and bow slipper or L. G. Wright's mini-slipper, daisy and button salt, and 5" robin covered dish with Degenhart pieces. They are close, but there are differences. See Gene Florence's *Degenhart Glass and Paperweights: A Collector's Guide To Colors And Values* (Degenhart Paperweight and Glass Museum: 1982) for a detailed list of Degenhart patterns.

Club: The Friends of Degenhart, Degenhart Paperweight and Glass Museum, Inc., P. O. Box 186, Cambridge, OH 43725.

Priscilla, Degenhart Green, $125.00.

Animal Dishes, covered

Hen, 3"

Dark Green **25.00**

Pigeon Blood	48.00
Robin, taffeta	50.00
Turkey	
Amethyst	50.00
Slag, gray	80.00
Bicentennial Bell	
Canary	15.00
Heatherbloom	4.00
Peach	8.50
Candy Dish, cov, wildflower, crystal	15.00
Creamer and sugar, Texas, pink	45.00
Cup Plate, Seal of Ohio, amethyst	15.00
Eldena Doll, blue–green slag	6.00
Hand	
Blue and White	20.00
Persimmon	8.00
Hat, Daisy and Button	
Custard	20.00
Opalescent	12.00
Jewelry Box, Heart, fawn	18.00
Owl	
Frosty Jade	45.00
Sunset	25.00
Willow Blue	48.00
Paperweight, Peacock Feather	50.00
Pooch Dogs	
April Green	15.00
Ivory Slag	20.00
Priscilla, Crown Tuscan	75.00
Salt, Daisy and Button, bittersweet	15.00
Salt and Pepper Shakers, pr, Birds, antique	
blue	20.00
Shoe, high button boot, light blue	25.00
Slipper, bow, caramel	30.00
Tomahawk	
Blue Bell	23.00
Emerald Green	23.00
Toothpick Holder	
Baby Shoe, pearl gray	15.00
Beaded Oval, teal	18.00
Daisy and Button, dichromatic	24.00
Forget–Me–Not, heatherbloom	20.00
Heart, crystal	7.50]

DEPRESSION GLASS

Specialize in one pattern or color. Once again, there is no way that you can own every piece made. Also, because Depression Glass was produced in vast quantities, buy only pieces in excellent or better condition.

Depression Glass refers to glassware made between 1920 and 1940. It was mass-produced by a number of different companies. It was sold cheaply and often given away as a purchasing premium.

A number of patterns have been reproduced. See Gene Florence's *The Collector's Encyclopedia of Depression Glass* (Collector Books, revised annually) for a complete list of reproductions.

Club: National Depression Glass Association, Inc., P. O. Box 1128, Springfield, MO 65808.

Newspaper: *The Daze*, Box 57, Otisville, MI 48463.

ADAM

Made by Jeannette Glass Company, 1932–1934. Made in pink, green, crystal, yellow, and delphite blue. Heavily reproduced.

Adam pattern, candlesticks, pink, 3¾" h, pr, $65.00.

Bowl	
4¾" d, dessert	
Green	8.75
Pink	10.00
9" d, cov, vegetable	
Green	60.00
Pink	40.00
Butter Dish, cov	
Green	225.00
Pink	72.00
Cake Plate, 10" d, ftd	
Green	18.00
Pink	18.00
Creamer	
Green	18.00
Pink	15.00
Cup and Saucer	
Green	20.00
Pink	18.00
Plate	
7¾", sq, salad	
Green	8.00
Pink	7.50
9", sq, dinner	
Green	17.50
Pink	18.00
Sherbet, 3"	
Green	30.00
Pink	20.00
Sugar	
Green	15.00
Pink	12.00

AMERICAN SWEETHEART

Made by MacBeth–Evans Glass Co, 1930–1936. Made in pink, monax, red, blue, cremax, and color-trimmed monax.

Bowl
3¾" d, berry, pink 25.00
6" d, cereal
  Cremax 8.00
  Monax 12.00
  Pink 10.00
11" l, oval, vegetable
  Monax 45.00
  Pink 32.00
Creamer
  Monax 8.00
  Pink 7.00
Cup and Saucer
  Blue 90.00
  Monax 9.50
  Pink 12.00
  Red 130.00
Plate
8" d, salad
  Monax 6.00
  Pink 15.00
9¾" d, dinner
  Monax 13.00
  Pink 15.00
  Smoke, black rim trim 50.00
Platter
  Monax 40.00
  Pink 31.00
  Smoke, black rim trim 95.00
Salt and Pepper Shakers, pr
  Monax 210.00
  Pink 275.00
Sherbet, 4¼", ftd
  Monax 13.00
  Pink 10.00
  Smoke, black rim trim 30.00
Sugar, open, ftd
  Blue 70.00
  Monax 5.00
  Pink 5.00
  Smoke, black rim trim 60.00

BLOCK OPTIC

Hocking Glass Co, 1929–1933. Made in green, pink, yellow, crystal, and blue.

Bowl
5¼" d, cereal
  Green 10.00
  Pink 6.00
7" d, salad, green 17.00
Butter Dish, cov, green 40.00
Creamer
  Green 10.00
  Pink 9.00
  Yellow 10.00
Cup and Saucer
  Green 12.00
  Pink 10.00

Goblet, 4½"
  Green 28.00
  Pink 25.00
Pitcher, 8½" h, 54 oz
  Green 25.00
  Pink 27.50
Plate
8" d, luncheon
  Green 3.00
  Pink 2.50
  Yellow 3.75
9" d, dinner
  Green 13.00
  Pink 20.00
  Yellow 30.00
9" d, grill
  Green 9.00
  Pink 12.00
  Yellow 30.00
Salt and Pepper Shakers, pr, ftd
  Green 25.00
  Pink 55.00
  Yellow 60.00
Sherbet, 3¼" d
  Green 4.50
  Pink 6.00
  Yellow 7.00
Tumbler, 9 oz, ftd
  Green 12.00
  Pink 11.00
  Yellow 18.00

CHERRY BLOSSOM

Jeannette Glass Co, 1930–1939. Made in pink, green, delphite, crystal, jadite, and red. Heavily reproduced.

Bowl
4¾" d, berry
  Delphite 10.00
  Green 12.50
  Pink 13.00
9" d, vegetable
  Delphite 38.00
  Green 22.00
  Pink 20.00
Butter Dish, cov
  Green 75.00
  Pink 65.00
Cake Plate, 10¼" d
  Green 16.00
  Pink 15.00
Creamer
  Delphite 16.50
  Green 18.00
  Pink 15.00
Cup and Saucer
  Delphite 15.50
  Green 20.00
  Pink 16.50
Plate
7" d, salad
  Green 16.00
  Pink 14.50

9" d, dinner
Delphite 13.00
Green 17.50
Pink 15.00
Sherbet
Delphite 11.00
Green 13.50
Pink 14.00
Sugar
Delphite 15.00
Green 14.00
Pink 10.00
Tumbler, 9 oz, round foot, all over pattern
Delphite 15.00
Green 27.00
Pink 26.00

COLUMBIA
Federal Glass Co, 1938–1942. Made in crystal
and pink. Prices for both colors are very similar.

Columbia pattern, saucer, clear, $2.00.

Bowl, 5", cereal, crystal 13.50
Butter Dish, cov, ruby flashed cov 18.00
Cup and Saucer, crystal 6.00
Plate, 9½" d, luncheon, crystal 5.00
Snack Plate, crystal 30.00
Tumbler, 2⅛" h, juice, crystal 15.00

DAISY
Indiana Glass Co. Made in crystal, 1933;
fired–on red, 1935; amber, 1940; dark green
and milk glass, 1960s and 1970s.

Bowl
4½" d, berry
Amber or red 7.00
Crystal or green 4.00
6" d, cereal
Amber or red 22.50
Crystal or green 10.00
10" l, oval, vegetable
Amber or red 12.00
Crystal or green 8.00
Creamer, ftd
Amber or red 7.00

Crystal or green 5.00
Cup and Saucer
Amber or red 6.00
Crystal or green 3.50
Plate
6" d, sherbet
Amber or red 2.00
Crystal or green 1.00
8⅜" d, luncheon
Amber or red 5.00
Crystal or green 2.00
9⅜" d, dinner
Amber or red 7.00
Crystal or green 3.50
Relish Dish, three part
Amber or red 20.00
Crystal or green 10.00
Sherbet
Amber or red 8.50
Crystal or green 3.50
Sugar, ftd
Amber or red 6.50
Crystal or green 3.00

FLORAL
Jeannette Glass Co, 1931–1935. Made in pink,
green, delphite, jadite, crystal, amber, red, and
yellow.

Bowl
4" d, berry
Delphite 25.00
Green 12.00
Pink 11.00
9" d, vegetable
Green 12.00
Pink 10.00
Butter Dish, cov
Green 75.00
Pink 70.00
Candy Jar, cov
Green 34.00
Pink 27.50
Creamer
Cremax 50.00
Delphite 65.00
Green 10.00
Pink 9.00
Cup and Saucer
Green 15.00
Pink 12.50
Pitcher, 8" h, 32 oz, ftd, cone
Green 25.00
Pink 20.00
Plate
8" d, salad
Green 8.00
Pink 7.50
9" d, dinner
Delphite 110.00
Green 13.50
Pink 11.00
Relish Dish, 2 part, oval
Green 11.00
Pink 10.00

Sherbet
Delphite	**75.00**
Green	**13.00**
Pink	**11.00**

Sugar
Cremax	**50.00**
Delphite	**55.00**
Green	**8.50**
Pink	**7.50**

Tumbler, 9 oz, ftd
Green	**35.00**
Pink	**32.50**

FOREST GREEN
Anchor Hocking Glass Co, 1950–1957. Made in forest green.

Ashtray	**3.00**

Bowl
4¾" d, dessert	**4.00**
6" d, soup	**9.00**
Creamer	**4.50**
Cup and Saucer	**3.25**
Mixing Bowl Set, 3 nested bowls	**25.00**

Plate
6¾" sq, salad	**2.00**
8⅜" sq, luncheon	**4.00**
10" sq, dinner	**15.00**
Punch Bowl	**10.00**
Punch Cup	**1.75**
Sugar	**5.00**
Vase, 4" d, ivy	**3.00**

IRIS
Jeannette Glass Co, 1928–1932; 1950s, 1970s. Made in crystal, iridescent, pink, recently in bi–colored red/yellow and blue/green, as well as white.

Bowl
5" d, sauce, ruffled
Crystal	**6.00**
Iridescent	**15.00**

7½" d, soup
Crystal	**80.00**
Iridescent	**35.00**

11½" d, fruit, ruffled
Crystal	**8.50**
Iridescent	**6.00**

Butter Dish, cov
Crystal or iridescent	**27.50**
Coaster, crystal	**40.00**

Creamer, ftd
Crystal	**7.00**
Iridescent	**8.00**

Cup and Saucer
Crystal	**15.00**
Iridescent	**14.00**

Plate
5½" d, sherbet
Crystal	**8.00**
Iridescent	**7.00**
8" d, luncheon, crystal	**37.50**

9" d, dinner
Crystal	**35.00**

Iridescent	**30.00**

Sherbet, 2½"
Crystal	**15.00**
Iridescent	**10.00**

Sugar
Crystal	**6.00**
Iridescent	**6.50**

Tumbler, 6" h, ftd
Crystal	**12.00**
Iridescent	**12.50**

MAYFAIR
Hocking Glass Co, 1931–1937. Made in ice blue, pink, green, yellow, and crystal.

Bowl
5½" d, cereal
Blue	**37.50**
Green	**60.00**
Pink	**17.50**
Yellow	**60.00**

7" l, vegetable
Blue	**38.00**
Green	**100.00**
Pink	**17.50**
Yellow	**100.00**

Butter Dish, cov
Blue	**225.00**
Pink	**45.00**

Celery Dish
Blue	**32.00**
Green	**90.00**
Pink	**25.00**
Yellow	**90.00**

Creamer, ftd
Blue	**50.00**
Green	**175.00**
Pink	**18.00**
Yellow	**150.00**

Cup
Blue	**37.00**
Green	**125.00**
Pink	**15.00**
Yellow	**125.00**

Plate
6½" d, round, off center indent
Blue	**20.00**
Green	**100.00**
Pink	**20.00**

8½" d, luncheon
Blue	**27.50**
Green	**60.00**
Pink	**17.50**
Yellow	**60.00**

9½" d, dinner
Blue	**48.00**
Green	**100.00**
Pink	**37.50**
Yellow	**100.00**

9½" d, grill
Blue	**27.50**
Green	**60.00**
Pink	**27.50**
Yellow	**60.00**

Salt and Pepper Shakers, flat, pr
Blue **200.00**
Pink **45.00**
Yellow **750.00**
Sugar, ftd
Blue **50.00**
Green **165.00**
Pink **17.50**
Yellow **165.00**
Tumbler
3½" h, 5 oz, juice
Blue **80.00**
Pink **32.00**
4¾" h, 11 oz, water
Blue **85.00**
Green **150.00**
Pink **115.00**
Yellow **160.00**
5¼" h, 13½ oz, iced tea
Blue **135.00**
Pink **35.00**

MISS AMERICA (DIAMOND PATTERN)
Made by Hocking Glass Company, 1935–1937. Made in crystal, pink, some green, ice blue jadite, and red.

Bowl
6¼", berry
Crystal **6.00**
Pink **14.00**
Green **10.00**
10", oval, vegetable
Crystal **10.00**
Pink **17.50**
Butter Dish and Cover
Crystal **190.00**
Pink **435.00**
Cake Plate, 12", ftd
Crystal **17.50**
Pink **29.00**
Celery Dish, 10½", oblong
Crystal **8.00**
Pink **16.00**
Creamer, ftd
Crystal **6.50**
Pink **13.00**
Red **145.00**
Cup
Crystal **7.50**
Pink **16.00**
Green **8.00**
Pitcher, 8"
Crystal **40.00**
Pink **90.00**
Plate
8½", salad
Crystal **5.00**
Pink **15.00**
Green **8.00**
Red **65.00**
10¼", dinner
Crystal **10.00**
Pink **18.00**

Platter, 12¼", oval
Crystal **10.00**
Pink **18.00**
Salt and Pepper Shaker, pr
Crystal **22.50**
Pink **42.50**
Green **275.00**
Saucer
Crystal **2.50**
Pink **4.00**
Sugar
Crystal **6.00**
Pink **12.50**

OLD CAFE
Made by Hocking Glass Company, 1936–1938, 1940. Made in pink, crystal, and Royal Ruby.

Bowl
3¾", berry
Crystal **2.00**
Pink **2.00**
Royal Ruby **4.00**
5½", cereal
Crystal **4.00**
Pink **4.00**
Royal Ruby **8.50**
9", closed handles
Crystal **7.50**
Pink **7.50**
Royal Ruby **11.50**
Cup
Crystal **3.00**
Pink **3.00**
Royal Ruby **6.00**
Pitcher, 6"
Crystal **50.00**
Pink **50.00**
Plate
6", sherbet
Crystal **1.50**
Pink **1.50**
10", dinner
Crystal **20.00**
Pink **20.00**
Saucer
Crystal **1.50**
Pink **1.50**
Tumbler, 3", juice
Crystal **8.00**
Pink **8.00**
Royal Ruby **7.50**
Vase, 7¼"
Crystal **9.50**
Pink **9.50**
Royal Ruby **14.00**

OLD ENGLISH, THREADING
Made by Indiana Glass Company. Made in green, amber, pink, crystal, and forest green. Prices listed are for pink, green, and amber which all have the same value.

Bowl
4" **12.00**

9", fruit	22.50
Candlesticks, 4", pr	22.50
Compote, 7"	14.00
Creamer	14.00
Pitcher	50.00
Plate, indent for compote	17.50
Sandwich Server, center handle	40.00
Sugar	12.00
Vase, ftd	
8¼"	35.00
12"	40.00

PARROT, SYLVAN
Made by Federal Glass Company, 1931–1932.
Made in green, amber, some crystal and blue.

Bowl	
5", berry	
Amber	11.00
Green	14.00
7", soup	
Amber	25.00
Green	30.00
10", oval, vegetable	
Amber	50.00
Green	35.00
Butter Dish and Cover	
Amber	1,000.00
Green	240.00
Creamer, ftd	
Amber	35.00
Green	22.00
Cup	
Amber	25.00
Green	25.00
Pitcher, 8½", green	1,200.00
Plate	
5¾", sherbet	
Amber	12.00
Green	20.00
7½", salad, green	18.00
9", dinner	
Amber	27.50
Green	32.00
10¼", sq, green	25.00
Platter, 11¼", oblong	
Amber	50.00
Green	27.50
Saucer	
Amber	8.50
Green	8.50
Sugar	
Amber	20.00
Green	20.00
Tumbler, 5½", ftd, amber	110.00

PETALWARE
Made by MacBeth–Evans Glass Company,
1930–1940. Made in Monax, Cremax, pink,
crystal, cobalt and fired–on red, blue, green, and
yellow. Cremax, Monax, Florette, and fired–on
decorations have the same value as does pink
and crystal.

Bowl	
4½", cream soup	
Cremax	8.50
Pink	4.00
Plain	7.50
5¾", cereal	
Cremax	6.50
Pink	3.50
Plain	4.50
7", soup, plain	40.00
9", large berry	
Cobalt	40.00
Cremax	15.00
Pink	7.50
Plain	12.50
Red Trim Floral	45.00
Creamer, ftd	
Cobalt	25.00
Cremax	8.00
Pink	2.50
Plain	4.50
Red Trim Floral	15.00
Cup	
Cremax	6.00
Pink	2.50
Plain	4.50
Red Trim Floral	12.00
Mustard, metal cov, cobalt blue	8.00
Pitcher, pink, crystal dec bands	22.00
Plate	
6", sherbet	
Cremax	4.00
Pink	1.50
Plain	2.00
8", salad	
Cremax	6.00
Pink	1.75
Plain	3.00
Red Trim Floral	10.00
9", dinner	
Cremax	8.00
Pink	3.50
Plain	5.00
12", salver	
Cremax	15.00
Plain	6.50
Red Trim Floral	22.50
Platter, 13", oval	
Cremax	15.00
Pink	7.50
Plain	12.00
Saucer	
Cremax	2.50
Pink	1.00
Plain	1.50
Red Trim Floral	3.00
Sugar, ftd	
Cobalt	25.00
Cremax	7.50
Pink	2.50
Plain	4.50
Red Trim Floral	15.00

ROULETTE, MANY WINDOWS

Made by Hocking Glass Company, 1935–1939. Made in green, pink, and crystal. Pink and green have the same value.

Bowl, 9", fruit
Crystal	8.50
Pink	10.00

Cup
Crystal	34.50
Pink	4.25

Pitcher, 8"
Crystal	22.50
Pink	25.00

Plate

6", sherbet
Crystal	2.00
Pink	2.25

8½", luncheon
Crystal	4.00
Pink	4.00

12", sandwich
Crystal	9.00
Pink	9.00

Saucer
Crystal	1.25
Pink	2.25

Tumbler, 3¼", juice
Crystal	6.50
Pink	12.50

SANDWICH

Made by Hocking Glass Company, 1939–1964, 1977. Made in crystal, forest green, and white/ivory (opaque) 1950–1960, amber 1960s, pink 1939–1940, royal ruby 1939–1940.

Bowl

4 5/16"
Crystal	4.00
Forest Green	2.00

4⅞", ruffled, crystal ... 9.50

5¼", scalloped
Crystal	6.00
Ruby Red	15.00

6½", cereal
Crystal	20.00
Desert Gold	9.00

7", salad
Crystal	6.50
Forest Green	45.00

8", scalloped
Crystal	6.50
Ruby Red	30.00
Forest Green	50.00
Pink	13.00

8¼", oval, crystal ... 6.00

9", salad
Crystal	20.00
Desert Gold	22.50

Butter Dish, crystal ... 32.50

Cookie Jar
Crystal	30.00
Desert Gold	30.00

Forest Green	16.00

Creamer
Crystal	4.00
Forest Green	20.00

Cup
Crystal	1.50
Desert Gold	3.50
Forest Green	13.00

Custard Cup
Crystal	3.50
Forest Green	1.50

Pitcher, 6", juice
Crystal	45.00
Forest Green	95.00

Plate

7", dessert
Crystal	8.00
Desert Gold	8.00

8", crystal ... 3.00

9", dinner
Crystal	12.00
Desert Gold	7.00
Forest Green	52.50

12", sandwich
Crystal	9.00
Desert Gold	10.00

Punch Bowl, 9¾", crystal ... 15.00

Saucer
Crystal	1.00
Desert Gold	3.00
Forest Green	6.00

Sugar
Crystal	12.50
Forest Green	17.00

Tumbler
Juice, crystal	10.00

Water
Crystal	6.50
Forest Green	3.25

WINDSOR, WINDSOR DIAMOND

Made by Jeannette Glass Company, 1936–1946. Made in pink, green, crystal, some Delphite, amberina red, and ice blue.

Bowl

4¾", berry
Crystal	2.50
Green	7.00
Pink	5.00

5", cream soup
Crystal	4.50
Green	20.00
Pink	15.00

5⅛", cereal
Crystal	7.00
Green	15.00
Pink	12.00

8", pointed edge
Crystal	8.00
Pink	25.00

8½", large berry
Crystal	4.50
Green	12.00

Pink 10.00
9½", vegetable, oval
Crystal 5.00
Green 17.50
Pink 12.00
10½", salad, crystal 6.00
12½", fruit console
Crystal 20.00
Pink 75.00
Butter Dish
Crystal 22.50
Green 70.00
Pink 37.50
Candlesticks, 3", pr
Crystal 15.00
Pink 65.00
Creamer
Blue 55.00
Crystal 3.00
Green 8.00
Pink 7.50
Cup
Blue 55.00
Crystal 2.50
Green 7.00
Pink 6.00
Pitcher, 6¾"
Crystal 11.00
Green 40.00
Pink 18.50
Red 400.00
Plate
6", sherbet
Crystal 1.50
Green 3.50
Pink 2.50
7", salad
Crystal 3.00
Green 13.50
Pink 9.50
9", dinner
Blue 55.00
Crystal 3.50
Green 13.50
Pink 9.50
10¼", sandwich, handle
Crystal 4.00
Green 10.00
Pink 9.00
13⅝", chop
Crystal 7.50
Green 30.00
Pink 30.00
Platter, 11½", oval
Crystal 4.50
Green 12.00
Pink 10.00
Relish Platter, 11½", divided
Crystal 9.50
Pink 175.00
Salt and Pepper Shaker, pr
Crystal 12.50
Green 40.00
Pink 30.00
Saucer
Crystal 1.50
Green 3.00
Ice Blue 15.00
Pink 2.50
Sugar
Crystal 4.50
Green 22.00
Pink 17.50
Tray
4", sq, handles
Crystal 2.50
Green 8.00
Pink 6.00
8½" x 9¾"
Crystal 12.50
Green 35.00
Pink 75.00
Tumbler
3¼"
Blue 55.00
Crystal 6.00
Green 25.00
Pink 15.00
5"
Crystal 7.50
Green 37.50
Pink 20.00
7¼", ftd, crystal 10.00

DISNEYANA

"Steamboat Willie" introduced Mickey Mouse to the world in 1928. Walt and Roy Disney, brothers, worked together to create an entertainment empire filled with a myriad of memorable characters ranging from Donald Duck to Zorro.

Early Disney is getting very expensive. No problem. Disney continues to license material. In thirty years the stuff from the 1960s and 1970s is going to be scarce and eagerly sought after. Now is the time to buy it.

Club: Mouse Club, 2056 Cirone Way, San Jose, CA 95124.

Ashtray, Disneyland, 5" d, white china, pictures Tinkerbell and castle, gold accents, 1950s–1960s 20.00
Bank
Donald Duck, ceramic, Leeds, 1940s 45.00
Pluto, 6½" h, ceramic, figural, late 1940s 50.00
Book, *Mickey And His Friends*, 6" x 8", hard cov, published by Thomas Nelson and Sons, 1937, 104 pgs 40.00
Card Game, Ferdinand the Bull, 5" x 6½" x 1" orig box, Whitman, copyright 1938 Disney Enterprises 35.00

Toy, fire truck, Sun Rubber Co, Mickey and Donald, painted red, yellow, black, and silver, $65.00.

Charm, Mickey Mouse, 1¼", disc, enamelled, full body, WDP **12.00**

Charm Bracelet, Cinderella, brass link, five painted brass charms, orig 2" x 5½" brass box and cellophane slip cover, copyright Disney Productions, c1950. . . . . **35.00**

Crayon Holder, Dopey, ceramic, figural **50.00**

Figurine

Bambi

Flower, American Potteries **45.00**

Owl, American Potteries **145.00**

Thumper, 2½", American Potteries. **55.00**

Tramp, Lady and the Tramp, Japan. . . . **55.00**

Flashlight, Mickey Mouse, 6" l, tin litho, USA–Lite, mid-1930s **100.00**

Glass, 5" h, Maleficent, black, purple, fleshtone, and yellow, sword and shield on back, inscribed "Maleficent Bestows The Terrible Gift From Walt Disney's Sleeping Beauty," from set of 6, 1958. . . . . **30.00**

Hand Puppet, Donald Duck, Gund, 1949. . . . . **15.00**

Little Golden Book, *Walt Disney's Pinocchio*, copyright 1948 . . . . **12.50**

Lunch Box, The Fox and the Hound, steel, emb, Aladdin, copyright 1981. . . . . **25.00**

Magic Slate, Winnie the Pooh, 8½ x 13½", cardboard, two plastic sheets, missing stylus, 1965 . . . . **10.00**

Map, 18 x 24", Peter Pan's Neverland, premium, aerial view of island, inscribed "This Map Is A Collectors Limited Issue, Dedicated to the users of Peter Pan Beauty Bar with Chlorophyll," c1953. . . . . **100.00**

Marionette, Alice in Wonderland **65.00**

Milk Pitcher

Dumbo, 6" h, ceramic, white glaze, 1940s **65.00**

Mickey Mouse, 7" **60.00**

Mug, Minnie Mouse, 3" h, china, white glazed, colorful transfer, Minnie holding mirror and hairbrush, Patriot China. **85.00**

Pillow, Mickey Mouse, Vogue, 1932 . . . . **95.00**

Program, serviceman's, wartime Mickey and Minnie, 1944 . . . . **40.00**

Puzzle, 10" x 12" x 1", Sleeping Beauty, copyright 1958, set of 3 . . . . **40.00**

Salt and Pepper Shakers, pr, 5" h, figural, Alice in Wonderland, white glazed china, gold accents, c1951. . . . . **125.00**

Song Sheet, *Mickey Mouse Wedding Party*, 1936. . . . . **75.00**

Valentine, Donald Duck, 3½" x 4½", mechanical, diecut cardboard, copyright 1939. . . . . **30.00**

Wallet, 3" x 4", Davy Crockett, plastic, pictures trees and Indian teepees, colorful, c1955. . . . . **25.00**

Wristwatch, Mickey Mouse

Bradley, Swiss made **46.00**

Ingersoll, red leather band, WDP. **125.00**

DOG COLLECTIBLES

The easiest way to limit your collection is to concentrate on the representations for a single breed. Many collectors focus only on three-dimensional figures. Whatever approach you take, buy pieces because you love them. Try to develop some restraint and taste and not buy every piece you see. Easy to say, hard to do!

Advertising mirror, Mascot Crushed Cut Tobacco, 2⅛" d, $25.00.

Bank, cast iron

Retriever, 3⅜" h, with pack, traces of black paint **50.00**

Scottie, 5" h, white, no key. **60.00**

Candy Container, glass **10.00**

Doorstop

Airedale, 4¾" **90.00**

Boston Bulldog, full figure. **50.00**

German Shepherd, standing **40.00**
Russian Wolfhound **155.00**
Figure
Bone China
Boxer, 3½"h **5.00**
Chihuahua, 3¼"h **4.00**
Cast Metal, Scottie, 1¾"h **10.00**
Chalkware, Rin Tin Tin, 19" **50.00**
Composition, Scottie, 8½"x 10½" **30.00**
Earthenware, Springer Spaniel, 3¾" x
5¾", hp nose and eyes, airbrushed . . . **6.00**
Glass, 2¾" h, frosted, gold collar, red
eyes **11.00**
Porcelain
Collie, 5½" x 8¼", "Made in Ja-
pan" **10.00**
English Bulldog, 3⅛"h **7.00**
Poodle, 9½" x 9½", "Made in Aus-
tria" **75.00**
Planter, Scottie, 5"x 6", chalkware **9.00**
Pin, Scottie, Bakelite, black **75.00**
Record, "Train Your Dog," Lee Duncan,
12¼" sq cardboard album, 33 1/3 rpm,
1961, produced by Carlton Record
Corp. **15.00**
Tape Measure, red and white, collie and
company slogan on one side, Armco
Steel logo on other, inscribed "Lyle Cul-
vert and Road Equipment Co, Minne-
apolis" **18.00**

Note: The dolls listed date from the 1930s through the present. For information about antique dolls, see Jan Foulke's *10th Blue Book Dolls and Values* (Hobby House Press: 1991) and R. Lane Herron's *Herron's Price Guide To Dolls* (Wallace—Homestead: 1990).

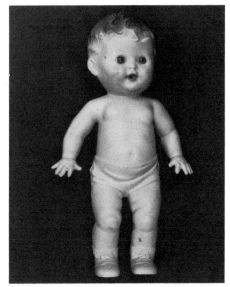

Sun Rubber, Tod–L–Dee, one pc body, molded painted hair, molded diaper and shoes, 10½" l, $25.00.

DOLLS

People buy dolls primarily on the basis of sentiment and condition. Most begin by buying back the dolls with which they remember playing as a child.

Speculating in dolls is risky business. The doll market is subject to crazes. The doll that is in today may be out tomorrow.

Place great emphasis on originality. Make certain that every doll you buy has the complete original costume. Ideally, the box or packaging also should be present. Remember, you are not buying these dolls to play with. You are buying them for display.

Magazines: *Doll Reader*, Hobby House Press, Inc., 900 Frederick Street, Cumberland, MD 21502; *Dolls—The Collector's Magazine*, P. O. Box 1972, Marion, OH 43305.

Clubs: Madame Alexander Fan Club, P. O. Box 146, New Lenox, IL 60451; Ginny Doll Club, 305 West Beacon Road, Lakeland, FL 33803; United Federation of Doll Clubs, P. O. Box 14146, Parkville, MO 64152.

Advertising
Aunt Jemima, rag doll, stuffed. **45.00**
Campbell Kids, vinyl, partially dressed,
pr **25.00**
Choo Choo Charlie, Good 'N Plenty . . . **24.00**
Conchita Banana, cloth, 1970s **10.00**
Green Giant Sprout **22.00**
Smokey Bear, cloth, Ideal, 1950s **60.00**
(Madame) Alexander Doll Co, plastic and
vinyl
Caroline, 15" **225.00**
Jenny Lind and Cat, 14" **300.00**
Marlo Thomas, 17" **350.00**
Peter Pan, 15" **250.00**
Sound of Music, Marta, 8" **150.00**
American Character Doll Co
Annie Oakley, 17", hard plastic **190.00**
Chuckles, 23" **125.00**
Composition Babies, 14", cloth body,
marked "AC" **90.00**
Little Miss Echo, 30", talker **115.00**
Ricky Jr, 13" **45.00**
Arranbee Doll Co
Nanette, 14", hard plastic **130.00**
Storybook Dolls, 10", composition,
molded hair, painted eyes **105.00**

125

Cabbage Patch, Coleco
  1983, #2, bald, small eyes, freckles,
    blue stripe sleeper **150.00**
  1984, #1, Black preemie, knit outfit . . . **45.00**
  1986, #12, cornsilk hair **30.00**
Celluloid Dolls
  Baby, 12″, jointed, painted hair and
    features, orig clothes, marked "Ja-
    pan". **75.00**
  Blonde Hair, 8″, sleepy eyes, organdy
    dress. **55.00**
  Twin Black Babies, pr **27.50**
Character and Personality
  Captain and Tenille, pr **70.00**
  Angela Cartwright, 15″ h. **35.00**
  Cher. **35.00**
  Farrah Fawcett **32.00**
  Laverne and Shirley, pr **80.00**
  Lone Ranger **10.00**
  Diana Ross **55.00**
  Fred Sanford, rag. **32.00**
Comics Dolls
  Fred Flintstone, 6½″, cloth, Knicker-
    bocker **14.00**
  Huckleberry Hound, Knickerbocker,
    1959. . . . . **25.00**
  Skeezix, 13″, oilcloth. **85.00**
  Snoopy, plush, eleven outfits, orig
    bag. **20.00**
  Sweet Pea, "The World of Popeye,"
    MIB **18.00**
Effanbee Doll Co
  Babykin, 10″, composition **45.00**
  Button Nose, 18″, vinyl, cloth **35.00**
  Fluffy, 10″, Girl Scout, vinyl. **32.00**
E. I. Horsman Co
  Baby Tweaks, 20″, cloth, vinyl, inset
    eyes, 1967 . . . . **26.00**
  Betty Jane, 25″, plastic, vinyl. **45.00**
  Crawling Baby, 14″, vinyl, 1967 . . . . . . **25.00**
  Jackie   Kennedy,   25″,   marked
    "Horsman   JK,"   plastic,   vinyl,
    1961. . . . . **110.00**
Ideal Novelty and Toy Co
  Bizzy Lizzy, 17″, plastic, vinyl **22.00**
  Goody Two Shoes, 18″. **70.00**
  Tammy, 12″, 1962 . . . . **34.00**
Mattel, Inc
  Baby Go Bye Bye, 12″ **15.00**
  Barbie
    1969, Twist 'n Turn **85.00**
    1971, Growing Pretty Hair, bendable
      knees **250.00**
    1975, Free Moving. **65.00**
    1978, Super Size, 18″. **95.00**
    1981, Western **25.00**
  Chatty Cathy, 20″ **57.00**
  Ken, Live Action **60.00**
  Midge, 11½″, bendable legs, 1965 . . . . . **85.00**
Raggedy Ann and Andy Dolls
  Andy, 19″, Georgene, tag, orig
    clothes **135.00**

Ann
  Georgene, 14″, no tag. **75.00**
  Handmade, 1930s **95.00**

DOOR HARDWARE

Door hardware is collected for its ornate
and unusual design. The same is true for
doorknobs and knockers. Push plates fall
largely within the advertising sphere.

Stress condition. A rusted and pitted example should be avoided unless extremely
rare. Excellent sources are individuals and
firms who make a living tearing down old
buildings. Talk to them before they start.
Once they get rolling, they destroy things
quickly and with little concern for salvage.

Watch   out   for   reproductions   and
copycats. They can be identified by the
poor detail in the castings and a difference
in weight when felt.

*Door Push, American Special Flour, emb litho
tin, red, white, and blue, $50.00.*

Door Push, adv, Kellam's teas and cof-
  fees. **50.00**
Hinges, ironware
  18″, pr **40.00**
  36″, pr **85.00**
Knockers
  Brass
    Bust of Will Rogers. **65.00**
    Dog's head, 7″ **65.00**
    Eagle, figural, large **55.00**
    Owl, 3½″ h **35.00**
  Bronze
    Grecian head, 4½″ **80.00**

Lion's head, loose ring knocker **50.00**
Cast Iron
Couple kissing **80.00**
Fruit cluster **22.00**
Ram's head, English **65.00**
Latch
Brass, $7\frac{1}{2}''$, iron bar, keeper **35.00**
Ironware, butterfly **75.00**
Lock, 4" x 6", ironware, turn handle with key, c1840 .... **100.00**

DOORSTOPS

Doorstops have gone through a number of collecting crazes over the past twenty years. The last craze occurred just a few years ago. The latest craze has driven prices up to a level where you now are more likely to find doorstops at an antiques show than at a flea market.

Reproductions abound. A few helpful clues are: (1) check size (many reproductions are slightly smaller than the period piece); (2) check detail (the lesser the detail, the more suspicious you need to be); and (3) check rust (a bright orange rust indicates a new piece).

Golfer, red coat, gray pants, green grass, 10" h, $450.00.

Boston Terrier, $8\frac{1}{4}''$ **75.00**
Cape Cod, $5\frac{3}{4}''$ x $8\frac{3}{4}''$, Albany Foundry ... **125.00**
Cat, by flower, 5" x $6\frac{1}{4}''$ **100.00**
Cinderella Carriage, $9\frac{3}{4}''$ x 19" **175.00**
Conestoga Wagon, 8" x 11" **95.00**
Cornucopia and Roses, $10\frac{1}{4}''$, cast iron, orig paint **85.00**
Doll on Base, $4\frac{1}{2}''$ x $4\frac{7}{8}''$ **100.00**
Flower Basket, $5\frac{7}{8}''$ x $5\frac{5}{8}''$, National Foundry **75.00**
Frog, 3" x $5\frac{1}{4}''$ **45.00**
Little Girl by Wall, $4\frac{1}{4}''$ x $3\frac{1}{4}''$, Albany Foundry **160.00**
Pansy Bowl, 7" x $6\frac{1}{2}''$, Hubley **125.00**
Parrot, in ring, 8" x 7" **100.00**
Peacock, $6\frac{1}{4}''$ x $6\frac{1}{4}''$ **150.00**
Poppies and Cornflowers, $7\frac{1}{4}''$ x $6\frac{1}{2}''$, Hubley **115.00**
Shepherd, 9", iron, sitting, bronzed, #275 .... **95.00**
Ship, cast iron **50.00**
Shoe, high heel **75.00**
Whippet, $6\frac{3}{4}''$ **110.00**

DRINKING GLASSES, PROMOTIONAL

It is time to start dealing seriously with promotional glasses given away by fast food restaurants, garages, and other merchants. The category also includes drinking glasses that start out life as product containers.

Most of the glasses are issued in series. If you collect one, you better plan on keeping at it until you have the complete series. Also, many of the promotions are regional. A collector in Denver is not likely to find a Philadelphia Eagles glass at his favorite fast food restaurant.

Just a few washings in a dishwasher can seriously change the color on promotional drinking glasses. Collectors insist on unused, unwashed glasses whenever possible. Have the glass put in a paper bag, drink your drink out of a paper cup.

A & W, The Great Root Beer **9.00**
Arby's, name in stain glass look, 5" h..... **3.50**
Big Boy, 50th anniversary............. **3.00**
Burger Chef, Burger Chef and Jeff Go Trail Riding, 1976 .... **8.00**
Burger King
1978, See These Burgers **11.00**
1979, Sir Shake A Lot **5.00**
Domino's Pizza, Noid at the Beach **3.00**
Kentucky Fried Chicken, bucket and balloon **6.50**
MacDonald's
1977, MacDonaldland Series, Big Mac on roller skates, $5\frac{5}{8}''$.............. **3.50**
1980, Adventureland Series, Grimace climbs a mountain **6.50**
1983, Camp Snoopy **3.00**

Pizza Hut, ET Collector Series, Be Good,
1982.......................... **2.50**
Pizza Time Theater, Chuck E Cheese..... **4.50**
Popeye's Fried Chicken, Swee' Pea,
1979.......................... **10.00**
Wendy's, Cleveland Browns, Brian Sipe,
1981.......................... **5.00**

DRUGSTORE COLLECTIBLES

The corner drugstore, especially those with a soda fountain, was a major hangout center in almost every small town in the United States. Almost all of them dispensed much more than drugs. They were the 7–11s of their era.

This category documents the wide variety of material that you could acquire in a drugstore. It bearly scratches the surface. This is a new collecting approach that has real promise.

Box, Deer Skin Prophylactic Rubbers, silver and red, 2¼" × 2" × ¾", $5.00.

Blotter, Smith Brothers.............. **25.00**
Booklet, Royal Tooth Powder, 1890s **23.00**
Bottle
  Mrs Allen Hair Restorer, amber....... **10.00**
  Woodwards Chemist, cobalt......... **7.00**
Box
  Bootjack Plug Tobacco, labels, plug still
  inside....................... **68.00**
  Cutex Deluxe, wood, art Deco, gift
  set......................... **85.00**
  Feen–A–Mint Chewing Gum Laxa-
  tive........................ **20.00**
  Smith Brothers Cough Drops, 39" x 18"
  x 10", wood **75.00**
Calendar, Colgate, miniature, flower,
1901......................... **15.00**
Chalkboard, Hambone 5¢ Cigar, 13" x
20"......................... **65.00**
Clock, Rexall, double face, lights up **155.00**

Display, Peter Rabbit Safety Pins, colorful
cartoon **25.00**
Fan
  666 Laxative **17.50**
  Tums, 1920s **18.50**
Glass, Bromo Seltzer................ **25.00**
Honing Stone, pocket size, Bagley's Sweet
  Tips Tobacco **30.00**
Lunch Pail, Tiger Chewing Tobacco,
  red **125.00**
Mirror
  People's Drug, birthstones, pocket **20.00**
  Pond's Extract, 15" x 17", bevel edge,
  oak frame..................... **165.00**
  Star Soap, pocket................. **20.00**
Needle Case, Bromo Seltzer **10.00**
Playing Cards, Speedy Alka Seltzer...... **30.00**
PostCard, Speedy Alka Seltzer **15.00**
Shaker, Blue Rexall Foot Powder, tin **15.00**
Sign
  Dolly Madison Cigar, 6" x 20", tin **20.00**
  Keen Kutter, 27", tin **55.00**
  Nature's Remedy, porcelain **265.00**
Song Book, Alka–Seltzer, 1937 .... **10.00**
Thermometer
  Ex–Lax, 8" x 36", porcelain.......... **135.00**
  Ramon's Kidney & Laxative Pills, 8½" x
  21", wood, c1930............... **175.00**
Tin
  Bayer's Aspirin, 7" d............... **100.00**
  Century Tobacco, factory graphics, flat,
  pocket **110.00**
  Golden Pheasant Condom **88.00**
  Lucky Strike Cut Plug, flat **16.00**
  Ramsey's Condoms, 1929.......... **60.00**
  Three Merry Widows, condoms **25.00**
  Velvet Night Talc **26.00**

EASTER COLLECTIBLES

Now that Christmas and Halloween collectibles have been collected to death, holiday collectors finally are turning their attention to Easter Collectibles. The old Easter bonnet still hangs in the Clothing Collectibles closet, but chicken and rabbit collectors now have to contend with Easter collectors for their favorite animal collectible.

Newsletter: *Hearts to Holly: The Holiday Collectors Newsletter*, P. O. Box 105, Amherst, NH 03031.

Basket
  3" x 5", printed cardboard, pastel colors,
  trimmed with colored eggs, USA,
  1930s....................... **7.00**
  8" d, yellow metal, metal handle, rabbits
  and chicks painted on outside, Chein
  Toy Co **15.00**

Candy Mold, four eggs, $80.00.

Collectors place a premium on character eggcups. You can make a great collection consisting of egg cups from breakfast services of hotels, railroads, steamships, or restaurants. As tourists, many of our ancestors has a bad case of sticky fingers.

Finally, do not forget the various scissorlike devices designed to decapitate the egg. Would you even recognize one if you saw one? I saw one once at a flea market marked as a circumcision device. *Ouch!*

Candy Container
Chick and Egg, 6" h, papier mache, yellow chick, black glass eyes, standing next to egg candy container, USA ... **55.00**
Duck, 4" h, yellow composition, ribbon around neck, standing on 3" d round cardboard box, opens at base, Germany **35.00**
Rabbit, 8" h, pot belly, white, head and ears on wire spring, white glass beaded trim, separates at belt line, marked "US Zone, Germany" **15.00**
Chick, 2" h, cotton batting, wire legs, paper beak, marked "Japan" **18.00**
Egg
Bisque, 2 pc, cupid, dove with letter, German **150.00**
China, daisies, gold dec, Dresden **35.00**
Glass, 5" l, white, opaque, painted spring scene, "Happy Easter" painted in gold trim. **25.00**
Postcard, "Bright and Happy Easter for You," Gibson Girl kissing chick in garden. **1.25**
Rabbit
1½" h, diecut, multicolored, marked "Germany" **1.25**
5" h, plastic, hard, mother rabbit dressed in yellow, brown glasses **7.00**

EGGCUPS

Where modern Americans would be hardpressed to recognize, let alone know how to use, an eggcup, their European counterparts still utilize the form as an everyday breakfast utensil. Their greatest period of popularity in America was between 1875 and 1950 — long before cholesterol became a four-letter word.

A plain white porcelain eggcup works just as well as a fancifully decorated one. The fact that so many different and highly decorative eggcups exist show our unwillingness to accept the mundane at the breakfast table.

Willow Ware, marked "Japan," 3¾" h, $18.50.

Belleek, Irish, basketweave, pink rim, first black mark...................... **150.00**
Character, ceramic
Lone Ranger, 2½" h, raised portrait, Lone Ranger Inc. copyright on base, c1950...................... **35.00**
Supercar, 2¼" h, white, raised Supercar, marked "Keele St. Pty. Co, Ltd., England," 1962 AP Film Ltd copyright........................ **80.00**
French Porcelain, blue floral dec, white ground, marked "Made In France," pr........................... **30.00**
Indian Tree Pattern, 4" h, marked "John Maddock & Sons, Ltd" **25.00**
Limoges, 2½" h, multicolored florals, marked "Limoges, France".......... **12.00**
Meissen, Blue Onion pattern **20.00**
Quimper, peasant man, yellow ground, marked "Henriot Quimper, France"... **35.00**
Torquay, 1¾" h, cottage dec, motto "Straight From The Nest," Watcombe Pottery...................... **12.00**
Wedgwood, Caneware, brown scrolling vine dec, c1820 .... **275.00**
Willow Ware, blue, marked "Wood and Sons".......................... **15.00**

ELEPHANT COLLECTIBLES

Public television's unending series of documentaries on African wildlife have destroyed the fascination associated with wild animals. By the time parents take their children to the zoo or circus, elephants are old hat, blasé. Boo, hiss to public television — those pompous pachyderms. We want the mystery and excitement of wildlife returned to us.

Things were different for the pretelevision generations. The elephant held a fascination that is difficult for us to comprehend. When Barnum brought Jumbo from England to America, English children, and a fair amount of adults, wept.

There are a few elephant-related political collectibles listed. It is hard to escape the G.O.P. standard–bearer. However, real elephant collectors focus on the magnificent beasts themselves or cartoon representations ranging from Dumbo to Colonel Hathi.

Club: The National Elephant Collector's Society, 380 Medford Street, Somerville, MA 02145.

Figurine, ceramic, white ground, rust, yellow, and blue dec, marked "China," 2" × 3", $.50.

Advertising Trade Card, Clark's O N T Spool Cotton, Jumbo Aesthetic, elephant walking on hind legs 5.00
Bank, 6½", Elsie, metal, head figure, Master Caster Mfg Co, Chicago, 1950 . . . . . 75.00
Bookmark, 7½", cardboard, triangular shape, text "Here's Walt Disney's Dumbo Of The Circus And His Little Pal Timothy," c1940 . . . . 25.00
Cheese Cutting Board, 8" x 13", elephant shape, cherry hardwood 85.00
Chocolate Mold, tin, three cavities 75.00
Doorstop, 10", cast iron 25.00

Figure
Dumbo, 5½", china, Shaw Pottery, mid 1940s 100.00
Fantasia Elephant, 5½" h, ceramic, wearing pink dress, American Pottery 150.00
Pin, 3 /4" x 1", elephant shape, inscribed "Carlsberg Beer," diecut, silvered brass 15.00
Pinback Button, 1½", elephant shape, inscribed "Willkie," silvered brass 10.00
Toy
Squeaker, 6½", Dumbo, rubber, moveable head, Walt Disney Productions copyright, 1950s 20.00
Windup, 3" x 6" x 4½", tin litho, red, yellow, and green design, riding blanket on bank, c1930 . . . . 125.00

ELVIS

Dad grew up with Elvis and ignored him. Always knew he was a bit of a prude. Fortunately, millions of others did not. Elvis was hot, is hot, and promises to be hot well into the future. Elvis is a collectible that is bought from the heart, not the head. A great deal of totally tacky material has been forgiven by his devoted fans.

Elvis material breaks down into two groups: (1) items licensed while Elvis was alive and (2) items licensed after his death. The latter are known as "fantasy" items. Fantasy Elvis is collectible, but real value rests with the material licensed during his lifetime.

Beware of any limited edition Elvis. It was manufactured in such large numbers that its long-term prospect is very poor. If you love it, fine. If you expect it to pay for your retirement, forget it.

Belt, metal, gold colored, intricate mesh, two eagle head fasteners, "Russian Double Eagle" 48.50
Book, *The Elvis Presley Story*, 160 pgs, 1960, Hillman Books. 35.00
Bracelet, dog tag, 2' x 6½", orig insert card and plastic bag, 1956 . . . . 40.00
Calendar, 11" sq, full color glossy, 1963, RCA 30.00
Decanter, musical, 1955 . . . . 55.00
Necklace, chain, heart, dated 1956 . . . . . . 45.00
Poster, 21' x 27", Girls! Girls! Girls!, color, 1960, Paramount film 5.00
Purse, clutch, 1956 . . . . 35.00
Scarf, concert souvenir 10.00
Sheet Music, *Love Me Tender*, pinktone

Whiskey Bottle, McCormick, second in series, $90.00.

Plastic, white ovals with winglike flair at
upper edge on each side, c1950s **3.00**

FAIRY TALE COLLECTIBLES

Thank goodness for fairies. They keep the
line between myth and reality blurred.
Where would children be without the
tooth fairy or Cinderella without her fairy
godmother? I have told some fairy tales in
my time that I hoped the listener would
believe were true.

This category is a celebration of the characters and the tales. It also celebrates the
spirit of fairy tales — the hopes and
dreams. There is a pot of gold at the end of
rainbows, isn't there?

Clock, Snow White, Walt Disney, Bayard/Blance Neige, marked "Made in France Par autorisation Walt Disney," $75.00.

photo cov, copyright 1956 Elvis Presley
Music Inc, 2 pgs **25.00**
Tab Pin, 2" d, tin, litho, orange and blue
lettering on white ground, "I Love
Elvis," c1970s **20.00**

EYEGLASSES

Look around. Eyeglasses come in all shapes
and sizes. There are even designer models.
Form and shape changes to correspond
with subsequent fashion shifts. Yet, given
all this, the number of eyeglass collectors is
relatively small. Existing collectors love
this, it keeps prices very low.

Do not forget those cool shades. I am
constantly amazed at what people are
willing to wear when it comes to protecting
their eyes from the sun. You could create a
pizazz collection if you simply concentrated
on 1950s sunglasses.

Eyeglasses
Driving glasses, white leather side
pieces **25.00**
Plastic tortoise shell rims, near round
glasses, c1950s **75.00**
Safety glasses, round glasses, mesh
protection pieces on side, original
box **20.00**
Wire rims, oval glass, c1900, nerd glasses **5.00**
Sunglasses
Plastic, purple frames with round glasses, c1965 .... **2.00**

Big Little Book, *The Laughing Dragon of Oz,*
Whitman, 1934 .... **75.00**
Book
A Year With The Fairies, Anna Scott, P F
Volland, 1914, 99 pgs **95.00**
Dance of the Hours from Fantasia, Walt
Disney, Harper, 1940 .... **40.00**
Once Upon A Monday, Dixie Willson,
Volland, 1931 .... **16.00**
Rumpelstiltskin, Edith Tarcov, Four
Winds, 1974, 46 pgs **45.00**
The Black Stallion Races, Walter Farley,
Random House, 1955 .... **18.00**
The Land of Oz, 64 pgs, Rand McNally,
1939 copyright. **40.00**
The Legend of the Tulip and Other Fairy

Flowers, Isidora Newman, Whitman,
1926. . . . .   **9.00**
Bracelet, "Who's Afraid of the Big Bad
Wolf," silvered brass, black, green, and
yellow accents, early 1930s. **125.00**
Case, Alice In Wonderland, 4″ × 11″ ×
8½″, heavy cardboard, white plastic
handle, Neevel, Disney copyright
1951. . . . . **40.00**
Children's Dishes, dinnerware set, Alice in
Wonderland, 17 pcs, service for four,
beige, Plasco **40.00**
Christmas Card, Peter Pan, 4″ × 5″, diecut,
orig envelope, c1953 . . . . **10.00**
Doll, Limited Edition, Edwin M. Knowles,
Heroines from the Fairy Tale Forests of
the Brother's Grimm
Goldilocks, 1989 . . . . **65.00**
Little Red Riding Hood **70.00**
Figure, Snow White, 5″ h, china, Japan,
c1960. . . . . **20.00**
Game, The Wonderful Game of Oz, 1921
Parker Brothers **300.00**
Plaque, 13″ × 16″, figural, Cinderella,
diecut laminated cardboard, 1951 copy-
right. **20.00**
Puppet, hand, Pinocchio, 10″, velvet body,
molded cardboard head with flocking,
c1940. . . . . **125.00**
Sheet Music, *Over The Rainbow*, 9¼″ ×
12¼″, brown tone photo **30.00**
Snowdome, Jiminy Cricket, 3″ × 3″ ×
1½″, plastic, black base, diecut red and
white figure, inscribed on base "Jiminy
Cricket Award For Outstanding Com-
munity Chest Service 1958" **100.00**

FARM COLLECTIBLES

The agrarian myth of the rugged individual
pitting his or her mental and physical talents against the elements remains a strong
part of the American character in the
1990s. There is something pure about returning to the soil.

The Country look heavily utilizes the objects of rural life, from cast-iron seats to
wooden rakes. This is one collectible where
collectors want an aged, i.e., well worn,
appearance. Although most of the items
were factory-made, they have a
handcrafted look. The key is to find objects
that have character about them, a look that
gives them a sense of individuality.

Club: Cast Iron Seat Collectors Association, RFD #2, Box 40, Le Center, MN
56057

Pinback button, black work horse, white
ground, 1¼″ d, $10.00.

Chick Feeder, tin **15.00**
Corn Dryer, wrought iron **15.00**
Egg Candler, 8″ h, tin, kerosene burner,
mica window. **20.00**
Feed Bag, cotton, black illus of sheep **7.50**
Hay Rake, varnished, 48½″ l **50.00**
Hinge, barn, wrought iron, strap, 27″ l . . . **60.00**
Implement Seat, cast iron, Hoover &
Co **65.00**
Milking Stool, wooden, three short
legs. **50.00**
Pinback Button, Brinker Ranch, 1″ d,
multicolored, woman in Western outfit,
feeding chickens, c1930 . . . .   **8.00**
Sap Spout, wood, carved. **5.00**
Sheep Shears, 13¾″ l, steel, marked "Cast
Steel, W P Ward". **20.00**
Shovel, cast iron, wooden handle **25.00**

FARM TOYS

The average age of those who play with
farm toys is probably well over thirty. Farm
toys are adult toys. Collectors number in
the tens of thousands. The annual farm toy
show in Dyersville, Ohio, draws a crowd in
excess of 15,000.

Beware of recent limited and special edition farm toys. The number of each toy
being produced hardly qualifies them as
limited. If you buy them other than for enjoyment, you are speculating. No strong resale market has been established. Collectors who are not careful are going to be
plowed under.

Magazines: *Miniature Tractor and Implement*, R. D. #1, Box 90, East Springfield,
PA 16411; *The Toy Farmer*, R. R. #2, Box 5,

LaMoure, ND 58458; *The Toy Tractor Times,*
P. O. Box 156, Osage, IA 50461.

Club: Ertl Replica Collectors' Club, Highways 136 and 10, Dyersville, IA 52040

Tractor, Ertl Co, International, metal and plastic, 1:32 scale, $55.00.

Baler, International Harvester, diecast, 1/
  16 scale, four bales, Ertl, 1967 . . . . **18.00**
Bulldozer, Caterpillar, driver, yellow,
  Matchbox, 1963 . . . . **20.00**
Combine, Marx, tin, friction, MIB. **25.00**
Corn Picker, Tru–Scale, pressed steel, 1/
  16 scale, Carter, 1971 . . . . **70.00**
Disc, International Harvester, diecast, 1/
  16 scale, sure–lock hitch blades, Ertl,
  1965. . . . . **20.00**
Elevator, John Deere, pressed steel, 1/16
  scale, Carter, 1960. . . . . **85.00**
Harrow, tandem disc, Corgi, 1967,
  MIB **12.00**
Industrial Crawler, Lionel, plastic, 1/43
  scale, 1950. . . . . **35.00**
Planter, White **15.00**
Tractor
  Allis Chalmers, plastic, 1/25 scale, Beaver Falls Show insert, Yoder. **75.00**
  Ford, red, rubber tires, Tootsietoy **25.00**
Truck, Dodge Farm Truck, Dinky,
  1950s. **25.00**
Wagon, Minneapolis Moline, pressed
  steel, 1/32 scale, rubber wheels, Slik,
  1950. . . . . **20.00**

FAST FOOD COLLECTIBLES

If you haunt fast food restaurants for the food, you are a true fast food junkie. Most collectors haunt them for the giveaways. If you stop and think about it, fast food collectibles are the radio and cereal premiums of the second half of the twentieth century. Look at what you have to eat to get them.

Whenever possible, try to preserve the original packaging of the premiums. Also, save those things which are most likely to be thrown out. I see a great many Happy Meals toys and few Happy Meals boxes. Dad saves fast food company bags. There is no accounting for taste.

Club: For Here or To Go, P. O. Box 162281, Sacramento, CA 95816.

*McDonald's, Ronald McDonald, cloth, 16½" h,
$7.50.*

A & W
  Decals, sheet, iron–on, Root Beer Bear
    and A & W logo, 1977 . . . . **2.50**
  Puppet, hand, Root Beer Bear, cloth . . . **6.50**
Burger King
  Frisbee, plastic, 3¾" d, emb with Burger
    King character **6.50**
  Pinback, ¾" d, metal, "Happy Face,"
    eyes made of the Burger King Corporate logo **3.50**
  Crown, jewellike design, "Have It Your
    Way" slogan **7.00**
Carl's Jr
  Meal Box, Star Flyer, flying saucer,
    cardboard, 1985. . . . . **2.50**
  Ring, plastic, Happy Star character in
    center of circle **2.75**
Dairy Queen, toy, 5", Noid, plastic,
  poseable and bendable, 1987 . . . . **5.00**
Kentucky Fried Chicken
  Meal Box, "Colonel's Kids," features
    Foghorn Leghorn, 1987. . . . . **2.00**
  Nodder, Colonel Sanders, plastic, early
    1970s. **10.00**
McDonald's
  Bank, plastic, McDonaldland,
    wastebasket, 1975 . . . . **7.50**
  Colorforms Playset, premium, 1986 . . . **2.00**
  Radio, french fry, 1st version, AM,
    1977. . . . . **25.00**

133

FENTON ART GLASS

Frank L. Fenton founded the Fenton Art Glass Company as a glass-cutting operation in Martins Ferry, Ohio, in 1905. In 1906 construction began on a plant in Williamstown, West Virginia. Production began in 1907 and has been going on ever since.

The list of Fenton glass products is endless. Early production included carnival, chocolate, custard, pressed, and opalescent glass. In the 1920s stretch glass, Fenton dolphins, and art glass were added. Hobnail, opalescent, and two–color overlay pieces were popular in the 1940s. In the 1950s Fenton began reproducing Burmese and other early glass types.

Throughout its production period, Fenton has made reproductions and copycats of famous glass types and patterns. Today these reproductions and copycats are collectible in their own right. Check out Dorothy Hammond's *Confusing Collectibles: A Guide to the Identification of Contemporary Objects* (Wallace–Homestead: 1979, revised edition) for the clues to spotting the reproductions and copycats of Fenton and other glass manufacturers of the 1950s and 1960s.

Club: Fenton Art Glass Collectors Of America, Inc., P. O. Box 384, Williamstown, WV 26187.

Cruet, Opalescent Hobnail, cranberry shading to white, applied clear handle, orig clear hobnail stopper, $65.00.

Basket, Burmese, Maple Leaf **35.00**
Bowl, 11", jade, flared **40.00**
Cake Plate, Spanish Lace, green pastel . . . **40.00**

Candlesticks, Silver Crest, cornucopia, pr **45.00**
Candy Dish, Rosalene, Ogee, 3 pc **85.00**
Compote, orange, Roses pattern **8.00**
Creamer and Sugar, French opalescent, hobnail, mini **15.00**
Cruet, Jamestown blue **32.00**
Egg, pedestal, ebony, white flowers **50.00**
Goblet, Colonial amber, Empress, sticker **7.50**
Hat, Black Crest, #1923 . . . . **55.00**
Lamp, boudoir, Coin Dot, blue opalescent **40.00**
Kettle, hobnail, milk glass, #3990 . . . . . . **7.00**
Perfume, Silver Crest, melon rib **10.00**
Vase, Dolphin, jade, 6"

FIESTA WARE

Fiesta was the Melmac ware of the mid-1930s. The Homer Laughlin China Company introduced Fiesta dinnerware in January 1936, at the Pottery and Glass Show in Pittsburgh, Pennsylvania. It was a huge success.

The original five colors were red, dark blue, light green (with a trace of blue), brilliant yellow, and ivory. Other colors were added later. Redesigned in 1960, discontinued in 1972–1973, and reintroduced in 1986, Fiesta appears destined to go on forever.

Values rests in form and color. Forget the rumors about the uranium content of early red colored Fiesta. No one died of radiation poisoning from using Fiesta. However, rumor has it that they glowed in the dark when they went to bed at night.

Fruit bowl, cobalt blue, 11⅝" d, $90.00.

Ashtray, turquoise............... 25.00
Bowl
   4¾", rose..................... 22.00
   5½", green 3.00
   6½", gold 4.00
   9", green..................... 10.00
Candlesticks, pr
   Bulbous, ivory................ 45.00
   Tripod, pink, pr 85.00
Chop Plate, 13", ivory.............. 17.00
Compote, 12", turquoise............ 75.00
Creamer, red, stick handled 27.00
Cup
   Chartreuse.................... 25.00
   Light blue.................... 12.00
Deep Plate
   Light Green 20.00
Egg Cup, turquoise 25.00
Gravy Boat, light blue............. 32.00
Jug, 2 pint, light green............. 39.00
Juicer, cobalt.................... 20.00
Mug
   Forest green.................. 40.00
   Gray........................ 40.00
Nappy, 8½", red 32.00
Pitcher
   Disc, juice, yellow 27.00
   Disc, water, red 75.00
Plate
   6", dessert, yellow 3.00
   7½", bread and butter, chartreuse 9.00
   9", luncheon, yellow............ 6.00
   10", dinner
      Light Green 17.00
      Rose...................... 30.00
Platter, chartreuse................ 35.00
Refrigerator Dish, lid, Kitchen Kraft,
   round, blue 75.00
Relish Tray, light blue.............. 18.00
Salt and Pepper Shakers, red–orange,
   pr.......................... 15.00
Saucer
   Chartreuse.................... 4.00
   Rose........................ 3.00
Soup, lid, cobalt and cream.......... 35.00
Sugar, cov, red................... 28.00
Tumbler, light blue 22.50
Vase, red, 6½"................... 25.00

FIGURINES

Looking for a "small" with character? Try collecting ceramic figurines. Collecting interest in the colorful figurines produced by firms such as Ceramic Arts Studio, Florence Ceramics, Vernon Kilns, and others has grown considerably during the past ten years. Pieces are starting to become pricy. However, there are still bargains to be found. A surprising number of these figu-rines are found at garage sales and flea markets at prices below $10.00.

Fair Lady, #2193, Royal Doulton, $100.00.

Accordion Boy, Ceramic Arts Studio 68.00
Alden, John, Florence Ceramics, 9¼" 70.00
Alice in Wonderland with White Rabbit,
   pr, Ceramic Arts Studio............ 60.00
Archibald the Dragon, Ceramic Arts Stu-
   dio 70.00
Arthur, boy with chicken, Brayton Pot-
   tery......................... 35.00
Baby Weems, Vernon Kilns 250.00
Bali Hai, Ceramic Arts Studio 35.00
Bedtime Boy and Girl, pr, Ceramic Arts
   Studio 30.00
Bernhardt, Sarah, Florence Ceramics,
   13¼".......................375.00
Blynken, Florence Ceramics, 5½" 55.00
Bride and Groom, Brayton Pottery 45.00
Cat, Kay Finch Ceramics, 6" 45.00
Comedy and Tragedy, pr, Ceramic Arts
   Studio 85.00
Dumbo, Vernon Kilns 110.00
Figaro, playing, tail up, Brayton Pot-
   tery......................... 95.00
Fruit Girl, Abingdon Pottery, 10" 90.00
Genevieve, Florence Ceramics 95.00
Geppetto, Pinocchio on lap, Brayton Pot-
   tery.........................300.00
Hiawatha, Ceramic Arts Studio........ 22.00
Kneeling Nude, Abingdon Pottery, 7" 160.00
Lady Diana, Florence Ceramics, 10" 140.00
Mary and Lamb, pr, Ceramic Arts Stu-
   dio 30.00
Pioneer Sam and Susie, pr, Ceramic Arts
   Studio 40.00
Russell, Lillian, Florence Ceramics,
   13¼".......................300.00

Scarf Dancer, Abingdon Pottery, 13" **160.00**
Shepherdess and Fawn, Abingdon Pottery, 11½" **90.00**
Spanish Dance Man and Woman, pr, Ceramic Arts Studio **75.00**
Sprite, Vernon Kilns **135.00**
The Girls, three girls, one with doll, Brayton Pottery **90.00**
Unicorn, Vernon Kilns **300.00**

FIREARMS

A majority of Americans own firearms. However, many have them and do not use them. Neglecting to properly care for a firearm can seriously damage its value. Avoid any weapons that show heavy use or the slightest signs of rust.

Before selling or buying a handgun, check federal, state, and local laws. Modern handguns must be sold only by a licensed federal firearms dealer. Do not take a chance by selling outside the law.

Gun collectors are a world unto their own. They buy and sell through specialized gun shows. Check your local paper for the one closest to you.

A surprising number of firearms have low value. Do not be deceived by age. Age alone does not make a gun valuable. The key is collectibility.

The following sampling bearly scratches the surface. For antique firearms consult Norman Flayderman's *Fladyerman's Guide To Antique American Firearms....And Their Values, 4th Edition* (DBI Books, 1987). For modern weapons, see Russell and Steve Quetermous's *Modern Guns: Identification & Values, Revised 8th Edition* (Collector Books: 1991).

Newspaper: *Gun List*, 700 East State Street, Iola, WI 54990.

Handgun
Beretta Model 1923, .9mm Luger, semi−automatic, exposed hammer, 9−shot clip, 4" barrel, blued, wood grips **250.00**
Charter Arms Bulldog, .44 Special, single action, 5−shot swing out cylinder, 4" barrel, blued, checkered walnut bulldog grips **135.00**
Colt Peacemaker, .22 caliber, single action, 6−shot cylinder, side load, 7½" barrel, case-hardened frame, black composite rubber grips **175.00**
High Standard Sentinel Mark II, .357

Magnum, single action, 6−shot swing out, 4" barrel, blued, checkered walnut grips **150.00**
Ruger Mark I Target, .22 long rifle, semiautomatic, concealed hammer, thumb safety, 9−shot clip, 6" tapered round barrel, blued, checkered hard rubber grips **125.00**
Sterling, Model 283, .22 long rifle, semi−automatic, exposed hammer, adjustable trigger, rear safety lock, 10−shot clip, 8" heavy bull barrel, blued, checkered plastic grips **120.00**
Rifle
Colt Coltsman, Sako−Medium, .308 Winchester, medium stroke, Sako−type bolt action, repeating, five shot box, 24" blued barrel, checkered walnut Monte Carlo one piece pistol grip stock **275.00**
Marlin Model 65, .22 caliber, bolt action, single shot, 24" round barrel, pistol grip stock and grooved forearm **50.00**
Military, British, Lee−Enfield, No. 1 SMLE MK1, .303 caliber, bolt action, curved bolt handle, 10−shot detachable box with cut−off, 25¼" barrel, plain wood military stock **140.00**
Military, United States, U.S. M1 Carbine, .30 M1 caliber, semi−automatic, gas operated, 30 shot staggered row detachable box, 18" barrel, one-piece wood stock and forearm **350.00**
Remington Nylon 11, .22 caliber, bolt action, repeating, 10 shot clip, 19½" round barrel, polished brown nylon one piece stock **75.00**
Shotgun
Bretta Model A−301, 12 gauge, gas−operated, semi−automatic, hammerless, 3−shot tubular, 30" full barrel, checkered walnut pistol grip stock and forearm **300.00**
High Standard Supermatic Field, 20 gauge, semi-automatic, gas operated, hammerless, 3−shot tubular, 26" barrel, plain walnut semi−pistol grip stock and fluted forearm **150.00**
Remington Model 27, 20 gauge, slide action, hammerless, bottom ejection, repeating, 3−shot tubular, 32" stell in full barrel, checkered walnut pistol grip and forearm **225.00**
Savage, 12 guage, regular, slide action, hammerless, side ejecting, repeating, 4−shot tubular, 28" modified barrel, hardwood semi−pistol grip stock and grooved side handle **150.00**
Winchester, Model 23 Pigeon Grade, lightweight, 20 gauge, magnum, box lock, top lever, breaks open, hammerless, selective automatic

ejectors, double barrel, 26″ modified barrel, Winchoke, checkered walnut semi–pistol grip stock and forearm **900.00**

FISH SETS

The Victorians had special china and silver serving pieces for every type of fruit, vegtable, and meat. There is no reason to expect fish to be treated any differently. Victorian and early twentieth century fish serving sets are desirable and elegant.

Some dealers break up sets feeling there is more profit in the individual piece than in the set. Do not buy from them. A minimum set consists of a serving platter and four to six plates. A sauce boat and other accessory pieces are a bonus.

Plate, brown fish, green border, blue flowers, marked "Austria," 8 ⅜″ d, $25.00.

8 pcs, four plates, 24″ platter, sauce boat with attached underplate, cov tureen, Rosenthal **350.00**
11 pcs, ten plates, platter, Limoges **350.00**
13 pcs, twelve sq plates with six different fishing scenes, rect sauce boat, cobalt blue border, gilt dec, underglaze green Limoges mark **275.00**
14 pcs, twelve plates, platter, gravy boat, hp bass, blue beehive mark **250.00**
15 pcs, twelve 9″ plates, 24″ platter, sauce boat with attached underplate, cov tureen, hp, raised gold dec edge, artist sgd, Limoges **750.00**

FISHING COLLECTIBLES

There has been a lot written recently about the increasing value of fishing tackle of all types. What has not been said is that high ticket items are very limited in number. The vast majority of items sell below $5.00.

Fishing collectors place strong emphasis on condition. If a rod, reel, lure, or accessory shows heavy use, chances are that its value is minimal. The original box and packaging are also important, often doubling value.

You will make a good catch if you find early wooden plugs made before 1920 (most that survive were made long after that date), split bamboo fly rods made by master craftmen (not much value for commercial rods), and reels constructed of German silver with special detail and unique mechanical action. Fishing collectors also like to supplement their collection with advertising and other paper ephemera. Find a pile of this material and you have a lucky strike.

Club: National Fishing Lure Collectors Club, P. O. Box 1791, Dearborn, MI 48121.

Creel, wicker, ribbed bow front, straight back, 12″ l, $25.00.

Advertising
Catalog, Heddon Co, color illus, 1934. . . . . **45.00**
Sign, South Bend Co, boy holding stringer of fish **65.00**
Bobber, 5″ l, panfish float, hp, black, red, and white stripes **10.00**
Creel, crushed willow, 14″ × 9″ × 7″, leather bound, form fit. **24.00**
Decoy
Oliver Reigstad, 1960 . . . . **17.00**
Sletten, cast aluminum, unopened, 1950s. **22.00**

Lure, wood
  Creek Chub Co, baby beetle, yellow and
    green wings 35.00
  Heddon, Frog pattern, crazy crawler,
    wood 35.00
  Paw Paw, underwater minnow, green
    and black, tack eyes, three hook 15.00
  Shakespeare Co, Mouse, 3⅝" l, white
    and red, thin body, glass eyes. 27.00
Reel
  Hendryx, raised pillar type multiplying,
    nickel over brass, fancy handle, horn
    knob, two buttons on back plate drag/
    click 25.00
  Winchester, Model #1135, fly, black
    finish 60.00
Rod, Split Bamboo Fly
  Horrocks & Ibbotson, 9' l, 3 pc, two tips,
    maroon wraps 40.00
  Union Hardware, Kingfisher, 7½' l,
    saltwater boat rod, dark brown
    wraps 25.00

FLAGS AND FLAG COLLECTIBLES

There certainly has been a great deal of flag waving as a result of operations Desert Shield and Desert Storm. Collectors have already salted away "yellow ribbon" flags. They have forgotten a basic rule of collecting — the more made, the less likely to have value in the future. Ask anyone who owns a forty-eight star flag.

Flags themselves are difficult to display. Old flags are quite fragile. Hanging them often leads to deterioration. If you own flags, you should be aware of flag etiquette as outlined in Public Law 829, 7th Congress, approved December 22, 1942.

Many collectors do not collect flags

Automobile Ornament, tin, red, white, and blue litho, 6" × 4", $5.00.

themselves but items that display the flag as a decorative motif. A flag-related sheet music collection is one example.

Club: North American Vexilological Association, 3 Egdehill Road, Winchester, MA 01890.

Advertising Trade Card, Major's Cement,
  two American flags decorating display
  of 125 lb weights 10.00
Bread Plate, flag. 22.00
Catalog, Detra Flag Company, Catalog
  #24 . . . . 40.00
Flag
  4" × 5¾", silk, child's parade, 49 stars,
    wood stick 18.00
  7½" × 12", silk, 46 stars 25.00
  16" × 24", muslin, parade, 37 stars,
    1867–1877 . . . . 40.00
  12½" × 22", coarse muslin, 38 stars,
    mounted on stick 12.00
Handkerchief, US and France flags, embroidered, "To My Dear Sweetheart,"
  WWI 5.00
Pin, 1", diecut, brass, flying flag shape,
  "God Bless America" inscription 12.00
Plate, 10" d, "Washington's Headquarters, Newburg, NY, 1783–1883," crossed flags under house, cream, brown printing 25.00
Poster, 14" × 29", lithograph, "History of Old Glory". 145.00
Sheet Music, "The Triumphant Banner,"
  E T Paull 25.00
Stickpin, brass, diecut, enameled, flag centered in victory wreath, c1898 . . . . 15.00

FLUE COVERS

When someone hears "flu" in the 1990s, they immediately think of a cold. There aren't many individuals left who remember wood– and coal–burning kitchen and parlor stoves. When the stovepipe was removed for the summer, for cleaning, or for repair, the exhaust flue in the wall needed to be covered. The answer was a flue cover.

A flue cover is generally round with a small section of chain attached to the back so that the cover can be hung from a nail in the wall. They were made from a variety of materials. Covers that sport a pretty woman or advertising have the most value.

Girl Holding Flowers, glass 30.00
"Hoover For President," tin, litho, 8" d,
  c1928. . . . . 40.00
Mountain Landscape, glass. 38.00
Parlor Scene, Victorian, glass, 9" d. 40.00
Rural Winter Landscape, brass 15.00
Seasons, multicolor, stamped, tin 15.00

138

FOOD MOLDS

Commercial ice cream and chocolate molds appear to be the collectors' favorites. Buying them is now a bit risky because of the large number of reproductions. Beware of all Santa and rabbit molds.

Country collectors have long touted the vast array of kitchen food molds, ranging from butter prints to Turk's head cake molds. Look for molds with signs of use and patina.

Do not forget the Jell–O molds. If you grew up in the 1950s or 1960s, you ate Jell–O and plenty of it. The aluminum Jell–O molds came in a tremendous variety of shapes and sizes. Most sell between ten cents and one dollar, cheap by any stretch of the imagination.

Chocolate, rabbit, marked "E & Co, 4746," 8¹/₂" × 9¹/₂", $75.00.

Butter, 4¹/₄" h, hexagonal, cased, strawberry design, pewter bands **75.00**
Cheese, 5" × 13", wood, carved design, branded "Los," carved date 1893 . . . . . **45.00**
Chocolate
  Basket, single cavity **45.00**
  Hen on basket, clamp type, 2 pcs, marked "E & Co/Toy" **45.00**
  Rabbit, 12" × 10", four cavities **48.00**
Cookie, pewter, wood back, six classical heads **45.00**
Ice Cream
  Black child killing turkey, marked "E & Co" **75.00**
  Castle, chess game piece, marked "S & Co" **60.00**
Pudding, 6", tin, fluted sides **10.00**
Turk's head
  Redware, 7", brown sponged rim **40.00**
  Yellow ware, 8", brown splotches **45.00**

FOOTBALL CARDS

Football cards are "hot." It was bound to happen. The price of baseball cards has reached the point where even some of the common cards are outside the price range of the average collector. If you cannot afford baseball, why not try football?

Football card collecting is not as sophisticated as baseball card collecting. However, it will be. Smart collectors who see a similarity between the two collecting areas are beginning to stress Pro-Bowlers and NFL All-Stars. Stay away from World Football material. The league is a loser among collectors, just as it was in real life.

Newspapers: *Current Card prices*, P. O. Box 480, East Islip, NY 11730; *Sports Collectors Digest*, 700 East State Street, Iola, WI 54990.

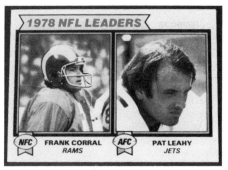

Topps, NFL Leaders, Frank Corral and Pat Leahy, $.10.

Bowman Gum Company
  1948
    Common Card **2.25**
    Harry Gilmer **15.00**
  1951
    Common Card **1.50**
    Tom Landry **20.00**
  1953
    Common Card **1.20**
    Frank Gifford **18.00**
  1955
    Common Card **1.00**
    Norm Van Brocklin **8.00**
Fleer Gum Company
  1960
    Common Card . . . . **.35**
    Sammy Baugh **6.50**
  1962
    Common Card . . . . **.30**
    George Blanda **5.50**
Philadelphia Gum Company
  1964
    Common Card . . . . **.25**
    Jim Brown **18.00**

1966
  Common Card 20
  Fran Tarkenton 5.25
1967
  Common Card 20
  Don Meredith 5.00
Topps Chewing Gum Inc
1950
  Common Card 2.25
  Joe Paterno 20.00
1955
  Common Card 1.00
  Knute Rockne 10.00
1958
  Common Card 30
  John Unitas 5.00
1961
  Common Card 25
  Jack Kemp 4.50
1964
  Common Card 25
  Len Dawson 4.00
1967
  Common Card 20
  Joe Namath 6.00
1970
  Common Card 15
  Bart Starr 2.25
1974
  Common Card 05
  Fran Tarkenton 1.50
1978
  Common Card 05
  Tony Dorsett 3.00

Tape Measure, Yale, blue bulldog and football, made by "Ehrmann Mfg Co, Boston, MA," $30.00.

Bubble Gum Card, Joe Namath, #96,
  Topps Chewing Gum, 1966 . . . .   12.00
Game, Vince Lombardi's Game, Research
  Games Inc, 1960s 40.00
Nodder, 5½", composition
  Baltimore Colts, 1961–62 NFL se-
  ries 75.00
  Green Bay Packers, inked "1961 Cham-
  pions" 50.00
Pennant
  Los Angeles Rams, 29½", blue and white
  felt, National Football League logo
  and 1967 date 20.00
  St Louis Cardinals, red and white felt,
  c1967 . . . .   15.00
Sign, 7¾" × 11½", cardboard, Dallas Cow-
  boys, big sign set by Fleer Gum, 1968
  copyright 15.00

FOOTBALL COLLECTIBLES

At the moment, this category is heavily weighted toward professional football. Do not overlook some great college memorabilia.

Local pride dominates most collecting. Taking an item back to its "hometown" often doubles its value. Because of their limited production and the tendency of most individuals to discard them within a short time, some of the hardest things to find are game promotional giveaways. Also check the breweriana collectors. A surprising number of beer companies sponsor football broadcasts. Go Bud Light!

Newspaper: *Sports Collectors Digest,* 700 East State Street, Iola, WI 54990.

Ashtray, 7½", 1958 Baltimore Colts Cham-
  pionship, china, boxed 50.00
Beer Can, 5", 1975 Steelers Commemo-
  rative, aluminum, Iron City Beer, 12
  oz 15.00

FOSTORIA GLASS

The Fostoria Glass Company began in Fostoria, Ohio, and moved to Moundsville, West Virginia, in 1891. In 1983 Lancaster Colony purchased the company and produced glass under the Fostoria trademark.

Fostoria is collected by pattern, with the American pattern the most common and most sought after. Other patterns include Baroque, Georgian, Holly, Midnight Rose, Navarre, Rhapsody, and Wister. Hazel Weatherman's *Fostoria, Its First Fifty Years,* published by the author about 1972, helps identify patterns.

Club: Fostoria Glass Society of America, P. O. Box 826, Moundsville, WV 26041.

Compote, marigold, 5½" d, 4¾" h, $15.00.

Almond Dish, American, 3¾" l, oval 15.00
Animal
   Gosling 25.00
   Mermaid 100.00
   Polar Bear, clear. 75.00
Ashtray
   Coin, ruby, 8". 24.00
   Pioneer, blue, 3¾" 12.00
Bowl
   8½" oval, Coin, crystal 25.00
   11" d, Baroque, rolled edge 35.00
   12" d, Navarre, flared.............. 40.00
   12¾" d, Willow Etch. 65.00
   18" d, American.................. 265.00
Butter, dish, ¼ lb, Colony 30.00
Cake Plate, Navarre, 10" 35.00
Candlesticks, pr
   Coin, olive green, 4½" 28.00
   Colony........................ 45.00
Candy Dish, cov, Coin, olive green 28.00
Celery, Midnight Rose, crystal 25.00
Champagne
   Chintz 18.00
   Georgian 8.00
   Holly 12.00
Cigarette Urn, Coin, olive green 20.00
Cordial
   Colonial Dame, emerald green bowl. . . 18.00
   Coral Pearl, irid 22.00
   Midnight Rose, crystal. 45.00
Cream Soup, Mayfair, amber 8.50
Creamer, Vesper, green. 15.00
Creamer and Sugar
   Colony, individual size 12.00
   Coronet, crystal 12.00
   Meadow Rose 28.00
   Midnight Rose, matching tray........ 60.00
Cup and Saucer
   Baroque, crystal. 12.50
   Dolly Madison................... 12.00
   June, yellow 25.00
   Mayfair, amber 7.50

Dresser Compact, fan shape, amber, pearlized celluloid 38.00
Goblet
   American, 5½". 8.50
   Chintz 20.00
   Colonial Dame, emerald green bowl. . . 12.00
   Coral Pearl, irid 14.00
   Corsage 16.00
   Navarre 20.00
   Wistar, crystal 15.00
Gravy, attached underplate, Mayfair, yellow............................ 65.00
Ice Bucket, Willowmere, crystal, bail handle 85.00
Iced Tea, ftd
   Jamestown, amber 6.00
   Rhapsody, turquoise, crystal stem..... 8.00
Jelly, Coin, crystal, ftd 8.00
Juice Tumbler
   Coral Pearl, irid 12.00
   Gadroon 4.50
   Rhapsody, turquoise, crystal stem..... 6.00
Luncheon Set, Mayfair, black, crystal cups, four 8" plates, cups and saucers, 9¾" handled tray 85.00
Mayonnaise, American.............. 39.95
Nappy, American, 5", cov 30.00
Olive Dish, American 7.50
Oyster Cocktail
   American....................... 10.00
   Versailles, yellow................. 22.00
Pin Box, Jenny Lind, milk glass....... 38.00
Pitcher, Coin, amber 45.00
Plate
   7" d, Mayfair, amber 5.00
   8" d, Argus, clear 7.00
   9½" d, June, yellow 16.00
Punch Cup, American................ 9.00
Relish, Meadow Rose, divided 45.00
Salad Plate, American, crescent 45.00
Salt and Pepper Shakers, pr, matching tray, individual size, Century 20.00
Server, Chintz, center handle 37.50
Sherbet
   Coral Pearl, irid 12.00
   Laurel, crystal 14.00
   Navarre 18.00
Sundae, American, 3⅛". 9.50
Toothpick, Coin, olive green 18.00
Torte Plate, American, 14". 32.00
Tumbler
   American....................... 15.00
   Chintz 20.00
Vase
   7" h, Colony, ftd................. 45.00
   8" h, Coin, olive green 2.00
Wine
   Coral Pearl, irid 16.00
   Laurel, crystal 24.95
   Rhapsody, turquoise, crystal stem..... 12.00
   Ringlet........................ 8.00

FRANKART

Every time there is an Art Deco revival, Frankart gets rediscovered. Frankart was founded by Arthur Von Frankenberg, a sculptor and artist, in the mid-1920s. The key is to remember that his pieces were mass produced.

Frankart figures are identified through form and style, not specific features. Do I have to tell you that the nudes are most collectible? Probably not. Nudes are always collectible. Do not overlook other animal and human figures.

Almost every Frankart piece is marked either with the company name followed by a patent number of "pat. appl. for." Avoid unmarked pieces that dealers are trying to pass as Frankart. Frankenberg experienced plenty of knockoffs during the late 1920s and early 1930s.

Ashtray, chrome Scottie, black enamel base, marked "Frank Art Inc/Pat Appld For," $100.00.

Ashtray, horse, standing, orig paint, label **100.00**
Bookends, 5½" h, angel fish, exaggerated fins, stylized **90.00**
Figurine, 6¼" h, elk, bronze patina finish **120.00**
Lamp, 11" h, standing nude, embracing orig 8" candlelight bulb **310.00**
Night–light, 11", sailor leaning against lamppost, bronze patina, orig shade ... **250.00**

FRANKOMA

This is one of those pottery groups, such as Gonder and Hull, that runs hot and cold. At the moment, it is cold. In fact, it may be downright freezing. Not much price advance over the last several years. Sounds bad, doesn't it. If you stop and think about it, now is a great time to buy if you like the stuff.

In 1933, John N. Frank, a ceramics art instructor at Oklahoma University, founded Frankoma, Oklahoma's first commercial pottery. Originally located in Norman, it eventually moved to Sapulpa, Oklahoma, in 1938. A series of disastrous fires, the last in 1983, struck the plant. Look for pieces bearing a pacing leopard mark. These are earlier than pieces just marked "FRANKOMA."

Vase, wheel, mottled green, imp mark, 6¾" h, $15.00.

Ashtray, Horseshoe, green **10.00**
Bean Pot, cov, Plainsman, green and brown **9.00**
Bookends, boots, #433, pr **24.00**
Bottle, 11½", morning glory blue, white int, 1979 .... **28.00**
Bowl
    Divided, 7" × 13". **8.00**
    Shell, 12" **20.00**
Christmas Card, 1975 .... **30.00**
Figure
    English Setter, 5" **48.00**
    Swan, 9", open tail, brown glaze **20.00**
Honey Pot **4.00**
Mug
    Donkey, 1977 .... **8.00**
    Elephant, 1976 .... **5.00**
    Uncle Sam, red, 1976. .... **5.00**
Planter
    Elephant **6.00**
    Turtle. **6.50**

Plate
 Bicentennial Series, 1976 . . . . **7.00**
 Easter, 1972. . . . . **15.00**
 Largemouth Bass, Wildlife Series,
  1975. . . . . **20.00**
Toby Mug, baseball player, 1980. . . . . . . **15.00**
Trivet
 Centennial, yellow **5.00**
 Lazybones **30.00**
Vase
 6¾", wagon wheel, mottled green **18.00**
 9½", octagonal, red **10.00**

FRATERNAL ORDER COLLECTIBLES

In the 1990s few individuals understand the dominant societal role played by fraternal orders and benevolent societies between 1850 and 1950. Because many had membership qualifications that were prejudicial, these "secret" societies often were targets for the social activists of the 1960s.

As the 20th century ends, America as a nation of joiners also seems to be ending. Many fraternal and benevolent organizations have disbanded. A surprising amount of their material has worked its way into the market with lodge hall material often given a "folk art" label and corresponding high prices.

The symbolism is fun. Some of the convention souvenir objects are downright funky. Costumes are great for dress—up. Do not pay big money for them. Same goes for ornamental swords.

Masonic, glass, Syria, Pittsburgh, PA, 1909, Louisville, KY, amber and white, 4½" h, $30.00.

Benevolent & Protective Order of Elks
(BPOE)
 Ashtray, bronze **30.00**
 Bookmark, emb, elk's head, SS **18.00**
 Shaving Mug, elk, gold letters **30.00**
Fraternal Order of Eagles (FOE)
 Ashtray **12.00**
 Watch Fob, bronze, FOE, Liberty,
  Truth, Justice, Equality, 1918 . . . . . . **8.00**
Independent Order of Odd Fellows
(IOOF)
 Teaspoon, IOOF, SS, 1915 . . . . **25.00**
 Trivet, 8¼" l, insignia and heart in hand
  in laurel wreath **30.00**
Knights of Columbus, Plate, Vienna Art,
 1905. . . . . **38.00**
Loyal Order of Moose, watch fob, double
 tooth **75.00**
Masonic
 Belt Buckle, SP. **22.00**
 Ring, man's, gold, 19th C. **145.00**
Order of Eastern Star (OES) Cup and Saucer, emblem **15.00**
Shrine
 Hat, fez, brass scarab **22.00**
 Pin, lapel, 32nd emblem, SS **12.00**

FROG COLLECTIBLES

A frog collector I know keeps her collection in the guest bathroom. All the fixtures are green also. How long do you think it took me to find the toilet? Thank goodness I have good bladder control.

In fairy tales frogs usually received good press. Not true for their cousin, the toad. Thank goodness television finally wised up and introduced us to Kermit the Frog, thus putting to rest the villanous frog image of Froggy the Gremlin. I am willing to bet Froggy's "magic twanger" would not get past today's TV censors.

Newsletter: *Flower Frog Gazette*, P. O. Box 106, Trumbull, CT 06611.

Club: The Frog Pond, P. O. Box 193, Beech Grove, IN 46107.

Advertising Trade Card, French Laundry
 Soap, diecut frog **4.50**
Basket, figural **30.00**
Doorstop, 3", full figure, sitting, yellow
 and green. **50.00**
Figure, 5" l, cast iron, old paint **35.00**
Key Chain, 1", metal, frog riding bicycle,
 c1940. . . . . **8.00**
Paperweight, celluloid and iron, advertising **35.00**
Salt and Pepper Shaker, figural, tray, 3 pcs,
 Occupied Japan. **12.50**

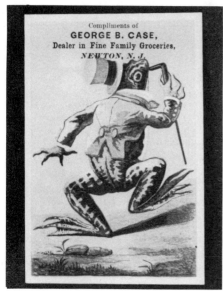

Advertising Trade Card, G B Case, Family Grocer, Newton, NJ, adv on back, 4¼" × 2 15/16", $3.00.

Stuffed Animal
  5", velvet, glass eyes **85.00**
  8", smoking pipe **45.00**
Toothpick Holder, silverplated, frog pulling snail shell. **55.00**
Vase, 6", figural, floral top, Occupied Japan. **12.00**

FRUIT CRATE LABELS

They are colorful and plentiful. While there are a few serious collectors who collect them by age, region, and/or product, most buy them for their decorative value. Chances are that you can find labels that work for you priced at well under $5.00.

Many dealers mat and frame labels and charge prices ranging from $25.00 to over $100.00. In almost every case, you are paying for the matting and framing and not the label. Most framed labels that you find fit the under $5.00 rule.

Club: Citrus Label Society, 16633 Ventura Blvd., No. 1011, Encino, CA 91436.

AK–SAR–BEN, oranges, blue background, Lemon Cove. **1.00**
Better 'N Ever, half sliced grapefruit, blue background . . . . **.50**
Caledonia, thistle spray, tartan plaid background, Placentia **1.00**

Lemons, La Patera, Santa Barbara County, black ground, green, red, and blue letters, $1.00.

Desert Bloom, grapefruit, desert scene, white blooming yucca, blue sky background, Redlands **2.00**
Don't Worry, little boy holding apple, black background **1.00**
Forever First, red holly berries, greens, and plump juicy pears, blue background . . . **2.00**
Eat One, arrow pointing to juicy orange, aqua background, Lindsay **2.00**
Great Valley, scenic, orange orchard, Orange Cove **1.00**
L–Z, smiling boy holding green grapes . . . **.50**
Littlerock, bunch of pears, orchard **1.00**
Morning Smile, lemon on opened Sunkist wrapper, blue background **1.00**
Red Diamond, red and yellow apples, red diamond, blue background **1.00**
Sea Coast, two lemons, blue triangle brown background, Ventura. **2.00**
Sunkist California lemons, lemon, yellow letters, black background **1.00**
Tell, red apple pierced by arrow, gray background. **1.00**
Wilko, red apple, yellow background, red border **1.00**
Yokohl, Indian brave fishing by stream, oranges, red background, Exeter. **3.00**

FRUIT JARS

Most fruit jars that you find are worth less than $1.00. Their value rests in reuse through canning, rather than in the collectors' market. Do not be fooled by patent dates that appear on the jar. Over fifty different types of jars bear a patent date of 1858 and many were made as much as fifty years later.

However, there are some expensive fruit jars. A good pricing guide is Alice M. Creswick's *Red Book No. 6: The Collector's Guide To Old Fruit Jars* published privately by the author in 1990.

Newsletter: *Fruit Jar Newsletter*, 364 Gregory Avenue, West Orange, NJ 07052.

Whitney, Mason, clear, 1½ qt, patent 1858, $4.50.

Atlas E–Z Seal, cornflower blue, pt	10.00
Ball, Masons' Patent 1858, green, qt	5.00
Double Safety, pt	5.00
Faxon, blue, qt	8.00
Garden Queen, qt	4.00
Mason's, Improved, light green, qt	15.00
Reverse Ball, aqua, qt	5.00
Smalley's Royal Trademark Nu–Seal, pt	10.00
Texas Mason, clear, qt	15.00
White Crown Mason, milk glass, aqua, pt	10.00

FULLER BRUSH

The Fuller Brush man paved the way for the Avon Lady. To the best of my knowledge, they were not married.

Fuller Brush men, a fair number of whom actually were women, sold household products door to door. Although still in existence, the golden age of the Fuller Brush man was the 1930s through the 1950s.

Most collectors focus on Fuller Brush advertising and promotional giveaways. Look for the actual products themselves. Most examples are not very expensive.

I'll include a "Door to Door Salesman" category in a future edition. Meanwhile, keep eyes peeled for Fuller Brush material.

GAMBLING COLLECTIBLES

Casino and other types of gambling are spreading across the country, just as they did over a century ago. Gaming devices, gaming accessories, and souvenirs from gambling establishments, from hotels to riverboats, are all collectible.

Gambling collectors compete with Western collectors for the same material. Sometimes the gunfight gets bloody. With the price of old, i.e., late 19th– and early 20th–century gambling material skyrocketing, many new collectors are focusing on more modern material dating from the speakeasies of the 1920s to the glitz of Las Vegas in the 1950s and 1960s.

You might as well pick up modern examples when you can. Some places last only slightly longer than a throw of the dice. Atlantic City has already seen the Atlantis and Playboy disappear. Is Trump's Taj Mahal next?

Good Luck Charm, horseshoe, Gold Club, Sparks, Nevada, 1971, $2.50.

Bingo Cage, 9" h, metal, red celluloid handle, eleven wood balls, 9 cards, 1941 copyright	12.00
Card Counter, plated, imitation ivory face, black lettering	18.00
Card Press, 9½" × 4½" × 3", dovetailed, holds ten decks, handle	140.00
Catalog, KC Card Co, Blue Book No. 520, Gambling Equipment, 68 pgs	40.00
Dice	
Poker, celluloid, set of 5	24.00
Weighted, always total 12, set of 3	35.00
Faro Cards, sq corners, Samuel Hart & Co, New York, complete	110.00
Poker	
Chip	
Inlaid, four crosses	4.00

Ivory, scrimshawed, eagle	30.00
Molded Rubber, dollar	4.00
Chip Rack, 11½" × 4" h, revolving, wood, holds four decks of cards and 400 chips	35.00
Roulette Ball, set of three, one metal, two composition	15.00
Shot Glass, ribbed dec, porcelain dice in bottom	24.00
Slot Machine	
Liberty Bell, 5¢, 3 reel, orig red, white, and blue, decal	160.00
The Puritan Ball, 5¢, 10¼" h	135.00
Tray, 11" d, tin, red, black, and white, martini center, card border	50.00

GAMES

Many game collectors distinguish between classic games, those made between 1840 and 1940, and modern games, those dating after 1940. This is the type of snobbishness that gives collecting a bad name. In time 1990s games will be one hundred years old. I can just imagine a collector in 2090 asking dealers at a toy show for a copy of the Morton Downey "Loudmouth" game. I am one of the few who have one put aside in mint condition.

Condition is everything. Games that have been taped or have price tags stickered to the face of their covers should be avoided. Beware of games at flea markets where exposure to sunlight and dirt causes fading, warping, and decay.

Avoid common games, e.g., "Go to the Head of the Class," "Monopoly," and "Rook." They were produced in such vast quantities that they hold little attraction for collectors.

Most boxed board games are found in heavily used condition. Box lids have excessive wear, tears, and are warped. Pieces are missing. In this condition, most games are in the $2.00 to $10.00 range. However, the minute a game is available in fine condition or better, value jumps considerably.

Club: American Game Collectors Association, 4628 Barlow Drive, Bartlesville, OK 74006.

Addams Family, Ideal, 1965, boxed board game, very fine condition 100.00
Barbie "Keys To Fame" Career Game, Mattel, 1963, boxed board game, mint 40.00
Charlie's Angels, Milton Bradley, 1977,

Battlestar Galactica, Parker Bros, 1978 Universal City Studios, Inc. copyright, $5.00.

boxed board game, very good condition 4.00
Captain Gallant, Transogram, 1955, boxed board game, fine condition 40.00
Dukes of Hazzard, Ideal, 1981, boxed board game, good condition 2.50
Dr. Kildare, Ideal, 1962, boxed board game, very fine condition 35.00
Fall Guy, Milton Bradley, 1982, Milton Bradley, boxed board game, very good condition 3.00
Felix The Cat, Milton Bradley, boxed board game, fine condition
1960 .... 35.00
1968 .... 20.00
Flintstone "Stone Age," Transogram, 1961, boxed board game, fine condition 20.00
Go To The Head Of The Class, Milton Bradley, 1955, boxed board game, near mint condition 15.00
I–Spy, Ideal, 1965, boxed board game
Mint 125.00
Near Mint 95.00
Fine 45.00
Good 20.00
Land of the Giants, Ideal, 1968, boxed board game, great graphics of attacking cat, very good condition 50.00
Laverne & Shirley, Parker Brothers, 1977, boxed board game, very good condition 4.00
Magilla Gorilla, Ideal, 1964, very fine.... 75.00
Mr. Ree Murder Mystery, Selchow & Righter, 1948, boxed board game, very fine 55.00
Nancy Drew, Parker Brothers, 1959, boxed board game, very good condition 22.50
Napoleon Solo, Milton Bradley, 1964, card game, very fine condition 20.00

Park & Shop, Milton Bradley, 1960, boxed
board game, very fine condition **37.50**
Rat Patrol, Transogram, 1967, boxed
board game, very fine condition **65.00**
Restless Gun, Milton Bradley, 1959,
boxed board game
Fine condition **55.00**
Unusued condition **135.00**
Twilight Zone, Ideal, 1964, boxed board
game, great box graphics, fine condi-
tion **150.00**
Video Village TV Quiz Game, Milton Brad-
ley, 1960, boxed board game......... **25.00**
Voyage to the Bottom of the Sea, Milton
Bradley, 1964, boxed board game, very
fine condition **45.00**

Gas Globe
Glass, Texaco, black border, T Hull
body........................ **300.00**
Plastic, Pemco **110.00**
Key Holder, Dezol **5.00**
Lubricant Can, Badger **85.00**
Oil Can, Marble's Nitro Solvent **45.00**
Padlock, Gas Pump, Standard Oil,
brass......................... **40.00**
Sign
Champlin Motor Oil **75.00**
Husky, fiberglass, graphics, pump..... **85.00**
Mobil Gas Special, porcelain, pump ... **95.00**
Pan–Am Gas, porcelain **65.00**
Thermometer, Lube King Motor Oil **125.00**
Tin
Arco Kid, metal polish............. **45.00**
Prestone Antifreeze, car, unused,
1927........................ **40.00**

GAS STATION COLLECTIBLES

Approach this from two perspectives —
items associated with gas stations and gasoline company giveaways. Competition for
this material is fierce. Advertising collectors
want the advertising; automobile collectors
want material to supplement their collections.

Beware of reproductions ranging from
advertising signs to pump globes. Do not
accept too much restoration and repair.
There were hundreds of thousands of gasoline stations across America. Not all their
back rooms have been exhausted.

Newspaper/Magazine: *Hemmings Motor
News*, Box 100, Bennington, VT 05201.

Clubs: Autombile License Plate Collectors
Association, Box 712, Weston, WV 26452;
Internalional Petrolina Collectors Associa-
tion, 2151 East Dublin–Granville Road,
Suite G292, Columbus, OH 43229.

*Booklet, Tydol Flying A Gasoline, cardboard,
dirigible shape, 9 ³/₈″ l, c1935, $20.00.*

Bank, pump, Sinclair **22.50**
Coin Set, Shell Oil Co, fifty states, complete, 1969..................... **35.00**

GEISHA GIRL

Geisha Girl porcelain is a Japanese export
ware whose production began in the last
quarter of the 19th century and still continues today. The only manufacturing gap is
1940 to 1945, the period of World War II.

Collectors have identified over 150 different patterns from over one hundred
manufacturers. When buying a set, check
the pattern of the pieces carefully. Dealers
will mix and match in an effort to achieve a
complete set.

Beware of reproductions that have a very
white porcelain, minimal background
washes, sparse detail coloring, no gold, or
very bright gold enameling. Some of the
reproductions came from Czechoslovakia.

*Tea cup and saucer, Child Reaching for Butter-
fly, variation B, $12.00.*

Bowl, 6½″, red, gold lacing, Flag **23.00**
Creamer, 4″, Feeding The Carp, ribbed,
hourglass shape, red **18.00**
Cup and Saucer, Kite A, brown and
gold **12.00**
Dish, 7″, oval, Mother and Son C,
red–orange **25.00**

147

Plate, 6", Chinese Coin **15.00**
Relish Dish, Picnic B, red–orange, floret
edge **25.00**
Salt and Pepper Shakers, pr, Visiting with
Baby, bulbous, blue and gold **20.00**
Salt, To the Teahouse, red, fluted, han-
dle **20.00**
Sugar Bowl, Flower Gathering B, green,
gold lacing **15.00**
Teapot, Butterfly, apple green and gold,
ftd. **30.00**

GOLD

24K gold is pure gold. 12K gold is fifty
percent gold and fifty percent other elements. Many gold items have more weight
value than antiques or collectibles value.
The gold weight scale is different from our
regular English pounds scale. Learn the
proper conversion procedure. Review the
value of an ounce of gold once a week and
practice keeping that figure in your mind.

Pieces with gold wash, gold gilding, and
gold bands have no weight value. Value
rests in other areas. In many cases the gold
is applied on the surface. Washing and
handling leads to its removal.

The only way to buy gold is to take the
time to learn what you are doing. This is
not an area in which to speculate. How
many times have you heard that an old
pocket watch has to be worth a lot of
money because it has a gold case? Many
people cannot tell the difference between
gold and gold plating. In most cases, the
gold value is much less than you think.

Gold coinage is a whole other story. Every coin suspected of being gold should first
be checked with a jeweler and then in coin
price guides.

GOLF COLLECTIBLES

Golf was first played in Scotland in the 15th
century. The game achieved popularity in
the late 1840s when the "guttie" ball was
introduced. Although golf was played in
America before the Revolution, it gained a
strong foothold in the recreational area
only after 1890.

The problem with most golf collectibles is
that they are common while their owners
think they are rare. This is an area where
homework pays, especially when trying to
determine the value of clubs.

Do not limit yourself only to items used
on the course. Books about golf, decorative
accessories with a golf motif, and
clubhouse collectibles are eagerly sought
by collectors. This is a great sports collectible to tee off on.

Club (no pun intended): Golf Collectors's
Society, 235 East Helena Street, Dayton,
OH 45404.

*Cigarette Lighter, score keeper, chrome, Japan,
2¾" × 1½", $20.00.*

Ashtray, metal, trophy, figural golfer **45.00**
Book
   Anderson, John, *The American Annual
   Golf Guide*, 1924 . . . . **40.00**
   Nelson, Byron, *Winning Golf*, 1947 . . . . **7.50**
   Ray, Edward, *Driving, Approaching and
   Putting*, 1922 . . . . **30.00**
Bag, leather, Tony Lema, 1964 British
   Open Champion **50.00**
Ball
   Bramble ball, The Crown. **15.00**
   Chemico Bob, yellow dot **35.00**
   Gutty, Mitchell, Manchester **35.00**
Bookends, 4" × 6", golfer in relief **55.00**
Cigarette Box, bronze, Art Deco, Silver
   Crest. **130.00**
Cigarette Lighter, Craftsman, golfer on
   front. **50.00**
Club
   Iron, Burke juvenile mashie, wood
   shaft **22.00**
   Putter, Spalding Cash–in, steel shaft. . . **45.00**
   Wood, Auchterlonie scared–head bras-
   sie, wood shaft **30.00**
Game, Golf–o–matics, Royal London . . . **18.00**
Paperweight, glass, US Open, 1980. . . . . . **25.00**
Plate, golfing rabbits, Royal Doulton Bun-
   nykins **140.00**
Print
   "The First Tee," Dendy Sadler, etching,
   colored. **30.00**
   "In the Sand, St Andrews," after Mi-
   chael Brown. **35.00**
Sketches, Gene Sarazen, black chalk,
   Ridgewell. **35.00**

Souvenir Spoon, SS, golfer, Milford,
PA **80.00**
Towel, bag, 1980 US Open **7.00**

GONDER POTTERY

In 1941 Lawton Gonder established
Gonder Ceramic Arts, Inc., at Zanesville,
Ohio. The company is known for its glazes,
such as Chinese crackle, gold crackle, and
flambé. Pieces are clearly marked. Gonder
manufactured lamp bases at a second plant
and marketed them under the trademark
"Eglee." Gonder Ceramic Arts, Inc. ceased
production in 1957.

*Basket, leaf pattern, turquoise, pink coral int.,
8" w, $25.00.*

Basket, 6½", leaf pattern, ext turquoise, int
pink coral, marked "H–39 Gonder,
USA" **30.00**
Bowl, 6½", ribbed, yellow **8.50**
Candlestick, 4¾", ext. turquoise, int. pink
coral, marked "E–14, Gonder," pr **18.00**
Cornucopia, 6", gray, pink int. **10.00**
Ewer, 7½", bulbous, mottled maroon **25.00**
Figure, elephant, 10½", raised trunk, rose
and gray **40.00**
Planter, Madonna, mottled pink and
gray **15.00**
Vase
6½", greenish blue glaze, handles **10.00**
12", glossy yellow, mottled red glaze,
emb leaves **35.00**

GOOFUS GLASS

Goofus glass is a patterned glass where the
reverse of the principal portion of the pattern is colored in red or green and covered
with a metallic gold ground. It was distributed at carnivals between 1890 and 1920.

There are no records of it being manufac-
tured after that date. Among the companies
who made Goofus glass are: Cresent Glass
Company, Imperial Glass Corporation, La-
Belle Glass Works, and Northwood Glass
Company.
Value rests with pieces that have both
the main color and ground color still intact.
The reverse painting often wore off. It is not
uncommon to find the clear pattern glass
blank with no painting on it whatsoever.
Goofus glass had other names: Mexican
Ware, Hooligan Glass, and Pickle Glass.
Says a lot, doesn't it?

Plate, gold, red flowers, 10¾" d, $12.00.

Ashtray, red rose dec, emb adv **8.00**
Bowl, 8½", floral, red dec, gold ground ... **20.00**
Coaster, 3", floral, red dec, gold
ground **10.00**
Dresser Tray, 6", Cabbage Rose, red roses,
gold foliage **28.00**
Mug, Cabbage Rose, gold ground **30.00**
Pin Dish, 6½", oval, red and black flo-
rals **15.00**
Plate
7¾", red carnations, gold ground **18.00**
8", red poppies, gold ground **25.00**
Toothpick Holder, red rose and foliage,
gold ground **20.00**

GRANITEWARE

Graniteware, also know as agateware, is
the name commonly given to iron or steel
kitchenware covered with enamel coating.
American production began in the 1860s
and still is going on today.
White and gray are the most common
colors. However, wares can be found in

shades of blue, brown, cream, green, red, and violet. Mottled pieces, those combining swirls of color, are especially desirable.

For the past few years a deliberate attempt to drive prices upward has been taking place. The dealers behind it were quite successful until the 1990 recession. Never lose sight of the fact that graniteware was inexpensive utilitarian kitchen and household ware. Modern prices should reflect this humble origin.

Club: National Graniteware Society, 4818 Reamer Road, Center Point, IA 52213.

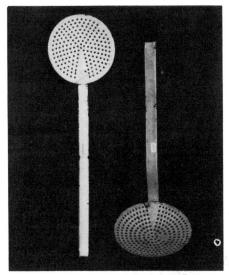

Skimmers, top: white, 16" l, $25.00; bottom: tan, 13½" l, deeply turned, $15.00.

Berry Pail, 4¼" h, robin's egg blue, black trim, lid, bail handle.	**35.00**
Bundt Pan, gray.	**15.00**
Coffee Pot, medium blue.	**35.00**
Colander, gray.	**12.00**
Cup, child's, green, cat on side	**22.00**
Dipper	
Gray and White	**20.00**
Red and White.	**15.00**
Funnel, gray	**24.00**
Measure, gray, 8".	**40.00**
Milk Pan, blue and white swirl	**45.00**
Muffin Pan, gray	**22.00**
Pie Pan, gray	**20.00**
Pitcher and Bowl Set, white, black trim	**45.00**
Plate	
Blue and white swirl	**15.00**
Gray mottled	**9.00**
Potty, child's, light blue	**12.50**

Pudding Pan, emerald green, white specks, 10⅝ × 7¾".	**35.00**
Roaster, cream and red, large	**30.00**
Soap Dish, blue and white swirl	**25.00**
Spittoon, blue	**35.00**
Strainer Insert, 8½" d, wire bail, brown and white, large mottle, straight sides	**55.00**
Teapot, 8½", black and white flecks.	**67.00**

GREETING CARDS

Greeting cards still fall largely under the wing of postcard collectors and dealers. They deserve a collector group of their own.

At the moment, high ticket greeting cards are character-related. But some day collectors will discover Hallmark and other greeting cards as social barometers of their era. Meanwhile, enjoy picking them up for 25¢ or less.

Assortment, boxed set, Lil Abner, seven different, 1950s	**35.00**
Birthday	
Amos 'n' Andy, brown portraits, message includes song title "Check and Double Check," inked birthday note, Rust Craft.	**20.00**
Blondie, full color, Dagwood illus, 5" × 6", Hallmark, 1939 copyright	**15.00**
Golliwog, c1930	**9.00**
Snow White and the Seven Dwarfs, c1938.	**40.00**
Space Patrol Man, 5" sq, full color, diecut, small green transparent helmet, orig envelope	**20.00**
Christmas, AGFA–SCO, c1940, 10" × 12", orig photo, Flying Spinnakers	**75.00**
Get Well, Amos 'n' Andy, black and white photo, 4½" × 5 ½", Hall Bros, 1951 copyright	**30.00**
Mother's Day, Cracker Jack, diecut, full color, puppy, c1940.	**40.00**

GUNDERSON GLASS CO

This peachblow–type art glass was manufactured by the Gunderson Glass Company beginning about 1950. This special order glass resembled peachblow in color, shading from an opaque white with a hint of pink to a deep rose. Many pieces of Gunderson Glass are sold as "old peachblow" by dealers who cannot identify the copies from the period pieces. Gunderson Peachblow is collectible in its own right.

Box, cov, 5½" × 7", hinged puff lid, large finial, emb brass bindings, satin finish **250.00**
Compote, 7⅛" d, wide scalloped rim, swirled knob stem **175.00**
Creamer, ftd. **75.00**
Cruet, orig stopper, glossy finish **250.00**
Mug, dec, orig paper label, c1970 . . . . **125.00**
Sugar, ftd, open **75.00**
Tumbler, 4" h **125.00**
Vase
   5½" h, applied ribbon and acorn at neck **225.00**
   9½" h, lily form **175.00**

HAIR RECEIVERS

The nineteenth century toilet set usually contained a hair receiver, a device used to store milady's hair resulting from her vigorous daily brushing. I am certain the hair was put to some useful function, but I will be darned if I know what.

Judging from the number of hair receivers that have survived, the form also must have been sold as an independent bureau accessory. The Victorian craze has renewed interest in the form. Prices are strong.

Cut Glass, American
   4" d, 3" h, engraved SS top, floral and leaves, rayed base. **75.00**
   5" d, 3½" h, Harvard pattern **150.00**
Glass
   Fostoria, American pattern, 3" × 3" × 2⅞", crystal **85.00**
   Heisey, Winged Scroll pattern, opal, gold trim **80.00**
Ceramic
   Austria, small pink roses, pink and green accents, white ground, gold trim, "M Z Austria" **35.00**
   Germany, pink roses, blue shaded ground **20.00**
   Limoges, small blue flowers and butterflies, off–white ground, gold trim, "JP Limoges" **72.50**
   Majolica, pink and green raised flowers **50.00**
   Nippon China, 5", yellow and red roses, black ground, blue maple leaf mark **60.00**
   Royal Bayreuth
      3½" h, Snow Babies, 3–ftd, blue mark **135.00**
      4½" h, lady with ducks, light yellow ground, marked **100.00**
   Royal Rudolstadt, 4¼" d, yellow roses, green leaves on yellow ground, gold trim **75.00**

RS Germany, roses, raised gold leaves, green mark **60.00**
RS Prussia, pink roses, white ground, green border, 4–ftd, red mark **65.00**
Schafer and Vater, 3½" l, pink jeweled jasper, triangular **65.00**
Souvenir
   Bev, MA, made in Austria **25.00**
   Lincoln, NE **20.00**

HALL CHINA CO.

In 1903 Robert Hall founded the Hall China Company in East Liverpool, Ohio. Upon his death in 1904, Robert T. Hall, his son, succeeded him. Hall produced a variety of kitchenware, dinnerware in a wide variety of patterns, and refrigerator sets. The company was a major supplier of institutional (hotel and restaurant) ware.

Hall also manufactured some patterns on an exclusive basis: Autumn Leaf for Jewel Tea, Blue Bouquet for the Standard Coffee Company of New Orleans, and Red Poppy for the Grand Union Tea Company. Hall teapots are a favorite among teapot collectors.

For the past several years Hall has been reissuing a number of its solid color pieces as an "Americana" line. Items featuring a decal or gold decoration have not been reproduced. Because of the difficulty in distinguishing old from new solid color pieces, prices on many older pieces have dropped.

Water jug, Westinghouse, blue, $35.00.

Aristocrat
   Butter. **17.00**
   Water Server, lid, cobalt **70.00**
Bingo
   Butter. **70.00**
   Water Bottle, 7" h, cork tip. **60.00**
Blue Blossom
   Custard Cup. **16.00**
   Casserole, oval, handle **45.00**
   Salt and Pepper Shakers, pr, handles. . . **40.00**

Blue Bouquet
  Fruit Bowl, 5½" **6.00**
  Pie Baker **22.00**
  Platter, 11¼", oval **13.00**
Crocus
  Gravy **19.00**
  Jug, bell shape **45.00**
  Plate, 7¼", pie **7.00**
Emperor
  Butter **14.00**
  Leftover **10.00**
Hotpoint
  Leftover, rect **22.00**
  Water Server, cork tip **45.00**
Patrician
  Butter **12.00**
  Water Server, cov, delphinium **35.00**
Poppy
  Cake Server **65.00**
  Cereal Bowl, 6" **7.00**
  Mustard, 3 pcs **45.00**
  Souffle Dish **14.00**
  Vegetable Bowl, 9⅛" round **14.00**
Red Poppy
  Casserole, cov, 7" **18.00**
  Cake Plate **16.00**
  Mixing Bowl, set of 3 .... **35.00**
  Sugar **8.00**
  Teapot, Aladdin **50.00**
Rose Parade
  Bean Pot **35.00**
  Casserole **25.00**
  Drip, cov **16.00**
  Salad Bowl **16.00**
Taverne
  Coffeepot, china drip **110.00**
  Leftover, rect **20.00**
  Mug **30.00**
  Tea Tile, 6", round **90.00**
Yellow Rose, mixing bowl, 9" **15.00**
Teapot
  Apple, sky blue and gold **225.00**
  Adele, maroon **125.00**
  Baltimore, emerald **35.00**
  Parade, canary **18.00**
  Polka Dot, windshield, ivory gold label ... **25.00**

HARDY BOYS

In the 1920s a series of juvenile novels featuring the Hardy Boys was published. The novels themselves have limited value, most sell in the 50¢ to $2.00 range. Material associated with "The Hardy Boys Mysteries," an ABC television show between January 1977 and August 1979, is attracting collector attention. One of the reasons could well be that Shaun Cassidy played the role of Joe Hardy.

Game, "The Hardy Boys Mystery Game / The Secret of Thunder Mountain," Parker Brothers **15.00**
Lunch Kit, box and thermos, lithographed steel, King Seely Thermos **35.00**
Vehicle and miniature figures, Gorgi, 1969, based on Saturday morning cartoon series entitled "The Hardy Boys" **90.00**

HARKER POTTERY

In 1840 Benjamin Harker of East Liverpool, Ohio, built a kiln and produced yellow ware products. During the Civil War, David Boyce managed the firm. Harkers and Boyces played important roles in the management of the firm through much of its history. In 1931 the company moved to Chester, West Virginia. Eventually Jeannette Glass Company purchased Harker, closing the plant in March 1972.

Much of Harker's wares were utilitarian. The company introduced Cameo ware in 1945 and a Rockingham ware line in 1960. A wide range of backstamps and names were used.

Newspaper: *The Daze,* P. O. Box 57, Otisville, MI 48463.

Creamer, Cameoware, blue and white, 3" h, $4.50.

Amy
  Creamer and Sugar **7.00**
Plate
  7½", salad **4.00**
  9", dinner **6.00**
  Rolling Pin **55.00**
  Teapot **30.00**
Cameoware
  Bowl, 7", pink **9.50**
  Child's Feeding Dish **30.00**
  Pitcher, cov **15.00**
  Plate, 10", dinner, blue and white **5.00**
  Sugar, cov **5.50**

152

Modern Tulip				

Modern Tulip
Bowl, 9½". 7.00
Cake Server, brown 12.00
Pie Baker 8.00
Platter, 14" 7.00
Salad Fork 12.00
Pate Sur Pate
Creamer, green 2.50
Platter, 13", gray 5.75
Salt and Pepper Shakers, pr, gray 6.00
Red Apple
Bowl, 9", berry 15.00
Cake Server 12.50
Mixing Bowl, 10". 15.00
Tea Tile. 20.00
Teapot 28.00

HATPIN HOLDERS AND HATPINS

Hatpins were used by women to hold on their hats. Since a woman was likely to own many and they were rather large, special holders were developed for them. Hatpins became a fashion accessory in themselves. The ends were decorated in a wide variety of materials ranging from gemstones to china.

Club: International Club for Collectors of Hatpins and Hatpin Holders, 15237 Chanera Avenue, Gardena, CA 90249.

Rhinestones, 1¼" d, $10.00.

HOLDERS
Bluebirds, Bavaria. 55.00
Floral
Cobalt and pink, Japan 28.00

Cobalt and white 55.00
Hand Painted, 7", Bavaria 95.00
Jasperware medallion, woman's profile, 5"h, Schafer & Vater 125.00
Kewpie 159.00
White, gold decorated, RS Germany 42.00

PINS
Amethyst, rhinestones 29.00
Enamel
Bow shape, pearl center 45.00
St Louis World's Fair, 1904 . . . . 30.00
Kewpie 49.00
Mother–of–Pearl, snake motif, ruby head, gold top, American 175.00
Porcelain, ball, ceramic transfer, hp accents, gold overlay, c1895 . . . . 110.00
Rhinestone, butterfly, figural, blue body. 30.00
Silver Filigree, 12", lotus blossom 23.00
Sterling Silver, maple leaf 20.00
Tortoise Shell, pear shape, 1¼", ribboned pique work 120.00

HATS AND CAPS

No clothing accessory, except jewelry, mirrors changing fashion tastes better than the hat. Hats also express our individuality. How else do you explain some of the hats that grace peoples' heads? Hang twenty on a wall as decoration for a surefire conversation piece.

Formal hats are fine. Want some real fun? Start a collection of advertising baseball–style caps. The source is endless from truck stops to farm equipment dealers. Why, you can even collect baseball team hats. New, they cost between $5.00 and $7.50. At flea markets you can acquire them for a couple of dollars each.

Bowler, black, leather band, marked "John B Stetson, Phila," $35.00.

Beaded, shell beads and sequins, hand
  sewn, lady's c1925 . . . . **32.00**
Bonnet, silk, hand crocheted lace **36.00**
Railroad, agent, Boston & Maine, gold
  finish, curved top **38.00**
Satin, pillbox, black, netting **18.00**
Straw, cloche, lavender, lady's, Milan,
  1920s **8.00**
Top Hat, beaver, child's **37.50**

HEISEY GLASS

A. H. Heisey Company of Newark, Ohio,
began operations in 1896. Within a short
period of time, it was one of the major
suppliers of glass to middle America. Its
many blown and molded patterns were
produced in crystal, colored, milk
(opalescent), and Ivorina Verde (custard).
Pieces also featured cutting, etching, and
silver deposit decoration. Glass figurines
were made between 1933 and 1957.

Candy jar, cov, Recessed Panel, crystal, sgd,
$35.00.

Not all Heisey glass is marked. Marked
pieces have an "H" within a diamond.
However, I have seen non-Heisey pieces
with this same marking at several flea markets.

Plate, Old Colony, Sahara, 8½", sq **22.00**
Sherbet, Plantation Ivy, crystal **16.00**
Toothpick, Punty Band, ruby stained **55.00**
Vase, Ridgeleigh, triangle **40.00**

The key to Heisey glass is to identify the
pattern. Neila Bredehoft's *The Collector's En-*
cyclopedia of Heisey Glass, 1925–1938 (Collector Books: 1986) is helpful for early material. The best help for post-World War II
patterns are old Heisey catalogs.

HEISEY GLASS ANIMALS

Club: Heisey Collectors of America, P. O.
Box 4367, Newark, OH 43055.

Heisey produced glass animals between
1933 and 1957. It is difficult to date an
animal because many remained in production for decades.

Ashtray
  Grape Leaf, Moongleam **65.00**
  Horsehead **45.00**
  Orchid, sq **30.00**
Banana Split Dish, Yeoman, Moongleam,
  ftd **35.00**
Basket, Crystolite, 6" **165.00**
Bonbon, Lariat **25.00**
Bookends, fish, pr **150.00**
Bowl
  Crystal, rolled rim, black and gold trim,
    star base, 9" **30.00**
  Pineapple and Fan, 8" **35.00**
  Queen Anne, 9" **65.00**
Butter Dish, cov, Rose, crystal **160.00**
Candleblock, Crystolite, sq **8.00**
Candy Dish, cov, Empress, Flamingo, dol-
  phin base, ftd **27.50**
Celery, Twist pattern, Moongleam **35.00**
Compote, Waverly, orchid etching, 6 ¼",
  low standard **50.00**
Creamer and Sugar, Lariat, crystal **16.75**
Goblet, Duquesne, clear, 9 oz **10.00**

Although the animal line was introduced
in 1933, some forms made in the 1920s
featured animal motifs, e.g., Dolphin–footed and Dolphin finial articles and
Lion Head bowl with paw feet, marketed
under the pattern name Empress, later
Queen Anne. Other examples are the
Kingfisher and Duck flower frogs. Collectors believe that the Dolphin candlestick
was made from molds obtained from the
Sandwich Glass Company.

Royal Hickman and Horace King are two
of the Heisey employees who were involved in the design of the animal figures.
Many of King's designs resulted in animal
head stoppers.

The most commonly found color is crystal. Many other colors were used. In order
of rarity, these colors are Tangerine, Vase-
line, Cobalt, Alexandrite, Amber, Lime-

light, Dawn, Marigold, Moongleam, Sahara, and Flamingo.

One final note: Collecting Heisey animal figures is not for those with a limited pocketbook. As you can see from the prices below, they are on the expensive side.

Club: Heisey Collectors of America, P. O. Box 4367, Newark, OH 43055.

days. If I included special days, from Secretary's Day to Public Speaker's Day, I would fill this book with holiday collectibles alone. Besides, in fifty years, is anyone going to care about Public Speaker's Day? No one does now.

Newsletters: *Hearts to Holly: The Holiday Collectors Newsletter*, P. O. Box 105, Amherst, NH 03031; *Trick or Treat Trader*, P. O. Box 1058, Derry, NH 03038.

Decanter stopper, horsehead, crystal, orig label, $45.00.

Thanksgiving, candy container, papier-mâché, metal legs, 5" h, $40.00.

Asiatic Pheasant	250.00
Colt, rearing.	125.00
Cygnet	125.00
Donkey	200.00
Giraffe, head back	125.00
Goose, wings down	285.00
Mallard, wings up	150.00
Plug Horse	90.00
Pony, standing.	50.00
Rabbit	135.00
Rooster, fighting	125.00
Scottie	95.00
Sparrow	65.00

HOLIDAY COLLECTIBLES

Holidays play an important part in American life. Besides being a break from work, they allow time for patriotism, religious renewal, and fun. Because of America's size and ethnic diversity, there are many holiday events of a regional nature. Attend some of them and pick up their collectibles. I have started a Fastnacht Day collection.

This listing is confined to national holi-

FOURTH OF JULY

Postcard, "4th of July Greeting," red, white, and blue, gold ground, Germany, 1910.	2.00

GEORGE WASHINGTON'S BIRTHDAY

Candy Container, stump, 3" h, papier mache, surrounded by cherries, marked "Germany"	45.00
Diecut, 2½" h, George Washington, hatchet with cherry, flanked by stump with hatchet, set of 3	8.00

HALLOWEEN

Candy Container	
Cat, 4" h, hard plastic, orange and black, arched back, open area in back for candy, USA, 1950s.	7.50
Pumpkin Man, 3" h, orange head, green suit, standing on round box, marked "Germany"	85.00
Costume	
Clown, home made, baggy, yellow and black, trimmed in bells, matching pointed clown hat with bells, 1940s	8.00

155

Porky Pig, child's, large, plastic mask, cloth suit and cap, Warner Bros, orig box, 1950s 10.00

Mr Spock, Star Trek, 1967 .... 30.00

Jack–O–Lantern

Smiling Mouth, 5"h. 45.00

Glass Globe, battery operated, tin base, bail handle.................... 45.00

Papier Mache, bail handle, orig paper insert 62.00

Lantern, 7" h, papier mache, devil head, two tone red, paper insert behind cut out eyes and mouth, wire bail handle, Germany 100.00

Mask

Fritz, Katzenjammer Kids, molded 24.00

Pirate, papier mache, string ties, marked "Germany" 10.00

Noisemaker, 3" d, rattle, round, tin, wooden handle, orange, white, and green, pumpkin and cats litho, USA ... 7.50

ST PATRICK'S DAY

Diecut, 3" h, gold harp entwined with shamrocks and green ribbon, marked "Germany"..................... 1.50

Pin, "Erin Go Bragh" across face, Irish and American flags, shamrock, harp, green satin ribbon attached to pin, paper on back of pin marked "12th St Badge and Novelty House, Phila, PA".......... 6.50

Postcard

"Ireland Forever," shamrock with view of Ireland in each leaf, marked "Germany" 1.00

"To My Little Colleen," girl dressed in green, large shamrock for hair bow, marked "London".............. 1.50

THANKSGIVING

Candy Container, turkey, 6" h, composition, folded tail, glass eyes, metal feet, removable head, marked "Germany" 45.00

Figurine, 4" h, composition, man and woman Pilgrims, marked "Germany" 45.00

Postcard, "A Thanksgiving Greeting," large harvest pumpkin in background, three turkeys eating from dish outside a home, 1910 .... 1.00

Turkey, 4" h, celluloid, white, pink, and blue, weighted bottom, marked "Irwin, USA".......................... 25.00

VALENTINE'S DAY

Greeting Card

4½" h, "Best Wishes," shades of blue, picture of bird in center, poem beneath, no greeting inside 5.00

6" h, "To My Sweetheart," white dog, envelope in mouth, stand–up, marked "Germany" 3.50

6" × 10", mechanical, steamroller filled with children holding hearts, wheels turn and children move up and down, tab operated, marked "Germany" 18.00

6½" h, "To My Sweetheart," card style, small girl in green dress and hat, red wild rose border, verse inside....... 10.00

Postcard

Cupid on swing of roses, bordered by red hearts and gold scroll work, small verse, marked "E Nash" 1.25

"February 14th," trimmed in green ivy, cupids shooting hearts and arrows at two lovers, enclosed in heart, marked "Germany, 1910" 1.50

HORSE COLLECTIBLES

This is one of those collectible categories where you can collect the real thing, riding equipment ranging from bridles to wagons, and/or representational items. It is also a category where the predominant number of collectors are women.

The figurine is the most favored collectible. However, horse-related items can be found in almost every collectible category from Western movie posters to souvenir spoons. As long as there is a horse on it, it is collectible.

A neglected area among collectors is the rodeo. I am amazed at how much rodeo material I find at East Coast flea markets. I never realized how big the Eastern rodeo circuit was.

Figurine, black, raised mahogany base, Midwest Potteries, Inc., 7 ¼", $50.00.

EQUIPMENT AND RELATED ITEMS

Bridle, braided leather strips, 1930s **45.00**
Saddle Ring, sterling **35.00**
Stirrup, wood, rounded bottom, worn
 leather cover **15.00**
Wagon Seat, leather cov, springs and steel
 frame **150.00**

THEME ITEMS

Ashtray, White Horse Whiskey, white
 china, figural horse head, painted **10.00**
Belt Buckle, Roy and Trigger **35.00**
Binoculars, metal, Hopalong Cassidy on
 Topper **95.00**
Calendar, Iroquois Brewing Co, Indian on
 Painted Pony, 1897 . . . . **75.00**
Christmas Ornament, Hobby Horse,
 Dresden **80.00**
Cigarette Lighter, Dale Evans, horse
 head **15.00**
Doorstop, 5" l, cast iron, horse figure,
 Hubley **175.00**
Figure, Royal Doulton, chestnut mare and
 foal, HN2522 . . . . **450.00**
Game, Derby Day, board folds out to 72",
 six wooden horses and hurdles, Parker
 Brothers, copyright 1959. . . . . **40.00**
Horseshoe, Hopalong Cassidy, "Good
 Luck," orig insert card, 1950 . . . . **20.00**
Lunch Box
 Gene Autry and Champion, 1950s **50.00**
 Trigger **45.00**
Medal, Ohio horseshoer's, ribbon,
 1917. . . . . **57.50**
Photo, rancher on horse, mountain
 scene **15.00**
Pin Cushion, metal, horseshoe shape **10.00**
Spoon, sterling, Cheyenne, WY, bucking
 horse **22.00**
Toy
 Pull, 16" h, horsehair mane and tail,
  glass eyes, wood base, red wood
  wheels, late 19th C. **600.00**
 Tin, windup, Lone Ranger on rearing
  horse **95.00**

HOWDY DOODY

The Howdy Doody show is the most famous early television children's program.
Created by "Buffalo" Bob Smith, the show
ran for 2,343 performances between December 27, 1947 and September 30, 1960.
Among the puppet characters were Howdy
Doody, Mr. Bluster, Flub–A–Dub, and
Dilly–Dally. Princess Summerfall–Winter-
spring and Clarabelle, the clown, were
played by humans.

There is a whole generation out there
who knows there is only one answer to the
question: "What time is it?"

*Straw Holder, plastic, fifty orig cellophane
straws, orig box, $40.00.*

Alarm Clock, Howdy on Clarabelle fig-
 ural, Bob Smith wake up voice, MIB . . . **135.00**
Bank, Howdy on pig **200.00**
Board Game **58.00**
Cookie Jar, tin, merry–go–round,
 marked "Cookie–Go–Round,
 Krispy" **145.00**
Detective Disguises, Poll Parrot Shoes, cut
 out premium, mint, uncut **70.00**
Dot Book **20.00**
Figure, plastic **15.00**
Game
 Bean bag **125.00**
 Bowling, Howdy, Clarabelle, Dilly
  Dally, and Flub–A–Dub, MIB. **135.00**
 Flub–A–Dub Flip A Ring, orig pkg **95.00**
Hand Puppet **45.00**
Little Golden Book **15.00**
Marionette, orig box **275.00**
Night light, figural, sitting **115.00**
Pipe **16.00**
Plaque, 14", with Santa, orig box,
 1950. . . . . **95.00**
Plate, child's **35.00**
Plate, mug, and bowl set, porcelain,
 mint. **155.00**
Pocket Watch, toy **15.00**
Push–up figure, wood, jointed, Howdy in
 front of NBC mike, orig box **195.00**
Squeeze Toy, 13" h, cowboy outfit, near
 mint **125.00**
Sticker Book **22.00**
Transfer, unused **30.00**
Wall Walker **35.00**

HULL POTTERY

Hull Pottery traces its beginnings to the 1905 purchase of the Acme Pottery Company of Crooksville, Ohio, by Addis E. Hull. By 1917 a line of art pottery for flower and gift shops was added to its line of novelties, kitchenware, and stoneware. A flood and fire destroyed the plant in 1950. When the plant reopened in 1952, Hull products had a newer glossy finish.

Hull is collected by pattern. A favorite with collectors is the Little Red Riding Hood kitchenware line, made between 1943 and 1957. Most Hull pieces are marked. Pre–1950 pieces have a numbering system to identify pattern and height. Post–1950 pieces have "hull" or "Hull" in large script writing.

Cornucopia, green, high glaze pink int., marked, $20.00.

Bow Knot
Basket, B–21, 10½" **350.00**
Cornucopia, pink and blue, B–2, 5" . . . **55.00**
Jardiniere, B–18, 5¾" **65.00**
Butterfly, cornucopia, B–2, 6½" **40.00**
Camelia, (Open Rose)
Candleholder, doves, 117, 6½", pr. **90.00**
Console Bowl, bird handles, 116,
12" **125.00**
Pitcher, 128, 4¾" **35.00**
Iris
Basket, hanging, 412, 4" **50.00**
Bowl, oval, 409, 12" **95.00**
Vase, 16", tan **325.00**
Magnolia
Basket, 10½" **175.00**
Ewer, 5, 7" **50.00**
Teapot, orig paper label, 23, 6½" **55.00**
Vase, matte, pink and blue, 11, 6¼" **35.00**
Poppy
Bowl, boat shape, 604, 8" **75.00**
Jardiniere, 603, 4¾" **50.00**
Rosella
Ewer **40.00**
Pitcher, R, 6½" **45.00**
Sunglow, basket, pink, 84, 6¼" **25.00**

Tulip
Flower Pot, 116–33, 6" **75.00**
Vase, handles, 6½" **32.00**
Water Lily
Candleholder, pr, L–22 . . . . **50.00**
Console Bowl, L–21, 13½" **85.00**
Vase
L–1–6, 6½" **35.00**
12, 10½" **50.00**
Wildflower
Candleholder, double, 69, 4" **75.00**
Ewer, W–19, 13½" **250.00**
Vase, W–15, 10½" **75.00**
Woodland
Bud Vase, double, W–15, 8½" **50.00**
Planter, W–14, 10" **55.00**
Wall Pocket, pink, glossy **55.00**

HUMMEL

Hummel items are the original creations of Beta Hummel, a German artist. At the age of 18, she enrolled in the Academy of Fine Arts in Munich. In 1934 Beta Hummel entered the Convent of Siessen and became Sister Maria Innocentia. She continued to draw.

In 1935, W. Goebel Co. of Rodental, Germany, used some of her sketches as the basis for three-dimensional figures. American distribution was handled by the Schmid Brothers of Randolph, Massachusetts. In 1967 a controversy developed between the two companies involving the Hummel family and the convent that was eventually settled by the German courts. The Convent has the right to Beta Hummel's sketches made between 1934 and her death in 1964. Schmid could deal directly with the family for reproduction rights to any sketches made before 1934.

All authentic Hummels bear both the signature, M. I. Hummel, and a Goebel trademark. Various trademarks were used to identify the year of production. The Crown Mark (CM) was used in 1935, Full Bee (FB), 1940–1959; Small Stylized Bee (SSB), 1960–1972; Large Stylized Bee (LSB), 1960–1963; Three Line Mark (3L) 1964–1972; Last Bee Mark (LB), 1972–1980, and Missing Bee Mark (MMB), 1979–1990. Hummel has just announced a new mark for 1991 production.

Hummels are emotional collectibles. Collectors do not like to read or hear anything negative about them. At the moment, they are very unhappy campers. The Hummel market for ordinary pieces is flat, with little signs of recovery in the years ahead.

Hummel material was copied widely. These copycats also are attracting interest among collectors. For more information about them, see Lawrence L. Wonsch's *Hummel Copycats With Values* (Wallace–Homestead: 1987).

Christmas plate, 1973, orig box, $75.00.

Ashtray, Joyful, #33, CM **325.00**
Bookends, pr, Apple Tree Boy and Apple
   Tree Girl, #252 A&B, SSB **250.00**
Candleholder, Happy Pastime, #111/69,
   3L **125.00**
Figurine
   Accordion Boy, #185, FB **120.00**
   Baker, #128, SSB **85.00**
   Bird Duet, #169, 3L. **90.00**
   Chick Girl, #57/0, FB **100.00**
   Chimney Sweep, #122/0, LB **70.00**
   Heavenly Lullaby, #262, LB **110.00**
   Little Goat Herder, #200, FB **175.00**
   March Winds, #43, LB **75.00**
   Village Boy, #51/3/0, CM **115.00**
Font
   Angel Cloud, #206, LB **40.00**
   Seated Angel, #167, FB. **75.00**
Plaque, Mail Coach, #140, LB **135.00**
Table Lamp, Just Resting, #225/II, 3L. . . . **275.00**

ICE BOXES

You know the play "The Ice Man Cometh." Well, this listing is the legimate reason why the ice man came. Never offer to help an ice box collector move!

Acme, extra high, ash, solid brass locks. . . **750.00**
Economy, elm, golden finish, galvanized
   steel lining, brass hinges, 45 pounds of
   ice capacity, 41¼" h **500.00**
Northey Duplex, oak, four doors, 74½"
   h. **425.00**
Pine, zinc lining, lift lid, 42" h **300.00**

ICE HOUSE COLLECTIBLES

Dad still calls our refrigerator an "ice box." His eyes become misty when he talks about the two months that he spent in 1948 living with his mother's Aunt Naomi and Aunt Annie, who still used an ice box and a wood/coal-burning kitchen cook stove. He talks about spending the night in the ice house at Camp Minsi, a Boy Scout camp situated on an old ice-cutting lake in Pennsylvania's Pocono mountains. As we drive through the countryside near his home, he is constantly pointing out ice ponds and remains of ice houses. What the devil is he so fascinated with?

Tray, Falls City Ice and Beverage Co, Louisville, KY, 13" × 10," $60.00.

Album Card, cat in front of ice wagon,
   printed color, JC Beard, 1881 . . . . **8.00**
Chipper, "Crown," steel, wood handle,
   North Brothers, c1900. . . . . **12.00**
Chisel, "Crown Ice Chipper," steel, wood
   handle, American Machine Co, pat
   1884. . . . . **12.00**
Hatchet, round cutting edge, marked **10.00**
Pick, adv, steel, wood handle **10.00**

Pinback Button, ¾" d, tongs holding block of ice, "Sulzer–Vogt Mach Co, Ice Mchny, Lou KY," white lettering, blue ground, 1896–1900 .... 3.00
Scraper, "White Mountain," cast iron, wood handle 15.00
Shaver
Arctic Ice Shave No 33, cast iron, Grey Iron Casting Co, Mount Joy, PA 14.00
Enterprise Hardware, nickeled iron, saucepan shape, lid, replaceable blade 15.00
Shredder, Enterprise No 43, cone shape, blade in lid, c1900 .... 20.00
Stickpin, ⅝" × 1" h, adv, celluloid, oval, multicolor, "Indiana Ice Dealers Assn" on block of ice, 1911–1920 .... 13.00
Tongs
Adv, 14" l, "Dixie Gem Coal, Ice & Fuel Co," iron, wood handle 22.50
Wrought Iron, plain. 35.00

IMPERIAL GLASS

The history of Imperial Glass dates back to 1901. Initially the company produced pattern and carnival glass. In 1916 an art glass line, "Free-Hand," was introduced. However, Imperial's reputation rests primarily on a wide variety of household glassware products.

Imperial made a practice of acquiring molds from companies that went out of business, e.g., Central, Cambridge, and Heisey. The company used a variety of marks over time. Beware of an interlaced "I" and "G" mark on carnival glass. This is an Imperial reproduction.

Club: National Imperial Glass Collectors Society, P. O. Box 534, Bellaire, OH 43906.

Rose bowl, 5" d, $22.00.

Animal, donkey, cobalt. **65.00**
Animal Dish, cov
Hen on nest, amethyst slag **100.00**
Rooster, lacy basket base, amethyst slag. **125.00**
Turkey, milk glass **50.00**
Ashtray, End–O–Day, purple, 6" sq **25.00**
Bell, Suzanne
Carnival, cobalt. **50.00**
Lemon. **30.00**
Lemon, frosted. **35.00**
Butter, cov, Cape Cod **25.00**
Cake Plate, ftd, Molly pattern, opalescent green **45.00**
Cocktail Glass, Cape Cod. **5.00**
Cocktail Shaker, Big Shot, red. **75.00**
Console Bowl, Cape Cod. **30.00**
Decanter, cobalt blue, six shots, chrome tray, Schaeffer **165.00**
Goblet
Cape Cod. **5.00**
Tradition, 5½" **12.50**
Iced Tea Tumbler, Cape Cod **12.00**
Juice Tumbler, Cape Cod, ftd **10.00**
Old Fashioned, Cape Cod **9.00**
Punch Bowl Set, Cape Cod, 12" bowl, 16" d underplate, twelve cups, orig ladle ... **200.00**
Punch Cup, Candlewick **15.00**
Relish, Cape Cod, divided **30.00**
Salt Dip, Candlewick. **6.00**
Sherbet, Victorian, yellow. **9.50**
Sundae, Cape Cod, 6 oz. **5.00**
Tumbler, Big Shot, red, 5½". **20.00**
Whiskey, Cape Cod. **9.00**
Wine, Cape Cod. **7.00**

INK BOTTLES

In the 18th and early 19th centuries, individuals mixed their own ink. With the development of the untippable bottle in the middle of the 19th century, the small individual ink bottle arrived upon the scene. Ink bottles are found in a variety of shapes ranging from umbrella style to turtles. When the fountain pen arrived on the scene, ink bottles became increasingly plain.

Magazine: *Antique Bottle and Glass Collector*, P. O. Box 187, East Greenville, PA 18041.

Arnold, P & J, brown, pouring lip **12.00**
Billings, J T & Son, aqua **7.00**
Carter's Ink, amethyst, mold blown, applied lip **4.00**
Greenwood's, clear, sheared top. **8.00**
Higgins Inks, Brooklyn, NY, amethyst ... **4.00**
Moses Brickett, olive green **12.00**
Paul's, aqua. **12.00**
Sanford, clear, round, crown top **2.00**
Signet Ink, cobalt blue. **18.00**

Silverplated, dog's head, hinged, round, $75.00.

Traveling, 2", round, leather, cov, Russian 75.00
Wood, maple, cobalt blue glass liner 15.00

Aqua, applied lip and collar, c1880, 3" h, $10.00.

Todd, W B, green 6.00
Underwood, John & Co, cobalt blue 30.00
Wood's, aqua 25.00

INKWELLS

Inkwells enjoyed a "golden age" between 1870 and 1920. They were a sign of wealth and office. The common man dipped his ink directly from the bottle. The arrival of the fountain pen and ball point pen led to their demise.

Inkwells were made in a wide variety of materials. Collectors that seem to have the most fun are those collecting figural inkwells. Beware, there are some modern figural reproductions.

Club: Society For Inkwell Collectors, 5136 Thomas Avenue, Minneapolis, MN 55410.

Blown- Three- Mold, olive amber, cylindrical, disc mouth 40.00
Brass
  Art Nouveau stand, hinged lid, glass insert 80.00
  Egyptian bust, hinged lid, glass insert 60.00
Cast Iron, double well, storks on sides 50.00
Figural, two children playing, porcelain, German 85.00
Metal, cat's head on tray, glass insert 70.00
Pewter, floral dec on lid, pen rest with cherub dec, glass liner 65.00
Porcelain, domed, white glaze, multicolored floral dec, metal cap 30.00

INSULATORS

This trendy collectible of the 1960s has resided primarily in the collectors' realm since the early 1970s. As a result, prices have been stable.

Insulators are sold by "CD" numbers and color. Check N. R. Woodward's *The Glass Insulator In America* (privately printed, 1973) to determine the correct "CD" number. Beware of "rare" colors. Unfortunately, some collectors and dealers have altered color using heat and chemicals to increase the rarity value. The National Insulators Association is leading the movement to identify and stop this practice. They are one of the few clubs in the field that take their "policing" role seriously.

Club: National Insulators Association, 5 Brownstone Road, East Grandby, CT 06026.

Threaded
  CD 102, BGM Co, smooth base, purple 18.00
  CD 102, California, smooth base, blue 15.00
  CD 102.2, Westinghouse, smooth base, blue 130.00
  CD 106, Star, smooth base, olive green 8.00
  CD 112, New England Telegraph & Telephone, smooth base, green 80.00
  CD 122, McLaughlin, round drip points, apple green 7.50
  CD 138, Kerr, smooth base, clear 4.00
  CD 141, no name, smooth base, emerald green 9.00

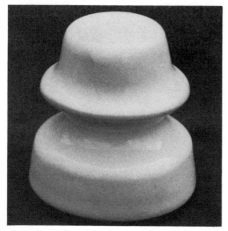

Ceramic, white, glazed, unmarked, 3¹/₂" × 3¹/₄", $2.00.

CD 154, White Tatum No 1, amethyst......................... **11.00**
CD 155, Armstrong's DPL, smooth base,
    clear........................... **1.00**
CD 160, Hemingray 14/Made in USA,
    dark smoke **10.00**
CD 162, SS & Co, smooth base, lime
    green **150.00**
CD 168, Hemingray, Made in USA/
    D510, carnival................. **25.00**
CD 168, Whitall Tatum Co No 11/Made
    in USA, ice blue................. **15.00**
CD 190/191, Am Telegraph & Telephone, smooth base, jade green,
    2–pc......................... **35.00**
CD 263, Hemingray, smooth base,
    blue **80.00**
CD 292.5, Boston, smooth base, dark
    green **95.00**
CD 317, Chambers, smooth base, lime
    green **150.00**
CD 320, Pyrex, smooth base, clear..... **10.00**
Threadless
    CD 718, no name, no embossing
        Aqua...................... **200.00**
        Black Glass................. **350.00**
    CD 728, Boston Bottle Works, smooth
        base, light aqua **60.00**
    CD 731, McKee, smooth base, aqua ... **150.00**
    CD 733, Brookfield, smooth base,
        aqua....................... **200.00**

IRONS

Country and kitchen collectors have kept nonelectric iron collecting alive. The form changed little for centuries. Some types were produced for decades. Age is not as important as appearance — the more unusual or decorated the iron, the more likely its value will be high.

There are still bargains to be found, but cast-iron and brass irons are becoming expensive. The iron collectible of the future is the electric. Check the appliance category for some listings.

Clubs: Friends of Ancient Smoothing Irons, Box 215 Carlsbad, CA 92008; Midwest Sadiron Collectors Club, 3915 Lay Street, Des Moines, IA 50317.

Charcoal, double spout, "New Plus Ultra/Pat'd July 29, '02," wood handle, $100.00.

Alcohol or Gas, Drammel, Akron Lamp &
    Mfg Co, crescent shape base, spherical
    tank, c1918 .... **45.00**
Billiard Table Iron, #20, English........ **175.00**
Charcoal, Ideal, 6¹/₂", snub chimney, rear
    vent, lift–off lid, early 1900s **70.00**
Flatiron and Sadiron
    Dover Mfg Co, sleeve style, detachable
        tin cov, sgd "Asbestos" **35.00**
    Sensible, Stueter, side latch mechanism....................... **25.00**
    Tailor, #20, twisted handle.......... **25.00**
Fluter
    Howell's Wave Fluter, wave pattern,
        brass base overlay **150.00**
    Streeter, T style roller, 1878.......... **85.00**
Goffering, 6" barrel, S shape stand,
    Kenrich **75.00**
Sleeve, Ober 1 .... **85.00**
Slug, brass, turned posts, triangular
    base, wood handle and knife gate,
    English........................ **120.00**

IRONSTONE POTTERY

This was the common household china of the last half of the 19th century and first two decades of the twentieth century. Its name came because the ceramic ware was supposed to wear like iron. Many different manufacturers used "ironstone" when marking their pieces. However, the vast majority of pieces do not bear the "ironstone" mark.

When plain white and patterned, it is known as "White Patterned Ironstone." Decoration was achieved by the transfer process.

IVORY

Ivory is a yellowish–white organic material that comes from the teeth and tusks of animals. In many cases, it is now protected under the Endangered Species Act of 1973, amended in 1978, which limits import and sale of antique ivory and tortoise shell items. Make certain that any ivory you buy is sold within the provisions of this law.

Vegetable ivory, bone, stag horn, and plastic are ivory substitutes. Do not be fooled. Most plastic substitutes do not approach the density of ivory nor do they have cross-hatched patterns. Learn the grain patterns of ivory, tusk, teeth, and bone. Once you have, a good manifying glass will quickly tell you if you have the real thing.

Gravy boat, cov, ladle, underplate, marked "Richard Alcock," 9" × 6 ½", $65.00.

Figurine, elephant, 1⅜" × 1¾", $45.00.

Bowl, white, leaf fan pattern, lid,
Alcock **85.00**
Chamber Pot, white, simple line pattern,
Johnson Bros. **50.00**
Cup and Saucer
Oriental transfer, polychrome
enamel **25.00**
White, grape and medallion pattern,
Challinor **35.00**
Gravy Boat, white, vintage pattern **30.00**
Plate, 9¼", purple transfer, polychrome
enamel, Maastricht **20.00**
Platter, white, Ceres, 16", Elsmore &
Forster **60.00**
Relish Dish, white, parish shape,
Alcock **20.00**
Soup Plate, 9", blue transfer, marked
"Adams" **20.00**
Sugar, white, fuschia pattern, Meakin . . . **40.00**
Tea Set, child's, red transfer of Punch and
Judy, three plates, four cups and sau-
cers, teapot, waste bowl, sugar **165.00**
Teapot
8¾", paneled, blue floral transfer, poly-
chrome enameling. **95.00**
8⅞", white, forget–me–not pattern,
Wood, Rathbone and Co, Cobridge,
Staffordshire **85.00**
Waste Bowl, white, Columbia pattern,
unmarked **75.00**

Bobbin, Victorian, carved flowers, Chi-
nese, pr **140.00**
Box, lid, 2¾" d, round, carved, high relief,
figures and pavilion, Chinese, late 19th
C **175.00**
Cane, 36½" l, bamboo form, horse foreleg
shape handle, 19th C **250.00**
Cane Handle, 4½" l, carved, monkey on
branch, holding egg away form bird,
c1900. . . . . **90.00**
Chess Set, carved, figural, 32 pcs, Chi-
nese **225.00**
Cigarette Holder, carved **25.00**
Cribbage Board, 5¼" l, engraved foliage
and two seals, three pegs **100.00**
Crochet Hook, 6¼" l, hand shaped
finial. **40.00**
Ladle, 7⅛", African. **100.00**
Memo Pad, 1½" × 2¾", silver fittings. **25.00**
Napkin Ring, 2" h, relief carved bird **10.00**
Needle Case
Chinese, carved dragons and clouds,
early 19th C **160.00**

Stanhope, ornate **90.00**
Netsuke
Duck, carved, sitting, Hakusen **150.00**
Man, crawling on bundle of cloth and
fan, sgd **110.00**
Thread Winder **16.50**
Tongue Depressor, 7¼" l, 1" w, eagle under
words "Union Forever" on one side,
wreath and "BP to LB 1841 AD" on
other **250.00**

JEWELRY

All jewelry is collectible. Check the prices on costume jewelry from as late as the 1980s. You will be amazed. In the current market, "antique" jewelry refers to pieces that are one hundred years old or older, although an awful lot of jewelry from the 1920s and 1930s is passed as antique jewelry. "Heirloom/estate" jewelry normally refers to pieces between twenty–five and one hundred years old. "Costume" refers to quality and type, not age. Costume jewelry exists for every historical period.

The first step to determining value is to identify the classification of jewelry. Have stones and settings checked by a jeweler or gemologist. If a piece is unmarked, do not create hope where none deserves to be.

Finally, never buy from an individual that you cannot find six months later. The market is flooded with reproductions, copycats, fakes, and newly made pieces. Get a receipt that clearly spells out what you believe you bought. Do not hesitate to have it checked. If it is not what it is supposed to be, insist that the seller refund your money.

Pin, sterling silver, Art Nouveau woman with flowing hair, 1½" w, $90.00.

Bar Pin
SS, "MIZPAH" and ribbon motif, English hallmarks **45.00**
YG, 15K, set with three cabochon garnets **200.00**
Bracelet
Gold, 18K yg, enameled blue and green dec, Art Nouveau, Tiffany **285.00**
Bangle, gold filled, etched band dec . . . **75.00**
Brooch, hp portrait on porcelain, gold filled frame **250.00**
Cuff Links
Fancy shamrock motif, SS **80.00**
Plain ball motif, 14K yg **90.00**
Earrings, hoop, small, 14K yg **130.00**
Locket
Gold, yellow, oval painted miniature, half pearl floral frame **225.00**
Silver, black onyx shield centered by turquoise and half pearl floral basket **200.00**
Necklace, Art Deco, enamel dec SS links, set with lapis color glass **165.00**
Pendant, figural, carved lava, gold fittings **250.00**
Pin
Art Deco, antelope motif, SS **55.00**
Arts and Crafts, SS, round orange petaled flowers, star points, hallmarked and stamped "JF," 1½" d, pr **140.00**
Victorian, floral carved ivory **35.00**
Ring, 10K yg, cabochon opal surrounded by six rose–cut diamonds **285.00**
Scarf Pin, gold, Etruscan bead work, pietra dura center **175.00**
Stick Pin, tie, 14K yg, gargoyle motif, set with ruby **125.00**
Watch, pocket, open face, 18K yg, Hamilton, Arabic numerals **275.00**
Watch Fob, 14K yg and mother of pearl, horn motif **80.00**

JEWELRY, COSTUME

Diamonds might be a girl's best friend, but costume jewelry is what most women owned. Costume jewelry is design and form gone mad. There is a piece for everyone's taste — good, bad, or indifferent.

Collect it by period or design — highbrow or lowbrow. Remember that it is mass-produced. If you do not like the price the first time you see a piece, shop around. Most sellers put a high price on the pieces that appeal to them and a lower price on those that do not. Since people's taste change, so does the price on an individual piece.

Costume jewelry often was sold in sets. A

164

piece from a broken set has much less value than the entire unit. Collectors have not placed a strong emphasis on original packaging. I think they are making a mistake. In many cases, the packaging provides the only identification of a maker.

Pin and earrings, plastic, wood grain pattern, $5.00.

Bracelet
Abalone 39.00
Bakelite, black, carved 25.00
Faux Pearls, three rows, sterling filigree
medallion 46.00
Bracelet and Earring Set
Bakelite, hinged, cream color, rhinestones 45.00
Rhinestones, green, Occupied Japan 32.00
Brooch, shell cameo, Rebecca 72.00
Brooch and Earrings Set, coral, gold overlay, branch 20.00
Choker, faux pearls, center drop 12.00
Charm, Santa, metal, red enamel 28.00
Earrings
Copper, enameled, Matisse 25.00
Lavender and rhinestones, Lisner 25.00
Rhinestone, drop 15.00
Sterling, swordfish, Taxco 20.00
Lapel Pin, Donald Duck, rhinestones, red
stones 35.00
Necklace
Agate, 15", large gold beads, green and
black enamel over brass trim 35.00
Amethyst, 31" 26.00
Black Jet 65.00
Coral, 16", three strand branch 45.00
Crystal, facet cut, sterling clasp 65.00
Deco, three enameled brass discs, four
alternating blue glass drops 48.00
Faux Cultured Pearls, double strand,
Ciner 45.00
Hawaiian seed 4.00

Lucite 50.00
Oyster Shell, three blue Venetian trade
beads 40.00
Plastic, pastel fruit 6.00
Rope Twist, 16", pearls, amethyst carnival beads 30.00
Turquoise, gold enameled, two
mermaids kissing 30.00
Necklace Set
Satin Glass, purple, necklace and earrings, 1930s 60.00
Rhinestone, center drop, 15" necklace,
earrings 35.00
Pendant
Bakelite, black cameo, clear base, 2" ×
2½", 26" clear chain 28.00
Cornucopia, 3", hanging pearls, Kramer 40.00
Faux topaz, Emmons 25.00
Marcasites, mother–of–pearl, chain . . 24.00
Pin
Arts & Crafts, sterling on copper 45.00
Bakelite, ivory, 3", flower, carved,
France 40.00
Brass, fly, amethyst stones 37.00
Holly man, Christmas, green, red
berries, Beatrix 14.00
Lucite, rooster 27.00
Marcasite, "Mother" 22.00
Pink Rhinestones, Weiss 30.00
Rhinestone, 2¼", figural, scissors 30.00
Sterling Silver
Floral and leaf 29.00
Spaceman, Taxco 30.00
Pin and Earrings Set, bakelite, metal, sea
horses, signed JHP Paris 45.00
Ring
Bakelite, red, white, and blue 19.00
Garnet, Bohemian, lady's 75.00
Silver, sterling, filigree, large jelly
opal 55.00

JUGTOWN

Jugtown is the pottery that refused to die. Founded in 1920 in Moore County, North Carolina, by Jacques and Julianna Busbee, the pottery continued under Julianna and Ben Owens when Jacques died in 1947. It closed in 1958 only to reopen in 1960. It is now run by Country Roads, Inc., a nonprofit organization.

The principal difficulty is that the pottery continues to produce the same type of wares using the same glazes as it did decades ago. Even the mark is the same. Since it takes an expert to tell the new from the older pieces, this is a category that novices should avoid until they have done a fair amount of study.

Carolina pottery is developing a dedicated core group of collectors. For more information read Charle G. Zug III's *Turners and Burners: The Folk Potters of North Carolina* (University of North Carolina Press: 1986).

Platter, orange wash glaze, 12¾" × 11½" × 1½", $24.00.

Bowl, 5" × 3", frogskin glaze **50.00**
Candlesticks, 3" h, Chinese Translation,
  Chinese blue and deep red, marked,
  pr **70.00**
Cookie Jar, cov, 12" h, ovoid, strap handles **75.00**
Creamer, cov, 4¾" h, yellow, marked **45.00**
Jar, 6¼" h, yellow ware, marked **45.00**
Mug, brown glaze **25.00**
Pitcher, 5" h, gray and cobalt blue salt
  glaze **75.00**
Sugar, cov, 3¾" h, Tobacco Spit glaze,
  marked **35.00**
Teapot, 5¼" h, Tobacco Spit glaze, sgd,
  c1930 . . . . **40.00**
Vase, 7" h, four small handles, salt

JUICERS

Dad lists them as "Reamers" in *Warman's Americana & Collectibles*. Here I call them "Juicers."
  They were used to make juice. Therefore, finding them in mint condition is next to impossible. The variety of material in which they are found is staggering, ranging from wood to sterling silver. As in many other categories, the fun examples are figural. Scholarly collectors might enjoy focusing on mechanical examples, although I am not

certain that I would mention on the cocktail circuit or the church social hall that I collect "mechanical reamers."
  Reamers are identified using a number system developed by Ken and Linda Ricketts in 1974. This cataloging system was continued by Mary Walker in her two books on reamers.
  Edna Barnes has reproduced a number of reamers in limited editions. These are marked with a "B" in a circle.

Club: National Reamer Collectors Association, Rt. #1, box 200, Grantsburg, WI 54840.

Porcelain, marked "Marutoware, Made In Japan," $48.00.

China
  Clown, figural, 4½" h, pastel yellow,
    Rising Sun Mark, Japan **35.00**
  Orange Shape, 3¼" h, 2 pcs, orange
    body, green leaves, England,
    (L−20) **24.00**
  Delft type dec, blue and white, Germany, (E−66) **42.00**
  Jiffy Juicer, 1 pc, large bowl with cone
    center, elongated loop handle, ten
    colors known, Pat 1938, USA,
    (A−5) **60.00**
Glass
  Green, floral etching, Cambridge **85.00**
  Light Jadite, two cup, 2 pc, Jeannette
    Glass Co **35.00**
  Milk Glass, Sunkist in block letters, McKee **20.00**
  Opal, fluted sides, 1 pc, Fry Glassware,
    c1920 . . . . **38.00**
  Pink, green tab handle, 1 pc, Hazel
    Atlas **36.00**
Metal
  Aluminum, 6" d, cast, skillet shape, long
    rect seed dams beneath cone, hole in
    handle, two spouts, Wagner Ware,
    (M−96) **18.00**

Iron, 9½" l, hinged, Dunlap's Improved, (M-17) **32.00**
Scissor type, 8¾" l, Ebaloy, handles marked "Ebaloy Juicer Pat Pend," (M-76) **12.00**
Stainless Steel, 2½" h, 2 pcs, flat, Hong Kong, (M-205) **8.50**
Pottery, grapefruit size, yellow, sgd Red Wing **150.00**

Door Knocker, brass **65.00**
Figure, 5", bisque, O'Neill **60.00**
Handkerchief **28.00**
Paper Dolls, Kewpies in Kewpieland, uncut book **20.00**
Post Card, 3½" × 5½", Valentine, Kewpie pair snuggled on chair, Gibson Art Co, c1920 . . . . **30.00**
Tea Cup, 2¼", white china, full color Kewpie with turtle at feet, Rose O'Neill copyright **25.00**

KEWPIES

Kewpies are the invention of Rose Cecil O'Neill (1876–1944), artist, novelist, illustrator, poet, and sculptor. The Kewpie first appeared in the December 1909 issue of *Ladies Home Journal*. The first Kewpie doll followed in 1913.

Many early Kewpie items were made in Germany. An attached label enhances value. Kewpie items also were made in the United States and Japan. The generations that grew up with Kewpie dolls are dying off. O'Neill's memory and products are being kept alive by a small but dedicated group of collectors

Club: International Rose O'Neill Club, P. O. Box 688, Branson, MO 65616.

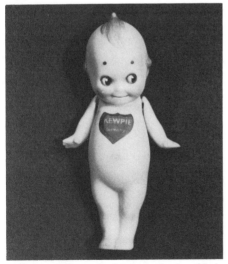

Doll, porcelain, orig label on back, 4¼" h, $100.00.

Bell, brass **65.00**
Crumb Tray, brass **30.00**
Christmas Plate, 1973, orig package **8.00**
Doll, 11", vinyl, glass eyes, orig clothes and tag, Cameo Dolls Products **85.00**

KEY CHAINS

Talk about an inexpensive collecting category. Most examples sell under $10.00. If you are really cheap, you can pick up plenty of modern examples for free. Why not? There are going to be collectible in thirty years and antiques in a hundred. Who knows, maybe you will live that long!

One of the favorite charity fund raising gimmicks in the 1940s and 1950s was the license plate key chain tag. Would you believe there is a collectors' club devoted to this single topic?

Club: Key Chain Tag Collectors Club, 888 8th Avenue, New York, NY 10019.

Newsletter: *The Chain Gang*, P. O. Box 9397, Phoenix, AZ 85068.

Advertising
Edsel **10.00**
GM Motorama of 1956, brass, rocketship, 1" × 2¼" **10.00**
Indian Bicycles, brass, detailed Indian in canoe, tree lined river scene, c1900, 1¼" **60.00**
Oilzum, brass, diecut trademark, 1½" **30.00**
Swift Premium Hams, enamel **12.00**
Automobile, inscription on back to return to owner
Chrysler, emb copper, Airflow model, 1934, ⅞" × 1¼" **20.00**
Studebaker, silvered brass, c1930, ⅞" × 1¼" **25.00**
Bicycle, A. I. A. M. Meet, brass, three balloon tires, eagle center, 1911, 1¼" × 1½" **35.00**
Good Luck
Horseshoe, Franklin Institute, aluminum, penny center **2.50**
Rabbit's foot, pink fur **5.00**
Identification, US Social Security, 1½" SS, raised wings design, engraved serial number on front, owner's name and address on back **18.00**
Souvenir, *Majesty's Ship Victoria*, brass, emb, Incress Line, c1960, 1¼" d **10.00**

World's Fair

Chicago, brass, emb city seal, 1893, 1"
× 1¾" **20.00**
New York, brass, 1939, Trylon and
Perisphere, rising run rays, inscribed
"In 1939/New York World's Fair,"
reverse with depiction of Geo Washington's inauguration, inscribed
"Souvenir Of The 150th Anniversary," 1¼" **15.00**
Pan–Am, brass, emb fair symbol, text
on back, 1901, 1 ¼" **18.50**

KEYS

There are millions of keys. The way to get a
handle on the category is to focus on a
special type of key, e.g., automobile,
railroad switch, etc. Few keys are rare;
prices above $10.00 are unusual.

Collect keys with a strong decorative
motif. These range from keys with advertising logos at the top to cast keys with animal
or interlocking scrolls at the top. If someone offers you a key to King Tut's Tomb,
Newgate Prison, or the Tower of London,
be suspicious.

Finally, if you are locked out of your
house or car, call a locksmith. Your key
collection is not likely to help. Either that
or find a good-sized brick.

Club: Key Collectors International, P. O.
Box 9397, Phoenix, AZ 85068.

Bureau, brass, double dolphin top, 2¾" l, $1.00.

Cabinet, barrel type

Brass

Decorative type, 2" **4.50**
Standard bow and bit, 2" **1.50**
Bronze
Art Deco design, 2" **12.00**
Decorative type, 2" **9.00**
Iron, painted, 3", plastic bow, Art Deco
design **9.50**
Nickel-plated, 2¼", lyre design bow.... **5.50**
Steel
Art Deco design, 2" **6.00**
Standard bow and bit, 2" .... **.50**

Car

Dodge, brass, reverse "Caskeey–
Dupree" **1.25**
Edsel, any maker **2.50**
Ford, Model "T," brass
C–D mark **2.00**
"V" in circle mark **12.00**
Nash logo key, Ilco #132 .... **5.00**
Packard logo key, gold plated, 50th an-
niversary **8.00**
Studebaker, Yale, Jr, logo key **1.50**
Car, Special
Auto Dealer Presentation Keys, sterling
silver **12.00**
Crest Key, Frazer **3.00**
Gas Company, premium type, alumi-
num .... **.75**
Casting Plate, bronze, 3" **18.00**
Door
Brass, standard bow and bit, 5" **8.00**
Bronze, Keen Kutter bow, 4" **5.50**
Steel, decorative bow, 3" **3.00**
Folding, Jackknife
Bronze and Steel, bit cuts, no maker's
name, 5" **15.00**
Steel, bit cuts, no maker's name, 5½"... **5.00**
Steel, uncut, maker's name, 5½" **6.00**
Gate, bronze, bit type, 6" **12.00**
Hotel
Bit type, bronze, hotel name and room
number on bow, 3" **4.50**
Bit type, steel, bronze tag **3.00**
Jail
Nickel–Silver, pin tumbler, Yale Mogul,
cut **15.00**
Spike Key, bronze bow, steel bit, serial
no, no maker's name, 5½" **35.00**
Steel, flat, lever tumbler,
Folger–Adams, uncut blank **12.00**
Keys to the City, Presentation, iron, brass
plated, Master Lock Co, 1933 World's
Fair, 2" **7.50**
Pocket Door, bow folds sideways, bronze,
Art Deco, triangular bow **15.00**
Railroad
ARR Alaska Railroad **20.00**
LM RR Little Miami Railroad **55.00**
SPTCO Southern Pacific **6.00**
Ship, bit type
Bronze, ship name on bow **10.00**
Iron/steel, bronze tags, 4" **3.00**
Watch
Brass, advertising type, shield, 1" **10.00**
Brass and steel, swivel, 1" **2.00**
Gold plated, decorative bow, 1" **8.00**
Sterling Silver, rose on bow, 1" **35.00**

KING KONG

Hairy gorillas do not turn me on the way
they did Fay Wray or Jessica Lange. Yet, I
must confess that like so many others, King

Kong has my vote for favorite monster/beast of all time.

You would have a great collection if you focused only on Kong-on-the-Tower items. But, the King appeared in many other places as well. Do not neglect the recent material. King Kong movies will be stock in trade on late night reruns and cable channels forever.

Autograph, Fay Wray, 5½" × 6" page,
  Wray and Bruce Cabot photo and King
  Kong illus. **50.00**
Glass, King Kong on Twin Towers **3.50**
Lunch Box, 7" × 9" × 4", metal, full
  color illus, copyright 1977 Dino De
  Laurentis **15.00**
Magazine
  Famous Monsters, King Kong Special
  Photo Filmbook Issue, #108 . . . . **12.50**
  King Kong, April, 1977, Sportscene
  Publications **3.50**
  Science Fiction Illustrated, 1977, L/C
  Print Publications **3.00**
Model, 9", assembled, unpainted, girl in
  right hand, Aurora, 1964 copyright . . . **40.00**
Movie Poster, 24" × 28", stiff paper, 1963
  Universal Pictures **50.00**
Pinback Button, Happy Anniversary Kong
  1933–1983, black, white, and red **4.00**

KITCHEN COLLECTIBLES

Kitchen collectibles are closely linked to Country, where the concentration is on the 1860–1900 period. This approach is far too narrow. There are a lot of great kitchen utensils and gadgets from the 1900 to 1940 period. Do not overlook them.

Kitchen collectibles were used. While collectors like to have the used look present, they also want an item in very good or better condition. It is a difficult balancing act in many cases. The field is broad, so it pays to specialize. Tomato slicers are not for me; I am more of a chopping knife personality.

Apple Peeler, Keen Kutter **175.00**
Basting Spoon, granite, cobalt handle. . . . **12.00**
Biscuit Cutter, 1½", tin, bail **6.00**
Blueberry Picker, wood, iron teeth, A D
  Makespeace & Co, West Barnstable,
  MA. **175.00**
Butter Churn, Dazey No 40, orig instruc-
  tions. **45.00**
Butter Paddle, 8¾"l, curly maple **45.00**
Coffee Grinder, 9¼", dovetailed case,
  pewter hopper, iron handle, nailed
  drawer **95.00**

Beater, measuring cup base, green, marked "Handy Maid, Torrington T & S," $30.00.

Cookie Board, 6⅜" × 9", wood, running
  horse on one side, star on other **100.00**
Cornstick Pan, Griswold **35.00**
Cranberry Scoop, 14", tin, hinged lid **25.00**
Dutch Oven, 18½", tin **50.00**
Egg Whip, handle, dated 1906 . . . . **12.00**
Eggbeater, red Bakelite trim, Androck . . . **22.00**
Food Chopper, Universal **6.00**
Meat Thermometer, 6", Taylor **8.00**
Nutmeg Grater, 5¼", tin, spring loaded
  hopper, turned wood handles **55.00**
Patty Molds, Griswold, MIB **18.00**
Pot Scraper, Babitts Cleanser. **225.00**
Raisin Seeder and Grinder, clamp type,
  Enterprise, c1895 . . . . **60.00**
Refrigerator Bowls, Kitchen Kraft, set of
  3. . . . . **75.00**
Strainer, wire mesh bowl, twisted wire
  and wood handle. **6.00**
Strawberry Huller, tin, dated 1906 . . . . . . **10.00**
Tomato Slicer, enameled wood handle,
  orig litho sleeve **10.00**
Trivet, 9¼" d, cast iron, geometric star
  flower design **25.00**
Waffle Iron, 29½", cast iron, wrought iron
  handle **65.00**
Whisk, 10", twisted wire handle **12.00**

KNOWLES CHINA

There are two Knowles companies who made china. The Edwin M. Knowles China Company, Newell and Chester, West Virginia, made dinnerware between 1900 and 1963. Knowles, Taylor, Knowles, East

Liverpool, Ohio, operated between 1854 and 1931. Edwin was the son of Isaac Knowles of Knowles, Taylor, Knowles.

The Edwin M. Knowles Company resurfaced in the 1970s when it acquired rights to the name and used it to front the Bradford Exchange collector plate series, such as Gone with the Wind and the Wizard of Oz. The company is also heavily into Rockwell items.

Plate, Yorktown shape, maroon, 11¾", $4.50.

Batter Jug, cov, Fruits	**18.00**
Bowl, Tia Juana, 5"	**8.00**
Casserole, cov, Fruits, 8½"	**7.50**
Collector's Plate	
Annie and the Orphans, 1984, Annie series	**20.00**
Easter, 1980, Americana Holiday series	**30.00**
Over The Rainbow, 1977, first edition, Wizard of Oz series	**65.00**
Scarlett's Green Dress, 1984	**50.00**
Creamer and Sugar, Tia Juana	**12.00**
Cup, Yorktown	**3.00**
Mixing Bowl, Fruits, 8½"	**7.50**
Plate, dinner	
Fruits	**3.50**
Tia Juana	**8.25**
Yorktown	**3.75**
Salt and Pepper Shakers, pr	
Fruits	**15.00**
Yorktown, blue	**8.00**
Saucer, Yorktown	**1.25**

LACE

While there are collectors of lace, most old lace is still bought for use. Those buying lace to reuse are not willing to pay high prices. A general rule is the larger the amount or piece in a single pattern, the higher the price is likely to be. In this instance, price is directly related to supply and demand.

On the other hand, items decorated with lace that can be used in their existing form, e.g., costumes and tablecloths, have value that transcends the lace itself. Learn to differentiate between handmade and machine made lace. Value for these pieces rests on the item as a whole, not the lace.

Ask yourself one basic question. When was the last time you used any lace or anything with lace on it? Enough said.

Club: International Old Lacers, Box 1029, West Minster, CO 80030.

LAW ENFORCEMENT

Do not sell this category short. Collecting is largely confined to the law enforcement community, but within that group collecting badges, patches, and other police paraphernalia is big. Most collections are based upon items from a specific locality. As a result, prices are regionalized.

There are some crooks afoot. Reproduction and fake badges, especially railroad police badges, are prevalent. Blow the whistle on them when you see them.

Badge, P. R. R. Co, Railway Police, nickel plated brass, c1920, $65.00.

Badge	
Boston Police, city skyline, nickel plated, c1880	**100.00**
Overland Park, KS, patrolman	**60.00**
Silver Lake, WI	**50.00**
Special Deputy Sheriff	**10.00**

Billy Club, wooden 20.00
Buckle, New York City, c1900 . . . . 75.00
Helmet, New York City, riot type,
  leather 200.00
Magazine Cover, Collier's, cov illus by Jay
  Irving, c1939 . . . . 15.00
Patch
  Maricopa County Deputy Sheriff, star
    center 2.00
  San Francisco, eagle 3.00
Sheet Music, *Police Parade March,*
  c1917 . . . . 25.00
Toy, litho tin wind–up, policeman on mo-
  torcycle, Unique Art 150.00
Whiskey Bottle
  Texas Ranger, Grenadier, 1977 . . . . 25.00
  US Marshall, McCormick, riding horse,
    c1979 . . . . 50.00

Bowl, oval, vegetable, Temple Blossom
  pattern 55.00
Cigarette Box, white apple blossoms,
  green ground, wreath mark 40.00
Cup and Saucer, Kingsley pattern 20.00
Honey Pot, 5" h, 6¼" underplate, ivory
  beehive, gold bee and trim 75.00
Mug, 5¼" h, Harvard College dec, dated
  1910 . . . . 85.00
Nappy, 4½" × 7", ftd, shell shape, pink
  tinged beige 35.00
Plate, dinner, Temple Blossom pattern . . . 32.00
Platter, 13"d, Temple Blossom pattern . . . 90.00
Salt, 3" × 2" × 1", ivory ground,
  molded seashells and coral, green
  wreath mark 35.00
Salt and Pepper Shakers, hp, green and
  gold bird dec, pr 65.00
Tea Strainer, hp, small roses dec 65.00
Vase, 11" h, corset shape, six leafy
  panels 85.00

LENOX

Johnathan Cox and Walter Scott Lenox founded the Ceramic Art Company in Trenton, New Jersey, in 1889. By 1906 Lenox had broken away and established his own company. Much of Lenox's products resemble Belleek, not unexpectedly since Lenox lured several Belleek potters to New Jersey.

Lenox has an upscale reputation. China service sets sell, but within a narrow price range, e.g., $600 to $1,200 for an ordinary eight-place setting service. The key are Lenox gift and accessory items. Prices are still reasonable. The category has not yet been truly "discovered."

Lenox made and makes limited edition items. Buy them because you like them, not as an investment. Potential for long-term value is limited.

Swan, salt, light coral, 3" × 2", $25.00.

Bouillon Cup and Saucer, gold band and
  handles, monogrammed 25.00

LETTER OPENERS

Isn't it amazing what can be done to a basic form? I have seen letter openers that are so large that one does not have a ghost's chance in hell of slipping them under the flap of a No. 10 envelope. As they say in eastern Pennsylvania, these letter openers are "just for nice."

Advertising letter openers are the crowd pleaser in this category. However, you can build an equally great collection based on

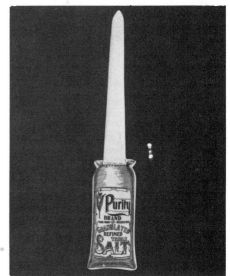

Purity Brand Salt, International Salt Co of NY, celluloid, made by Whitehead and Hoag, Newark, NJ, 7¾" l, $20.00.

material (brass, plastic, wood, etc.) or theme (animal shapes, swords, etc.)

Advertising
Boyertown Burial Casket Co, brass, early 1900s. **25.00**
Fuller Brushman **6.50**
Pacific Mutual **25.00**
Alligator, beige, black and white eyes, marked "Germany," c1900 . . . . **75.00**
Doctor's symbol, edge wear **5.00**
Dragon, brass. **40.00**
Elephant, ivory **30.00**
Indian, beige, black accents. **60.00**
Israel, Terra Cotta Guild, 1969 . . . . **7.50**
Owl, celluloid **65.00**
Seagull, bronze **24.00**
Tennis, racquet **6.00**

1977, metal, beige background, red and dark blue design **20.00**
Harrisburg Republican Club with Dewey–Bricker, fiberboard, dark blue background, yellow inscription, 1944. . . . . **25.00**
Jimmy Carter/A New Beginning, plastic, red, white, blue and green design, 6″ × 12″, c1976 . . . . **15.00**
State
Chicago, 1924, 4″, round, raised letters **30.00**
Michigan, 1923 . . . . **15.00**
Nebraska, 1930, enamel **15.00**
New York, 1912, porcelain **100.00**
North Dakota, 1933, pr **7.50**

LICENSE PLATES

They are mounted row after row on walls in their garage, den, and even living room. License plate collectors are truly among the possessed.

Collectors specialize. The most obvious approach is by state. But this just scratches the surface. Government plates, vanity plates, law enforcement plates, and special issue plates are just a few of the other potential collecting categories.

License plates are found most frequently at automobile flea markets. When they are found at general flea markets, they are generally encountered in large groups. Be prepared to buy the lot. Most sellers do not want them picked over. They know they can never sell the junk.

Club: Automobile License Plate Collectors Association, Inc., Box 712, Weston, WV 26452.

Philippines, green ground, white letters, Wheaties Premium, 1953, 3$\frac{1}{8}$ × 2$\frac{1}{4}$″, $1.00.

Novelty
District of Columbia, Inauguration

LIMITED EDITION COLLECTIBLES

Collect limited edition collectibles because you love them, not because you want to invest in them. While a few items sell well above their initial retail price, the vast majority sell between twenty-five and fifty cents on original retail dollar. The one consistent winner is the first issue in any series.

Whenever possible, buy items that still have their original box and inserts. The box adds another ten and twenty percent to the value of the item. Also, buy only items in excellent or better condition. Very good is not good enough. So many of each issue survive that market price holds only for the top condition grades.

Clubs: Foxfire Farm (Lowell Davis) Club, 55 Pacella Park Drive, Randolph, MA 02368; Gorham Collectors Club, P. O. Box 6472, Providence, RI 02940; Precious Moments Collectors' Club, 1 Enesco Plaza, Elk Grove Village, IL 60009.

Magazines: *Collector Editions*, 170 Fifth Avenue, New York, NY 10010; *Collectors Mart*, 15100 West Kellogg, Wichita, KS 67235; *Plate World*, 9200 North Maryland Avenue, Niles, IL 60648; *Precious Moments Collector*, P. O. Box 410707, Kansas City, MO 64141.

Bells
Bing & Grondahl, Christmas, 1980 . . . . **70.00**
Goebel
Angels, 1978, white. **6.00**
Mother's Day, FE, Crystal **38.00**
Gorham
1978, Currier & Ives. **20.00**
1983, Christmas Medley **30.00**
Noritake, 1982, Christmas **35.00**

Royal Copenhagen, 1921, Aabenraa Marketplace, $75.00.

Schmid
Peanuts, 1983, Peanuts in Concert 12.00
Raggedy Ann, 1976, Christmas 15.00
Wedgwood, 1985, Puffin 60.00
Dolls
Gorham
1984, Summer Holly Hobbie, 12″ . . . 65.00
1986, Jessica 150.00
Hamilton Collection
American Fashion Doll Collection,
1985, Victoria 125.00
Hakata, 1982, The Marionette 75.00
Royal Doulton by Nisbet, First Born . . . 175.00
Eggs
Anri, 1979, Beatrix Potter 5.00
Goebel, 1980, crystal 6.00
Noritake, Easter
1972 . . . . 35.00
1975 . . . . 10.00
Royal Bayreuth, 1977 . . . . 5.50
Veneto Flair, 1977 . . . . 15.00
Wedgwood, 1978 . . . . 25.00
Figurines
Burgues, 1982, Frosty 75.00
Cybis, 1976, Bunny, Muffet 125.00
Llardo, 1973, Going Fishing 90.00
Royal Doulton, Bunnykins, Clean
Sweep 14.00
Schmid, Lowell Davis artist, 1980,
Two's Company 45.00
Mugs
Bing & Grondahl, 1980 . . . . 25.00
Gorham, 1981, Bugs Bunny 8.00
Lynell Studios, 1983, FE, Gnome Series,
Mama Gnome 7.00
Royal Copenhagen, 1976, large 25.00
Wedgwood, 1973, Christmas 40.00
Music Box
Ferrandiz, Chorale 125.00
Walt Disney, 1982, Christmas 25.00

Plates
Bareuther, Germany, Christmas Series,
Hans Mueller artist
1970, Chapel in Oberndorf 15.00
1982, Bad Wimpfen 40.00
Bing and Grondahl, Denmark, Christmas Series, Henry Thelander artist
1970, Pheasants in Snow 20.00
1980, Christmas in Woods 42.00
1986, Silent Night, Holy Night 55.00
Franklin Mint, United States, Audubon
Society Series
1972, The Wood Duck, James
Fenwick artist 110.00
1976, Lion, Bernard Buffet artist 250.00
Gorham, United States, Christmas Series, Norman Rockwell artist
1974, Tiny Tim 50.00
1980, Letter to Santa 38.00
Haviland, France, Christmas Series,
Remy Hetrcau artist
1970, Partridge 110.00
1978, Nine Ladies Dancing 45.00
Haviland and Parlon, France, Russian
Fairy Tale Series, Boris Zvorykin artist
1980, The Snow Maiden 190.00
1982, In Search of the Firebird 70.00
Kaiser, Germany, Anniversary Series,
Toni Schoener artist
1976, Serenade 25.00
1982, Betrothal 40.00
Knowles, Edwin M, United States
Biblical Mother Series, Eve Licea
artist, 1984, Judgment of Solomon 75.00
Friends I Remember Series, Jeanne
Down artist, 1986, Flower Arrangement 22.00
Lenox, United States
Boehm Bird Series, Edward Marshall
Boehm artist
1970, Wood Thrush 225.00
1981, Eastern Phoebes 93.00
Christmas Series, Josef Neubauer artist, 1974, Peace 31.00
Pemberton and Oakes, United States
Childhood Friendship Series, Donald
Zolan artist, 1987, Beach Break . . . 25.00
Moments Alone Series, Robert
Bentley artist, 1980, The
Dreamer 45.00
Rosenthal, Germany, Classic Rose
Christmas Series, Helmut Drexel artist, 1984, City Hall of Stockholm 195.00
Royal Bayreuth, Germany, Mother's
Day Series, Leo Jansen artist
1974, Young Americans 130.00
1982, Young Americans IX 66.00
Royal Copenhagen, Denmark, Christmas Series, Kai Lange artist
1972, In the Desert 98.00
1980, Bringing Home the Christmas
Tree 76.00
Royal Doulton, Great Britain, Mother
and Child Series, Edna Hibel artist

173

1973, Colette and Child **460.00**
1976, Marilyn and Child **115.00**
Wedgwood, Enock, Great Britain,
Child's Birthday Series, Beatrix Potter
artist
1981, Peter Rabbit **24.00**
1988, Oakapple Wood. **29.00**

LINENS

Carefully examine linens for signs of wear, patching, and stains. Be cautious of estate linens that are unwashed and unironed. Question why the dealer has not prepared them for sale. Remember, you have no knowledge that the stains will come out. Also check all sets to make certain the pieces match.

Caring for Linens: If you are not planning to use your linens, store them unpressed, rolled, covered with an old pillow case, and stored out of bright sunlight. Rinse linens and the storage pillow case several times to make certain all detergent residue is removed.

If you are going to use your linen on a regular basis, wrap them in acid-free white tissue or muslin folders. Whenever possible, store linens on rollers to prevent creasing. You can get acid-free storage materials from Talas, 104 Fifth Avenue, New York, NY 10011.

Club: International Old Lacers, Box 1029 West Minster, CO 80030.

Bedding, linen, white, double bed, white
embroidered "P" in floral wreath
Pillow Sham, crocheted pointed
ends **45.00**
Sheet, crocheted hems. **40.00**

Bridge Cloth, cross–stitch dec, Quimper
pattern, green, blue, rose, and yellow,
c1920. . . . . **100.00**
Centerpiece, crocheted, white
4½″ × 11″, "Bread" in center. **15.00**
12″ × 20″, "God Bless Our Home" in
center. **25.00**
Doily, 38″ d, 5″ w crocheted trim, three
heavily beaded birds **50.00**
Dresser Set
Cotton, white, embroidered basket of
flowers, blue, yellow, rose, green, and
brown, crocheted edge **35.00**
Linen, white, embroidered "S," 3″ w
crocheted end panels **50.00**
Tablecloth
Damask, woven mustard geometric
borders, cinnamon ground, c1900,
53″ sq **600.00**
Linen, cream, cut work, overall floral
and scroll pattern, ecru embroidery,
132″ × 164″. **200.00**
Tea Towels, printed cotton, sq, primroses
and forget-me-nots, pr **20.00**

LITTLE GOLDEN BOOKS

Read me a story! For millions of children that story came from a Little Golden Book. Colorful, inexpensive, and readily available, these wonderful books are a hot collectible. You see them everywhere.

Be careful, you may be subject to a nostalgia attack because sooner or later you are going to spot your favorite. Relive your childhood. Buy the book. You won't be sorry.

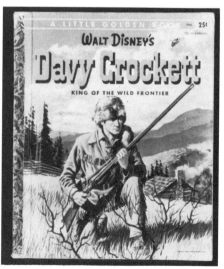

Walt Disney's Davy Crockett, King Of The Wild Frontier, *1955, $15.00.*

Doily, crocheted, Pineapple pattern, 30 wt cotton, 19″ d, $12.00.

A Day At The Playground, Miriam Schlein,
   illus Eloise Wilkin, c1951 . . . . **10.00**
Buffalo Bill Jr, Gladys Wyatt, c1956. . . . . . **5.50**
Doctor Dan at the Circus, Pauline Wilkins,
   c1960. . . . . **17.50**
Grandpa Bunny, Jane Werner, illus Walt
   Disney Studios, c1951. . . . . **15.00**
Huckleberry Hound Safety Signs, Ann
   McGovern, c1961 . . . . **7.00**
It's Howdy Doody Time, Edward Kean,
   c1955. . . . . **12.00**
Little Red Riding Hood, illus Sharon
   Koester, with paper dolls. **25.00**
Maverick, Carl Memling. **7.50**
Mickey Mouse Club Stamp Book, Kathleen N
   Daily, c1956, orig stamps **20.00**
Our Puppy, Elsa Ruth Nast, c1948 . . . . . . **10.00**
Rootie Kazootie Joins The Circus, Steve
   Carlin, c1955. . . . . **12.00**
Roy Rogers and the Mountain Lion, Ann
   McGovern, c1955 . . . . **10.00**
Rusty Goes to School, Pierre Probst,
   c1962. . . . . **5.00**
Tiger's Adventure, William P Gottlieb,
   c1954. . . . . **5.50**

LITTLE ORPHAN ANNIE

Little Orphan Annie is one of those characters that pops up all over the place — radio,
newspapers, movies, etc. In the early
1930s, "Radio Orphan Annie" was syndi-
cated regionally. It went network in 1933.
The show's only sponsor was Ovaltine.
Many Little Orphan Annie collectibles
were Ovaltine premiums.
   Actually Little Orphan Annie resulted
from a sex-change operation. Harold Gray,
an assistant on the "Gumps" strip, changed
the sex of the leading character and sub-
mitted the same basic strip concept as a
proposal to the New York News. The 1924
operation was a success.
   Annie's early companions were Sandy,
her dog, and Emily Marie, her doll.
"Daddy" Warbucks replaced the doll, and
the strip went big time. Gray died in 1968.
The strip was farmed out to a succession of
artists and writers. The result was disastrous.
   Radio and cartoon strip Little Orphan
Annie material is becoming expensive. Try
recent movie-and stage-related items if you
are looking for something a bit more
affordable.

Book, James Whitcomb Riley, The Little
   Orphan Annie Book, color illus by Ethel
   Betts, 1908. **25.00**

Bracelet, identification disc, 1934 . . . . **20.00**
Clicker, red, white, and black, Mysto
   members, 1941 . . . . **35.00**
Gravy Boat, lusterware, white, orange,
   yellow, and black. **175.00**

**Game, Little Orphan Annie Game, Milton Brad-
ley, 1927, $60.00.**

Manual, Radio Orphan Annie's Secret So-
   ciety, 1937 . . . . **30.00**
Mask, Annie, 1933 . . . . **30.00**
Mug, ceramic, 1932. . . . . **20.00**
Nodder, 3½" h, painted bisque, stamped
   on back "Orphan Annie," 1930s. **150.00**
Pastry Set, miniature baking utensils,
   Transogram "Gold Medal" Toy,
   1930s. **75.00**
Whistle, tin, signal, three tones **30.00**
Photo, 8" × 10", black and white, glossy,
   Shirley Bell, sgd "To My Friend/Radio's
   Little Orphan Annie/Shirley Bell,"
   1932. . . . . **40.00**

LLARDO PORCELAINS

Llardo porcelains are Spain's contribution
to the world of collectible figures. Some
figures are released on a limited edition basis; others remain in production for an extended period of time. Learn what kinds of
production numbers are involved.
   Llardo porcelains are sold through jewelry and "upscale" gift shops. However,
they are the type of item you either love or
hate. As a result, Llardo porcelains from
estates or from individuals tired of dusting
that thing that Aunt Millie gave for Christmas 1985 do show up at flea markets.

Bride and Groom, #4808 . . . . **175.00**
Bullfighter, #5117 . . . . **125.00**
Dove, #1915 . . . . **50.00**
Gypsy Woman, #4919 . . . . **165.00**
Girl, with calla lily, #4650 . . . . **75.00**
Harlequin, with cat, #1229. . . . . **185.00**
Hebrew Student, #4684 . . . . **375.00**

Japanese Girl, kneeling, #4840 . . . . **275.00**	Money Bag Lock, brass, 3". **35.00**
Mother, two children, #L4864 . . . . **400.00**	Trunk Hatch Lock, Eagle Lock Co **5.00**
Nuns, #2075 . . . . **150.00**	Value Lock, 5½", bronze **15.00**
Teasing The Dog, #5078 . . . . **160.00**	
Victorian Girl, reading, #5000 . . . . **150.00**	

LUGGAGE

LOCKS

Padlocks are the most desirable lock collectible. While examples date back to the 1600s, the mass production of identifiable padlocks was pioneered in America in the mid–1800s.

Padlocks are categorized primarily according to tradition or use: Combination, Pin Tumber, Scandinavian, etc. Cast, brass, and iron are among the more sought-after types.

Reproductions, copycats, and fakes are a big problem. Among the trouble spots are screw key, trick, iron lever, and brass lever locks from the Middle East, railroad switch locks from Taiwan, and switch lock keys from the U.S. Midwest. All components of an old lock must have exactly the same color and finish. Authentic railroad, express, and logo locks will have only one user name or set of initials.

Club: American Lock Collectors Association, 36076 Grennada, Livonia, MI 48154.

Money Bag Lock, brass, 3", $35.00.

Buckle Lock, brass	
1"	**8.50**
2"	**15.00**
Buckle Lock, iron	
1"	**6.00**
2"	**12.00**
Buckle & Strap, Tourist, 2"	**20.00**
Gate Lock	
Iron, handmade, large	**28.00**
Iron and Brass, manufacturer's name,	
10"	**70.00**
Hotel Lockout, ILCO	**14.00**
Locking Clamp, Backus	**22.50**
Lug Nut Lock, Chicago	**7.00**

Until recently luggage collectors focused primarily on old steamship and railroad trunks. Unrestored, they sell in the $50 to $150 range. Dealers have the exterior refinished and the interior relined with new paper and then promptly sell them to decorators who charge upwards of $400. A restored trunk works well in both a Country or Victorian bedroom. This is why decorators love them so much.

Within the past three years, there is a growing collector interest in old leather luggage. It is not uncommon to find early twentieth century leather overnight bags priced at $150 to $300 in good condition. Leather suitcases sell in the $75 to $150 range.

LUNCH KITS

Lunch kits, consisting of a lunch box and matching thermos, were the most price-manipulated collectibles category of the 1980s. Prices in excess of $2,500 were achieved for some of the early Disney examples. What everyone seemed to forget is that lunch boxes were mass-produced.

The lunch kit bubble is in the process of bursting. Price are dropping for the commonly found examples. A few dealers and collectors are attempting to prop up the market, but their efforts are failing. If you are buying, it will pay to shop around for the best price.

Buy lunch kits. Resist the temptation to buy the lunch box and thermos separately.

I know this is a flea market price guide, but lunch kits can get pricy by the time they arrive at a flea market. The best buys remain at garage sales where the kits first hit the market and sellers are glad to get rid of them at any price.

Newsletter: *Hot Boxing*, P. O. Box 87, Somerville, MA 02143.

Advertising	
Dixie Queen	**95.00**
Central Union	**75.00**
Bonanza	**20.00**

Space: 1999, King Seely Thermos Co, 1975, $25.00.

Denim, vinyl, jeans design with patches,
  c1960........................... **25.00**
Early West....................... **20.00**
Empire Strikes Back **10.00**
Flipper, metal, full color illus, 1966 Van
  Tors Films copyright **55.00**
Grizzly Adams, dome top **65.00**
Muppets **28.00**
Pac Man, metal, emb, full color illus, 1980
  Bally Midway Mfg Co **30.00**
Robin Hood, metal, full color illus, 1956
  copyright...................... **50.00**
Sesame Street, vinyl, full color illus, 1981
  Children's Television Workshop copy-
  right.......................... **20.00**
Submarine, metal, full color illus, 1960
  copyright...................... **25.00**
Super Heroes..................... **20.00**
Wags 'N Whiskers, metal, full color illus,
  1978 Norcross copyright **15.00**
Waltons......................... **20.00**

MAGAZINES

The vast majority of magazines, especially if they are less than thirty years old, are worth between 10¢ and 25¢. A fair number of pre–1960 magazines fall within this price range as well.

There are three ways a magazine can have value: (1) the cover artist, (2) the cover personality, and (3) framable interior advertising. In these cases, value rests not with the magazine collector, but with the speciality collectors.

At almost any flea market, you will find a seller of matted magazine advertisements. Remember that the value being asked almost always rests in the matting and not the individual magazine page being matted.

Newspaper: *PCM (Paper Collector's Market-place),* P. O. Box 127, Scandinavia, WI 54977.

Saturday Evening Post, May 24, 1958, Norman Rockwell cover, $4.00.

American Boy, 1928 .... **2.00**
American Home..................... **2.00**
Atlantic Monthly, 1914............... **1.00**
Cosmopolitan, 1942 .... **1.00**
Country Home...................... **.75**
Field and Stream **3.00**
Harper's Bazaar, illus cov............. **10.00**
Harper's Weekly, Dec 1900............. **15.00**
House Beautiful, illustrator cov......... **8.00**
Ladies' Home Journal, 1925 .... **5.00**
Life, artist sgd cov.................. **20.00**
Look, celebrity **5.00**
Newsweek, after 1950................ **.25**
Outdoor Life **1.00**
Playboy, 1958..................... **2.00**
The Theater Magazine, 1908 .... **5.00**
Time, 1941–1960 .... **1.00**
TV Guide, NYC–TeleVision Guide,
  1948–1953 .... **40.00**
Vogue, illus cov **10.00**

MAGIC

Presto, chango — the world of magic has fascinated collectors for centuries. The category is broad; it pays to specialize. Possible approaches include: children's magic sets, posters about magicians, slight of hand tricks, and many, many more.

When buying a trick, make certain to get instructions—if possible, the original.

Without them, you need to be a mystic, rather than a magician to figure out how the trick works.

Magic catalogs are treasure chests of information. Look for company names such as Abbott's, Brema, Douglas Magicland, Felsman, U. F. Grant, Magic Inc., Martinka, National Magic, Nelson Enterprises, Owen Magic Supreme, Petrie–Lewis, D. Robbins, Tannen, Thayer, and Willmann. Petrie–Lewis is a favorite among collectors. Look for the interwoven "P & L" on magic props.

Magicians of note include: Alexander, Blackstone, Carter The Great, Germain The Wizard, Houdini, Kar–MI, Kellar, Stock, and Thornston. Anything associated with these magicians has potentially strong market value.

Club: Magic Collectors Association, 19 Logan Street, New Britain, CT 06051.

Book
    Fred Keating/Magic's Greatest Entertainer,
      16 pgs, late 1940s, early 1950s...... **25.00**
    Magic Made Easy, 28 pgs, 1930 copy-
      right......................... **20.00**
    Magicdotes, Robert Orben, 44 pgs, 1948
      copyright..................... **15.00**
    Catalog, Heaney Company, 1924....... **20.00**
Magic Kit
    PF Fliers Blackstone Magic Wedge Kit,
      sealed bag with Balance Magic, Dis-
      appearing Coin Trick, and Defy Grav-
      ity, box with Blackstone Jr illus,
      1970s........................ **15.00**
    Scarecrow Magic Kit, Ralston Purina Co
      premium, 1960s **25.00**
Pinback Button
    Houdini Convention Club of Wiscon-
      sin, blue and white, 1930s........ **8.00**
    14th Annual International Brother-
      hood of Magicians Convention, Bat-
      tle Creek Michigan, blue and white,
      1939........................ **6.00**
    The International Brotherhood of Magi-
      cians, orange, 1930s **12.00**
Top Hat, beaver **35.00**

MAGNIFYING GLASSES

The vast majority of magnifying glasses that are offered for sale at flea markets are made–up examples. Their handles come from old umbrellas, dresser sets, and even knives. They look old and are highly decorative — a deadly combination for someone who thinks they are getting a one hundred-year-old-plus example.

There are few collectors of magnifying glasses. Therefore, prices are low, often a few dollars or less, even for some unusual examples. The most collectible magnifying glasses are the Sherlock Holmes types and examples from upscale desk accessory sets. These often exceed $25.00.

MARBLES

Marbles divide into handmade glass marbles and machine–made glass, clay, and mineral marbles. Marble identification is serious business. Read and re–read these books before buying your first marble: Paul Baumann, *Collecting Antique Marbles, Second Edition* (Wallace–Homestead, 1991); and Mark E. Randall and Dennis Webb, *Greenberg's Guide to Marbles* (Greenberg Publishing, 1988.)

Children played with marbles. The vast majority are found in a damaged state. Avoid these. There are plenty of examples in excellent condition.

Beware of reproductions and modern copycats and fakes. Comic marbles are just one type of marble that is currently being reproduced.

Clubs: Marble Collectors' Unlimited, 503 West Pine, Marengo, IA 52301; Marble Collectors Society of America, P. O. Box 222, Trumbull, CT 06611; National Marble Club of America, 440 Easton Road, Drexel Hill, PA 19026.

Swirl, white, red, blue, yellow, and green, 1⅝" d, $40.00.

Akro Agate, ½" d, bull's eye **20.00**
Bennington Type
    5/8" d, mottled blue **25.00**

7/8" d, mottled brown 30.00
Cat's Eyes, Vitro–Agate, bag of 100,
c1950. . . . . 35.00
Comic Strip, glass
  Koko 30.00
  Skeezix 45.00
  Tom Mix 55.00
Onionskin
  1/2" d, blue and white swirls 25.00
  2" d, red and yellow swirls 275.00
Sulphide
  1¼" d, pig 60.00
  1⅝" d, woman 150.00
  1¾" d, dog, Chow 75.00
Swirl
  1" d, blue, orange, and green 55.00
  2" d, multicolored 75.00

Perfume Bottle, 4⅝" h, little girl, cranberry,
  clear ball stopper 165.00
Pitcher, ruffled top
  10½" h, man in sailboat, clear. 125.00
  11" h, woman blowing trumpet, royal
  blue 325.00
Plate, 11" d, stag running, black ame-
  thyst. 285.00
Toothpick Holder, girl and floral sprays,
  cranberry 55.00
Tumbler, boy and girl, cranberry, facing
  pr 100.00
Vase
  4" h, boy and girl reading books,
  cranberry, pr 110.00
  10" h, man holding gun, woman hold-
  ing basket of fruit, lime green, pr 265.00
  11" h, herons in flight, sapphire blue . . . 300.00

MARY GREGORY GLASS

Who was Mary Gregory anyway? Her stuff
certainly is expensive. Beware of objects
that seem like too much of a bargain. They
may have been painted by Mary Gregory's
great–great granddaughter in the 1950s
rather than in the 1880s. Also, watch the
eyes. The original Mary Gregory did not
paint children with slanty eyes. Guess who
did?

*Pitcher, sapphire blue ground, white enameled
young child, 10" h, $325.00.*

Box, cov, 3⅛" d, round, hinged lid, girl and
  floral sprays, cranberry 265.00
Liqueur Glass, 3⅜" h, little girl, lime
  green 50.00

MATCHBOOKS

Don't play with matches. Save their covers
instead. A great collection can be built for a
relatively small sum of money. Matchcover
collectors gain a fair amount of their new
material through swapping.

A few collectors specialize in covers that
include figural shaped or decorated
matches. If you get into this, make certain
you keep them stored in a tin covered container and keep them in a cool location. If
you don't, your collection is going to catch
fire and go up in smoke.

Club: Rathkamp Matchcover Society,
1359 Surrey Road, Vandalia, OH 43577.

*Left: Heilman's Old Style Lager, Ohio Match Co,
Wadsworth, OH, $.25; right: Dr Pepper, Uni-
versal Match Corp, $.25.*

: There are over thirty regional clubs throughout the United States and Canada.

Airlines	.25
Banks	.02
Dated	.10
Diamond Quality	.50
Fairs	.15
Girlies, non stock	.40
Holiday Inns, stock design	.10
Joe Louis & Max Schmeling Championship Fight, Giant	18.00
Matchtones, Universal trademark	.10
Patriotic	.05
Political	1.00
Presidential Yacht, "Patricia"	10.00
Pull for Willkie, Pullquick Match	28.00
Pull Quick	1.00
Ship Lines	.10
Stoeckle Select Beer, Giant, Stoeckle Brewery	6.00
Whiskey	.30

Clubs: American–International Matchbox, 522 Chestnut Street, Lynn, MA 01904; Matchbox Collectors Club, 141 West Commercial Avenue, Moonachie, NJ 07075.

Airport Coach, 1978	4.00
BMW, sport coupe, orange, 1980	2.00
Cadillac, 1965	6.00
Cement Truck, 1977	7.50
Ferrari, green, 1970	5.00
Ford, Capri, red and silver, 1975	3.00
Hot Rod, 1971	5.00
Lotus, roadster, orange, 1961	5.00
Mercedes, convertible, 1982	3.00
Pepsi Truck	8.00
Pontiac, Trans Am, black, 1980	2.50
Rolls Royce, Yesteryears 2nd Series	20.00
Steam Roller, MIB	40.00
Train, Yesteryears Series, 3 pcs	24.00

MATCHBOX TOYS

Leslie Smith and Rodney Smith founded Lesney Products, an English company, in 1947. They produced the first Matchbox toys. In 1953 the trade name "Matchbox" was registered and the first diecast cars were made on a 1:75 scale. In 1979 Lesney produced over 5.5 million cars per week. In 1982 Universal International bought Lesney.

Land Rover Fire Truck, #57, diecast, red, $4.50.

McCOY POTTERY

Like Abingdon Pottery, this attractive pottery is sought after by those no longer able to afford Roseville and Weller pottery. Commemorative cookie jars and planters seem to be rapidly increasing in price, like the Apollo Spaceship cookie jar at $45.00. These speciality items bring more from secondary collectors than from McCoy collectors who realize the vast quantity of material available in the market.

Beware of reproductions. The Nelson McCoy Pottery Company is making modern copies of their period pieces. New collectors are often confused by them.

Planter, dog, light green, white, highlights, 7½" l, $10.00.

Ashtray, Seagram's advertising, black,
  gold letters 12.50
Baby Planter
  Cradle, pink 7.50
  Lamb, white, blue bow 8.00
  Stork, green 7.00
Bank, sailor, duffel bag over shoulder 20.00
Bookends, jumping horses, pr, marked
  "Nu–Art" 18.50
Centerpiece Bowl, blue, tulips dec, 8¾"
  d. 7.50
Cookie Jar
  Black Stove 20.00
  Mammy 45.00
  Picnic Basket 35.00
  Red Apple 20.00
  Yosemite Sam 40.00
Creamer, Elsie The Cow adv 15.00
Mug, Suburbia pattern, yellow 7.50
Planter
  Dog, light green and white 12.00
  Rabbit, ivory 7.00
  Smiley Face, yellow 4.00
  Sprinkling Can, white, rose decal 6.50
Teapot, Grecian pattern 25.00
Vase, 8" h, bud, matte green 5.00

MEDICAL ITEMS

Anything medical is collectible. Doctors often discard obsolete instruments, never realizing that the minute an object becomes obsolete, it also becomes collectible. Many a flea market treasure begins life in a garbage can behind the doctor's office.

Stress condition and completeness. Specialize in one area. Remember some instruments do not display well. Dad's wife will not let him keep his collection of rectal examiners in the livingroom.

Apothecary
  Bottle, 5⅞" h, pressed, amber, tole
  lid 25.00
  Mortar and Pestle, 9", turned ash
  burl, wide turned foot, plain birch
  pestle 125.00
  Pill Roller, 2 pcs, 7" × 14", walnut and
  brass, makes 24 pills. 100.00
Dental
  Cheek Retractor, carved, MOP handle 75.00
  Pliers, nerve canal 15.00
  Sterilizer, formaldehyde, wall
  mounted 50.00
Medical
  Anesthesia Mask, brass, folding,
  c1870 . . . .   75.00
  Bleeder, spring loaded, brass, "POL
  1842," etched on back, orig box 75.00

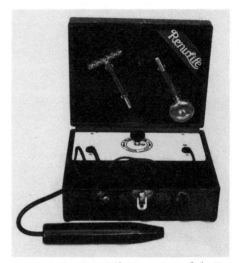

Quack device, Renu Life Generator, mfg by Renulife Electric Co, Inc., Detroit, Mich, patent September 30, 1949, $45.00.

Bottle
  Chlorate Potassique, pontil, clear,
  painted brown, 6 ½" 20.00
  Granular Citrate of Magnesia, kite
  with letter inside, ring top, cobalt,
  8" 30.00
  Pine Tree Tar Cordial, Phila, tree and
  patent 1859 on one panel, LQG
  Wisharts on other, blob top, green,
  8" 50.00
Hearing Aid, silk tubing 85.00
Saw, amputation, bow blade, ebony
  handle 120.00
Stethoscope, monaural, metal 100.00
Optical
  Book, *Optical Dictionary and Encyclopedia*, 1908 . . . .   25.00
  Eyelid Retractor, ivory handle, marked
  "Hills King St," c1853 . . . . 125.00
  Ophthalmoscope, Morton, cased 100.00

MILITARIA

Soldiers have returned home with the spoils of war as long as there have been soldiers and wars. Look at the Desert Storm material that is starting to arrive in the market. Many collectors tend to collect material relating to wars taking place in their young adulthood or related to re-enactment groups to which they belong.

It pays to specialize. The two obvious choices are a specific war or piece of equipment. American collectors have never

181

overlooked the enemy. Nazi material remains the strongest segment of the market. Reproductions abound. Be especially careful of any Civil War and Nazi material.

Magazines: *Military Collectors' News*, P. O. Box 702073, Tulsa, OK 74170; *North South Trader*, P. O. Drawer 631, Orange, VA 22960.

Clubs: American Society of Military Insignia Collectors, 1331 Bradley Avenue, Hummelstown, PA 17036; Association of American Military Uniform Collectors, 446 Berkshire Rd, Elyria, OH 44035; Company of Military Historians, North Main Street, Westbrook, CT 06498; Imperial German Military Collectors Association, Box 38, Keyport, NJ 07735.

Document and discharge papers, reverse painting under glass, US Army, Warren Bennethum, 1919, 16⅛" × 20⅛" framed, $50.00.

CIVIL WAR

Bullet Mold, picket pattern bullet	**45.00**
Cartridge Box, Weston	**300.00**
Field Glasses, 7½", brass, made by Lemaire Fabt, Paris	**125.00**
Insignia, brass, lieutenant	**25.00**
Muster roll, 20th Regt Illinois, August to October 1863, folds out to 20" × 30", document entries	**100.00**
Shell Jacket, Union cavalry, buttons, lining, and inspector's marks	**425.00**
Tintype, full length, unidentified Confederate Cavalry man, gear, sword, and carbine	**450.00**

WORLD WAR I

Badge, Tank Corps, British cap, 8th Churka	**20.00**
Belt, webb	**15.00**

Gas Mask, carrying can, shoulder strap, canister attached to bottom, German **75.00**
Medal, Iron Cross **35.00**
Periscope, wood, used in trench warfare **75.00**
Poster, "Lend the Way They Fight, Buy Bonds to Your Utmost," full color action scene, red and black lettering, green border **50.00**
Uniform, U.S. Army, Engineer, coat, belt, pants, cap, canvas leggings, wood puttees, and leather gaiters, canteen . . . **300.00**

WORLD WAR II

Badge, Nazi, General Assault, silver, c1940	**30.00**
Binoculars, Army, M-17, field type, 7½" l, olive drab, 7 × 50 power, clear, fixed optics	**100.00**
Book, A. Hitler, *Mein Kampf*, 1933, 407 pgs, orig dust jacket	**15.00**
Envelope, Iwo Jima flag raising, 8/29/45, artist G F Hadley	**15.00**
Hat, Nazi SS, rabbit fur, quilted int., black ties at ear flaps, olive green wool body, RZM/SS, skull and eagle devices	**325.00**
Knife, Cumillus, USN Mark S Sheath Knife, black finish blade, light scabbard wear, USN and name marked on guard, gray web belt look, gray fiber scabbard	**50.00**
Manual, *Recognition Pictorial Manual*, Bureau of Aeronautics, Navy Department, Washington, DC, June 1943, contains silhouettes and technical information on Allied and Axis aircraft, 6" × 10", 80 pgs, black and white	**45.00**
Patch, pilot's wings, leather, AAF, emb, standard design, flying jacket attachment type	**30.00**
Ring, Nazi, silver, crossed swords, helmet, and swastika	**50.00**
Shirt, Nazi, brown, S.A., black collar tabs, black piping, eagle buttons, c1933	**150.00**
Sweater, sleeveless, olive drab, "V" neck	**25.00**

KOREA

Jacket, Sergeant's OD, Ike style, pile lined cap with ear flaps	**40.00**

VIETNAM

Helmet, US tanker, fiberglass, dark green, intercom system on side	**50.00**
Medal, Vietnam Service	**15.00**
Tunic, US Army, sergeant, 5th Division, red diamonds insignia, green, gold stripes	**40.00**

MILK BOTTLES

There is an entire generation of young adults to whom the concept of milk in a bottle is a foreign idea. In another fifteen years a book like this will have to contain a chapter on plastic milk cartons. I hope you are saving some.

When buying a bottle, make certain the glass is clear of defects from manufacture and wear and the label and/or wording in fine or better condition. Buy odd-sized bottles and bottles with special features. Don't forget the caps. They are collectibles too.

Newsletter: *The Milk Route*, 4 Ox Bow Road, Westport, CT 06880.

R. M. Deger, Phoenixville, PA, Pure Milk, clear glass, $2.50.

Alden Bros, round, emb	**25.00**
Borden's Golden Crest, amber	**18.00**
Dunmyer Dairy	**20.00**
Gold Spot, green	**40.00**
Grasslands Dairy	**10.00**
Hoeier Dairy, Springfield, IL, red painted "Hey Mom, I want my glass of milk". . .	**6.00**
Murphy's Dairy, Neenah.	**30.00**
Palmer Dairy, dripless	**25.00**
Price's Dairy Co, clear	**5.00**
Shelton Bros Dairy, clear, pt	**4.00**
The Croney Dairy, Clymer, NY, baby reaching for bottle	**4.00**

MILK GLASS

Milk glass is an opaque white glass that became popular during the Victorian era. A scientist will tell you that it is made by adding oxide of tin to a batch of clear glass. Most collect it because it's pretty.

Companies like Atterbury, McKee, and Westmoreland have all produced fine examples in novelties, often of the souvenir variety, as well as household items. Old timers focus heavily on milk glass made before 1920. However, there are some great pieces from the post-1920 period that you would be wise not to overlook.

Milk glass has remained in continuous production since it was first invented. Many firms reproduce old patterns. Be careful. Old timers will tell you that if a piece has straw marks, it is probably correct. Some modern manufacturers who want to fool you might have also added them in the mold. Watch out for a "K" in a diamond. This is the mark on milk glass reproductions from the 1960s made by the Kemple Glass Company.

Milk glass is practical. A glass sitting beside a plate of cookies gives others in the room the impression that you are drinking milk. Hint, hint!

Club: National Milk Glass Collectors Society, P. O. Box 402, Northfield, MN 55057.

Children's dishes, Thumbelina pattern, Westmoreland Glass Co, $50.00.

Animal Covered Dish	
Dog, split ribbed base	**50.00**
Dove, basketweave base, marked "McKee".	**90.00**
Hen, nest base	**75.00**
Rabbit, octagonal base.	**65.00**
Appetizer Plate, Paneled Grape pattern, Westmoreland.	**40.00**
Bottle, Statue of Liberty, metal lid	**150.00**

Bowl, cov, Beaded Grape, Westmoreland.................... 20.00
Creamer, Sunflower pattern, Atterbury........................ 65.00
Dish, snare drum shape, cannon finial ... 70.00
Egg Cup, bird cover, round, fluted, Atterbury.......................135.00
Inkwell, Daisy and Button pattern, figural, high back chair 90.00
Miniature Lamp, applied multicolored flowers.........................100.00
Nappy, Roses & Bows pattern, hp flowers 30.00
Pickle Dish, fish shape, 9⅝" l, Atterbury...................... 25.00
Plate, Three Kittens 35.00
Spooner, Monkey pattern, scalloped top 115.00
Sugar, Old Quilt pattern, Westmoreland................... 10.00
Toothpick Holder, figural, swan 20.00

Chair, cast iron, painted green, Victorian, American, 4⅛" h, $50.00.

MINIATURES

If you want to find miniatures at flea markets, look in the cases because the size that you are most likely to find is "doll house." The other two sizes are child's and salesman's sample. These rarely show up at flea markets.

Beware. Miniatures have been sold for years. Modern crafts people continue to make great examples. Alas, their handiwork can be easily aged so that it will fool most buyers. Also Cracker Jack giveaways, charms, etc. should not be confused with miniatures.

Magazines: *Miniature Collectors*, Collector Communications Corp., 170 Fifth Ave., New York, NY 10010; *Nutshell News*, Clifton House, Clifton, VA 22024.

Clubs: International Guild of Miniature Artisans, P. O. Box 842, Summit, NJ 07901; National Association of Miniature Enthusiasts, 123 N. Lemon Street, Fullerton, CA 92632.

Ashtray on stand, wooden, c1910....... 30.00
Bathroom Set, wood, painted white, Strombecker 35.00
Bedroom Suite, Victorian style, metal, veneer finish, faux marble tops, bed, night stand, commode, armoire, mirror, cradle, Biedermeier clock, washstand 650.00
Bird Cage, brass, stand, tiny bird, 7"h 60.00
Candelabra, Petite Princess 20.00
Clock, metal 20.00
Cup and Saucer, china, floral decal, c1940.......................... 8.50

Desk, Chippendale style slant front...... 50.00
Dining Room Suite, French style, gilded wood, round faux marble top table, six chairs, upholstered damask settee, pier mirror, fireplace.................800.00
Living Room Suite, Victorian style, upholstered red velvet, settee, two chairs, foot stool, two plant stands, two gilt filigree tables, screen, Gone with the Wind style lamp...........................500.00
Measuring Cup, Pyrex............... 10.00
Piano, grand, wood, 5"h 30.00
Silhouettes, Tynietoy, c1930, pr 15.00
Typewriter, moving carriage, silver plated......................... 20.00
Umbrella Stand, brass ormolu, sq emb palm fronds 50.00

MORTON POTTERIES

Morton is an example of a regional pottery that has a national collecting base. Actually, there were several potteries in Morton, Illinois: Morton Pottery Works and Morton Earthenware Company, 1897–1917; Cliftwood Art Potteries, 1920–1940; Midwest Potteries, 1940–1944; and, Morton Pottery Company, 1922–1976.

Prior to 1940 local clay that fired to a golden ecru was used. After 1940 clay was imported and fired white. Few pieces are marked. The key to identifying Morton pieces is through the company's catalogs and Doris and Burdell Hall's book, *Morton's Potteries: 99 Years*, (published by the authors, 1982).

Planter, rabbit with basket, white, pink ears, gold dec, $18.00.

MOTHER'S DAY COLLECTIBLES

It's not fair. The amount of Mother's Day memorabilia is about ten times the amount of Father's Day memorabilia. It has something to do with apple pie.

A great deal of Mother's Day memorabilia seen at flea markets is "limited edition." The fact that you see so much is an indication that few of these issues were truly limited. Insist on excellent or better condition and the original box when buying.

Since so many collectors are focusing on limited edition material, why not direct your efforts in another direction, for example, greeting cards or pinback buttons. Your costs will be lower, and your collection will be out of the ordinary, just like your mother.

Royal Copenhagen, 1979, A Loving Mother, $30.00.

Morton Pottery Works and Morton Earthenware Co
Bank, 3" h, acorn shape, brown Rockingham glaze 20.00
Chamber Pot, 9" d, yellow ware, handled 50.00
Creamer, 1¾" h, miniature, brown Rockingham glaze 20.00
Cliftwood Art Potteries, Inc
Compote, 6" h, 9" d, #226, old rose glaze 15.00
Figurine, Lioness, 12" × 7", green glaze 25.00
Vase, 10" h, #109, six side panels, arched top, cobalt 22.00
Midwest Potteries, Inc
Figurine, Tiger, 7" × 12", natural colors 40.00
Miniature, figurine, polar bear, 1¾" h, white 7.00
Salt and Pepper Shaker, Scottie dog, matte white, pr. 10.00
Morton Pottery Company
Ashtray, square, 12", dark brown, cigarette snuffer in center 16.00
Bank, Elephant, pink 15.00
Cookie Jar, hen, chick finial on lid 50.00
Planter, Mother Earth Line, sweet potato, natural colors, #390 . . . . 3.00
American Art Potteries
Flower Bowl, 10"l, S shape, yellow 8.00
Flower Frog, turtle, white, green and yellow spray glaze 12.00
Vase, 7½" h, shamrock shape, peach, orchid spray glaze, stemmed base . . . 10.00

Bell, limited edition, Schmid
1976, Mother's Day Series, Devotion for Mothers 55.00
1977, Peanuts Mother's Day, Dear Mom 15.00
Doll, limited edition, Reco, 1990, Precious Memories of Motherhood series, Loving Steps 125.00
Figurine
Artaffects, 1987, limited edition, musical, Motherhood 65.00
Avon, 1983–84, Little Things, 3¾" h, porcelain boy, hp, MIB 18.00
Byers' Choice Ltd, 1988, Mother's Day, daughter 175.00
Pinback Button
3/4" d, bust of woman in center, carnation on either side, "Mothers

Day" on banner below, multicolored,
1920s **3.50**
3/4" d, carnation, "Anna Jarvis Founder
Philadelphia, Mother's Day,"
multicolored, 1920s. **3.00**
1¼" d, carnation behind heart in-
scribed "Mother," "May, 2nd Sunday, Mothers Day," red and white,
1920s **5.00**
Plate
Anri, 1973, Mother's Day Series, Alpine
Mother and Children **55.00**
Avon, 1981, Cherished Moments, 5" d,
porcelain, MIB. **10.00**
Kaiser, 1981, Mother's Day Series, Safe
Near Mother **40.00**
Svend Jensen, 1970, Mother's Day Se-
ries, Bouquet for Mother **75.00**

MOTORCYCLES

Some of these beauties are getting as expensive as classic and antique cars. This
category is personal. I owned motorcycles,
until an elderly lady who ran a light and
my dad put a stop to my motorcycling career.

Motorcycles are generational. My grandfather would identify with an Indian, my
dad with a BMW or Harley Davidson, and I
with the Japanese imports. I suspect that
most users of this book are not likely to buy
an older motorcyle. However, just in case
you see a 1916 Indian Power Plus with
sidecar for a thousand or less, pick it up. Its
book value is $15,000.00.

Magazine: *Hemmings Motor News*, P. O. Box
100, Bennington, VT

Toy, cast iron, Harley Davidson, painted blue,
silver wheels, 7" × 4½", $120.00.

MOVIE MEMORABILIA

The stars of the silent screen have fascinated audiences for over three–quarters of
a century. In many cases, this fascination
had as much to do with their private lives
as their on-screen performances.

This is a category where individuals focus on their favorites. There are super stars
in the collectibles area. Two examples are
Charlie Chaplin and Marilyn Monroe.

Posters are expensive. However, there
are plenty of other categories where a major collection can be built for under $25.00
per object. Also, do not overlook the pres-
ent-day material. If it's cheap, pick it up.
Movie material will always be collectible.

Newspapers: *Big Reel*, P. O. Box 83, Madison, NC 27025;

Club: Studio Collectors Club, P. O. Box
1566, Apple Valley, CA 92307.

Game, Hollywood Movie Bingo, Whitman Pub-
lishing, 1937, $42.50.

Almanac, *International Motion Picture Al-*
manac, 6 ½" × 9¼", 1026 pgs, Quigley
Publishing co, 1946–1947 . . . . **25.00**
Book, *Screen Personalities*, biography pic-
ture book, Grosset & Dunlap, 1933
copyright **40.00**
Handbill, Spellbound, Gregory Peck and
Ingrid Bergman, 8" × 11", 4 pgs **20.00**
Lobby Card, M*A*S*H, Donald
Sutherland. **5.00**
Movie Poster
Horrors of the Black Museum, 27" ×
41", black and white illus, English,
1959. . . . . **50.00**
Jungle Drums of Africa, 27" × 41", fea-
tures Clayton Moore, 1952 . . . . **30.00**
Not As A Stranger, 27" × 41", 1955
United Artist film **25.00**
Sands of Iwo Jima, 14" × 36", paper,
pictures John Wayne, John Agar, and
Adela Mara **50.00**

Paint Book, Ziegfeld, 10¼" × 15", Merrill, 1941.	25.00
Photograph, Rock Hudson, color, brass frame, 1950s	15.00
Program	
Gone With The Wind, 6¼" × 9½", buff paper, brown illus, 1939	50.00
MacBeth, 9" × 12", 16 pgs, includes film scenes and photos and biography pages of Orson Welles and stage production, 1948.	25.00
Sheet Music	
Casablanca, *As Time Goes By*, 9" × 12", 8 pgs, 1931 copyright	50.00
Thin Man, *Smoke Dreams*, 9¼" × 12¼", William Powell and Myrna Loy pictures on cov, 1936	15.00
Sticker Book, My Fair Lady, 8½" × 11", 1965, Ottenheimer Inc	5.00

MUGS

The problem with every general price guide is that they do not cover the broad sweeping form categories, e.g., wash pitchers and bowls, any longer. A surprising number of individuals still collect this way.

If you stay away from beer mugs, you can find a lot of examples in this category for under $10.00. Look for the unusual, either in form or labeling. Don't forget to fill one now and then and toast your cleverness in collecting these treasures.

Club: Advertising Cup and Mug Collectors of America, P. O. Box 182, Solon, IA 52333.

Norman Rockwell's "A Boy and His Dog" series, 1984, $12.00.

A & W Root Beer, clear glass, logo	5.00
Big Boy Restaurant, clear glass	3.00
Carebear, days of week, American Greeting Corp	2.00
Carter Carburetor, stoneware	15.00
Frosty Root Beer, clear glass, set of 6	30.00
Grog, BC Comics	3.00
Mickey Through The Year	
1937 Brave Little Tailor	2.00
1955 Mickey Mouse Club	3.00
Nestle's, globe shape, clear, set of 6	40.00
Whataburger, nickel	12.00
Whitetower Restaurant.	22.00

MUSICAL INSTRUMENTS

Didn't you just love music lessons? Still play your clarinet or trumpet? Probably not! Yet, I bet you still have the old instrument. Why is it that you can never seem to throw it out?

The number of antique and classic musical instrument collectors is small, but growing. Actually, most instruments are sold for reuse. As a result, the key is playability. Check out the cost of renting an instrument or purchasing one new. Now you known why prices on "used" instruments are so high. Fifty dollars for a playable instrument of any quality is a bargain price. Of course, it's a bargain only if someone needs and wants to play it. Otherwise, it is fifty dollars ill-spent.

Drum, base, complete with carrying strap and sticks, $65.00.

Banjo, Edgemere, birch neck with imitation mahogany, c1900.	320.00
Castanets, Argentinian, early 19th C.	170.00

Cornet, Marceau E–Flat, brass, 1905–1910 . . . . 110.00
French Horn, King, sgd "USMC," 1890s 200.00
Guitar, Stanford, imitation rosewood finish 85.00
Piccolo, Meyer, grenadilla wood, c1900 . . . . 275.00
Tambourine, Brazilian, 19th C 180.00
Ukulele, birch, white celluloid binding, c1920 . . . . 50.00
Violin
Chester Langdon, 1940 . . . . 150.00
John Jusek, ¾ size 200.00
Stradivarius, Germany 230.00
Suzuki, ¾ size 165.00

NAPKIN RINGS

If you get lucky, you may find a great Victorian silver-plated figural napkin ring at a flea market. Chances are that you are going to find napkins rings used by the common man. But do not look down your nose at them. Some are pretty spectacular.

If you do not specialize from the beginning, you are going to find yourself going around in circles. Animal-shaped rings are a favorite. Avoid Bakelite. Bakelite rings carry an extremely high value because of the Bakelite jewelry craze of a few years ago. The craze is now over, but prices seem to remain high. They will come down when no one buys.

Ceramic, dog, marked "Japan," 2" × 2¾", $20.00.

Art Nouveau, girl with flowing hair, SS 25.00
Bear, figural, celluloid 6.00
Cherub in shell, figural 65.00
Dragon, cloisonne, white ground 25.00
Eagles, SS, two 55.00
Flowers and butterfly, Noritake 15.00
Grand Rapids, MI, scenic 10.00
Lady with stick, metal, c1942 . . . . 15.00
Nursery rhyme figures 25.00
Parrot, SP, rect base, Rogers Mfg Co 50.00
Ring, SP, etched dogwood branch 20.00
Scottie, SS 35.00

NAUTICAL

There is magic in the sea, whether one is reading the novels of Melville, watching Popeye cartoons, or standing on a beach staring at the vast expanse of the ocean. Anyone who loves water has something nautical around the house.

This is one case where the weathered look is a plus. No one wants a piece of nautical material that appears to have never left the dock.

Magazine: *Nautical Brass*, P. O. Box 744, Montrose, CA 91020.

Price Annual: *Conklin's Guide: Maritime Auction Annual*, Leeward Shore Press, P. O. Box 838–-20, Brisbane, CA 94005.

Tile, porcelain, SCIRA/WLIS Fleet, 1937, dark blue ground, framed, $35.00.

Bag, sailor's, macrame, 19th C 90.00
Book, *Whaling Masters*, Old Dartmouth Historical Society, New Bedford, MA, 1938 . . . . 225.00
Crew List, whale ship *Montpelier*, Sept 6,

1853, names, position, number of
shares in voyages to be received. **125.00**
Fog Horn, 30″ l, brass, 19th C. **85.00**
Harpoon Head, 3⅛″ l, whale ivory, incised
designs. **100.00**
Log Book, bark *Manchester,* between Bos-
ton and New Orleans, c1884 . . . . **125.00**
Navigation Scale, 24″ l, boxwood, B Dodd,
19th C **210.00**
Quarterboard, *Edith Nute,* traces of black
paint, orig gold lettering **200.00**
Rudder, 59″, orig white paint traces, 19th
C **50.00**
Signal Horn, 15″, foot operated, "E A Gill,
Gloucester, MA" **110.00**
Station Pointer, brass, cased, sgd "Coxe &
Coombes/Davenport & Plymouth". . . . **150.00**

NEWSPAPERS

"Read All About It" is the cry of corner
newspaper vendors across the country.
Maybe these vendors should be collected.
They appear to be a vanishing breed.

Some newspapers are collected for their
headlines, others because they represent a
special day, birthday, or anniversary. Everybody saved the newspaper the day JFK
was shot. Did you save a paper from the
day war was declared against Iraq? I did.

Magazine: *PCM—Paper Collectors' Marketplace,* P. O. Box 127, Scandinavia, WI
54977.

1969, July 21, **Daily News,** *Man Lands On The
Moon,* $20.00.

Club: Newspaper Collectors' Society of
American, Box 19134, Lansing, MI 48901.

1885, July 23, death of Ulysses S Grant. . . **70.00**
1898, Feb 15, sinking of the *Maine* **40.00**
1901, Sept 14, death of McKinley **35.00**
1906, April 18, earthquake in San Fran-
cisco. **40.00**
1926, Sept 23, Jack Dempsey defeated by
Tunney **25.00**
1927, May 21, Atlantic crossing by
Lindbergh **35.00**
1929, Oct 28, crash of the Stock Mar-
ket **65.00**
1934, May 23, Bonnie and Clyde
killed **70.00**
1941, Dec 7, Pearl Harbor attacked **45.00**
1945, April 12, death of Roosevelt **18.00**
1954, May 17, school segregation deci-
sion **10.00**
1962, Feb 20, John Glenn's space
flight **15.00**
1963, Nov 22, Kennedy assassination. . . . **25.00**

NILOAK POTTERY

When you mention Niloak, most people
immediately think of the swirled brown,
red, and tan stuff, formally known as Mission Ware. However, Niloak also made
items in a host of other designs through
1946. These included utilitarian wares and
the kind of ceramics florists used. These
later items can be found reasonably priced.
If Niloak prices follow the trend established
by Roseville prices, now might be the time
to stash some of these later pieces away.

Ashtray, marbleized swirls, Mission
Ware **25.00**
Bowl, 7½″, marbleized swirls, Mission
Ware **65.00**
Candlestick, 2″ h, brown, blue, and cream,
Mission Ware **24.00**
Cornucopia, light pink **5.00**
Hat, ashtray type, glossy blue **7.50**
Match Holder, figural, duck, brown and
white swirl. **15.00**
Pitcher, 7″ h, glossy pink **25.00**
Planter
Camel, 3″, glossy **22.00**
Elephant, 6″, white, glossy **20.00**
Swan, 3″, light brown, glossy. **10.00**
Urn, 4½″, marbleized brown and blue
swirls, Mission Ware **35.00**
Vase
4″ h, bud, matte blue and pink **22.00**
5¼″ h, Mission Ware, as is **15.00**
6″ h, green, wing handles. **25.00**

Plate, castle scene, purple castle, green–yellow trees, browns, tan, and brown, rim pierced for hanging, $100.00.

Vase, purple over white ground, four tulip shaped openings, 6 ¾" h, $22.50.

6½" h, wing handles
  Glossy blue.................... **25.00**
  Matte green and orange.......... **25.00**
7½" h, matte green, ribbed, full length
  handles, orig paper label.......... **35.00**

NIPPON

Nippon is hand-painted Japanese porcelain made between 1891 and 1921. The McKinley tariff of 1891 required goods imported into the United States to be marked with their country of origin. Until 1921, goods from Japan were marked "Made in Nippon."

Over two hundred different manufacturer's marks have been discovered for Nippon. The three most popular are the wreath, maple leaf, and rising sun. While marks are important, the key is the theme and quality of the decoration.

Nippon has become quite expensive. Rumors in the field indicate that Japanese buyers are now actively competing with American buyers.

Club: International Nippon Collectors Club, P. O. Box 88, Jericho, NY 11753.

Bouillon Cup, 5" h, cobalt and gold, green
  mark.......................... **90.00**
Bowl
  4¾" d, pink floral, gold trim, blue
  mark........................ **30.00**

7" d, molded peanuts, two handles,
  green mark....................**150.00**
7½" d, pink floral, gold trim, blue
  mark........................ **80.00**
8¾" d, gold leaves, blue mark......... **90.00**
Cake Set, pink roses, 10½" d cake platter,
  six 6¼" d plates, green mark..........**200.00**
Candy Dish, 7" d, gold dec and handle,
  blue mark....................... **55.00**
Cigar Holder, oval tray, sailboat design,
  green mark.....................**135.00**
Cinnamon Stick Holder, 4½" h, ftd cylinder shape, blue mark...............**200.00**
Coaster, 3¾" d, floral, blue mark........ **28.00**
Compote, 4½" d, moriage dec,
  unmarked..................... **95.00**
Cup and Saucer, Azalea pattern, blue
  mark......................... **18.00**
Dish
  5" l, rect, souvenir, Portland, ME, landscape scene, blue mark............ **35.00**
  7½" w, three compartment, green
  mark........................ **90.00**
Doll
  3¾" h, Dutch Boy, incised mark....... **80.00**
  4¼" h, girl, pink bow in hair, incised
  mark **110.00**
Dutch Shoe, 3" l, sailboats, green mark ...**145.00**
Egg Cup, 2½" h, green mark........... **55.00**
Feeding Dish, child's, 8" d, girl and dog
  illus, blue mark **75.00**
Ferner, 4½" w, floral design, ftd, blue
  mark **85.00**
Flask, talcum powder, 5" h, pink flowers,
  white ground, blue mark...........**140.00**
Gravy Boat, 6" l underplate, gold handle,
  marked...................... **70.00**
Hatpin Holder, 4½" h, WW I airplane illus,
  green mark **175.00**
Incense Burner, 3¼" h, blue, red mark.... **125.00**

Ink Blotter, 4¼" h, gold sticker, red
   mark 140.00
Inkwell, 3" sq, inner well, horse and rider,
   green mark 165.00
Lemon Dish, 5½" w, blue birds, white
   ground, two handles, blue mark 25.00
Mayonnaise, 4½" d, Azalea pattern, ladle,
   blue mark...................... 45.00
Mug, child's, 3" h, girl holding basket,
   green trim, blue mark 75.00
Napkin Ring, 2" d, green mark......... 60.00
Nappy
   6¼" w, three gold handles, blue
   mark 75.00
   7" w, white flowers, gold trim, handle,
   green mark.................... 55.00
Novelty, comic face of Jiggs, green
   mark 120.00
Nut Cup, 2¾" d, three geisha girls in old
   fashioned car, green mark.......... 40.00
Pancake Server, 8¾" d, cov, pink floral,
   gold trim, red mark 115.00
Pin Box, 2" d, 1¼" h, souvenir, Capitol
   Building, Washington, DC, green
   mark 60.00
Powder Box, 3" h, souvenir, Newport, RI,
   green mark 85.00
Plate
   6¼" d, yellow birds, pink flowers, green
   mark 25.00
   6½" d, Azalea pattern, blue mark 12.00
   7½" d, green mark 50.00
Relish Dish, 8½" l, landscape scene, green
   mark 125.00
Salt and Pepper Shakers, pr, pink flowers,
   blue ground, green mark............ 40.00
Sauce Dish, 7" l, pink floral, handle, blue
   mark 60.00
Shaving Mug, 3¾" h, yellow flowers, gold
   trim, green mark 120.00
Spoon Holder, 7¾" l, blue mark........ 85.00
Sugar Shaker, 4" h, pink floral, gold trim,
   green mark 115.00
Toothpick Holder, 2¼" h, landscape scene,
   three handles, green mark.......... 80.00
Trivet, 5" sq, landscape scene, green
   mark 50.00
Vase
   3½" h, floral dec, two gold handles, blue
   mark 80.00
   4½" h, cobalt and floral, blue mark..... 185.00
   5" h, moriage dec, green matte, dragon,
   green mark.................... 60.00
   6¾" h, yellow, green mark 70.00

NORITAKE AZALEA

Noritake china in the azalea pattern was
first produced in the early 1900s. Several
different backstamps were used. You will
find them listed in *Warman's Americana &*

Collectibles (Wallace–Homestead). They
will help date your pieces.

Azalea pattern wares were distributed as
a premium by the Larkin Company of Buffalo and sold to the public via Sears,
Roebuck. As a result, it is the best known of
the Noritake patterns.

Each piece is hand-painted, thus adding
a bit of individuality to the pieces. Hard-to-
find examples include the child's tea set
and salesmen's samples. Also, do not ignore the hand-painted glassware in the
azalea pattern that was manufactured to
accompany the china service.

Creamer, $15.00.

Bonbon Dish, 6¼" (184) 35.00
Bouillon Cup and Saucer, 5¼" (124) 15.00
Bowl, deep (310).................... 42.00
Butter Chip, 3¼" (312)................ 65.00
Cake Plate, 9¾" (10)................. 25.00
Casserole, cov (16) 60.00
Cheese Dish, 6¼", cov (314) 85.00
Condiment Set, 5 pcs (14)............. 35.00
Creamer (7)...................... 15.00
Cup and Saucer (2) 14.00
Egg Cup (120) 32.00
Gravy Boat (40).................... 28.00
Lemon Plate (121).................. 12.00
Mayonnaise Set, 3 pcs (3) 25.00
Mustard Jar (191) 45.00
Plate
   6¼", bread and butter (8) 8.00
   7½", tea (4)..................... 7.50
   8½", breakfast (98)................ 15.00
   9¾", dinner (13).................. 18.00
Platter, 12" (56)................... 40.00
Relish Dish, 8½", oval (18)............ 12.50
Salad Bowl, 10", round (12) 28.00
Sauce Dish (9) 8.00
Sugar, cov (7) 15.00
Tile, 6" (169) 30.00
Toothpick Holder (192) 75.00
Vase, fan, ftd (187) 120.00
Vegetable Bowl, 9½ × 6¾", oval (172) ... 32.00

191

NORITAKE CHINA

Noritake is quality Japanese china imported to the United States by the Noritake China company founded by the Morimura Brothers in Nagoya in 1904. The company is best known for its dinnerware lines. The company also used over one hundred different marks. These are helpful in dating pieces.

The Larkin Company of Buffalo, New York, used Noritake china as a premium. This is why Azalea, Briarcliff, Linden, Savory, Sheridan, and Tree in the Meadow patterns are found in quantity.

Be careful. Not all Noritake china is what it seems. The company also sold blanks to the home decorator. Check the art before deciding that a piece left Japan painted.

Easter Egg, 1978, $18.00.

Ashtray, 5" d, horses dec, green border, red
  cigarette rests, red mark **65.00**
Basket, 7", handles, floral, multi-col-
  ored **30.00**
Bowl, 8½", gold, wood scene border **65.00**
Bread Plate, 14" × 6¼", white, pale green
  and gold floral border, open handles . . . **24.00**
Candy Dish, 6½" d, orange flowers, gold
  trim, black ground **135.00**
Condiment Set, salt and pepper shakers,
  mustard, and round tray, red ground,
  blue and yellow birds on perch **75.00**
Cup and Saucer, 3" d cup, 5" d saucer,
  white, pink and blue flowers, gold
  trim **25.00**
Demitasse Cup and Saucer, orange and
  blue flowers **18.00**
Ferner, 6", triangular **75.00**

Hatpin Holder, 4½" h, gold luster, black
  band at top with multicolored flow-
  ers **45.00**
Lemon Dish, 6" d, relief molded, lemon
  hp blossoms and leaves, M in wreath
  mark **50.00**
Mustard Jar, underplate, orange luster fin-
  ish, blueberries finial **45.00**
Perfume, orange luster bottle, blue flower
  stopper **85.00**
Plaque, 10", hp, cottage, trees, and pastel
  flowers, brown rim **65.00**
Tile, hp, scenic, water, willow tree, rushes,
  and man in boat **38.00**
Tray, 8" l, two handles, hp, blue violets,
  red M in wreath mark **40.00**
Vegetable Bowl, Wild Ivy pattern **12.00**
Wall Pocket, 8¼", cylindrical, floral dec. . . **48.00**

NORITAKE TREE IN THE MEADOW

If you ever want to see variation in a pattern, collect Tree in the Meadow. You will go nuts trying to match pieces. In the end you will do what everyone else does. Learn to live with the differences. Is there a lesson here?

Tree in the Meadow was also distributed by the Larkin Company of Buffalo, New York. Importation began in the 1920s, almost twenty years after the arrival of azalea pattern wares. Check backstamps to identify the date of the pieces in your collection.

Vegetable Dish, 9⅜" l, $40.00.

Berry Set, large bowl, open handles, six
  small bowls **68.00**
Bowl, 6½", green mark **25.00**
Cake Plate, 10", pierced handle **30.00**
Condiment Set, mustard pot, ladle, salt
  and pepper shakers, tray **40.00**
Creamer. **25.00**

Dish, 6", pierced handles, blue luster border **40.00**
Lemon Dish, 5½", center ring handle **15.00**
Plate
  7½" **12.00**
  8½" **15.00**
Platter, 12" **30.00**
Relish Dish, divided **40.00**
Salt and Pepper Shakers, marked "Made in Japan," pr **30.00**
Sugar, cov **25.00**
Tea Tile, 5" w, chamfered corners, green mark **25.00**
Toothpick Holder **55.00**
Waffle Set, sugar shaker and syrup jug . . . **70.00**

NUDES

Mom, Dad made me put this category in. Honest, Mom! He really did, Mom! He really did!

Ashtray, Meridan Steel Co Inc., NY, 3¾" × 4¾", $15.00.

Ashtray, 10", nude holding tray over head, marked "Rembrandt" **185.00**
Bookends, pr, figural, cast iron, woman kneeling, leg extended forward, bronze finish **70.00**
Figure, female, 9½" × 10½", Sanzio **25.00**
Knife, 3¼", silvered metal, black and white female portrait, dark red glitter accents, c1920 . . . . **25.00**
Lamp, 9", nude sitting on top ribbed column, arms support crackle glass globe **370.00**
Pin, ⅞", female standing, brass frame, early 1900s **20.00**

Playing Cards, Royal Flushes, nudes, king size, boxed **14.00**
Postcard, woman shown waist up, arms folded over chest, divided back **10.00**
Print, woman sitting on red bench, marked "Copr C Moss 1947 Litho in USA" **50.00**
Rose Bowl, full figure nude sitting on edge, sgd "Clio Huneker" **195.00**
Statue, 7", ivory, three women embracing each other, sgd "G R" **85.00**
Vase, 3" h, cameo white relief nude, brown side handles **15.00**

NUTCRACKERS

Fast food and time did in the nut cracking community. From the mid–19th through the mid–20th century it was not uncommon to find a bowl of nuts awaiting cracking in the kitchen, living room, or dining room.

Just as there is a never ending search for a better mousetrap, so was man never content with his nutcracker design. The variety is endless, from cast iron dogs of the turn-of-the-century to brass legs from the Art Deco period.

Many modern collectors like the wooden military and civilian figures that come from Germany. Have you ever tried cracking a nut in them? Useless, utterly useless.

Monkey, carved wood, 6¾", $90.00.

Brass, figural
Jester 75.00
Lady's legs 35.00
Rooster 40.00
Cast Iron, figural
Dog, bronzed 45.00
Elephant, painted 145.00
Squirrel 48.00
Wood, figural
Bear, glass eyes 100.00
Bird, curved neck, long tail, worn finish 100.00
Man's head, neat carved mustache 115.00
Monkey, painted eyes 80.00
Toy Soldier, red, black, and white paint, furry beard, German 75.00

OCCUPIED JAPAN

America occupied Japan from 1945 to 1952. Not all objects made during this period are marked "Occupied Japan." Some were simply marked "Japan" and "Made in Japan." Occupied Japan collectors ignore this latter group. They want to see their two favorite little words.

Beware of falsely labeled pieces. Rubber-stamped marked pieces have appeared on the market. Apply a little fingernail polish remover. Fake marks will disappear. True marks are under glaze. Of course, if the piece is unglazed to begin with, ignore this test.

Clubs: Occupied Japan Collectors Club, 18309 Faysmith Avenue, Torrance, CA 90504; O. J. Club, 29 Freedom Street, Newport, RI 02840.

Ashtray, 4" sq, porcelain, green floral 12.00
Cigarette Box, 3¾ × 4" × 5", multicolored, gold floral and scroll 10.00
Cigarette Lighter, metal, cornucopia. 15.00
Demitasse Cup and Saucer, floral, pink and lavender 8.00
Figure
Bird, 4½" × 4¾" l, pink body, gray wings, yellow beak 20.00
Boy, 4" h, playing violin, seated, white shirt, brown shorts, green hat 12.50
Colonial Girl, 6¼" h, orange and blue dress, pink bow, gold trim holding skirt 18.00
Dog, 4" l, brown 15.00
Man and Woman, 3½" h, man wearing red coat, yellow pants, holding hat, woman wearing blue, green, and purple dress, pedestal base. 17.00
Monkeys, 2½" × 2¼" l, see no evil, hear no evil, speak no evil 18.00

Oriental Girl, 10" h, blue and green outfit, gold trim 28.00
Swan, 3¾" h, wings spread. 10.00
Jewelry Box, 1" h, metal, twelve drawers 12.00
Pin Cushion, tin, red velvet top, mirror inside lid 20.00
Pitcher, 4½" h, windmill scene. 17.50
Planter
Dog, 2½" h 8.00
Donkey, pulling wagon, 4¾" l 10.00
Reamer, 3¾" h, 2 pcs, strawberry shape, red, green leaves and handle 65.00
Teapot, 6½" h, floral dec on brown ground. 22.00
Toby Mug, 2½" h, black hat, blue collar . . . 15.00
Toy, 3½" × 4½ × 8½", dancer, litho tin and celluloid, windup, man standing by black and white tin sign "Hollywood" and "Vine" 165.00
Tray, 5" × 3", metal, souvenir, Chicago 6.00
Vase
3¾" h, bud vase, cherub playing tuba. . . 14.00
4½" h, landscape scene. 12.00
Wall Pocket, 5½" × 4", flying goose. . . . 18.00

OCEAN LINER COLLECTIBLES

Although the age of the clipper ships technically fits into this category, the period that you are most likely to uncover at flea markets is the age of the ocean liner. Don't focus solely on American ships. England, Germany, France, and many other foreign companies had transoceanic liners that competed with and bested American vessels.

Today is the age of the cruise ship. This aspect of the category is being largely ignored. Climb aboard and sail into the sunset.

Clubs: Steamship Historical Society of America, Inc., 345 Blackstone Boulevard, Hall Building, Providence, RI 02906; Titanic Historical Society, P. O. Box 53, Indian Orchard, MA 01151-0053.

Ashtray, *Princess*, glass, Swedish 8.00
Booklet, White Star Line Sailing List, 1933. . . . . 38.00
Log, Lykes Bros 1938 Ripley SS, New Orleans to Calcutta 8.00
Menu
Johnson Line 10.00
Matson Line. 7.00
SS City of Omaha, Christmas 1940 . . . . . 5.00
SS Oakwood, American Export Lines, Christmas, 1939. . . . . 5.00

194

Ashtray, **Normandie,** *French Line, porcelain, black lettering, backstamp, 4⅝" d, $120.00.*

Passenger List
 SS *Leviathan,* 1924 . . . . **15.00**
 Transylvania II, Anchor Line, June 22,
 1938 . . . . **18.00**
Pocket Mirror, Steamship *Augustus,*
 emb **52.00**
Stock Certificate, Cunard Steam Ship Co,
 Ltd **7.50**
Ticket Folio, Cunard Line, c1928 . . . . **50.00**
Tin
 Bremen, coffee, *Bremen* at sea on front
 panel, tin, litho, 1930s **50.00**
 Queen Mary, candy, full color *Queen
 Mary* illus on lid, tin, litho, 1930s **40.00**

OLD SLEEPY EYE

The Old Sleepy Eye Flour Company of Sleepy Eye, Minnesota, began offering Sleepy Eye premiums in the early 1900s. Many of the early stoneware products were made by the Weir Pottery Company, which eventually became the Monmouth Pottery Company.

The company's advertising is just as popular as its giveaway premiums. Beware of fantasy items, e.g., pocket mirrors, glass plates, toothpick holders, and more, as well as reproduction stoneware pitchers, marked "Ironstone" on the bottom, that are coming from Taiwan.

Club: Old Sleepy Eye Collectors Club, P. O. Box 12, Monmouth, IL 61462.

Barrel Label, framed **300.00**
Butter Crock, stoneware, Flemish, slight
 hairline **400.00**

Tea tile, cobalt blue and white stoneware, wood frame, $1,000.00.

Calendar, 1904 . . . . **200.00**
Cook Book, bread loaf shape **125.00**
Mug, green and brown, cream ground,
 marked "Brush–McCoy" **250.00**
Pillow Cover, Before The Great Father,
 unused **350.00**
Pitcher, blue rim, #5 . . . . **400.00**
Vase, stoneware, 8½" h, cylindrical **185.00**

OWL COLLECTIBLES

Most people do not give a hoot about this category, but those who do are serious birds. Like all animal collectors, all owl collectors care about is that their bird is represented.

Newsletter: *The Owl's Nest,* Howard Alphanumeric, P. O. Box 5491, Fresno, CA 93755.

Club: Russell's Owl Collector's Club, P. O. Box 1292, Bandon, OR 97411.

Bank, brass, glass eyes **65.00**
Cookie Jar, Woodsey Owl **95.00**
Creamer, Sugar, and Shakers, combina-
 tion, gold, green trim **20.00**
Doll, 6½", plush, "Give A Hoot, Don't
 Pollute" **10.00**
Figurine
 Audubon **45.00**
 Ceramic, glass eyes **15.00**
Letter Opener, bronze **30.00**
Pin, blue, green, and gold enamel, amber
 eyes, pearl tail feathers **15.00**
Salt and Pepper Shakers, pr, china, brown

Advertising trade card, Colburn's Phila Mustard, diecut, 3³⁄₈" × 3¹⁄₂", $7.50.

Animal
Cottontail Rabbit, clear **60.00**
Rooster **70.00**
Bowl, Caliente, yellow, 6¹⁄₂" **5.00**
Cake Stand, Black Forest, low foot **60.00**
Candy Dish, Mrs B, three part, ruby, gold
trim **50.00**
Cheese and Cracker Server, Glades, cobalt
blue **45.00**
Compote, Gazebo pattern, 8"h **40.00**
Creamer, Cupid **20.00**
Cup and Saucer, Largo, dark green **10.00**
Goblet, Penny Line **8.50**
Plate, dinner
Cupid, 10"d **15.00**
Popeye and Olive, ruby **18.50**
Salt and Pepper Shakers, pr, Penny Line,
cobalt blue **50.00**
Sugar, Nora Bird, Cheriglo **35.00**
Tumbler, Party Line, ruby **15.00**
Vase, California Poppy, 12" **125.00**

and white, scholarly expression, horn
rim glasses **6.50**
Toothpick Holder **22.00**
Trivet, Frankoma Pottery **4.00**

PADEN CITY

The Paden City Glass Manufacturing Company was founded in 1916 and located in Paden City, West Virginia. The plant closed in 1951, two years after acquiring the American Glass Company.

Paden City glass was handmade in molds. No free blown examples are known. Most pieces were unmarked. The key is color. Among the most popular are opal (opaque white), dark green (forest), and red. The company never made opalescent glass.

Newsletter: *Paden City Party Line*, 1630 Colby Avenue, #5, Los Angeles, CA 90025.

Bowl, apple green, wide gold overlay dec, 11¹⁄₄" d, $25.00.

PADLOCKS

Padlocks in all shapes and sizes were made in Europe and Asia as early as the 17th Century. America pioneered the mass production of padlocks in the mid–19th century. Over six hundred manufacturers have been identified.

The most desirable padlocks are cast brass or iron locks with embossed company names, logos, and decorative figures, florals, and scrolls. Avoid padlocks that have been repaired, cracked, dented, pitted by corrosion, or damaged internally.

Reproductions abound. For a partial list see the introduction to the padlock category in *Warman's Americana & Collectibles.*

Club: American Lock Collectors Association, 36076 Grennada, Livonia, MI 48154.

Lever, Slaymaker #25, key #65, 2¹⁄₂", $7.50.

Combination
  JBMKL, steel, 3¼"h............... 5.00
  Junkunc Safe & Lock Co, brass, round,
  1¼"h......................... 50.00
  Sesamee, brass, dials on bottom, 2½"
  h........................... 15.00
Commemorative, Missouri state seal
  front, 1904 Exposition, brass, emb, 2"
  h............................ 75.00
Eight Lever, Goliath, steel 10.00
Lever, Iron & Steel
  Bear, emb, steel, 2⅞"h.............. 5.00
  Dragons, emb, steel, 2¼"h.......... 10.00
  Pyes Patent, iron, 3½"h 25.00
Lever Push Key
  Champion Six Lever, brass, emb, 2¼"
  d............................ 5.00
  Romer & Co, 86, brass, 1¼"h........ 20.00
Lever Wrought Iron, S & Co, brass drop,
  3½"h 5.00
Logo, B of E, brass lever type 10.00
Pin Tumbler
  Ellis Lock Co, steel, 2¾"h........... 20.00
  Unit, brass, 3"h 35.00
Railroad, B P and Signal
  ICRR, emb, brass, 2¼"d............ 80.00
  Missouri Pacific, emb, brass......... 35.00
Railroad, Switch
  CRI & P RR, stamped, brass 40.00
  PRR, emb back, brass..............100.00
Scandinavian, J H W Climax, iron, 3½"
  h........................... 20.00
Six Lever, Winchester, emb, steel 60.00
Story, cast iron, emb, floral and scroll,
  shield shape, 2⅜"................. 90.00
Warded, Fordloc, emb, brass case 10.00

PAPER DOLLS

Paper dolls have already been through one craze cycle and appear to be in the midst of another. The recent publication of Mary Young's *A Collector's Guide To Magazine Paper Dolls: An Identification & Value Guide* (Collector Books, 1990) is one indication of the craze. It also introduces a slightly different approach to the subject than the traditional paper doll book.

The best way to collect paper dolls is in uncut books, sheets, and boxed sets. Dolls that have been cut out sell at fifty percent or less, providing all the dolls, clothing, and accessories are present.

Paper doll collectors have no desire to play with their dolls. They just want to admire and enjoy the satisfaction of owning them.

Magazine: *Doll Reader*, Hobby House Press, 900 Frederick Street, Cumberland, MD 21502.

Newsletter: *Paper Doll News*, P. O. Box 807, Vivian LA 71082.

Club: United Federation of Doll Clubs, P. O. Box 14146, Parkville, MO 64152.

Three Sisters, Whitman Publishing Co, 1942, 12¾" × 12½", $20.00.

Books
  Arlene Dahl, five dolls, eight pgs,
    Saalfield Publishing Co 50.00
  Barbie's Boutique, Whitman, 1973.... 7.50
  Betsy McCall, Biggest Paper Doll, Ga-
    briel & sons, 1955............... 20.00
  Buffy, six pgs, Whitman, 1969 ...... 18.50
  Carol & Her Dresses, Gabriel & Sons ... 18.00
  Cinderella, four dolls, four pgs, Saalfield
    Publishing Co.................. 15.00
  Deanna Durbin, Merrill Publishing Co,
    1940.........................170.00
  Janet Leigh Cutouts & Coloring, two
    dolls, Merrill Publishing Co 45.00
  June Allyson, eight pgs, Whitman,
    1953......................... 60.00
  Let's Play Paper Dolls, McLoughlin,
    1938......................... 20.00
  Miss America Magic Doll, Parker Bros,
    1953......................... 18.00
  Nanny & Professor, six dolls, four pgs,
    Artcraft, 1971.................. 20.00
  Patty's Party, Stephens Publishing Co,
    c1950........................ 8.00
  Sally Dimple, Burton Playthings,
    1935......................... 25.00
  Shari Lewis, five pgs, Treasure
    Books....................... 32.00
  Wendy Walks, Merry Mfg, 1965...... 10.00
Folder
  Dolly's Wardrobe, chromo litho, Dean
    & Son, c1910 .... 75.00
  Paul, McLoughlin Bros, c1870 .... 90.00
Uncut Sheets
  Betsy McCall, Dress n' Play, McCall's
    Magazine, 1963................ 12.00

Lucille Ball and Desi Arnaz, Whitman,
1953. . . . . **75.00**
Valentine's Day Boy and Girl, McCall's
Magazine, Barbara Hale artist, Feb
1921. . . . . **15.00**

PAPER MONEY

People hid money in the strangest places.
Occasionally it turns up at flea markets.
Likewise early paper money came in a variety of forms and sizes quite different from
modern paper currency.

Essentially paper money breaks down
into three groups — money issued by the
federal government, states, and private
banks, businesses, and individuals. Money
from the latter group is designated as obsolete bank notes.

As with coins, condition is everything.
Paper money that has been heavily circulated has only a small fraction of the
value of a bill in excellent condition. Proper
grading rests in the hands of coin dealers.

Krause Publications (700 East State
Street, Iola, WI 54990) is a leading publisher in the area of coinage and currency.
Among Krause's books are *Standard Catalog
of World Paper Money* in two volumes,
*Standard Catalog of United States Obsolete
Bank Notes, 1782–1866* in four volumes,
Standard Catalog of United States Paper Money
now in its ninth edition, *Standard Catalog of
National Bank Notes* in its second edition,
and *Early Paper Money of America*. Recently
Krause published the *Standard Catalog of
Depression Scrip of the United States*. As you
can see, there is a wealth of help to identify
and price any bill that you find. *Bank Note
Reporter*, a Krause newspaper, keeps collectors up–to–date on current developments
in the currency field.

Before you sell or turn in that old bill for
face value, do your homework. It may be
worth more than a Continental, which by
the way, continues to be a "dog" in the
paper money field.

PAPERBACK BOOKS

This is a category with millions of titles and
billions of copies. Keep this in mind before
paying a high price for anything.

A great deal of the value of paperbacks
rests in the cover art. Great art can make up

for a lousy story by an insignificant author.
However, little makes up for poor condition, a fate which has befallen a surprising
number of paperbacks. A risque lady helps.

Rather than list a dozen or two titles that
barely scratch the surface, I recommend
that you consult Kevin Hancer's *Hancer's
Price Guide To Paperback Books, Third Edition*
(Wallace–Homestead, 1990) and Jon
Warren's *The Official Price Guide Paperbacks,
First Edition* (House of Collectibles), 1991.
Both are organized by company and then
issue number. Hence, when trying to locate
a book, publisher and code number are
more important than author and title.

The vast majority of paperbacks sell in
the 50¢ to $2.50 range, even those from the
1950s.

Buffalo Bill's Spy Shadower *Buffalo Bill Stories, Gold Star Books, $10.00.*

PAPERWEIGHTS

This is a tough category. Learning to tell the
difference between modern and antique
paperweights takes years. Your best approach at a flea market is to treat each
weight as modern. If you get lucky and pay
modern paperweight prices for an antique
weight, you are ahead. If you pay antique
prices for a modern paperweight, you lose
and lose big.

Paperweights divide into antique (prior

to 1945) and modern. Modern breaks down into early modern (1945 to 1980) and contemporary (1980 and later). There is a great deal of speculation going on in the area of contemporary paperweights. It is not a place for amateurs or those with money they can ill afford to lose. If you are not certain, do not buy.

Newsletters: *Paperweight Gaffer*, 35 Williamstown Circle, York, PA 17404; *Paperweight News*, 761 Chestnut Street, Santa Cruz, CA 95060.

Club: Paperweight Collectors, P. O. Box 468, Garden City Park, NY 11010.

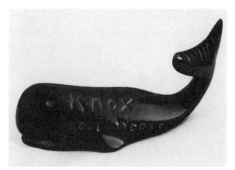

Advertising, Knox Stove Works, Whale of A Stove, cast iron, black, red letters, 3¾" l, $50.00.

Celluloid, adv
  Chelton Trust Co, 2½", celluloid over metal, bright green, red, and white design, diecut celluloid perpetual calendar disk wheel on bottom, orig box, early 1900s. **40.00**
  Eagle Electric, 2½", celluloid over metal, revolving celluloid disk wheel mounted on top, diecut opening reveals fuse adv, c1920s **35.00**
  Speyer Building, 2¾", black and white, tin band, detailed drawing of building **30.00**
Ceramic, adv, Laco Drawn Wire Quality, white ground, black letters, half-a-lightbulb shape, backstamped "Rosenthal". **60.00**
Glass
  Advertising
    Bell System, bell shape, blue **95.00**
    Best Pig Forceps, compliments J Reimers, Davenport, IA, pig shape, 6" **100.00**
    Columbia National Bank. **10.00**
    Lehigh Sewer Pipe & Tile Co, Ft Dodge, IA. **12.00**
    Pike Sharpening Stones, ½" × 2" × 3", whetstone block, fused glass cov on

oilstone base, multicolored paper label pictures pike and sharpening tools, c1900s **65.00**
The Ransbottom Bros Pottery Co, Roseville, OH, dome type, illus of brothers **70.00**
Personality, 1" × 2½" × 4" rect
  McKinley, sepia photo, inscribed "Pres McKinley, Wife and Home, Canton, O," marked "Cent Glass & Nov Co" on reverse, 1900s. **50.00**
  Col Albert A Pope, dated '87 . . . . **50.00**
Souvenir & Commemorative, 1" × 2½" × 4" rect
  Chicago World's Fair, Hall of Science, full color image **30.00**
  Factory Scene, NY office 7 Cedar St **50.00**
  Independent Press Room, Los Angeles. **15.00**
  Pan–American Expo, Temple of Music, small caption, 1901 . . . . **35.00**
Metal
  Advertising
    Consolidated Ice Co, 3" × 5½" × 3½" h, white metal, figural, polar bear sitting on block of ice, inscribed "Pure Ice" and "Distilled Water," company name on sides of base, early 1900s. **65.00**
    El Roco Gas, iron, figural **25.00**
    Hoover Ball & Bearing Co, 1¾" d, 2" h, chromed steel, eight ball bearings in channel around one large bearing **35.00**
    National Surety Co, bronze, eagle on world globe **45.00**
    Parke–Davis, pewter, baby in womb. **25.00**
    Purdue Foundry, cast iron, Kewpie. **35.00**
    St John Mill, ½" × 1½" × 3½", brass, figural, inscribed "Extra," issued by Furber, Stockford & Co, Boston, MA, early 1900s. **30.00**
    Star Line Goods, 1¾" × 2¼" × ½" h, cast iron, brass colored, figural, turtle, 1" oval celluloid shell, inscription in center of shell, 1904 copyright **80.00**
  Souvenir and Commemorative
    Crane Co, Chicago, 75th Anniversary, brass, 2⅛" d, round **30.00**
    New Deal, 2" × 3", high relief portrait on front, flat back, copyright 1932. . . . . **45.00**
    New York World's Fair, 1¼" × 4" × 2" h, silvered, figural, Unisphere in front of small suspension bridge, New York City skyline with Statue of Liberty, made in Japan **40.00**

199

PARKING METERS

I have seen them for sale. I have even been tempted to buy one. The meter was a lamp base, complete with new lamp wiring and an attractive shade. To make the light work, you put a coin in the meter. Can you imagine my date's face when I ran out of quarters? I'm not sure why, but they are rather pricey, usually in the $50 to $100 range. Maybe it has something to do with the fine that you will pay if you obtain one illegally.

Might be a good idea to stash a few coin-operated meters away. Have you experienced one of the new electronic meters? Isn't progress wonderful?

PATRIOTIC COLLECTIBLES

Americans love symbols. We express our patriotism through eagles, flags and shield, the Liberty Bell, Statue of Liberty, and Uncle Sam. We even throw in a few patriots, such as Benjamin Franklin. The symbols of America are currently being displayed with pride across the country as a result of the success of Operation Desert Storm. It's great to see.

Sheet music, **Star Spangled Banner,** *Calumet Publishing, $7.50.*

Advertising, tray, 12", Jacob Metzger, American Brewing Co, Indianapolis, IN, trademark on star in center of flag.......................... **150.00**
Bank, Dime Register, Uncle Sam, 1941... **38.00**
Bread Plate, glass, Constitution signer's names, emb 1776–1876, clear **80.00**
Cookie Cutter, 6½", tin, Eagle **85.00**
Figure, 16", Uncle Sam rolling up sleeves, plaster **30.00**
Hat, paper, "Liberty," red, white, and blue, picture of Statue, c1918 .... **20.00**
Needle Case, Statue of Liberty.......... **12.00**
Pin, diecut silvered metal eagle with shield symbol on chest, holding miniature replica brass alarm clock, c1890 .... **30.00**
Pinback Button, 1¼"
  Centennial Celebration, log cabin under red, white, and blue bunting, gold eagle design, early 1900s **12.00**
  Columbus Day, Columbus illus, white background, black lettering, 1920s........................ **15.00**
Reverse Painting on Glass, Statue of Liberty, oval **100.00**
Seals, "Patriotic Decorations," diecut gummed seals, red, white, and blue, Dennison, ten of orig 25, c1925....... **15.00**
Sheet Music, "Liberty Bell Time to Ring Again," 1918.................... **3.50**

PENCIL CLIPS AND PAPER CLIPS

Paper clips clip pieces of paper together; Pencil clips hold pencils in one's pocket. Both were popular; both were used to advertise products. Neither form is used much today. After seeing several hundred examples, I think they should be missed.

The listings below are for paper clips with celluloid buttons and metal spring clips, all dating from the early 1900s. Pencil clips have celluloid buttons with metal pencil holders.

PAPER CLIP

Bickmore's Gall Cure, black and white,⅞".................... **20.00**
Bissel Company, multicolored, red inscriptions, 1" **30.00**
Boston Varnish Co, multicolored, gold inscriptions, 1¼"................... **30.00**
Eureka Jewelry Co, sepia photo portrait of woman wearing pearl necklace, sheer off-the-shoulder white gown, light green and white inscriptions on dark brown border, 1¼".................. **40.00**
Farm & Home, black and white,⅞" **18.50**

McKibbin Hat, brown portrait of gentleman, tinted fleshtone face, light blue–green ground, 1¾" **45.00**
Star Egg Carriers and Trays, multicolored, dark olive green ground, red, yellow, and white inscriptions, 1¾" **60.00**

PENCIL CLIP

Baseball, black and white celluloid, photo portrait, silvered metal clip, c1948–1951,¾"
  Al Rosen, Cleveland Indians **20.00**
  Thurman Tucker, Cleveland Indians. . . **18.50**
Diamond Crystal Salt **8.00**
God Bless America, red, white, and blue, white ground, blue inscription,½" **12.00**
Keller's Butter/Eggs, red, white, and blue, celluloid, silvered tin clip, c1940,⅞" . . . **15.00**
Morton's Salt **6.00**
Ritz Crackers, litho tin, yellow, blue, and red, Nabisco logo, c1930,⅞" **8.50**
The Edwin Clapp Shoes/East Weymouth, MA, silvered brass, early 1900s **15.00**
Viking Snuff, blue and white celluloid, silvered tin clip, c1930. .... **20.00**

PENS AND PENCILS

Forget the ordinary and look for the unusual. The more special the object or set is, the more likely it is that it will have a high value. Defects of any kind drop value dramatically.

When buying a set, try to get the original box along with any instruction sheets and guarantee cards (you will be amazed at how many people actually saved them).

Clubs: American Pencil Collectors Society, 603 East 105th Street, Kansas City, MO 64131; Pen Fancier's Club, 1169 Overcash Drive, Dunedin, FL 33528.

Sheaffer, fountain pen and pencil set, White Dot, Triumph Valiant Pen, 14K point, 1948, $75.00.

Pencil
  Adlai Stevenson, plastic, mechanical, red, white, and blue, "Win With Adlai Stevenson/Stevenson For President" **15.00**
  Chicago Cubs, wood, mechanical, baseball bat shape, red "Atlantic" premium sponsor, 1940–1950. .... **15.00**
  Disneyland, 11" l, wood, white, red, yellow, and blue figures of Mickey, Donald, and Pluto **12.00**
  Elsie, 5", mechanical, Secretary Pen Co, Borden Co copyright, 1930–1940 .... **60.00**
  Fire Chief, mechanical. **20.00**
  Joe DiMaggio, 6", wood, mechanical, baseball bat shape, black signature, 1940–1950 .... **50.00**
  Pearl Harbor, mechanical **18.00**
  Popeye, 10½" l, metal, mechanical, silver gray, black and dark red illus and text, Eagle Pencil Co, 1930–40 ..... **25.00**
  Wahl–Eversharp, lady's **14.00**
Pen
  Epenco, black case, gold-plated trim. . . **20.00**
  Hopalong Cassidy, 6", black plastic and silvered metal, 3–D plastic portrait, Parker Pen Co, c1950. .... **50.00**
  Mother–of–pearl, Victorian, lady's **26.00**
  Parker, maroon, stainless steel cap, chrome-plated trim, 1950 .... **30.00**
  Sheaffer, Lifetime, black, brown stripe **50.00**
  Tom Mix, 4¾", marbleized, rope script, 14k gold plated by Southern Pen Co point, c1920. .... **75.00**

PERFUME BOTTLES

Perfume bottles come in all shapes and sizes. In addition to perfume bottles, there are atomizers (a bottle with a spray mechanism), colognes (large bottles whose stoppers often have an application device), scents (small bottles used to hold a scent or smelling salts), and vinaigrettes (an ornamental box or bottle with a perforated top). The stopper of a perfume is used for application and is very elongated.

Perfume bottles were one of the hot collectibles of the 1980s. As a result of market manipulation and speculative buying, prices became very high. The wind started to blow in the wrong direction. The field began to stink. Many prices collapsed.

Club: Perfume and Scent Bottle Collectors, 2022 East Charleston Blvd, Las Vegas, NV 89104.

Golliwogg, painted glass, black puff hair, orig box marked "Houbigant," 3½" h, $75.00.

Avon, 3¼" h, California Perfume Co, violet sachet, half full, violet paper label, 1912. . . . . 125.00
Baccarat, Rose Teinte, 1½" d, 4½" h, swirl. 65.00
Blown Three Mold, pale aqua glass, Gothic Arch, cork stopper, c1825 . . . . . 110.00
China, figural
  1¼" w, 2" d, 3⅜" h, lady and parrot, blue, white, black, yellow, green, and orange, metal and cork stopper. 70.00
  2" d, 4¼" h, child, seated in yellow bag, purple collar and black hat, metal and cork stopper, marked "Germany". . . 40.00
Cranberry
  2" d, 5¼" h, gold bands, small blue and white florals, gold ball stopper. 120.00
  2⅜" d, 3¾" h, bulbous, enameled blue and gray flowers, blue, orange, and white leaves, clear flattened ball stopper 90.00
  2¼" d, 5½" h, cut, beveled, clear cut faceted bubble stopper. 110.00
Cut Glass
  4" h, 2½" sq, Harvard pattern, atomizer, gold washed top. 125.00
  5½" h, ¼" d, heart shape, clear, cut flowers on front and back, clear cut faceted stopper 75.00
  5¾" h, Harvard pattern and panels of cut florals. 125.00
  6½" h, Button and Star pattern, rayed base, faceted stopper, Brilliant period. 100.00
Czechoslovakian, glass
  3½" h, clear and frosted 100.00
  3⅝" h, opaque black, clear stopper. 85.00
Moser Glass, blue, white enamel and gold trim, gilded metal rose shaker stopper, c1900. . . . . 110.00

Pairpoint, 5½" h, heavy crystal, controlled bubbles 60.00
Porcelain, floral dec, marked "Germany". 40.00
Pressed Glass, figural, dog, clown collar, gray, c1890 . . . . 40.00
Russian, clear glass, green box opens with silk cords and weights, mid 19th C 45.00
Spatter Glass, cranberry, leaf mold, bulbous, orig stopper 100.00

PIANO STOOLS

They are around. How's that for a grade "D" pun? All kidding aside, there are some great piano stool forms, especially from the Victorian era. Most individuals focus on the wooden stools. Do not overlook the great metal examples.

Adjustable seat, metal, claw feet holding glass ball, c1880–1915
  Ornate 125.00
  Plain. 65.00
Adjustable seat, wooden, c1880–1915
  Ornate 150.00
  Plain. 50.00
Salesman Sample, 12" h 85.00

PICKLE CASTERS

Imagine a matched table setting elaborate enough to include a pickle caster. When was the last time that you were served pickles with your evening meal? What's wrong with the pickle lobbyists?

Almost all the emphasis is on the Victorian pieces, i.e., casters from the 1870 to 1915 period. Deduct 25 percent if the pickle fork is missing. Even more if the lid is missing. No one wants a fly in his pickles anymore than he does in his soup.

Amethyst, applied floral dec, SP frame and lid. 275.00
Blue, 11", IVT insert, white enamel flowers, orig tongs. 250.00
Cranberry, 3¼" × 10⅛", enameled white band of flowers and leaves, gold trim, SP frame, lid and tongs 235.00
Northwood, Netted Apple Blossom insert, ornate SP ftd frame 275.00
Pattern Glass
  Beaded Dart, sapphire blue insert, resilvered ftd Meriden frame and tongs 250.00
  Cupid and Venus, clear insert, ftd

Daisy and Button pattern amber insert, silver plated Tufts frame, orig tongs, $185.00.

Folk art style, assorted soft woods, 14" × 17", $125.00.

Pairpoint frame stylized swan head tongs **85.00**

Daisy and Button, blue insert, SP Wilcox frame, lid and tongs **235.00**

Opalescent, Daisy and Fern, blue, apple blossom mold, ornate ftd SP frame, orig tongs **250.00**

Pigeon Blood, Bulging Loop pattern, 8", SP ftd frame, marked "Empire Mfg Co" **285.00**

Rubena, vertical optic pattern insert, ornate Pairpoint ftd fretwork frame and bail handle **225.00**

PICTURE FRAMES

We have reached the point where the frame is often worth more than the picture in it. Decorators have fallen in love with old frames. If you find one with character and pizazz at a flea market for a few dollars, pick it up. It will not be hard to resell it.

Who said picture frames have to be used for pictures? They make great frames for mirrors. Use your imagination a little.

Brass, Art Nouveau style, two oval openings, easel back, 7" × 12" **125.00**

Curly Maple, refinished, 16¾" × 20½" ... **90.00**

Mahogany, laminated, folk art pyramid dec, old varnish finish, 9" × 12¾" **45.00**

Silver Plated, 2" wide border with raised

peasant figures, houses, trees, village scene, rough textured finish, 9¾" × 17 ½" **100.00**

Tramp Art, Philadelphia area, 1915, 19½" × 17¼" **48.00**

Veneer, rosewood, beveled, 7⅝" × 8¾"... **50.00**

Walnut, chip carved edge, applied hearts, 16" × 19 ½" **50.00**

PIEBIRDS

They were never meant to whistle, although they look like they could. Piebirds were inserted in the middle of pies when baking them to stop the contents from overflowing.

They come in a variety of shapes and are usually made of porcelain. Many are collected as secondary objects by collectors from other categories.

Bird
  Big Mouth
    Black **28.00**
    White........................ **30.00**
  Black, black base **22.00**
  Black, white base **22.00**
  Blue Willow..................... **15.00**
  Royal Worcester, black **335.00**
Chicken.......................... **48.00**
Chinaman........................ **50.00**
Crow, black **40.00**
Duck, blue **23.00**

Elephant
Nut Brown.......................... **55.00**
White, standing on back feet, English............................. **50.00**
English Bobby, blue uniform, English.... **54.00**
Funnel, round, white, yellow top, pie man followed by three children and dog.... **50.00**
Man, black suit and hat, white face, black features.......................... **52.00**
Owl, white, on stump, English......... **50.00**
Penguin, green scarf and hat........... **54.00**
Rooster, Blue Willow................ **17.00**
Woman, holding pie................. **50.00**

PIG COLLECTIBLES

This is one animal that does better as a collectible than in real life. Pig collectibles have never been oinkers.

Established pig collectors focus on the bisque and porcelain pigs of the late 19th and early 20th centuries. This is a limited view. Try banks in the shape of a pig as a specialized collecting area. If not appealing, look at the use of pigs in advertising. If neither please you, there is always Porky. "That's all, folks."

Postcard, child riding pig, $30.00.

Bank, white clay, seated, clear glaze..... **30.00**
Chocolate Mold, tin, two parts......... **65.00**
Figure
Mama bathing baby at pump, pink.... **75.00**
Pig in washtub.................... **54.00**
Gravy Boat, porcelain, two pink pigs swinging....................... **45.00**

Matchsafe, pink pig poking head through fence........................... **60.00**
Paperweight, pig shape, glass, Best Pig Forceps, compliments J Reimers, Davenport, Iowa....................**100.00**
Pillow, pig shape................... **15.00**
Pinback Button, 1¼", Weilands/The Finest Pork Products, dancing yellow pig named Willie, light blue background, 1930s........................... **25.00**
Soaky Bottle, Porky Pig, 9½", figural, 1960s........................... **15.00**
Statue, 7", Porky Pig, plaster, painted, 1940–1950..................... **50.00**
Stickpin, brass..................... **5.50**
Tape Measure, celluloid, figural........ **25.00**
Toy, stuffed, velvet, Steiff............. **60.00**

PIN-UP ART

The stuff looks so innocent, one has to wonder what all the fuss was about when it first arrived upon the scene. Personally, I like it when a little is left to the imagination.

George Petty and Alberto Vargas (the "s" was dropped at *Esquire's* request) have received far more attention than they deserve. You would be smart to focus on artwork by Gillete Elvgren, Billy DeVorss, Joyce Ballantyne, and Earl Moran. While Charles Dana Gibson's girls are also pinups, they are far too respectable to be considered here.

Calendar, Esquire Girl, Alberto Vargas, 1947, $75.00.

Calendar
Armstrong, Rolf
1944, Truly Yours, 16" × 33", full pad........................ **80.00**
1947, See You Soon, 11" × 23", salesman's sample, Sept pad......... **45.00**
Elvgren, 1955, Stepping Out, 16" × 33", dec pad..................... **85.00**

Moran, Earl, 1946, Evening Star, 16″ ×
33″, full pad **175.00**
Varga, 1946, pocket folder, 3″ × 4½″
closed, opens to 4 ½ × 21½″ strip,
Varga and Esquire copyrights **60.00**
Christmas Card, 5½″ × 8″, multicolored,
MacPherson **22.00**
Cigarette Lighter
1/2 x¾ × 1″ h, miniature, keychain
charm, two tinted color pin up photos
on side, Japan, c1950s **30.00**
3″ d, 6½″ h, Torchee, figural aluminum
can, lighter wheel under removable
top cap, pin up in red dress and two
Scottie dogs around outside, inscribed "The Light of Your Life," attached card reads "For Dad as Adver-
tised in *Esquire*," c1950s **30.00**
Date Book, 1945 *Esquire*, 5″ × 7″, spiral
bound, calendar, subtitled "G I Edition", pin up art by Varga, photos of
movie stars. **60.00**
Folder, Sally of Hollywood & Vine, card-
board, sliding insert changing from
dress to underwear to nude **22.00**
Hairpin, Petty, orig 4″ × 5½″ yellow,
red, black, and white card, 1948, artist
sgd **20.00**
Illusion Glass, 5″ h, full color decal of pin
up in sheer clothing, outer clothing disappears when glass sweats, set of five,
c1938. . . . . **100.00**
Keychain
2¼″ h, souvenir, plastic, painted, figural,
female bather drying herself with
towel, white towel, yellow suit, red
hair, attached to cardboard tag,
c1940s **14.00**
3″ h, plastic, liquid filled cylinder, 1¼″ h
pin up figure inside, sheds clothing
when cylinder is tilted, c1940s. **35.00**
Letter Opener, 8½″ h, plastic, figural, flat
back, standing nude holding adv disk
overhead, designed by Elvgren,
c1940s–1950s. **18.00**
Magazine, WWII, girlie cartoons, 7 pg
"Whiz Bang Cuties' section, sepia photos by Murray Korman, Vol 1, #4, Sept
2, 1942. . . . . **35.00**
Match Book Cover, Petty girl, "Snug As A
Bug," Martins Tavern, Chicago, late
1940s **3.00**
Note Pad, 3 × 4½″, pastel, 1944 calendar
on back **6.00**
Playing Cards, Pretty Pippins, ¾ × 2½ ×
3½″ orig box, cowgirl leaning against
fence, signed Petty, complete deck,
c1940s **62.50**
Poster, 17 × 33″, full color, woman in
shorts walking wire–haired terrier,
c1951, Walt Otto **50.00**
Punch Board Label, 3¾″ × 8″, Elvgren,
unused. **10.00**

PLANTER'S PEANUTS

Amedeo Obici and Mario Peruzzi organized the Planter's Nut and Chocolate
Company in Wilkes–Barre, Pennsylvania,
in 1906. The monocled Mr. Peanut resulted
from a trademark contest in 1916. Standard Brands bought Planter's only to be
bought themselves by Nabisco.

Planter's developed a wide range of premiums and promotional items. Beware of
reproductions.

Club: Peanut Pals, 3065 Rumsey Drive,
Ann Arbor, MI 48105.

*Nut set, tin, 6 × 9″ master dish, 3″ d individual
dishes, 5 pcs, $20.00.*

Bank, 8½″ h, figural, Mr Peanut, plastic,
dark red, removable hat. **35.00**
Bookmark, die-cut, cardboard,
1920–1930 . . . . **20.00**
Bracelet, charm, three beige and blue Mr
Peanut figures, c1930 . . . . **12.00**
Counter Container, 12″ h, figural, Mr Pea-
nut, plastic, hollow, amber base, raised
facial features, blue hat, blue and yellow
Mr Peanut paper sticker label, dated
1979. . . . . **20.00**
Doll, 20″ h, Mr Peanut, cloth, stuffed,
orig clear plastic mailer, unopened,
c1960s **20.00**
Figure, 10″ h, cardboard **6.00**
Keychain Figure, 2¼″, figural, Mr Peanut,
plastic, day glow, molded keychain
loop, c1940s **25.00**
Mug, pewter **20.00**
Nut Tray, 5½″ d, 1¼″ h, plastic, green,
divided, 3″ Mr Peanut in center, matching 3″ l serving spoon with figural han-
dle **40.00**
Paint Book, 7½″ × 10½″, "Colorful Story
of Peanuts as Told by Mr Peanut," soft
cov, 28 pg, copyright 1957. . . . . **30.00**

Pinback Button, 1⅛" d, black and white illus and "Mr Peanut" on white ground, "Vote for the Peoples Choice" in white lettering on red rim, 1930s 12.50

Ring, Mr Peanut, metal, adjustable, yellow and black enamel figure, c1960s 30.00

Salt and Pepper Shakers, pr, 3" h, plastic, figural Mr Peanut, silver flashing, removable top hats, made in USA, c1940s 18.00

Serving Spoon, 5¼" l, SP, Carlton, c1930. . . . . 12.00

Souvenir Set, 1939 New York World's Fair, one large and four small peanut serving dishes, tin litho, Mr Peanut, Trylon, Perisphere, and inscription in center of each dish 70.00

Swizzle Stick, figural 3.50

Tab, 1½", metal, litho, diecut, yellow, black, and white Mr Peanut, 1920–1930 . . . . 12.00

Whistle, plastic, red and white, chain loop, "Mr Peanut" on hat brim, 1940–1950 . . . . 10.00

Wrapper, Planter's Bar, 6" × 7¾", textured wax paper, yellow and blue, Mr Peanut and lady in peanut shape canoe, inscribed "Scenes from Old Virginia Where the Peanut Grows," 1927 copyright 30.00

PLAYBOY

The Playboy empire of the 1960s and 1970s is dead. The clubs and casino are closed. Hugh got married. Is there no God?

Playboy was promotion-minded. Anything associated with it is collectible. Most Playboy magazines sell in the $1.00 to $3.00 range except for very early, (1953 to 1960) issues. The key magazine to own is Volume One, Number One, but isn't this always the case?

Cake Pan, bunny logo shape, Wilton Enterprises 10.00

Calendar
1961, 5½" × 6½", desk, MIB 45.00
1964, 8½" × 12½", spiral bound, photo for each month. 25.00

Car Freshener, Playboy logo, black and white 2.00

Magazine
1955, September, includes black and white Marilyn Monroe photos 30.00
1957. . . . . 4.00
1966. . . . . 3.00

Mug, black, white Playboy logo 4.00

Puzzle, Miss October, Majken Haugedal, canister, 1967 copyright 40.00

PLAYING CARDS

The key is not the deck, but the design on the deck surface. Souvenir decks are especially desirable. Look for special decks such as Tarot and other fortune-telling items.

Always buy complete decks. There are individuals who just collect Jokers and have a bad habit of removing them from a deck and then reselling it. If you are buying a playing card game, make certain that the instructions are available.

Magazine: *Playing Card World*, 188 Sheen Lane, East Sheen, London SW1 48LF, England.

Clubs: Chicago Playing Card Collectors, Inc., 1559 West Platt Boulevard, Chicago, IL 60620; Playing Card Collectors Association, Inc., 3621 Douglas Avenue, Racine, WI 53404.

Advertising, Reese's Peanut Butter Cups, Brown & Bigelow, St Paul, MN, poker size, $10.00.

Airline, complete deck 2.50

Charlie Chan Card Game, complete 35 playing cards and instruction card, boxed, Whitman, 1939 . . . . 50.00

Coca–Cola, 1943 . . . . 65.00

Eastern/Ryder, MIB. 5.00

Holland/America, orig box 25.00

Nile Fortune Cards, boxed, c1900 . . . . 45.00

Ozark Airlines, 1984 World's Fair, sealed deck 2.00

Poker Taurino, Mexican, complete deck, Spanish inscription on box, c1950 . . . . 12.00

Squadron Insignia Card Game, 17 pairs of duplicated cards and single "Enemy" titled card, orig box, All–Fair, mid–1940s 75.00

Tee Up, golf cartoon on each card, complete deck, orig box, c1950 . . . . 10.00

The Vista Dome, complete deck, 1950–60 . . . . 15.00

206

Whirlaway, race horse, two complete decks and joker cards, orig box, early 1940s, Fanfare................... **30.00**

World War II...................... **4.00**

World's Fair, 1934 New York, complete deck, orig box, complimentary gift from Markwell Staplers................ **25.00**

POLITICAL ITEMS

Collect the winners. For whatever reason, time has not treated the losers well, with the exception of the famous Cox–Roosevelt pinback button.

This is a good category to apply my Dad's Thirty Year Rule — "For the first thirty years of anything's life, all its value is speculative." Do not pay much for items less than thirty years old. But, do remember that time flies. The Nixon–JFK election was over thirty years ago.

Also concentrate on the nontraditional categories. Everyone collects pinbacks and posters. Try something unusual. How about political ties, mugs, or license plates?

Newspaper: *The Political Collector Newspaper*, 444 Lincoln Street, York, PA 17404.

Club: American Political Items Collectors, P. O. Box 340339, San Antonio, TX 78234.

Button, pinback, Coolidge–Dawes, Full Dinner Pail, red, white, and blue, $8.50.

Autograph, Cox, letter, addressed to Ohio judge, raised blue letterhead "State of Ohio/Executive Department/Columbus".........................**100.00**

Bandanna, JFK, 31" sq, rayon type fabric, full color portrait, white ground, red, white, and blue flag border, 1965 copyright tag......................... **20.00**

Bell, brass, Ring for Coolidge........... **15.00**

Button, pinback
Eisenhower/Nixon, Ike and Dick, Sure To Click, 3½" d, black and white slogan, 1952..................... **27.50**
Johnson, 6" d, inauguration, full color portrait, red, white, and blue rim.... **10.00**
Reagan/Bush, '84, flashing red lights, musical, 2¼" d red, white and blue button, 3½" × 6" colorful orig card, clear plastic cov, battery operated, pr..................... **20.00**

Coloring Book, 1973, titled "Watergate Coloring Book/Join The Fun/Color The Facts," 8" × 11", 48 pgs............. **25.00**

Comb, McGovern, plastic, blue, smiling face.......................... **4.00**

Convention Badge, National
1948, Democratic, Phila, 1½" × 5½", brass hanger with Betsy Ross house, fob with City Hall and Wm Penn statue, blue enameled "Press" bar, white fabric ribbons............. **18.00**
1968, Republican, Miami, brass, state-shaped top hanger, PA/Press, lower hanger keystone shaped, raised state seal, white fabric ribbon.......... **20.00**

Jewelry, pin, Willkie, red, white, and blue enameled white metal, 2" × 3½", ribbonlike design, ten inset rhinestones and center Willkie button.......... **35.00**

Lapel Stud, McKinley–Protection '96, brass, diecut, ⅞" l, Napoleon's hat shape..................... **25.00**

License Plate, Willkie, 4 × 13½", orange, gold letters outlined in dark blue, blue edge......................... **20.00**

Necktie, Wilson/Marshall, black fabric, 1½" w, 47" l, white embroidered names, red, white, and blue flag........... **50.00**

Pen, Eisenhower, 5" l, brass, black and white plastic, slogan "For The Love Of Ike–Vote Republican"............. **25.00**

Pennant, Dewey, olive green felt, white portrait and inscription, 11" × 30".... **20.00**

Pocket Mirror, Teddy Roosevelt, flesh tone sepia portrait................. **65.00**

Postcard, Taft, 3½" × 5½", black, white, gray, and dark brown, "Our Presidents/Past/Present/Future," portraits of McKinley, TR, and Taft, Sept 1908 postmark...................... **15.00**

Poster, Goldwater, "A Choice. . . Not An Echo," 14" × 21", red, white, and blue........................... **15.00**

Ribbon, For President Gen. W. S. Hancock, 3" × 5¾" dark pink ribbon, large gold design, 1" sepia paper photo of Hancock..................... **81.00**

Sheet Music, *Dedicated To The GOP/A Victory Is Ours/A Rousing Republican Cam-*

207

paign Song, 1904 copyright, blue and
white, 7" × 11" **15.00**
Sticker, diecut foil, 3½" × 6", silver, blue,
and red, inscribed "Willkie/The Hope of
America" **15.00**
Tab, Humphrey, 2", blue, green, red,
white, and black, "Labor for
Humphrey" **4.50**
Tray, McKinley, 3" × 5", aluminum,
center jugate photos of McKinley
and Teddy Roosevelt, red and blue
shield **18.00**
Watch Fob
  Bryan and Kern, enamel, eagles and
  flags center, orig strap **35.00**
  Roosevelt and Fairbanks, brass, 1¾" ×
  2" **20.00**

POSTCARDS

This is a category where the average golden
age card has gone from 50¢ to several dollars in the last decade. Postcards golden age
is between 1898 and 1918. As the cards
have become expensive, new collectors are
discovering the white border cards of the
1920s and 30s, the linens of the 1940s, and
the early glossy photograph cards of the
1950s and 1960s.

It pays to specialize. This is the only way
that you can build a meaningful collection.
The literature is extensive. It is worth re-
viewing before buying. Jack Smith's
Postcard Companion: The Collector's Reference
(Wallace–Homestead, 1989), not a favorite
among serious collectors and dealers, can
be used for a quick overview before moving
on to better specialized books.

Newspapers: *Barr's Postcard News*, 70 S.
6th Street, Lansing, IA 52151; *Postcard Collector*, Joe Jones Publishing, P. O. Box 337,
Iola, WI 54945.

Clubs: *Barr's* and *Postcard Collector* list
over fifty regional clubs scattered across the
United States.

Advertising
  Bulova Watch, government postal
  back **6.00**
  Moxie, two children with cutouts and
  sign **25.00**
Burlington Zephyr, stationed at 1934 Cen-
tury of Progress Exposition, inscription,
unused........................ **12.00**
Christmas, Santa, red suit **8.00**
Fourth of July, red, white, and blue, gold
ground, Germany, 1910 .... **2.00**
George Washington, multicolored **3.75**

*Bethlehem, PA, Trombone Choir of Moravian
Church, Announcing A Death, A. C. Bosselman
& Co, NY, made in Germany, $5.00.*

Halloween, orange pumpkin, artist sgd
"Ellen Clapsaddle" **8.00**
Hitler, glossy black and white cartoon pic-
ture, penciled note, May 15, 1943
postmark **15.00**
McKinley's death **6.00**
Roy Rogers, "Apple Valley Inn," full color
photo, unused, c1970 .... **15.00**
State
  Alabama **1.00**
  Idaho .... **.50**
  South Carolina .... **.75**
Truman, campaign card **25.00**
Valentine, children and women **4.00**
World's Fair, Chicago, unused **1.50**

POSTERS

Want a great way to decorate / use posters.
Buy ones you like. This can get a bit expensive if your tastes run to old movie or advertising posters. Prices in the hundred of
dollars are not uncommon. When you get
to the great lithography posters of the late
19th and early 20th century, prices in the
thousands are possible.

Concentrate on one subject, manufacturer, illustrator, or period. Remember that
print runs of two million copies and more
are not unknown. Many collectors have
struck deals with their local video store and
movie theater to get their posters when

they are ready to throw them out. Not a bad idea. But why not carry it a step further? Talk with your local merchants about their advertising posters. These are going to be far harder to find in the future than movie posters.

Because so many people save modern posters, never pay more than a few dollars for any copy below fine condition. A modern poster in very good condition is unlikely to have long-term value. Its condition will simply not be acceptable to the serious collector of the future.

Club: Poster Society of America, Inc., P. O. Box 43171, Montclair, NJ 07043.

Advertising
Buy A Poppy, American Legion Auxiliary, silk screen, 14" x 20"......... **40.00**
Coca–Cola–Yes, Harold Sundblum, 1946 bathing beauty, 11" × 27" **150.00**
Hilton–The Starched Collar For Fall–Tooke Brothers Ltd, c1915, 11" × 21"....................... **50.00**
Use Virginia Dare Double Strength Extracts, smiling 1925 housewife making cookies, 21 × 28".............**175.00**
Welch's Wine Coolers–Wouldn't This Hit The Spot Right Now? Taste It...You'll Love It, Says Eddie Cantor, 1952, 11" x 21".................**100.00**
Movie and Theater
Andy Hardy Comes Home, MGM, Mickey and Teddy Rooney, 1958, 41" × 81"....................... **80.00**
Carter Beats The Devil, Otis Litho, 1920, 14" × 22".................... **75.00**
Dangerous When Wet, MGM, Esther Williams, Fernando Lamas, Jack Carson, 1953, 41 × 81".......... **65.00**
King Kong, RKO, Fay Wray, Robert Armstrong, Bruce Cabot, 1936, 27" × 41".......................**800.00**
Three Penny Opera, Paul Davis, 1976, 41" × 81", two panels **275.00**
Tim McCoy Two Gun Justice, Monogram, 1938, 27 × 41".......... **65.00**
Zombies of the Stratosphere, Republic Serial, 1952, 41" × 81" **75.00**

PUZZLES

The keys to jigsaw puzzle value in order of importance are: (1) completeness (once three or more pieces are missing, forget value); (2) picture (no one is turned on by old mills and mountain scenery); (3) surface condition (missing tabs, paper, and silver fish damage cause value to drop dra-

matically); (4) age (1940 is a major cut off point); (5) number of pieces (the more, the better for wood; anything over 500 for cardboard, not so good); and (6) original box and label (especially important for wooden puzzles). Because of the limitless number of themes, jigsaw puzzle collectors find themselves competing with collectors from virtually every other category.

Jigsaw puzzle collectors want an assurance of completeness, either a photograph or a statement by the seller that they actually put the puzzle together. "I bought it as complete" carries no weight whatsoever. Unassembled cardboard puzzles with no guarantees sell for $1.00 or less, wooden puzzles for $3.00 or less. One missing piece lowers price by 20 percent, two missing pieces by 35 percent, and three missing pieces by 50 percent or more. Missing packaging (a box or envelope) deducts 25 percent from the price.

Clubs: American Game Collectors Association, 4628 Barlow Drive, Bartlesville, OK 74006; International Society for Jigsaw Puzzle Enthusiasts, 5093 Vera Cruz Road, Emmaus, PA 18049.

Note: The following retail prices are for puzzles that are complete, in very good condition, and have their original box.

Chicago World's Fair, bass wood, Marshall Field Co, Electrical Building, 3½" × 5 9/16", $25.00.

ADULT PUZZLES
Cardboard
Depression Era, late 1920s through 1940
Milton Bradley, Movieland, four puzzle set **30.00**
Movie stars and movie-related **12.00**
Nonweeklies **2.00**
Perfect Picture Puzzles **3.00**
Tuco......................... **3.00**
Weeklies **8.00**

World War II theme		6.00
Post World War II		
Up to 500 pieces		.50
500 to 1,000 pieces		1.00
Over 1,000 pieces		1.50
Springbok, circular box		2.50
Springbok, square box		1.50

Wood
1908–1910 craze

Up to 200 pieces		25.00
200 to 500 pieces		30.00
Over 500 pieces		35.00

Mid–1920s to mid–1930s craze

Up to 200 pieces		15.00
200 to 500 pieces		20.00
500 to 1,000 pieces		30.00
Over 1,000 pieces		50.00

Post–1945

Up to 500 pieces		15.00
Over 500 pieces		20.00

Par

Up to 500 pieces		50.00
Over 500 pieces		100.00

CHILDREN'S PUZZLES

Cardboard
Pre–1945

Less than 20 pieces		2.00
Over 20 pieces		3.00
Puzzle set, three to four puzzles		10.00

Post–1945

Less than 20 pieces		1.00
20 to 200 pieces		1.50
Over 200 pieces		2.00
Frame Tray, cartoon		6.00
Frame Tray, cowboy		12.00
Frame Tray, general		3.00

Composition, 1880s to 1920s
McLoughlin Brothers

General scene		75.00
Transportation theme		150.00

Others

Fairy Tale		25.00
General scene		50.00
Transportation scene		100.00

Wood
Madmar

General scene		15.00
Patriotic scene		20.00

Map

Pre–1880		75.00
1880 to 1915		50.00
1915 to 1940		20.00

Others

General scene		12.50
Transportation scene		17.50

Parker Brothers

Dolly Danty series		35.00
General scene		20.00

ADVERTISING & NOVELTY PUZZLES

Cardboard

1930s		10.00

Post–1945		5.00
Wood		
Pre–1945		35.00
Pseudo		25.00

RADIO CHARACTERS AND PERSONALITIES

Radio dominated American life between the 1920s and the early 1950s. Radio characters and personalities enjoyed the same star status as their movie counterparts. Phrases such as "The Shadow Knows" or "Welcome Breakfast Clubbers" quickly date an individual.

Many collectors focus on radio premiums, objects offered during the course of a radio show and usually received by sending in proof of purchase of the sponsor's product. Make certain an object is a premium before paying extra for it as part of this classification.

Many radio characters also found their way into movies and television. Trying to separate the products related to each medium is time consuming. Why bother? If you enjoyed the character or personality, collect everything that is related to him or her.

Game, Eddie Cantor's New Game, Tell It To The Judge, Parker Bros, copyright 1936, 10¾" × 5⅞" box, 19¼" sq board, $30.00

Jimmie Allen
Model, 19" l, 24" wingspan, Thunder-
bolt, orig box, unused, 1930s 100.00

Pocketknife, $3\frac{1}{4}''$ l, plastic simulated
wood grips, pair raised wings marked
"Jimmie Allen" on one side, two
blades, 1930s **285.00**

Amos 'n' Andy
Ashtray, 5" × 5" × 8", plaster, Amos
and Andy standing on either side of
barrel, "Ise Regusted" incised on
front edge, c1930s **90.00**
Pinback Button, $\frac{7}{8}''$ d, black and white,
photo, "Amos 'n' Andy Pantages" on
rim, 1930s **35.00**

Jack Armstrong
Ring, Egyptian Siren, brass, siren on
top, Egyptian symbols on side,
1938 . . . . **75.00**

Captain Midnight, record, "The Years to
Remember," 7" d, flexible vinyl, punch
out decoder, Longines Symphonette
Society, #6 from "The Silver Dagger
Strikes" series, 1960s **35.00**

Chandu the Magician, Svengali Mind-
Reading Trick, Beech–Nut premium,
orig mailing box, c1932–1935 . . . . **60.00**

Mitzi Green, pinback button, $1\frac{1}{4}''$ d, photo
and "I'm on the Air, Mitzi Green, in
Happy Landings" in center, "Ward's
Soft Bun Bread, WKAN, Tues & Thurs,
6:00 P.M." in white lettering on rim,
1930s **5.00**

The Gumps, book, *The Gumps in Radio
Land*, $3\frac{1}{2}''$ × $5\frac{1}{2}''$, soft cov, Pebeco
Toothpaste premium, 96 pgs, 1937
copyright **35.00**

Little Orphan Annie
Bandanna, 17" × 19", black, white, and
red, Ovaltine premium, c1934 . . . . . . **65.00**
Bottle, bubble bath, $10\frac{1}{2}''$ h, vinyl, figural, Annie holding bouquet, remov-
able molded hair cap, paper sticker on
base, 1977 copyright **20.00**
Doll Pattern, 5" × 10", fabric, printed
design, Harold Gray copyright, J
Pressman & Co of New York City,
c1930s **60.00**
Manual, Secret Society, 6" × $8\frac{1}{2}''$, 8 pgs,
1937 . . . . **55.00**

Lone Ranger
Album, $33\frac{1}{3}$ rpm, $12\frac{1}{4}''$ × $12\frac{1}{4}''$ card-
board sleeve, two radio broadcasts,
Adventures #1 and #2, written by
Fran Striker, color illus of Lone
Ranger on Silver, issued by Wrather
Corp, Detroit, c1950s **12.50**
Silver Bullet Compass, $1\frac{1}{4}''$, silvered
brass, hollow, compass in remov-
able end cap, orig card and mailer,
c1948 . . . . **58.00**

Charlie McCarthy
Dummy, 8" × $18\frac{1}{2}''$, cardboard, diecut,
multicolored, movable lever controls
mouth and eyes, late 1930s–early
1940s **58.00**
Game, Put and Take Bingo, #2931,

Whitman, orig box, 1938 copy-
right **35.00**

Perfume Bottle, $3\frac{1}{2}''$ h, clear glass, removable black plastic hat, late
1930s **40.00**

Statue, $15\frac{1}{2}''$ h, carnival chalkware,
multicolored, glitter accents,
1930s–1940s **85.00**

Fibber McGee and Molly
Game, The Amazing Adventures of Fib-
ber McGee, Milton Bradley, 1936 . . . **35.00**
Photo, $8\frac{1}{4}''$ × 12", black and white,
glossy, cast members, Fibber and
Molly pictured at top, late 1930s **25.00**

Joe Penner, pinback button, $\frac{7}{8}''$ d, "I'm a
Joe Penner Quacker," black illus of
duck and rim lettering on yellow
ground, 1930s **6.00**

Sgt Preston
Distance Finder, $2\frac{1}{2}''$ × $3\frac{1}{2}''$, diecut,
silver, Quaker Cereal premium,
1955 . . . . **35.00**
Map, Yukon Territory, $7\frac{1}{2}''$ × $9\frac{1}{2}''$,
c1955 . . . . **40.00**

The Shadow
Lapel Stud, $\frac{3}{4}''$, impressed image of
Shadow in cape and hat, silvered,
1930s **275.00**
Pinback Button, $1\frac{1}{4}''$ d, celluloid, yellow
and green, "The Shadow of Fu Man-
chu," 1930s **75.00**

Red Skelton, post card, $3\frac{1}{2}''$ × $5\frac{1}{2}''$, radio
show cast photo, matte finish,
postmarked 1948 . . . . **20.00**

Uncle Don, pinback button, black and
white photo center, "Uncle Don's Radio
Club" in white lettering on blue rim,
1930s **7.00**

RADIOS

If a radio does not work, do not buy it
unless you need it for parts. If you do, do
not pay more than $10.00. A radio that
does not work and is expensive to repair is
a useless radio.

The radio market has gone through a
number of collecting crazes in the 1980s
and 1990s. It began with Bakelite radios,
moved on to figural and novelty radios,
and now is centered on early transistors
and 1940s plastic case radios. These crazes
are often created by manipulative dealers.
Be suspicious of the prices in any specialized price guide focusing on these limited
topics. There are several general guides that
do a good job of keeping prices in perspec-
tive.

Magazines: *Radio Age*, 636 Cambridge
Road, Augusta, GA 30909.

RCA Victor, Art Deco, brown case, $40.00.

Newspaper: *Antique Radio Classified*, 9511 Sunrise Blvd., Cleveland, OH 44133.

Clubs: Antique Radio Club of America, 81 Steeplechase Road, Devon, PA 19333; Antique Wireless Association, 17 Sheridan Street, Auburn, NY 13021.

A–C Electrical, Model XL–30, table, battery, six tubes, two dials, 1929 . . . . **100.00**
Acme Apparatus, Model S, table, battery, five tubes, single dial, 1925 . . . . **75.00**
Atwater Kent, Model 46, table, green metal case, 1929 . . . . **115.00**
Crosley, Superheterodyne, three tubes, slant front **165.00**
Delco, car, Xstar Transportable **35.00**
FADA, model #790, working order **450.00**
Freed Eisenmann, Model NR–95, console, eight tubes, one dial, 1929 . . . . . . **125.00**
Novelty, figural
   Annie **20.00**
   Cabbage Patch Kids **15.00**
   Coke Bottle **17.50**
   Fire Chief **20.00**
   Pepsi, cooler, c1960, MIB **320.00**
Philco, Model PT–91, mantle, plastic, 1941 . . . . **30.00**
Philips, brown and ivory Bakelite case, shortwave **30.00**
RCA, Model U–25, console, broadcast and shortwave, push button, 1939 . . . . **50.00**
Stromberg–Carlson, Model 635, table, treasure chest, seven tubes, one dial, 1928 . . . . **165.00**
Westinghouse, Model WR–14, cathedral, 1931 . . . . **150.00**
Zenith, Model 5–G–401D, portable, gray, handle, 1949 . . . . **25.00**

RAILROADIANA

Most individuals collect by railroad, either one near where they live or one near where they grew up. Collectors are split about even between steam and diesel. Everyone is saddened by the current state of America's railroads. There are Amtrak collectors, but their numbers are small.

Railroad collectors have been conducting their own specialized shows and swap meets for decades. Railroad material that does show up at flea markets is quickly bought and sent into that market. Collectors use flea markets primarily to make dealer contacts, not for purchase.

Railroad paper from timetables to menus is gaining in popularity as railroad china, silver-plated flat and hollow wares, and lanterns rise to higher and higher price levels. The key to paper is that it bear the company logo and have a nice displayable presence.

Newsletters: *Key, Lock and Lantern*, P. O. Box 15, Spencerport, NY 14559; *U. S. Rail News*, P. O. Box 7007, Huntingdon Woods, MI 48070.

Clubs: Railroad Enthusiasts, 456 Main Street, West Townsend, MA 01474; Railroadiana Collectors Association, P. O. Box 365, St. Ignatius, MT 59865; Railway and Locomotive Historical Society, 3363 Riviera West Drive, Kellseyville, CA 95451.

Game, Twentieth Century Limited, Parker Bros, c1910, 21½" × 14 ½" wooden box, $125.00.

Book, *History of Burlington Route*, Overton, NY, 1st edition, 1965 . . . . **30.00**
Booklet, Santa Fe RR, 1927 . . . . **15.00**
Catalog, Vulcan Gasoline Locomotives, Vulcan Iron Works, Wilkes–Barre, PA, 28 pgs, illus, 1926–1927 . . . . **30.00**
Hat, conductor's, PRR **60.00**
Match Holder, Burlington Zephyr, stainless steel **22.00**
Napkin, Seaboard Railway, linen, pr **50.00**
Pass, Erie RR **8.00**
Playing Cards, California Zephyr, 1950–1960 . . . . **15.00**
Print, Santa Fe RR, pictures Indians, framed, 1949 . . . . **35.00**

Schedule

Pennsylvania Railroad Express, 4-page
folder, June 21, 1885 . . . . **20.00**
Philadelphia–Erie, 1869, framed **85.00**
Sugar Bowl, cov, Burlington Railroad, sil-
ver, double handles, Reed & Barton . . . **75.00**
Switch Key, Chicago & Northwestern. . . . **13.00**
Tape Measure, N & W RR, 50 ft **23.00**
Tumbler, Pennsylvania Railroad,
weighted clear glass, c1940 . . . . **15.00**

RECORDS

Most records are worth between 25¢ and
$1.00. A good rule to follow is the more
popular the record, the less likely it is to
have value. Who does not have a copy of
Bing Crosby singing "White Christmas?"
Until the mid-1980s the principal emphasis was on 78 rpm records. As the decade ended 45 rpm records became increasingly collectible. By 1990 33⅓ rpm albums,
especially Broadway show related, were
gaining in favor.

To find out what records do have value,
check L. R. Dock's *1915–1965 American Pre-
mium Record Guide, Third Edition* (Books
Americana, 1986) and Jerry Osborne's *The
Official Price Guide To Records, Ninth Edition*
(House of Collectibles, 1990).

By the way, maybe you had better buy a
few old record players. You could still play
the 78s and 45s on a 33 ⅓ machine. You
cannot play any of them on a compact disc
player.

Newspapers: *Discoveries*, P. O. Box 255,
Port Townsend, WA 98368; *Goldmine*, 700
East State Street, Iola, WI 54990.

Children's

Barbie Sings, 45 rpm, sung by Barbie
and Ken, Mattel Stock No. 840, 1961
copyright **35.00**
Bugs Bunny in Storyland, 78 rpm, Capi-
tol Records, voices by Mel Blanc, two
record set, 1949 copyright **35.00**
Donald Duck Fire Chief/Donald Duck
Song, 78 rpm, yellow plastic, Golden
Record, early 1950s **15.00**
Popeye the Sailorman, 33⅓ rpm, Rock-
ing Horse Series, Diplomat Records,
orig cardboard cov, 1960–1970 . . . . **20.00**
The Shmoo Club/The Shmoo is Clean,
The Shmoo is Neat, 33 ⅓ rpm, Music
You Enjoy, Inc, 7" × 7" paper enve-
lope, 1949 copyright **50.00**
Super Heroes Christmas Album, 33⅓
rpm, Peter Pan Label, copyright DC
Comics, 1977 . . . . **35.00**

Top Cat Theme Song, 45 rpm, Little
Golden Record, orig paper cov, 1962
Hanna–Barbera copyright **15.00**
Yogi Bear TV Theme Song/Before Yogi,
78 rpm, Little Golden Record, orig
paper cov, 1961 Hanna–Barbera
copyright **20.00**

Comedy

Sam 'N' Henry at the Fortune Tellers/
Sam's Speech at the Colored Lodge,
78 rpm, Victor, comedy sketches,
later known as Amos 'N' Andy, orig
unmarked sleeve, c1920s **70.00**
The Three Stooges Sing Six Happy
Yuletide Songs, 45 rpm, Little
Golden Record, parody songs, orig
cardboard cov, 1959 Norman Mauer
copyright **40.00**

Commemorative and Souvenir

Man on the Moon, 33⅓ rpm, CBS
News, narrated by Walter Cronkite,
1961. . . . . **20.00**
There's a Great Big Beautiful Tomor-
row, 33⅓ rpm, New York World's
Fair, General Electric/Walt Disney
Studios Exhibit, 1964 . . . . **22.50**

Miscellaneous

The Making of a Marine, Documentary
Record Co, boot camp reception
through completion, c1950s **10.00**
Move Over Babe (Here Comes Henry),
Richard (Popcorn) Wylie, 45 rpm,
Carla label, 1973 . . . . **17.50**

Television

The Addams Family, The Lurch/Wesley,
Ted Cassidy, 45 rpm, Capitol Records,
mid–1960s **24.00**
Batman and Robin, 33⅓ rpm, 12 songs
including "Batman Theme" and
"Joker is Wild," orig cov **18.00**
George Burns Sings, 45 rpm, Colpix
label, orig cardboard sleeve,
c1950s **18.00**
Captain Video and His Video Rangers,
78 rpm, eight page storybook,
punch–out figures, RCA Victor, two
record set, c1950s **80.00**
Dark Shadows, Curtis Records Inc, 11"
× 22" poster featuring Barnabas and
Quentin, copyright 1969 . . . . **40.00**
It's Howdy Doody Time, 33⅓ rpm, RCA
Victor, TV broadcast recordings, orig
cardboard sleeve, 1971 copyright . . . **22.00**
Mr Ed Theme Song/Pretty Little Filly, 45
rpm, Golden Record label, copyright
1962 The Mr Ed Co **35.00**
Songs from the Days of Rawhide, Sheb
Wooley, 33 ⅓ rpm, orig cov **15.00**
Charlie Weaver Sings for His People,
33⅓ rpm, Columbia, orig sleeve and
cardboard jacket with note from
Weaver's Mama, c1960s **18.00**

Western

The Ballad of Davy Crockett, The

Sandpipers, 78 rpm, Little Golden
Record, orig jacket, 1955 . . . . **20.00**
The Chisholm Trail, Gene Autry, 78
rpm, Playtime label, Columbia Rec-
ords, orig paper cov, early 1950s **20.00**

Merrileaf **12.00**
Vegetable, divided Merrileaf **15.00**
Wall Pocket, bird on grapevine,
gray—green **18.00**

ROBOTS

RED WING

Red Wing, Minnesota, was home to several
potteries. Among them were Red Wing
Stoneware Company, Minnesota Stoneware Company, and The North Star Stoneware Company. All are equally collectible.

Red Wing has a strong regional base. The
best buys are generally found at flea markets far removed from Minnesota. Look for
pieces with advertising. Red Wing pottery
was a popular giveaway product.

Club: Red Wing Collectors Society, Route
3, Box 146, Monticello, MN 55362.

This category covers the friction, windup,
and battery-operated robots made after
World War II. The robot concept is much
older, but generated few collectibles. The
grandfather of all modern robot toys is
Atomic Robot Man, made in Japan between 1948 and 1949.

Robots became battery operated by the
1950s. Movies of that era fueled interest in
robots. R2D2 and C3PO from *Star Wars* are
the modern contemporaries of Roby and
his cousins.

Robots are collected internationally. You
will be competing with the Japanese for
examples.

When buying at a flea market, take time
to make certain the robot is complete, oper-
ates (carry at least two batteries of different
sizes with you for testing), and has the original box. The box is critical.

*Robot, driving cream colored Mercedes, litho,
tin, friction, gun sparks, $350.00.*

*Teapot, green, wicker style handle, 7½" h,
$18.50.*

Bookends, pr, fan and scroll, green **15.00**
Bowl
  Lute Song, fruit **7.50**
  Pompeii, cereal **7.00**
Bread Tray, Merrileaf **28.00**
Cup and Saucer
  Capistrano **12.00**
  Merrileaf **10.00**
Gravy, cov, handle, Merrileaf **20.00**
Plate
  Capistrano, chop, 12" **15.00**
  Lotus, dinner, 10" **5.00**
  Pompeii, bread and butter, 6½" **3.00**
Salt and Pepper Shaker, pr
  Bob White **25.00**

Atom, 6", tin litho, silver, red and blue
  arms and accents, yellow plastic eyes,
  c1960 . . . . **100.00**
Ding—A—Lings, 5½", plastic, Boxer, or-
  ange, black arms, blue legs, Topper
  Corp, c1970 . . . . **45.00**
Dr Who Talking K—9, 6", plastic,
  gray, battery operated, BBC, Palitoy,
  1978 . . . . **100.00**
Estracter, 9½", plastic, blue, tin litho chest
  plate, silver accents, marked "made In
  Japan," c1970 . . . . **50.00**
Geag, 8", tin litho, soft rubber head, blue,
  green, yellow, and red, built—in key,
  orig box, Takara, c1970 . . . . **125.00**
Lost In Space, 12", plastic, black and red,
  Remco **400.00**

Mr Robot, 11", tin litho, silver, red arms, clear plastic head, Cragstan **400.00**
Robert The Robot, 14", battery–operated, eyes light, orig box, Ideal, 1950s **200.00**
Television, 14½", battery–operated, metal, large antenna, gold red eyes spin, screeching sound **350.00**
Toto, 8", plastic and tin litho, dark gray, orange feet and accents, marked "Made In Japan," c1960 . . . . **120.00**
Windup Radar robot, 6½", hard plastic, built–in key, orig box, S H, marked "Made In Japan," c1980 . . . . **75.00**
Zerak, 6", hard plastic, forward and reverse movement, orig box, Okay, marked "Made In Hong Kong,' c1970 . . . . **110.00**

ROCK 'N' ROLL

My Dad ought to be forced to do this category. He grew up in the Rock 'n' Roll era, but tuned it out. He claims this is why he can hear, and I cannot. I have heard rumors that he actually went to Bandstand in Philly, but he refuses to confirm them.

Most collectors focus on individual singers and groups. The two largest sources of collectibles are items associated with Elvis and the Beatles. As revivals occur, e.g., the Doors, new interest is drawn to older collectibles. The market has gotten so big that Sotheby's and Christie's hold Rock 'n' Roll sales annually.

Monkees, bubble gum box, 24 packs, copyright 1967, Raybert Productions, Inc., Screen Gems, Inc., $115.00.

Autograph, Chubby Checker, 8" × 10" glossy black and white photo, black felt tip "It Ain't Over Till It's Over, Keep It Up, Love Chubby Checker 86" **30.00**
Book, *Woodstock 69*, Scholastic Book Services, copyright 1970, Joseph J Sia, 124 pgs **25.00**
Doll
  Diana Ross, 19", molded hard plastic body, vinyl face and arms, gold glitter dress, orig box with the Supremes picture, Ideal, copyright 1969 Motown Inc **100.00**

Dick Clark, 25", plush stuffed body, molded vinyl head and hands, marked "Juro" on back of neck, c1950 . . . . **150.00**
Game
  Duran Duran Into The Arena, Milton Bradley, copyright 1985 . . . . **15.00**
  Kiss On Tour, 1978 copyright Aucoin Management **25.00**
Hat
  Purple People Eater, 11" × 13½", plastic, two diecut plastic pointed ears, orig display card **50.00**
  Rock Around The Clock, 9" l, blue felt, removable cardboard record on top, marked "Manufactured by Bing Crosby Phonocards Inc," c1950 . . . . **60.00**
Jacket, tour, silver/gray satin, yellow and white embroidered girl and guy dancing with black "Rock and Roll" above, gold, black, and white, "The Drifters On Broadway" on back, embroidered 1963, tag inside marked "Ragtime Collection" **150.00**
Magazine
  Dick Clark Official American Bandstand Yearbook, 9" × 12", 40 pgs, color and black and white photos, c1950 . . . . **25.00**
  Rock and Roll Songs, 8½" × 11", Vol 3 #11, Dec 1957 . . . . **15.00**
Postcard, Rolling Stones, 4½" × 6½", two, perforated, "The Rolling Stones Exile On Main Street" in red, marked "Scene 1" and "Scene 2," c1972 . . . . **15.00**
Poster
  Doors, 24" × 36", full color, green bottom border, white Doors logo, copyright 1968 Doors Production Corp **20.00**
  Fleetwood Mac, 33" × 46", full color, Jan 1970 concert, Deutsches Museum, Munich, West Germany **30.00**
  Grateful Dead Fan Club, 14" × 20", gold and blue, black and white photo, marked "The Golden Road To Unlimited Devotion," late 1960s **50.00**
  Jefferson Airplane, 13" × 19", Fillmore, April 11–13, late 1960s **50.00**
  Moody Blues, 18½" × 25½", stiff paper, April 1, 1970 concert, Terrace Ballroom, Salt Lake City, UT **50.00**
Record, Buddy Holly, Peggy Sue/Every Day, 78 rpm, Coral label, 1957 . . . . . . **25.00**
Thermos, Monkees, 6½", metal, full color illus, copyright 1967 Rayburt Productions Inc **25.00**

NORMAN ROCKWELL

The prices listed below are retail prices from a dealer specializing in Rockwell and/or limited edition collectibles. Rockwell items are one of those categories for which it really pays to shop around at a flea market. Finding an example in a general booth at ten cents on the dollar is not impossible or uncommon.

When buying any Rockwell item, keep asking yourself how many examples were manufactured. In many cases, the answer is tens to hundreds of thousands. Because of this, never settle for any item in less than fine condition.

Stein, River Pilot, Rockwell Museum, $15.00.

Bell
  Ben Franklin Bicentennial, 1976, Dave
    Grossman. **28.00**
  Christmas Medley, 1983, Gorham **30.00**
  Lovers, 1972, Gorham. **30.00**
Figurine
  After the Prom, 1980, Gorham **125.00**
  Antiques Dealer, 1983, Gorham **130.00**
  Artist's Daughter, 1980, Lynell Stu-
    dios **75.00**
  Bedtime, 1978, Rockwell Museum. . . . **50.00**
  Bride and Groom, 1979, Rockwell Mu-
    seum **100.00**
  Exasperated Nanny, 1980, Dave Gros-
    sman **125.00**
  Giving Thanks, 1982, Rockwell
    Museum **155.00**
  No Swimming, 1973, Dave Gros-
    sman **45.00**
  Saying Grace, 1976, Gorham **150.00**
  Snow Queen, 1979, Lynell Studios **85.00**
Plate
  A Scout Is Loyal, 1976, Gorham **55.00**
  Baby's First Step, 1978, Rockwell Mu-
    seum **80.00**
  Christmas Dream, 1978, Rockwell Soci-
    ety **50.00**
  Cooking Lesson, 1982, Rockwell
    Society **25.00**

Little Mother, 1979, Rockwell Mu-
  seum **65.00**
Mother's Blessing, 1981, Lynell Stu-
  dios **30.00**
Music Maker, 1981, Rockwell Soci-
  ety **30.00**
Scotty Plays Santa, 1980, Rockwell
  Society **32.50**
Spring Flowers, 1979, River Shore **115.00**
Surprises For All, 1980, Lynell Stu-
  dios **30.00**
The Carolers, 1972, Franklin Mint **175.00**
The Secret, Huckleberry Finn, 1979,
  Dave Grossman **50.00**
Tiny Tim, 1974, Gorham **65.00**
Trimming The Tree, 1973, Franklin
  Mint **175.00**
Under The Mistletoe, 1971, Franklin
  Mint **175.00**
Young Love, 1972, Gorham, set of 4 . . . **200.00**
Stein, For A Good Boy, Rockwell Mu-
  seum **85.00**

ROSEVILLE POTTERY

Roseville rose from the ashes of the J. B. Owen Company when a group of investors bought Owen's pottery in the late 1880s. In 1892 George F. Young became the first of four generations of Youngs to manage the plant.

Roseville grew through acquisitions, another Roseville firm and two in Zanesville. By 1898 the company's offices were located in Zanesville. Roseville art pottery was first produced in 1900. The trade name Rozane was applied to many lines. During the 1930s and 1940s, art pottery production was limited. Utilizing several new high gloss glazes in the 1940s, Roseville revived its art pottery line. Success was limited. In 1954 the Mosaic Tile Company bought Roseville.

Pieces are identified as early, middle (Depression era), and late pieces. Because of limited production, middle period pieces are the hardest to find. They also were marked with paper labels that have become lost over time. Some key patterns to watch for are Blackberry, Cherry Blossom, Faline, Ferella, Futura, Jonquil, Morning Glory, Sunflower, and Windsor.

Basket
  Peony, 10" yellow **65.00**
  Poppy, pink, hanging **45.00**
Bowl
  Clematis, blue **50.00**
  Laurel, 9", oval, gold **60.00**

Ewer, Bleeding Hearts, turquoise ground, pink flowers, 6³⁄₈" h, $50.00.

Candleholder, pr	
Magnolia, green	35.00
White Rose, 2¼"	30.00
Compote, Florentine	40.00
Ewer	
Bushberry, blue, 6"	65.00
Freesia, 6", green	35.00
Jardiniere, Poppy, 3", green	25.00
Planter, Velmoss, 16"	35.00
Sugar, Snowberry, pink	20.00
Teapot, Peony, green	85.00
Vase	
Clematis, green	65.00
Donatello, 4"	45.00
Magnolia, brown	35.00
Mostique, 10½"	60.00
Pine Cone II, brown, 8"	75.00
Snowberry, 4", blue	35.00
White Rose, 6", green	35.00
Wall Pocket	
Florentine, 9½", brown	75.00
Tuscany, pink	65.00
Window Box, Wincraft, blue, 13" × 4"	55.00

ROYAL DOULTON

Chances of finding Royal Doulton at flea markets are better than you think. It often is given as gifts. Since the recipients did not pay for it, they often have no idea of its initial value. The same holds true when children have to break up their parent's household. As a result, it is sold for a fraction of its value at garage sales and to dealers.

Check out any piece of Royal Doulton that you find. There are specialized price guides for character jugs, figures, and toby jugs. A great introduction to Royal Doulton is the two-volume videocassette entitled *The Magic of a Name,* produced by Quill Productions, Birmingham, England.

Newsletter: *Jug Collector,* P. O. Box 91748, Long Beach, CA 90809.

Club: Royal Doulton International Collectors Club, P. O. Box 1815, Somerset, NJ 08873.

Figurine, Bon Appetit, #HN2444, matte finish, 6½" h, $265.00.

Animal Mold	
English Setter, HN1050	85.00
Terrier, reclining, front paws crossed, HN1101	65.00
Ashtray, Barleycorn	90.00
Bowl, 9¼" d, 2¼" h, marked "Rosalind"	70.00
Candlesticks, 10¼", floral, blue ground, pr	150.00
Character Jug, tiny, 1¼"	
Gardener	40.00
Paddy	100.00
Character Jug, miniature, 2¼" to 2½"	
Granny	50.00
Toby Philpots	45.00
Character Jug, small, 3½" to 4"	
Mr Micawber	85.00
St George	65.00
Character Jug, large, 5¼" to 7"	
Drake	120.00
Pied Piper	20.00
Child's Feeding Dish, boy pushing wheelbarrow at beach, c1908	60.00
Cup and Saucer, hp, c1892	80.00
Dickens Ware	
Ashtray, Tony Weller	35.00
Demitasse cup and saucer, Mr Pickwick on cup, Sam Weller on saucer	55.00

Sauce Dish, Fat Boy, 5¼″ 45.00
Tray, 4″ × 5⅜″, Barnaby Rudge 50.00
Figurine
  Balloon Girl 115.00
  Bridesmaid 70.00
  Centurion 180.00
  Country Lass 125.00
  Fair Maiden 70.00
  Gameskeeper. 165.00
  Genie 95.00
  Grand Manner. 210.00
  Home Again. 95.00
  Little Pig. 45.00
  Lobsterman 135.00
  Mary Had A Little Lamb, #2048 ...... 75.00
  Mask Seller 145.00
  New Companions 140.00
  Queen of the Ice, #2435 .... 110.00
  Schoolmarm 155.00
  Shore Leave 165.00
  Votes for Women, #2816 .... 150.00
  Wendy 70.00
Flambe, animal mold, cat 65.00
Jug
  Rip Van Winkle 250.00
  Sairey Gamp, small A mark 65.00
Mug, Captain Ahab 55.00
Pitcher, 8″, Old Bob Ye Guard, pinch–in
  type 95.00
Plaque, 14″, Long John Silver 125.00
Plate
  6¾″, Coaching Days 60.00
  10″, Shakespeare Plays 45.00
Tankard, 6″, Queen Elizabeth at Old
  Moreton Hall, c1920 .... 20.00
Tile, Shakespeare Ware, Much Ado About
  Nothing 60.00
Toby Jug
  Beefeater, D6233. .... 45.00
  Happy John, 5½″, #6070, c1939 ...... 45.00
Tray, 5″ × 11″, Robin Hood Series. 85.00
Vase, 10″, bulbous, cream ground, young
  man, purple and rose dec. 135.00

Hooked, brown and black cat, pastel flowers, black border, yellow ground, 16 × 12½″, $165.00.

Character
  Donald Duck and Nephews, cotton,
    marked "Made in Belgium" 35.00
  Mickey Mouse, 22″ × 40″, Mickey
    launching rocket, Thumper watch-
    ing, white fringe, c1950 .... 50.00
Snow White, forest scene, 40″ × 21″. 65.00
Hooked
  Flowers, pink, green, and beige, 19″ ×
    41″ 75.00
  Pictorial, barnyard scene, red barn, pur-
    ple house, green tree, ducks, chicks,
    and birds, PA, early 20th C, 11″ ×
    39″ 275.00
  Sunburst design, yarn, 31″ × 86″ 200.00
Penny, felt, overlapping tan and brown
  petals, embroidered blue and red edges,
  center with applied oval brown panel
  embroidered with vase filled with three
  red and green floral sprigs, early 20th C,
  28″ × 34½″ 475.00
Rag, multicolored stripes, PA, 72″l 75.00

RUGS

You have to cover your floors with something. Until we have antique linoleum, the
name of the game is rugs. If you have to
own a rug, own one with some age and
character.

Do not buy any rug without unrolling it.
Hold it up in the air in such a way that there
is a strong light behind it. This will allow
you to spot any holes or areas of heavy
wear.

Braided, felt, alternating gray and blue
  squares, red and black squares border,
  52″ × 78″ 85.00

SALT AND PEPPER SHAKERS, PAIR

Hang on to your hats. Those great figural
salt and pepper shaker sets from the 1920s
through the 1960s have been discovered by
the New York art and decorator crowd.
Prices have started to jump. What does this
say about taste in America?

When buying a set, make certain it is a
set. Check motif, base, and quality of
workmanship. China shakers should have
no cracks or signs of cracking. Original
paint and decoration should be present on
china and metal figures. Make certain each
shaker has the right closure.

Salt and pepper shaker collectors must

compete with specialized collectors from other fields, e.g., advertising and black memorabilia. Dad keeps after me to find him a pair shaped like jigsaw puzzle pieces. I have not seen a pair yet nor found a dealer who has seen one. Do you think Dad will relent in his request? Forget it.

Club: Novelty Salt & Pepper Shakers Club, 581 Joy Road, Battle Creek, MI 49017.

Fish, glazed ceramic, one blue, one brown, Japan, 2⅝" h, $5.00.

Advertising, Kool, penguins, Willie and Millie, 3½" h, hard plastic, c1940s–1950s.................. **32.00**
Animal
Elephants, blue accents on gray bodies, trunks form letters "S" and "P," Ceramic Arts Studio, c1945.......... **28.00**
Frogs, ceramic, sitting on lily pad, one brown, one green, bulging eyes, Japan......................... **13.00**
Lobsters, red on green base, claws held above head, attached by springs, Japan........................ **24.00**
Penguins, 3¼" h, china, glazed, black and white, orange bill and webbed feet, marked Japan, c1930s........ **19.00**
Squirrels, brown, ceramic.......... **6.00**
Character
Aunt Jemima, Uncle Mose, 3½" h, plastic, yellow, black, and white accents on red ground, F&F Works, c1950..................... **35.00**
Captain Midnight and Joyce Ryan, plaster, painted, 1940s.............. **100.00**
Chilly Willy and Charlie Chicken, 4" h, china, 1958 Walter Lantz copyright....................... **80.00**
Donald Duck, 3" h, china, white glaze, blue, black, red, and yellow, Leeds, c1940s..................... **25.00**
Smokey the Bear, 4" h, china, yellow muzzle and hat, blue trousers, brown body, salt holding shovel, pepper holding bucket, c1960s.......... **20.00**
Toonerville Folks, 3½" h, china, two

men, smoking cigars, pepper has brown derby and coat, blue trousers, salt has white shirt and black trousers, marked Japan, c1930s........... **30.00**
Dick Tracy and Tess Trueheart, 3" h, plaster, painted, Famous Features copyright, 1942................ **65.00**
Don Winslow and Red Pennington, 3" h, plaster, painted, both have blue outfits with white hats and accents, c1940s...................... **40.00**
Household Items
Bed and Pillow, ceramic, Nester pattern, white with black trim.......... **10.00**
Candelabra, 5½" h, metal, silvered and black, clear plastic removable candle shakers, orig box, c1950s......... **18.00**
Gay 90's Hat Rack, 6½" h, plastic and metal rack, yellow straw boater hat salt, black derby pepper, hats hang on rack, base holds toothpicks, orig box, 1954....................... **15.00**
Hammer and Nail, ceramic, gray nail, brown and black hammer........ **12.00**
Telephone and Directory, ceramic, black phone, white book with black lettering.................... **8.00**
TV Set, 3" h, hard plastic, brown, gold accents and legs, black and white picture of Art Linkletter on screen, on/off switch raises and lowers shakers, orig box, c1950s................... **65.00**
Miscellaneous
Gondolas, 3 pc set, 5½" l, 2" h, china, shakers form hull and sit at front of gondola, hp, floral pattern on shakers, sgd "MK," Occupied Japan..... **23.00**
People
Black Children, 3 pc set, 3" high figures in 4" h yellow and pink nursery basket, sgd "Betson's Handpainted," Japan, c1930s................. **30.00**
Dutch Couple, ceramic, sitting on bench, kissing................. **12.50**
Hillbillies in Barrels, yellow, gray, black, and brown, male salt, female pepper..................... **14.00**
Indian and Squaw, 3" h, composition wood, yellow and green accents on natural brown ground, copyright 1947...................... **28.00**
Kitchen Witch, ceramic, blue dress, red hat, one figure has white apron and is holding broom, Taiwan, 1979..... **10.00**
Pixies, ceramic, blue outfit, yellow hair..................... **10.00**
Wrestlers, ceramic, one is held in body slam position above other wrestler's head........................ **21.00**
Souvenir
State of Maryland, Parkcraft, 48 state series, figural state and blue clam shell, manufactured by Taneycomo Ceramic Factory, c1957.......... **20.00**

World's Fair
  1933 Chicago Expo, 2¼" h, silvered white metal, tray, Hall of Science and Federal Building depicted in raised relief on each shaker, marked "1933," "1934," and "Chicago World's Fair," Japan ... **25.00**
  1939 NY World's Fair, 4" h, Perisphere and Trylon, hard plastic, one pc, orange, dark blue base **30.00**
  1964 NY World's Fair, 2" d, 3" h, Unisphere, glazed ceramic, light blue, white, and tan, dark blue base **40.00**

SCHOOL MEMORABILIA

"School Days, School Days, good old golden rule days." Dad's been singing this refrain since he moved his operation into the former elementary school at Vera Cruz, Pennsylvania. If you can't beat 'em, join 'em. Dad, this category is for you.

Magazine, **Saturday Evening Post**, *Norman Rockwell cov, 1958, $18.00.*

Alphabet Cards, a through z, circus train theme......................... **12.00**
Bell, 9" h, metal, turned wood handle.... **50.00**
Button, pinback, Village School Shoes, brown and red, c1900, 1" d **10.00**
Clock, Waterbury, calendar, needs work **200.00**
Desk
  Student's
    Formica, metal legs, rect top, c1950...................... **10.00**

Wood, cherry, top folds up, cast iron scrolled sides **125.00**
Teacher's, wood, six drawers **80.00**
Diploma, PA, 1915, framed, 19½" × 17¼"............................. **50.00**
Map, wall mount type, United States, orig wood case, varnished **45.00**
Penmanship Book, Palmer Penmanship, 1908, 135 pgs.................... **28.00**
Pin, horseshoe shape, "East Side School, Elk Rapids, Michigan" **25.00**
Pointer, wooden **18.50**
Post Card
  Lincoln Building, Quakertown Schools, PA, black and white **5.00**
  Pshawbetown School near Suttons Bay, MI, Beebe Photo, Indian children in front of one room school **30.00**
Report Card, Pupil's Report, 1900, neatly filled in......................... **3.00**
Reward of Merit
  Bookmark, Gibson, flowers **6.00**
  Card of Merit, Model Scholar, 1889, attached cut girl scrap **10.00**
  Reward of Merit, 1862, children and beehives...................... **10.00**
Sheet Music
  An Apple For The Teacher, Bing Crosby and other stars **10.00**
  Campus Rag, Richmond **7.00**

SEBASTIAN MINIATURES

Prescott Baston, the originator and first designer of Sebastian figures, began production in 1938 in a plant in Marblehead, Mas-

The Skipper, copyright 1966, P. W. Baston, 3¾" h, $30.00.

sachusetts. The hand-painted, lightly glazed figures, ranging in size from three to four inches, were usually based on characters from literature and history.

Club: Sebastian Collector's Society, 321 Central Street, Hudson, MA 01749.

Aunt Betzy Trotwood, Marblehead label **50.00**
Colonial Carriage **75.00**
Family Sing **200.00**
Gibson Girl **85.00**
House of Seven Gables **100.00**
Jefferson, Thomas.................. **95.00**
Lincoln, Abraham, seated **125.00**
Mary Had A Little Lamb **100.00**
Ross, Betsy........................ **85.00**
Santa Claus **100.00**
Twain, Mark **100.00**
Victorian Couple................... **85.00**

SEWING ITEMS

This is a wide open area. While many favor sterling silver items, only fools overlook objects made of celluloid, ivory, other metals, plastic, and wood. An ideal special collection would be sewing items that contain advertising.

Collecting sewing items has received a big boost as a result of the Victorian craze. During the Victorian era a vast assortment of practical and whimsical sewing devices were marketed. Look for items such as tape measures, pincushions, stilettos for punchwork, crochet hooks, and sewing birds (beware of reproductions).

Modern sewing collectors are focusing on needle threaders, needle holders, and sewing kits from hotels and motels. The general term for this material is "Twenty Pocket" because pieces fit neatly into twenty pocket plastic notebook sleeves.

Book, *Victorian Designs of Needlepoint,* Klinger, 1st ed, 88 pgs **14.00**
Bookmark, Merrick Spool Cotton....... **10.00**
Buttonhole Scissors, Germany **12.00**
Darner
  Egg, black **4.00**
  Slipper shape, maple wood base, 5½" **8.00**
Mending Kit, Bakelite, red and ivory **20.00**
Needle Book, A Century of Progress, complete......................... **6.00**
Needle Case
  Bestmaid **8.00**
  Boye Sewing Machines, 1929........ **15.00**
  Sewing Circle.................... **8.00**

Needle Case, Linco, Medium Motor Oil, white ground, blue and red, Lincoln Oil Refining Co, Robinson, IL, $4.75.

Pin cushion
  Doll, arms at head **10.00**
  Traveler's Insurance adv **8.00**
Tape Measure
  Advertising, Portland Cement....... **25.00**
  Figural, Indian, marked "Japan" **20.00**
Thimble, child's, pewter, "For A Good Girl".......................... **11.00**

SHAWNEE POTTERY

Between 1937, when it was founded, and 1961, when it closed, Shawnee Pottery produced approximately 100,000 pieces of pottery per working day at its plant, formerly home to the American Encaustic Tiling Company, in Zanesville, Ohio. Its chief products were kitchen-ware, dinnerware, and decorative art pottery.

Bookends, pr, Flying Geese........... **25.00**
Butter, cov, corn **30.00**
Casserole, cov
  Corn King **30.00**
  Fruits **22.00**
Cookie Jar
  Cookie House **65.00**
  Fruit.......................... **35.00**
  Mugsey, gold trim **150.00**
  Sailor Boy **50.00**
Cornucopia, gold trim, #835 .... **12.00**
Creamer
  Corn King **15.00**
  Daisy **15.00**
  Puss N Boots, gold trim **40.00**

Cookie Jar, Puss N Boots, ivory, red bow, yellow bird, $35.00.

Figural, elephant	10.00
Pitcher	
Chanticleer	45.00
Bo Peep, white	70.00
Smiley	50.00
Planter, cherub	10.00
Relish, Corn King, #79	22.00
Salt and Pepper Shakers, pr	
Corn King, large	20.00
Mugsey, small	15.00
Owls	10.00
Smiley, large	55.00
Shadow Box, yellow doe, green box, #850	14.00
Sugar, Corn King	18.50
Vase, Bow Knot, green	12.00

SHEET MUSIC

Just like postcards, this a category whose ten cent and quarter days are a thing of the past. Decorators and dealers have discovered the cover value of sheet music. The high ticket sheets are sold to specialized collectors, not sheet music collectors.

You can put a sheet music collection together covering almost any topic imaginable. Be careful about stacking your sheets on top of one another. The ink on the covers tends to bleed. If you can afford the expense, put a sheet of acid free paper between each sheet. Do not, repeat *do not*, repair any tears with Scotch and similar brand tape. It discolors over time. When removed, it often leaves a gum residue behind.

Clubs: National Sheet Music Society, 1597 Fair Park, Los Angeles, CA 90041; New York Sheet Music Society, P. O. Box 1126, East Orange, NJ 07019; Remember That Song, 5821 North 67th Avenue, Suite 103–306, Glendale, AZ 85301; The Sheet Music Exchange, P. O. Box 69, Quicksburg, VA 22847.

Jazzin' The Cotton Town Blues, *1917*, $7.50.

As Long As I Have You, 9″ × 12″, 1957 Gladys Music Inc copyright	15.00
By The Old Mill Where Waterlilies Grow, Morgan, 1912	2.00
Cryin' For The Moon, Conley, 1926	1.00
Good Bye Broadway Hello France, 1917	8.00
Heartbreak Hotel, 9″ × 12″, bluetone photo, 1956 Tree Publishing Co copyright	25.00
Hinky Dinky Parlay Voo, 1921 copyright, Ruth Wales and Doris Relyea photos	8.00
I'll Meet You In Chicago, 9″ × 12″ folder, 1933 copyright	15.00
Love Ain't Nothin' But The Blues, Alter, 1929	1.00
Military Waltz, 1917 copyright	8.00
Over There, George M Cohan, 1917 copyright	15.00
Peg O' My Heart, Bryan/Fisher, 1913	4.00
Sunbonnet Sue, Cobb, 1908	7.00
Teenage Crush, Tommy Sands, 1956 Central Songs Inc copyright	10.00
The Stars And Stripes Forever, John Philip Sousa, 1897 copyright	25.00

Who Will Care For Micky Now?, Eugene T Johnston **20.00**
Why Should I Fall For One Little Girl?, 9 × 12", 1936 copyright, music published by Fred Fisher Music Co **25.00**
Woofie Song, shows cat **1.50**

SHOE-RELATED COLLECTIBLES

This is a category with sole. Nothing more needs to be said.

Shoe Horn, Shinola Shoe Polish, Chas. W. Shonk Co., Litho, Chicago, $45.00.

Advertising Trade Card
  A. S. T. Co. Shoe Tips, Father Time, Donaldson Bros **9.00**
  Herrods $5.00 Shoes, drum shape, Bufford Litho **7.50**
  Johnson Shoes, santa, mechanical **35.00**
Alarm Clock, Star Brand Shoes, Gilbert **50.00**
Ball, Poll Parrot Shoes, rubber, 1930s **20.00**
Button, pinback
  Battle Axe Shoes, full color Confederacy flag, black, white, and red logo, white ground, black inscriptions, 1907, 1¼" **45.00**
  Buster Brown Shoes, multicolored, portrait of Buster and Tige, white ground, black letters, early 1900s, ⅞" **90.00**
  Griffiths Queen City Shoe, black and white, red logo, 1901–1912, ⅞" d. . . . **20.00**
  Omaha Made Shoes, black and white high button shoe, blue and white rim, early 1900s, 1½" d **40.00**
  Top Round Shoe, multicolored, winged cherubs scaling ladder to place high top shoe on top of world, ⅞" **22.50**

Clicker
  Peters Weatherbird Shoes, litho tin, multicolored, c1930 . . . . **25.00**
  Poll Parrot Shoes **13.00**
Counter Display, Cavalier Shoe Polish, revolving can display holder, orange, Cavalier man on top, tin **90.00**
Mirror, pocket
  Buster Brown Shoes, multicolored portrait of Buster and Tige holding wooden shoe last above inscription, 1¼" h, early 1900s **150.00**
  Shoe Worker's Union, c1910 . . . . **38.00**
Post Card, adv, Sterling Quality Shoes, Smith Wallace Shoe Co, c1907 . . . . **9.50**
Premium, Poll Parrot Shoes, Howdy Doody Detective Disguises, unused. . . . **70.00**
Puzzle, Red Goose Shoes **20.00**
Repair Box, wood, dovetailed, tools, soles, heels, and nails **85.00**
Repair Stand, iron **32.00**
Shoe Horn, Queen Quality, celluloid, curled handle, color portrait of lady, c1900, 2" × 6", pr **35.00**
Shoe Polish, American Shoe Polish Co, suede treatment, tin box, paper label. . . **20.00**
Shoe Shine Kit, child's, Shinola, 1953, MIB **20.00**
Stickpin, Red Fox Shoes, multicolored, hunting dogs chasing fox, brass back with inscription, early 1900s, 1" oval **40.00**
Store Display, US Royal Footwear, artist sgd, 38" × 23" **85.00**
String Holder, cast iron, Red Goose Shoes **1,200.00**
Whistle, Weatherbird Shoes, rooster weather vane **20.00**

SILVER FLATWARE

Popularity of pattern, not necessarily age, is the key to pricing. Since most individuals buy by pattern, buy only from dealers who have done the research and properly identified each piece that they are selling. Deduct 50 percent from the value if a piece has a monogram.

If you are planning to buy a set, expect to pay considerably less than if you were buying the pieces individually. Set prices should be bargain prices.

Alaska Silver, German Silver, Lashar Silver, and Nickel Silver are alloys designed to imitate silver plate. Do not be fooled.

Magazine: *The Magazine Silver*, P. O. Box 22217, Milwaukie, OR 97222.

Bacon Server, Old Maryland, Kirk–Steiff, engraved **87.00**

Cold meat fork, Astoria, 1835 R Wallace, patent 1868, $25.00.

Teaspoon
  Chapel Bells, Alvin **12.00**
  Formality, State House **13.00**
  Moselle **18.00**
Tomato Server, Edgewood, International **185.00**
Tongs, Fairfax, Durgin. **20.00**
Vegetable Fork, large, Queen, Howard . . . **195.00**

Berry Spoon, Chatham, Durgin **55.00**
Bonbon, Lady Sterling, Weidlich **11.00**
Butter Knife
  Damask Rose, Oneida **13.00**
  Dawn Mist, Wallace **14.00**
  Virginian, Oneida **13.00**
Carving Set, Cactus, Jensen. **300.00**
Cheese Knife, Allure, Rogers, 1939. . . . . .   **4.50**
Cheese Scoop, Gloria **60.00**
Cheese Spreader, Canterbury, Towle,
  monogrammed **15.00**
Citrus, Queen, Howard **25.00**
Claret Ladle, Mazerine, Dominick &
  Haff **150.00**
Cocktail Fork, Lady Sterling, Weidlich . . . **10.00**
Cocktail Stirrer, Royal Danish, International **75.00**
Cold Meat Fork
  Charter Oak **45.00**
  Moselle, monogrammed **55.00**
  Oxford **18.50**
Cream Ladle, Rococo, Dominick &
  Haff **40.00**
Cream Soup, Castle Rose, Royal Crest . . . **15.00**
Fish Knife, Acorn, Jensen **35.00**
Fork, dinner
  Gosvenor. **1.25**
  La Concorde Grape **10.00**
Fork, luncheon
  Romantique, Alvin **26.00**
  Spanish Lace, Wallace **14.00**
Fork, salad, Star, Reed & Barton **20.00**
Gravy Ladle
  Blossom, Jensen **125.00**
  Moselle **75.00**
  Oxford **20.00**
Gumbo, Bridal Rose, Alvin, monogrammed **38.00**
Knife, place
  Silver Spray, Towle **20.00**
  Star, Reed & Barton **18.00**
Lemon Fork, Normandie, Wallace **16.00**
Olive Fork, Chippendale, Alvin **25.00**
Oyster Ladle, Old Medici, Gorham **200.00**
Pie Server, Acorn, Jensen **125.00**
Preserve Spoon, Madame Morris,
  Durgin **16.00**
Sauce Ladle, Oxford **22.00**
Serving Spoon, Moselle **95.00**
Set
  24 pcs, Old Colony. **72.00**
  52 pcs, Meadowbrook **125.00**
Soup Ladle, Saratoga. **45.00**
Tablespoon, Medallion, Duhme **115.00**

SILVER PLATED

G. R. and H. Ekington of England are credited with inventing the electrolytic method of plating silver in 1838. In late–nineteenth century pieces, the base metal was often Britannia, an alloy of tin, copper, and antimony. Copper and brass also were used as bases. Today the base is usually nickel silver.

Rogers Bros., Hartford, Connecticut, introduced the silver–plating process to the United States in 1847. By 1855 a large number of silver plating firms were established.

Extensive polishing will eventually remove silver plating. However, today's replating process is so well developed that you can have a piece replated in such a manner that the full detail of the original is preserved.

Identifying companies and company marks is difficult. Fortunately there is Dorothy Rainwater's *Encyclopedia of American Silver Manufacturers, 3rd Edition* (Schiffer Publishing, 1989).

Syrup, floral relief and incising, monogram, made by Samson, Hall, Miller & Co, 7½" h, $85.00.

Ashtray, floral dec rim **10.00**
Baby's Cup, two handles, mono-
grammed **20.00**
Bread Basket, marked "US NAVY," offi-
cer's minor dents **12.50**
Butter Dish, three pcs, base, lid, insert,
delicate double rows of tiny beading,
cut glass drip trap, Meriden Silver Plate
Co **50.00**
Cheese Ball Frame, 5" d, mechanical, elab-
orate border, E G Webster & Sons **75.00**
Cigar Holder, 10½" h, champagne bottle,
beaded trim, engraved "CIGARS,"
Graham Silver marks **75.00**
Ice Bucket, Baroque pattern, thermos
lined, Wallace **225.00**
Sugar Shell, monogrammed **20.00**
Syrup, geometric and floral strap work
body, figural finial, Meriden, 1865, re-
plated **85.00**
Umbrella Stand, 20½", elongated trumpet
shape, interlaced flowering branches, H
Wilkinson & Co, copper showing **225.00**
Vase, bud, Three Pigs, Walt Disney **55.00**

SOAP COLLECTIBLES

At first you would not think that a lot of soap
collectibles would survive. However, once
you start to look around, there is no end to
the survivors. Many Americans are not as
clean as we think.

There is no hotel soap listed. Most survivors sell for 50¢ to $2.00 per bar. Think of
all the hotels and motels that you have
stayed at that have gone out of business.
Don't you wished you would have saved
one of the soap packets. You don't? What
are you—normal or something?

*Advertising trade card, B. T. Babbits, adv on
back, 4 15/16" × 3¼", $5.00.*

Advertising Trade Card
Bells Buffalo Soap, vegetable people,
1887 . . . . **12.00**
Lainds Bloom of Youth & White Lilac
Soap **5.00**

Lautz Bros Master Soap, baby on
pillow **7.50**
Bookmark, Dingman's Soap, illus of
baby **8.75**
Box
Capitol Scouring Soap, wooden **15.00**
Daylight Soap, wooden **20.00**
Brochure
Bon Ami, The Chick That Never Grew
Up **10.00**
Larkin Soap, 1885 . . . . **15.00**
Mirror, pocket, Dingman Soap, red
ground, white letters, 1⅞" d **30.00**
Poster, Packer's Tar Soap, barber shaving,
9" × 12", c1900 . . . . **30.00**
Ruler, Glory Soap Chips, folding celluloid,
5½" l, blue and orange Swift & Co trade-
mark, 1919 calendars **20.00**

SODA FOUNTAIN AND ICE CREAM COLLECTIBLES

The local soda fountain and/or ice cream
parlor was the social center of small town
America between the late 1880s and the
1960s. Ice cream items appeared as early as
the 1870s.

This is a category filled with nostalgia—
banana splits and dates with friends. Some
concentrate on the advertising, some on
the implements. It is all terrific.

Club: The Ice Screamers, 1042 Olde Hickory Road, Lancaster, PA 17601.

*Tray, Imperial Ice Cream, black and yellow,
17¼" × 12¼", $35.00.*

ICE CREAM

Advertising Trade Card, Reid's Ice Cream,
"She had but one tooth! And that was
for Reid's Ice Cream," old lady with one
tooth **14.00**
Carton, Hershey's Ice Cream, one pint, or-
ange and blue **15.00**
Condiment Set, 7½" **25.00**
Cone Dispenser, glass, copper insert **345.00**

Milk Shaker, Hamilton Beach, green **35.00**
Mold, pewter, star in circle **35.00**
Pinback Button, 7/8" d, Arctic Rainbow Ice
Cream Cones, celluloid, multicolored,
c1912......................... **20.00**
Sign, Rich Valley Ice Cream, yellow and
red, 9" d, 1940s **40.00**
Thermometer, Abbottmaid Ice Cream, 2"
× 6¼", 1920–1930, orig label........ **35.00**
Tray, Herron's Ice Cream, rect, mono-
gram **55.00**

SODA FOUNTAIN

Candy Scale, Exact Weight, orig
weights **75.00**
Dispenser
Dad's Root Beer, barrel shape, bronze
claw feet......................**250.00**
Hunter's Root Beer, milk glass........ **45.00**
Door Push, Whistle Cola, picture of bottle,
adjustable, 1940s.................. **55.00**
Funnel, Lash's Bitters, copper.......... **75.00**
Malt Jar, Borden's, aluminum **30.00**
Sign
Mt Kineo Ginger Ale, 12" × 24", tin,
emb, 1940s **30.00**
Whistle Soda, stand–up, cardboard,
diecut, elf and bottle, 1940s........ **20.00**
Straw Holder, jar, clear, Heisey **135.00**
Syrup Bottle, grapefruit, glass, red script
lettering on white enamel label, gold
border, plated metal measure cap, FM
Williams, 1913 copyright **70.00**
Syrup Dispenser, cherry, 10½" h **25.00**
Thermometer, Dr Pepper, tin, 20" h, 1960s
logo **50.00**

SOFT DRINK COLLECTIBLES

National brands such as Coca–Cola, Canada Dry, Dr. Pepper, and Pepsi–Cola dominate the field. However, there were thousands of regional and local soda bottling
plants. Their advertising, bottles, and
giveaways are every bit as exciting as those
of the national companies. Do not ignore
them.

Clubs: The Coca–Cola Collectors Club International, P. O. Box 546, Holmdel, NJ
07733; Pepsi–Cola Collectors Club, P. O.
Box 1275, Covina, CA 91722.

Banner, Lime Cola, canvas **40.00**
Bottle, Moxie, porcelain top **18.00**
Calendar
Pepsi, 1941, complete **200.00**
Sun Crest cola, 1957 .... **28.00**
Fan, Dr Pepper, green and red, six pack on
reverse......................... **50.00**
Match Dispenser, Dr Pepper, 1930s **65.00**

*Tray, Cherry Sparkle, Graf's, Northwestern Ex-
tract Co, Milwaukee, WI, yellow letters, red soda
bottle, green ground, 10½" × 13 ¼", $115.00.*

Mug
Dad's Root Beer, glass, barrel shape ... **30.00**
Graf's Root Beer, ceramic **55.00**
Pencil, Orange Crush, mechanical **20.00**
Sign
Canada Dry Hi–Spot, tin, 1940s **45.00**
Drink R–Pep 5¢ Bottle, tin, 1930s..... **88.00**
Nu Icy Soda, 17" × 35" **95.00**
Royal Crown, tin, 1930s **65.00**
7–Up, cardboard, girl on bike, 33½" ×
21", 1953 .... **55.00**
Tap, Pepsi, musical, 1940 ....**125.00**
Thermometer
Dr Pepper Hot & Cold.............. **75.00**
Orange Crush, Crushie, tin **95.00**
Pepsi, bottle cap shape.............. **65.00**
Vending Machine, Royal Crown, 27" ×
49".............................**260.00**

SOUTH OF THE BORDER
COLLECTIBLES

When you live on the East Coast and do
not roam west of Chicago, you are not
going to see South of the Border collectibles
except for the tourist souvenirs brought
home by visitors to Central and South
America. However, the growing Hispanic
population is beginning to look back to its
roots and starting to proudly display family
and other items acquired south of the border.

Within the past year there has been a
growing interest in Mexican jewelry. In
fact, several new books have been pub-

lished about the subject. Mexican pottery and textiles are also attracting collector attention.

At the moment, buy only high–quality, handmade products. Because of their brilliant colors, South of the Border collectibles accent almost any room setting. This is an area to watch.

SPACE COLLECTIBLES

This category deals only with fictional space heroes. My grandfather followed Buck Rogers in the Sunday funnies. Dad saw Buster Crabbe as Flash Gordon in the movies and cut his teeth on early television with Captain Video. I am from the Star Trek generation.

Do not overlook the real live space heroes, like the astronauts and cosmonauts who have and are yet to venture out into space. Material relating to these pioneers is going to be very collectible in the year 2091.

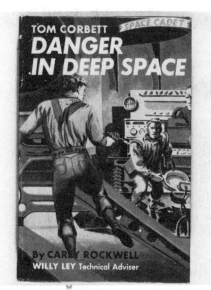

Book, **Tom Corbett Danger In Deep Space,** *Cary Rockwell, illus by Louis Glanzman, Grosset & Dunlap, 1953, 5″ × 7½″, $15.00.*

Buck Rogers
  Colorform Set, diecut vinyl figures, boxed, 1979 copyright. **15.00**
  Mask, 8″ × 11″, Wilma, face, paper, color. **65.00**
  Rubber Stamp, set of 11, yellow, wood back, Wilma, Buddy, Alura, and two different Buck Rogers, c1930. . . . . . . **90.00**

Captain Video
  Ring, Secret Seal **40.00**
  Watch, orig card **40.00**
Tom Corbett
  Flashlight, 7″, "Space Cadet Signal Siren Flashlight," full color illus, orig box, c1952. . . . . **50.00**
  Patch, 2″ × 4″, "Space Cadet," cloth, red, yellow, and blue, Kellogg's premium. **25.00**
Flash Gordon
  Costume, space outfit, c1950 . . . .**135.00**
  Game, orig box **25.00**
  Space Cadet, thermos, 1952 . . . . **25.00**
Space Patrol
  Drink Mixer, 8″, plastic, pink rocket ship, marked on side "XY7 Rocket," orig colored carton. **35.00**
  Handbook **150.00**
Star Trek
  Paint Set, 12″ × 16″ canvas portrait, boxed, slightly used, Hasbro, 1974 copyright **50.00**
  Utility Belt, phaser, tricorder, and communicator, Remco, 1975 . . . . **30.00**
Star Wars
  Children's Book, pop–up **15.00**
  Clock, alarm, talking **25.00**

SPORTS COLLECTIBLES

There has been so much written about sport cards that equipment and other sport-related material has become lost in the shuffle. A number of recent crazes, such as passion for old baseball gloves, indicates that this is about to change.

Decorators have discovered that old sporting equipment hung on walls makes a great decorative motif. This certainly helps call attention to the collectibility of the material.

Since little has been written outside of baseball and golf collectibles, it is hard to determine what exactly are the best pieces. A good philosophy is to keep expenditures minimal until this and other questions are sorted out by collectors and dealers.

Newspaper: *Sports Collectors Digest,* 700 East State Street, Iola, WI 54990.

Club: Golf Collectors' Society, P. O. Box 491, Shawnee Mission, KS 66202.

Book
  Guide to Good Golf, James Barnes **25.00**
  The Spectacle of Sports from Sports Illustrated, 1957, 320 pgs, dj **25.00**
Boxing Gloves, Jack Dempsey, brown, white vinyl trim, orig box, Everlast, c1950. . . . . **35.00**

227

Game, Bowling, A Board Game, Parker Bros, boxed board game, 1896, 15½" × 11½", $50.00.

Cigarette Lighter, figural, golf bag **45.00**
Dispenser, marbleized plastic bowling ball, chrome push top, six glasses, figural bowler handle **60.00**
Glass
   1932 Olympics, 5½", clear, frosted white picture **50.00**
   1986 Kentucky Derby, 5¼", clear, frosted white panel, red roses and green leaf accents, red and green inscriptions **10.00**
Handbook, women's, *Handbook of Light Gymnastics*, Lucy B Hunt, 1887, 92 pgs, hard cover **50.00**
Pennant, Derby Day, 18", felt, red, white lettering, red and white design with pink accents, 1939 . . . . **15.00**
Press Badge, Chicago Area Golf Tournament, 1950–1960 . . . . **12.00**
Program
   1948 Summer Olympic Trials, 8" × 10½", weight lifting trials, 20 pgs **15.00**
   1952 Olympic Tryouts, July 3–5, 1952, rowing tryouts, 72 pgs **20.00**
   1965 Harlem Globetrotters, 8" × 10½", 30 pgs, Magicians of Basketball Tour **15.00**
Puppet, Joe Louis, 8", fabric body, soft rubber boxing gloves and molded head, JV Co **55.00**
Puzzle, 1932 Olympic Games, 10 × 13¼", Toddy Inc, 1932 copyright. **30.00**
Score Pad, golf, 2½" × 4", cello cov, unused, 1900s **15.00**
Wristwatch, Muhammad Ali, gold colored metal, color photo on dial, black numerals, black inscriptions, Depraz–Faure America Corp, c1980 . . . . . **75.00**
Yearbook, Giant's, 1970 . . . . **10.00**

STANGL POTTERY

Stangl manufactured dinnerware between 1930 and 1978 in Trenton, New Jersey. The dinnerware featured bold floral and fruit designs on a brilliant ground of white or off–white shade.

The company also produced a series of three dimensional bird figurines that are eagerly sought by collectors. The bird figurines were cast in Trenton and finished at second company plant in Flemington. During World War II the demand for the birds was so great that over 60 decorators were employed to paint them. Some of the birds were reissued between 1972 and 1977. They are dated on the bottom.

Pitcher, Christmas Tree, light green ground, dark green tree, gold and silver decorations, 4½" h, $12.50.

BIRDS

3276 Double Bluebirds, 8½" h **70.00**
3404 Lovebirds, pr. **95.00**
3445 Rooster, gray, 9" **135.00**
3448 Blue Headed Vireo **40.00**
3584 Cockatoo, 8⅞" h **185.00**
3589 Indigo Bunting **36.00**
3595 Bobolink. **125.00**
3629 Broadbill Hummingbird, 6" **85.00**
3634 Allen Hummingbird. **48.00**
3810 Blackpoll Warbler **100.00**
3813 Evening Grosbeak **120.00**
3848 Golden Crowned Kinglet, 4" h **50.00**
3852 Cliff Swallow **60.00**

DINNERWARE

Colonial Green
  Bowl
    5½", fruit. **4.50**
    6", dessert. **1.75**
  Candlesticks, 3" **20.00**
  Creamer. **6.00**
  Cup and Saucer **6.75**
  Plate
    9", luncheon. **4.00**
    10", dinner. **5.00**
  Platter, 12" **10.00**
  Sugar, cov **10.00**

Jonquil
Bowl

8″	10.00
12″	17.50
Bread Tray	10.00
Casserole, cov	15.00
Chop Plate, 14½″	15.00
Coffeepot, 8 cup	12.50
Creamer	3.50
Gravy Boat	5.00
Pickle Dish, 10⅜″	7.50
Pitcher, 1 qt	10.00

Plate

6″	2.00
8″	5.00
10″	6.00
Platter, 15″, oval	15.00
Relish, 11⅜″	9.00
Soup, lug, 5¼″	5.00
Vegetable, divided	14.00

Terra Rose Fruit

Bowl, 10″	15.00
Bowl, divided	22.50
Butter, cov	20.00
Cereal Bowl	4.50
Chop Plate, 14¼″	27.00
Creamer and Sugar, cov	25.00
Cup and Saucer	4.00
Dessert	7.00
Gravy Boat	22.50
Pitcher	19.00

Plate

6″, bread and butter	3.50
8″, luncheon	4.50
10″, dinner	6.00

Platter

Large	25.00
Small	27.50
Relish, 3 tier	12.50
Salt and Pepper Shakers, pr	12.50
Vegetable Dish, divided	22.50

Thistle

Cereal Bowl	4.00
Chop Plate, 14″	10.00
Coaster	5.00
Coffeepot, cov	25.00
Creamer	6.00
Cup and Saucer	8.00
Fruit Bowl	5.00

Plate

6″, bread and butter	6.00
9″, dinner	8.00
Sherbet	12.00
Soup, flat	6.50
Sugar, cov	10.00
Teapot	25.00

"STRADIVARIUS" VIOLINS

In the late nineteenth century inexpensive violins were made for sale to students, amateur musicians, and others who could not afford an older, quality instrument. Numerous models, many named after famous makers, were sold by department stores, music shops, and by mail. Sears, Roebuck sold "Stradivarius" models. Other famous violin makers whose names appear on paper labels inside these instruments include Amati, Caspar DaSolo, Guarnerius, Maggini, and Stainer. Lowendall of Germany made a Paganini model.

All these violins were sold through advertisements that claimed that the owner could have a violin nearly equal to that of an antique instrument for a modest cost; one "Stradivarius" sold for $2.45. The most expensive model cost less than $15.00. The violins were handmade, but by a factory assembly line process.

If well cared for, these pseudo antique violins often develop a nice tone. The average price for an instrument in playable condition is between $100.00 and $200.00.

SUGAR PACKETS

Do not judge sugar packets of the 1940s and 1950s by those you encounter today. There is no comparison. 1940s and 1950s sugar packets were colorful, often containing full color scenic views.

Many of the packets were issued as sets, containing a dozen views or more. They often were gathered as souvenirs during a vacation trip.

There is a large number of closet sugar packet collectors. They do not write much about their hobby because they are afraid that the minute they draw attention to it, prices will rise. Most sugar packets sell for less than $1.00.

Its time to let the sugar out of the bag. No prices in this edition, but there will be next time. Get them cheap while you can.

Club: Sugar Packet Collectors Society, 105 Ridge Road, Perkasie, PA 18944.

SUPER HEROES

Super heroes and comic books go hand in hand. Superman first appeared in *Action Comics* in 1939. He was followed by Batman, Captain Marvel, Captain Midnight, The Green Hornet, The Green Lantern, The Shadow, Wonder Woman, and a host of others.

The traditional Super Hero was transformed with the appearance of The Fantastic Four—Mr. Fantastic, The Human Torch, The Invisible Girl, and The Thing. The mutant hero lives today with Teenage Mutant Ninja Turtles.

It pays to focus on one hero or related family of heroes. Go after the three-dimensional material. This is the hardest to find.

Toy, Spiderman, litho tin and plastic, Marx, orig box, $35.00.

Batman and Robin
Batmobile, 8″ × 19 × 6½″, molded plastic, 3–D figures, red striping, gold and black bat decals, c1966 .... **125.00**
Bat–Ray Gun, 8″ l, flashlight, four plastic disks project image, copyright DC Comics, 1978, orig box **35.00**
Helmet, 12″ h, molded plastic, diecut mouth and eye openings, black accents on blue ground, gold and black bat symbol, Ideal, copyright National Periodical Publications, 1966 ...... **100.00**
Mug, 3½″ h, plastic, clear, white insert, multicolored paper illus, copyright National Periodical Publications, 1966. .... **30.00**
Place Mats, 13″ × 18″, vinyl, foam backing, multicolored, copyright National Periodical Publications, 1966, set of two........................... **75.00**
Soaky, 10″ h, soft plastic body, hard plastic head, purple, blue, and yellow, copyright National Periodical Publications, 1966............... **75.00**
Captain America, badge, Sentinels of Liberty, brass, red and blue accents, 1941–1943 .... **225.00**
Captain Marvel
EZ Code Finder, 4″ d disk wheel, cardboard, Fawcett Comics premium, c mid–1940s **125.00**
Postcard, Captain Marvel's Secret Message, 3 × 5½″, blue, dip in water to reveal message, c1940s **75.00**

Flash Gordon
Lobby Card, 11″ × 14″, "Flash Gordon Conquers the Universe,' Universal Pictures **50.00**
Lunch Box, 7″ × 10″ × 5″ deep, plastic, color decals, Aladdin, copyright 1979 King Features Syndicate **65.00**
Spaceship, 3″ l, metal, diecast, blue, white accents, orig display card, LJN Toys, copyright 1975 .... **20.00**
Green Hornet
Coloring Book, 8″ × 11″, Watkins–Strathmore, copyright 1966, unused.................... **30.00**
Secret Print Putty, secret print book, magic print paper, Colorforms Toy, copyright 1966, unopened blister pack........................ **65.00**
Wallet, 3½ × 4½″, vinyl, green, Green Hornet on front, Kato on back, Green Hornet insect and logo on both sides, magic slate, pencil, and black and white photo of Kato inside, Mattel, copyright Greenway Productions, 1966........................ **60.00**
Spiderman
Bicycle Siren, 4″ h, plastic, red and yellow, decals, Empire Toys, copyright Marvel Comics Group, 1978 orig box and attachments, unused **40.00**
Doll, 20″ h, plush, red, white, and black outfit, orig Knickerbocker tag, copyright Marvel Comics Group, 1978 ... **20.00**
Spiderwoman, jewelry set, glasses, silver clip–on spider earrings, blue plastic butterfly barrettes, silver necklace with Spiderwoman in web medallion, Imperial Toy Corp, copyright Marvel Comics Group, 1979, orig blister pack **18.00**
Superman
Game, Sliding Square Puzzle, 5″ × 6″, black and white, Superman flying over buildings, orig display card **70.00**
Glass, Superman in Action, 4¼″ h, clear, blue illus, peach color inscriptions, copyright National Periodical Publications Inc, 1964 .... **50.00**
Hairbrush, 2½″ × 4½″, wood, red, white, and blue decal, c1940s **75.00**
Pencil Case, 3½″ × 8″, vinyl, zippered, red and blue illus and logo on yellow ground, Standard Plastic Products, copyright National Periodical Publications Inc, 1966 .... **58.00**
Pennant, 11 × 29″, felt, red, white logo, white, pink, and yellow illus of Superman, copyright National Periodical Publications Inc, 1966 .... **60.00**
Valentine, 4½″ × 4½″, diecut, multicolored, opens to 6″ w, 1940 Superman copyright **30.00**
Wonder Woman
Glass, 6¼″ h, clear, illus on front, logo

and name on back, issued by Pepsi, copyright DC Comics, 1978 . . . . **18.00**
Watch, 1¼" dial, color illus of Wonder Woman, gold case, Dabs, copyright DC Comics, 1977 . . . . **30.00**

SWANKYSWIGS

Swankyswigs are decorated glass containers that were filled with Kraft Cheese Spreads. They date from the early 1930s. See D. M. Fountain's *Swankyswig Price Guide* (published by author in 1979) to identify pieces by pattern.

Most Swankyswigs still sell for under $5.00. If a glass still has its original label, add $5.00 to the price.

Kiddie Cup, duck and pony, black, $2.50.

Antique, coffeepot and trivets, black	**4.50**
Bands, black and red	**3.00**
Bicentennial, green, Coin Dot design, 1975.	**10.00**
Bustlin' Betsy	**2.25**
Checkerboard, green, red, and dark blue	**25.00**
Cornflower	**3.00**
Dots & Circles	**4.50**
Forget–Me–Not	**3.00**
Jonquil, yellow flower, green leaves	**3.50**
Kiddie Cup	
Deer and squirrel, brown.	**2.00**
Kitten and bunny, green	**2.00**
Pony and duck, black.	**2.25**
Puppy and rooster, orange.	**2.00**
Tulip No 1, white leaves, 1937	**7.50**
Sailboat, blue.	**20.00**
Star, red	**6.00**
Texas Centennial, green	**10.00**

SWIZZLE STICKS

They just do not make swizzle sticks like they used to. There is no end to the ways to collect them—color, motif, region, time period, and so on.

You can usually find them for less than $1.00. In fact, you can often buy a box or glass full of them for just a few dollars. Sets bring more, but they have to be unusual.

Club: International Swizzlestick Collectors Association, Greenwood Village, 2150 Avenue A, No. 10, Yuma, AZ 85364.

Bird, Chez	**10.00**
Fruit, glass, set of 12, includes stand	**55.00**
Penthouse, set of 8	**20.00**

TEDDY BEARS

Teddy bear collectors are fanatics. Never tell them their market is going soft. They will club you to death with their bears. Do not tell anyone that you heard it here, but the Teddy Bear craze of the 1980s has ended. The market is flooded with old and contemporary bears.

The name "Teddy" Bear originated with Theodore Roosevelt. The accepted date for their birth is 1902–1903. Early bears had humps on their backs, elongated muzzles, and jointed limbs. The fabric was usually mohair; the eyes were either glass with pin backs or black shoe buttons.

The contemporary Teddy Bear market is as big or bigger than the market for antique and collectible bears. Many of these bears are quite expensive. Collectors who are speculating in them will find that getting their money out of them in ten to fifteen years is going to be a bearish proposition.

Game, Winnie–The–Pooh, Parker Bros, boxed board game, 1933, 17 × 9", $100.00.

Magazine: *The Teddy Bear And Friends,* Hobby House Press, Inc., 900 Frederick Street, Cumberland, MD 21502.

Club: Good Bears of the World, P. O. Box 8236, Honolulu, HI 96815.

4", plush, dark brown, jointed **40.00**

5", plush, standing, swivel head, "Character" label **40.00**

5½", Panda, mohair, black and white, googly glass eyes, yarn nose and mouth, felt pads, c1950s **95.00**

6", plush, jointed, fully dressed, orig clothes, "Berg" label **65.00**

8", mohair, dark brown, excelsior stuffed, fully jointed, black and white googly eyes, beige mohair snout and inner ears, open felt mouth, red felt tongue, beige felt foot pads, tagged "Fechter Spielwaren" on right ear **75.00**

9"

Mohair, Steiff Zotty, frosted curly light tan, pale yellow short mohair chest, glass eyes, open mouth, light yellow foot pads, c1950s **175.00**

Plush, blonde, black shoe button eyes, shoulder hump, small tail, straw filled, c1905 . . . . **165.00**

9½", Honey Bear, woolly mohair, chocolate brown and beige, kapok stuffed, fully jointed, glass eyes, horizontal stitched wool floss nose and mouth, embroidered tongue, beige velveteen pads, 1940 . . . . **80.00**

10", mohair, light gold, rigid neck, arms and legs wire-jointed in unison, tiny stalk eyes, yarn nose and mouth, sliced in velvet lined ears, squeaker in back, late 1920s. **85.00**

10½"

Chubby Shape, mohair, yellow, soft stuffed, fully jointed, short legs, clear glass eyes, vertical stitched square floss nose, red velveteen inner ears and pads, c1950–1960 . . . . **80.00**

Hermann Zotty, mohair, sand frosted, amber glass eyes, floss outlined upper lip, square floss nose, teardrop shape paw pads, c1960s **85.00**

11"

Cheeky Bear, honeysuckle nylon plush, fully jointed, glass eyes, white velvet snout, red velvet open mouth, overstitched brown felt pads, tagged "Merrythought Ironbridge Shop, Made in England, Reg & Design" on right foot, orig dress, jingle bell in ear, 1962. . . . . **95.00**

Cotton Plush, gold, rigid head, short jointed arms and legs, glass eyes, hemp–type floss nose and mouth, stubby feet, c1920s. **150.00**

12"

Plush, amber, swivel head, jointed arms

and legs, stitched on ears, felt paws, functioning growler, straw filled, c1915. . . . . **200.00**

Plush, white, woolly, clear glass eyes, coarse floss nose and mouth, worn pads, c1920–1930 . . . . **135.00**

13", plush, dark brown, jointed, long nose, felt paws, black sewn nose and mouth **25.00**

14"

Mohair, long brown, inset snout, kapok stuffed, fully jointed, floss nose and mouth, felt pads, windup music box, Knickerbocker, 1950s **175.00**

Plush, cotton, reddish brown and white, fully jointed, red felt behind red glass eyes with dark pupils, vertical stitched black floss nose, white felt snout, peach felt open mouth and red tongue, white curly mitten hands with thumb, cardboard reinforced white curly pads, three floss claws, growler, c1940s **100.00**

15"

Mohair, gold, "Old Yellow," excelsior stuffed, fully jointed, glass eyes, floss nose and mouth, felt pads, low set ears, curved paws, early 1930s **300.00**

Mohair, brown, black shoe button eyes, black embroidered nose, mouth, and claws, fully jointed, label "Bruin Mfg Co," c1907. . . . . **250.00**

16", walking bear, rayon plush, brown-tipped, beige flannel snout and inner ears, papier mache body, amber glass eyes, black floss nose, pink flannel open mouth, felt pads on hands, patterned heavy cotton foot pads, bear swings arms, turns head, and walks when a limb is moved manually, c1950s **165.00**

17", plush, brown, tan paws, molded muzzle, Ideal Toy **50.00**

18", mohair, gold, bat–eared, tail, velveteen snout and pads, jointed head, flat black eyes, horizontal stitched black floss nose and mouth, red floss tongue, squeaker, c1940s **150.00**

20", mohair, brown, jointed, flat face, Knickerbocker. **100.00**

21", mohair, long pile, gold, excelsior stuffed head and arms, soft stuffed body and legs, jointed arms, clear glass eyes, black yarn nose and mouth, made–to–body brown velveteen overalls, c1940–50. . . . . **165.00**

24", mohair, brown, glass eyes, black cloth nose, fully jointed, c1925 . . . . **600.00**

TELEPHONES AND TELEPHONE-RELATED

Ask a number of people when they think the telephone was invented. Most will give you a date in the early twentieth century. The accepted answer is 1876, when Alexander Graham Bell filed his patent. However, crude telegraph and sound–operated devices existed prior to that date.

Beware of reproduction phones or phones made from married parts. Buy only telephones that have the proper period parts, and a minimum of restoration, and that are in working order. No mass-produced telephone in the United States made prior to 1950 was manufactured with a shiny brass finish.

Concentrating on the equipment is only half the story. Telephone companies generated a wealth of secondary material from books to giveaway premiums. Dig around for examples from local companies that eventually were merged into the Bell system.

Clubs: Antique Telephone Collectors Association, Box 94, Abilene, KS 67410; Telephone Collectors International, P. O. Box 700165, San Antonio, TX 78270.

Candlestick, Western Electric, non–dial, patent Jan 26, 1915, $110.00.

Advertising
Mirror, pocket, 2½" l, blue and white, celluloid, issued for Missouri and Kansas Telephone Co of Bell System and American Telephone & Telegraph, early 1900s **65.00**

Paperweight, Bell Telephone, bell shape, cobalt blue glass **45.00**
Booth, wood, no doors **125.00**
Button, pinback
7/8" d
Blue and white rotary telephone dial, center inscribed "I'm For Automatic," issued by Auto Elec Co, early 1900s. **18.00**
Red and white, "Soldiers and Sailors' Comfort Club,' candlestick telephone with crossed military rifles, issued by Hawthorne Works of Western Electric, c1920 . . . . **20.00**
Red, white, and blue Independent Telephone logo on light blue ground, "Central Telephone & Electric Co, The Up–To–Date Telephone Company," early 1900s . . . **12.00**
1" d
Blue and white, "Have You Called Home To–Day?," c1920 . . . . **10.00**
Red, white, and blue, "Federal Telephone," shield logo, early 1900s **18.00**
Magazine, *Telephony*, 1955 . . . . **.50**
Notepad, Southern New England Telephone Co, simulated red good luck stamp on cov, black inscription, blue Bell System logo on back **20.00**
Pay Phone, Bell Telephone, beige, three slots, c1950 . . . . **150.00**
Pin, 7/8" d, celluloid, diecut, black and white, "Local and Long Distance Telephone" logo symbol on front, Bell System, c1905. . . . . **40.00**
Stand, Gossip Bench type **80.00**
Stickpin, 1" × 1" diecut celluloid hanger, blue and white, reverse inscribed "When In Doubt Telephone And Find Out/Use The Bell," Bell System, c1905 . . . . **42.00**
Switchboard, lightbulb type, pre–1935. . . . . **250.00**
Telephone
Candlestick, c1911 . . . . **100.00**
Dial, 1921 . . . . **125.00**
Field, World War II, US Army **25.00**
Wall, oak, hand crank, 23"l, c1908. . . . **285.00**

TELEVISION CHARACTERS AND PERSONALITIES

The golden age of television varies depending on the period in which you grew up. Each generation thinks the television of their childhood is the best there ever was.

TV collectibles are one category in which new products establish themselves as collectible quickly. The minute a show is canceled, something that happens rather rapidly today, anything associated with it is viewed as collectible.

The golden age of TV star endorsements was the 1950s through the 1960s. For whatever reason, today's toy, game, and other manufacturers are not convinced that TV stars sell products. As a result, many shows have no licensed products associated with them. Because of the absence of three dimensional material, collectors must content themselves with paper, such as *TV Guide* and magazines.

Captain Kangaroo, plastic drinking cup, maroon, copyright Robert Keeshan Assoc, $15.00.

Addams Family, lunch box, litho metal, black trim, full color scenes, 7" × 8½" × 4", King–Seeley, 1974 copyright. **30.00**
Allison, Fran, pinback button, adv, "Aunt Fanny's Bread/Fran Allison of Radio & TV, 1⅛" litho, full color, 1950s **20.00**
Ball, Lucille, magazine, *TV Guide*, April 30, 1966, full color cover art illus, artist Ronald Searle **10.00**
Beverly Hillbillies, book, Whitman #1572, 6" × 8" hard cover, color photo cover of Clampett Family. **15.00**
Bonanza, pinback button, 3" d, celluloid, redtone photo of Cartwright family, blue inscriptions, pre–1965 .... **35.00**
Crockett, Davy, plate, 7" d, white glass, dark red illus and words "Davy Crockett, Frontier Hero," mid–1950s **15.00**
Earp, Wyatt, big little book, Whitman #1644, 1958, 4½ × 5 ¾", full color cover with illus of Hugh O'Brien **20.00**
Fat Albert and the Cosby Kids, sticker book, Whitman #2865–66, 1973, 8½ × 11", unused **17.50**

Fischbeck, George, Eye Witness Weather, KOB–TV, pinback button, dark blue and white, 1⅛" d, Albuquerque, NM station, early 1950s **15.00**
Fury, comic book, Gold Key Comics, issue #1, Nov 1962, color photo cover and back, costar Bobby Diamond. **20.00**
Gunsmoke, game, Lowell Toy, 19¼" sq board, 10" × 20" × 2½" slightly scuffed box, late 1950s. **30.00**
Lassie, magazine, *TV Guide*, July 4, 1959, full color cov illus of Lassie, Jon Provost, article "The Life and Times of Lassie" with color photos. **7.50**
Rin–Tin–Tin, coloring book, Whitman #1257, 8¼" × 11", 1955, some pages neatly colored **15.00**
Rocky and His Friends, mug, 4" h, white ceramic, full color picture of Rocky, Mr Peabody, and Bullwinkle carrying signs, 1960 copyright. **75.00**
The Wild, Wild West, Robert Conrad, paperback, Signet Books, first printing, 1966. .... **25.00**
Welcome Back Kotter, book cover, unused. **12.00**

TELEVISIONS

Old television sets are becoming highly collectible. It is not unusual to see a dozen or more at a flea market. Do not believe a tag that says they work. Insist that the seller find a place to plug it in and show you.

A good general rule is the smaller the picture tube, the earlier the set. Pre–1946 televisions usually have a maximum of five stations, 1 through 5. Channels 7 through 13 were added in 1947. In 1949 Channel 1 was dropped. UHF appeared in 1953.

In order to determine the value of a TV, you need to identify the brand and model number. See *Warman's Antiques And Their Prices* for a more detailed list.

Newsletters: *TV Collector*, P. O. Box 188, Needham, MA 02192; *Sight, Sound, Style*, P. O. Box 2224, South Hackensack, NJ 07606.

Accessories
Figurine, panther, black, Frankoma ... **12.00**
On Screen Game, Winky Dink, official magic window, erasing mit, eight magic crayons, game book, MIB **60.00**
Parts Kit, Daven. **500.00**
TV Lamp, Scene–In–Action, Niagara Falls **95.00**
Television Set
Andrea, KTE–5 .... **2,500.00**
Dumont, 180. .... **2,000.00**
Motorola, VT–71 .... **225.00**

234

Philco Predicata, white **850.00**
RCA, 648PTK **200.00**
See–All, open frame **1,500.00**
Western Television Corp, ship's
wheel, cabinet type **2,500.00**

THERMOMETERS

The thermometer was a popular advertising giveaway and promotional item. Buy only thermometers in very good or better condition and that have a minimum of wear on the visible surface. Remember, thermometers had large production runs. If the first example that you see does not please you, shop around.

Old Reliable Whiskey, Daniel A Yoder Wines & Liquors, wood, $45.00.

Advertising
Borden Feed, orig box, 1952 . . . . **25.00**
Cash Value Tobacco, tin **22.50**
Champion Spark Plugs **20.00**
Coca–Cola, bottle shape, gold, orig box,
1950s **20.00**
Dr Pepper, tin, 20" h, 1960s logo **50.00**
Dr Pierce's Chemical Co, Bakelite,
1931 . . . . **18.00**
First National Bank, Fremont, OH,
wood, orig box **30.00**
Frog, Switch and Manufacturing Co,
Carlisle, PA, 36", dark blue trim,
white ground **45.00**
Georgia Real Estate Co, 21", wood,
1915 . . . . **70.00**
Happy Jim Chewing Tobacco, 35" **75.00**
Luminall, 39", 1950 . . . . **60.00**

Moxie, Old Fashion, metal **20.00**
Naco Fertilizer Co, Charleston, SC **22.00**
Nyal Drugstore Service, 38" **28.00**
Old Dutch Root Beer, 27", 1940 . . . . . . **65.00**
Pal Orange Ade, 26" **40.00**
Rislone **55.00**
Rochester American Insurance Co, NY,
porcelain **27.00**
Royal Crown Cola, cardboard, Santa
Claus and bottle, 20 × 10", 1950s . . . **35.00**
Salem Cigarettes **12.00**
Sauer's Vanilla, 1919, wooden **68.00**
Snow Goose Flour, 39", blue trim, white
ground **50.00**
Standard Oil, tin, orig box **20.00**
Stegmaier Beer, glass, round **43.00**
Winston Cigarettes, tin **36.00**
Other
1934 Chicago World's Fair, 2½" × 2½",
octagonal shape, silver and blue dial
symbol and lettering, brass rim, black
metal back and hanging **50.00**
Owl, 6" h, plaster body **75.00**

THINGS TOURISTS BUY

This category demonstrates that, given time, even the tacky can become collectible. Many tourist souvenirs offer a challenge to one's aesthetics. But they are bought anyway.

Tourist china plates and glass novelties from the 1900 to 1940 period are one of the true remaining bargains left. Most of the items sell for under $25.00. If you really want to have some fun, pick one form and

Cup and saucer, Souvenir of Wildwood By The Sea, NJ, multicolored, marked "Handpainted, Japan," $7.50.

see how many different places you can find from which it was sold.

Newspaper: *Travel Collector*, P. O. Box 40, Manawa, WI 54949

Newsletter: *The Antique Souvenir Collectors News*, P. O. Box 562, Great Barrington, MA 01230.

Clubs: American Spoon Collectors, 4922 State Line, Westwood Hills, KS 66205.

Ashtray, Everett (WA) Yacht Club, brass. **20.00**
Bottle Opener, 3⅞", cast iron, drunk at sign post, "Sequoia National Park" **25.00**
Creamer, 3", Saratoga, ruby stained, King's Crown pattern, etched "Nettie". **36.00**
Cup, china, white, St Charles Hotel, New Orleans, 2¾"h, 2¼"d **12.00**
Fan, Niagara Falls, silk. **8.50**
Hatchet, Hazelton, PA, white milk glass, red lettering, 6" **25.00**
Honey Pot, Belleville, KS. **10.00**
Jug, miniature, Valley Springs, SD **25.00**
Medallion, Souvenir of Wisconsin, green with gold, lacy **10.00**
Mug
  Colorado Springs, 2¾" h, ruby stained, Button Arches pattern **38.00**
  New Rockford, ND, custard glass. **330.00**
Paperweight, New Salem State Park, glass, round, 2¾"d. **30.00**
Pinback Button, Carnival Cruises **3.00**
Plate
  Bridge Over Illinois River, Beardstown. **10.00**
  Vanderbilt University, 10", rose, Jonroth **20.00**
Postcard, Main Street, large city **4.00**
Salt and Pepper Shakers, pr
  Empire State Building, Statue of Liberty, silvered cast metal, marked "Souvenir of NY". **8.00**
  Flamingos, 3" h, hp, pink, marked "Souvenir of FL" **6.50**
Shovel, Kearney, NE, glass, 6½", gold scoop and lettering, clear handle **20.00**
Snowdome
  The American Museum of Natural History, Hayden Planetarium, NY, 2¾" × 2¼" × 2", plastic dome, printing on back, camera and city sky line scene, 1980s. **4.00**
  Disneyland, 2¾" × 2¼" × 2", plastic dome, Tinkerbell and castle, 1970s. **8.00**
  Pocono Wild animal Farm, 2¼" × 2" × 2", plastic dome, deer and bear on seesaw, 1960s **7.00**
Spoon
  Baltimore, turtle handle, gold wash bowl, demitasse **20.00**
  Golden Gate, San Francisco. **30.00**

Teapot, Morrison Hotel, Chicago **25.00**
Tip Tray, Hotel Coronado, china **8.00**
Tray
  Rochester, MN, 2½ × 6", ruby stained, gold trim **10.00**
  Yellowstone Park, 4" oval, copper, silver wash **12.00**
Trivet, 9¾" l, cast iron, souvenir, hex design **5.00**
Tumbler, "Souvenir of Buffalo," sepia scenes **12.00**
Vase, Opera House, What Cheer, IA, china, colored scene, 4¾". **12.00**
Whimsey, potty shape, Stratton, ME, custard glass, gold trim **22.00**

TINS

The advertising tin has always been at the forefront of advertising collectibles. Look for examples that show no deterioration to the decoration of the surface and which have little or no signs of rust on the inside or bottom.

The theme sells the tin. Other collectors, especially individuals from the transportation fields, have long had their eyes on the tin market. Tins also play a major part in the Country Store decorating look.

Prices for pre–1940 tins are still escalating. Before you pay a high price for a tin, do your homework and make certain it is difficult to find.

Club: Tin Container Collectors Association, P. O. Box 440101, Aurora, CA 80014.

Black Cat Cigarettes, mild, English, green sides and center band, 4½" × 3" × 1½", $35.00.

Armour & Co Mince Meat, lid **35.00**
Band–Aid **10.00**
Cavalier. **22.50**
Chesterfield Cigarette, cat on lid **38.00**
Cleveland's Superior Baking Powder, lid, label. **25.00**
Dining Car Coffee, 1 lb, key wind **58.00**
Fitch Talc, c1930 . . . . **10.00**

Golden Pheasant Prophylactics......... **68.00**
Improved Trojans Prophylactics........ **28.00**
John Orderleys, Owl Drug Co.......... **25.00**
Log Cabin Syrup, no lid.............. **59.00**
Maxwell House Coffee, 1 lb, 1909....... **20.00**
New Bachelor Cigar, man playing cards
and dreaming of woman............**100.00**
Old English Curve Cut................ **15.00**
Philip Morris....................... **22.50**
Postmaster Cigar, "2 for 5¢ smokers".... **75.00**
Regulax........................... **15.00**
Snow Flake Crackers, hinged, 9" × 9".... **49.00**
Yellow Bonnet, 1 lb, key wind,
unopened **25.00**

TOBACCO-RELATED

The tobacco industry is under siege in the 1990s. Fortunately, they have new frontiers to conquer in Russia, Eastern Europe, Asia, and Africa. The relics of America's smoking past, from ashtrays to humidors, are extremely collectible.

Many individuals are not able to identify a smoking stand or a pocket cigar cutter. I grew up in York County, Pennsylvania, which along with Lancaster County was the tobacco center of the east. Today, tobacco growing and manufacturing have virtually disappeared. Is it possible that there will be a time when smoking disappears as well?

Club: International Seal, Label, and Cigar Band Society, 8915 East Bellevue Street, Tuscon, AZ 85715.

Tobacco Jar, porcelain, multicolored dec, 6¼" h, $85.00.

Cigar
Ashtray, adv, H Fendrick Cigar Co,
brass......................... **15.00**
Box
Linita Cigars, 1920.............. **45.00**
Oak, zinc liner.................. **25.00**
Holder, tortoise shell.............. **3.00**
Humidor, Don Porto Cigar, tin **17.50**
Matchbook Holder, Muriel Cigars,
blued metal, 1⅛" × 1⅝", multicolored
celluloid insert, woman in
multicolored portrait, small gold
frame, dark red ground, c1920 ..... **60.00**
Mirror, pocket, Union Made Cigars adv,
2⅛", celluloid, detailed union label,
light blue, black lettering, c1900 .... **50.00**
Notepad, Hemmeter Cigar Co, floral
and cigar design cover, calendar,
unused....................... **15.00**
Sign, Fame & Fortune 3¢ Cigars, 8" ×
14", tin...................... **55.00**
Tin
Los Ramos Cigars, 5" × 3¾"........ **8.00**
Ology Cigars, 3¼" × 5¼" **4.00**
Webster, 3½" × 5¼" × 1¼", litho,
multicolored lid illus, c1930 .....**220.00**
Tray, Red Earl Cigars, 3½", tip **50.00**
Cigarette
Ashtray, adv
Chesterfield, orig box............. **18.00**
Firestone, tire, copper **10.00**
Cigarette Card, American
Kinney Tobacco Co, military and naval
uniforms, 1887............. **2.00**
Wings Cigarettes, series B, set of
50........................ **40.00**
Case, black, envelope style, red stone
dec.......................... **15.00**
Clock, adv, Vantage Cigarettes, battery
operated...................... **20.00**
Lighter, adv
Pan Am **15.00**
United Lacquer, oil drum shape..... **9.00**
Pinback Button, Phillip Morris, 1" d, celluloid,
Johnny, c1930 .... **18.00**
Playing Cards, Camel Cigarettes **18.00**
Poster
Chesterfield Cigarettes, c1940...... **12.00**
Kool Cigarettes, 12" × 18", smoking
penguin points to pack, c1933.... **35.00**
Raleigh Cigarettes, 15" × 10",
1940..................... **25.00**
Silk, 1", Wm Randolph Hearst for Governor
.... **7.50**
Store Display, Chesterfield, Christmas,
1940s....................... **5.00**
Tin
Black Cat Cigarettes.............. **10.00**
Pall Mall, 7" × 8", Christmas dec.... **12.50**
Trade Card, Gypsy Queen Cigarettes,
1896........................ **2.00**
Tobacco
Box, Old Plug Tobacco, Irvin & Leedys,

Henry Country, VA, 4 × 7" × 12",
walnut **20.00**
Mirror, Mascot Tobacco **30.00**
Oilstone, Bagley's Tobacco, 2¾", celluloid, multicolored tobacco can, red
ground, mounted on back of emery
whetstone, c1900 .... **75.00**
Poster
Crusader Tobacco, 13" × 7",
c1900...................... **25.00**
Golden Eagle Tobacco, 13" × 7",
c1900...................... **30.00**
Pouch, Tiger Chewing Tobacco, black
and white, linen, stitched edge, tiger
illus on each side, early 1900s **20.00**
Sign
Brown's Mule Tobacco, mule reach-
ing in window pulling cover off
man **175.00**
Red Jacket Tobacco, cardboard, base-
ball scene, 22 × 28" **125.00**
Time Plug Tobacco, 12" sq, card-
board **25.00**
Thermometer
Cash Value Tobacco, tin........... **22.50**
Happy Jim Chewing Tobacco, 35". . . **75.00**
Tin
Blue Heaven Tobacco, beige and
blue **5.00**
Frishmuth's Whittle Cut Tobacco . . . **15.00**
Half & Half Tobacco, 1926 .... **6.00**
Union Leader Tobacco, red, gold ea-
gle. **25.00**

TOKENS

Tokens are an extremely diverse field. The
listing below barely scratches the surface
with respect to the types of tokens one
might collect.

The wonderful thing about tokens is
that, on the whole, they are very inexpensive. You can build an impressive collection

E. Keller & Sons, Allentown, PA, $7.50.

with a top spending limit of $2.00 per to-
ken.

Like the match cover and sugar packet
collectors, token collectors have kept their
objects outside the main collecting stream.
This has resulted in stable, low prices over a
long period of time in spite of an extensive
literature base. There is no indication that
this is going to change in the near future.

Club: Token and Medal Society, Inc., P. O.
Box 951988, Lake Mary, FL 32795.

Advertising
Breck Shampoo, Shirley Temple, Story
Book **10.00**
Guth Chocolate Co, eagle trademark,
inscribed "Gold Medal Chocolates,"
1⅛" d, brass................... **12.00**
Billiards
Aerial Billiard Parlors, Knoxville, TN,
blank back,⅞" d, brass, early
1900s...................... **12.00**
Pool & Cigars, Good For 5¢ In Trade, I J
Grove Pool & Cigars, 1" d, aluminum,
early 1900s................... **10.00**
Boy Scout, Good Luck, Excelsior Shoe Co,
luck symbols, inscription on back, 1¼"
d, brass, c1920.................. **10.00**
Campaign
Greeley, Horace, portrait, front in-
scribed "Sage of Chappaqua," re-
verse with eagle and slogan "Greeley,
Brown, and Amnesty 1872,"⅞" d,
brass....................... **30.00**
Lincoln, Abraham, portrait, front in-
scribed "1860 Republican Candidate
for President," reverse inscribed
"Free Territory For A Free People/
Let Liberty Be National & Slavery
Sectional," 1 ¼" d, copper, Hake
#3109 .... **85.00**
Sumner, Charles, MA Senator, portrait,
reverse with eagle and inscription
"Civil Rights For All,"⅞" d, brass **17.50**
Casino, Somers Casino, Atlantic City,
lighthouse next to casino, boardwalk,
reverse with city, bathing beach and sail
boats, 1" d, white metal, early 1900s . . . **20.00**
Railroad, C & O, brass, "Good for Sanitary
Cup" **14.00**

TOOTHPICK HOLDERS

During the Victorian era, the toothpick
holder was an important table accessory. It
is found in a wide range of materials and as
manufactured by American and European
firms. Toothpick holders also were popular
souvenir objects in the 1880 to 1920 period.

Do not confuse toothpick holders with match holders, shot glasses, miniature spoon holders in a child's dish set, mustard pots without lids, rose or violet bowls, individual open salts, or vases. A toothpick holder allows ample room for the toothpick and enough of an extension of the toothpick to allow easy access.

Club: National Toothpick Holder Collector's Society, P. O. Box 246, Sawyer, MI 49125.

California pattern, green, gold trim, 2½″ h, $55.00.

Advertising, Boothby's–Home of Seafood, Phila, celluloid	**8.00**
Brass, top hat, umbrella	**20.00**
Milk Glass, barrel, metal hoops	**25.00**
Opalescent, hobnail, blue	**28.00**
Pattern Glass	
Arched Fleur–De–Lis, clear	**30.00**
Beaded Bull's Eye and Drape, clear	**60.00**
Galloway, clear	**30.00**
Loop and Pillar, clear	**45.00**
Paneled Zipper, clear	**20.00**
Rising Sun	**35.00**
Swinger, clear and ruby	**22.00**
Royal Bayreuth, Black Corinthian	**85.00**
Souvenir	
Belvedere, IL, custard glass	**35.00**
Mother, 1947, button arches pattern, ruby stained	**20.00**

TORTOISE SHELL ITEMS

It is possible to find tortoise shell items in a variety of forms ranging from boxes to trinkets. Tortoise shell items went through several crazes in the nineteenth century, the last occurring near the end of the century.

Tortoise shell items, especially jewelry, also were popular in the 1920s.

Anyone selling tortoiseshell objects is subject to the Endangered Species Act and its amendments. Tortoise shell objects can be imported and sold, but only after meeting a number of strict requirements.

Bangle Bracelet, 3″ d, silver inlay	**30.00**
Box, 1½″ × 3½″, hinged cov	**135.00**
Cigarette Case, brass clips	**40.00**
Comb, side, applied metallic dec, simulated gemstones	**65.00**
Humidor, 4½″, rect, hinged lid	**150.00**
Match Safe, pocket, emb sides	**65.00**
Razor Case, sgd "Jefferson Steel"	**15.00**
Salt, SS rivets, orig spoon	**20.00**
Shaving Brush, inlaid MOP dec handle	**40.00**
Stickpin, carved fly perched on coral branch, gold filled pin	**75.00**
Straight Razor, Landers	**30.00**
Vase, 8¾″, pedestal base, flared top	**150.00**

TOYS

The difference between a man and a boy is the price of his toys. At thirty one's childhood is affordable, at forty expensive, and at fifty out of reach. Check the following list for toys that you may have played with. You will see what I mean.

Magazine: *Antique Toy World*, P. o. Box 34509, Chicago, IL 60634.

Newspaper: *Toy Shop*, 700 East State Street, Iola, WI 54990.

Club: Antique Toy Collectors of America, Two Wall Street, New York, NY 10005.

Hubley, telephone truck, white metal, painted olive green, $45.00.

Baby Toys	
Busy Box, Coleco	**6.00**
Musical Humpty Dumpty	**15.00**

Board Games
Alfred Hitchcock Game, Milton Bradley, copyright 1958 .... **35.00**
Beverly Hillbillies Game, Standard Toykraft, copyright Filmways TV Productions Inc, 1963 .... **35.00**
Combat Game, Ideal, copyright Selmur Productions Inc, 1963 .... **30.00**
Patty Duke Game, Milton Bradley, 1963........................ **30.00**
Uncle Wiggily, 1954, Milton Bradley, 1954........................ **25.00**
The Waltons, Milton Bradley, copyright Lorimar Productions Inc, 1974 ..... **25.00**
Building Sets
Architecture Jr, stone blocks, instructions, wood box **75.00**
Erector Set, Gilbert, illustrated instruction manual, 1954 .... **6.00**
Lincoln Log, #1, orig box **20.00**
Wunder Lumber, interlocking wood blocks, instructions, orig box....... **25.00**
Games
DX Getaway Chase, 1960s, orig box ... **50.00**
Giant Wheel Cowboys and Indians, Remco, 1958, orig box............ **25.00**
Pinball, Sears, 1960s, orig box........ **35.00**
Tudor True Action Electric Football, 1949, orig box **40.00**
Homemaker
Ironing Board, 20″ l, metal, Ohio Art, folding legs, 1958............... **15.00**
Kitchen Set, coppertone, bread box, covered cake, cookie, two covered canisters..................... **15.00**
Sadiron, asbestos, nickel finish, black wooden handle **57.50**
Sewing Machine, Singer, orig green box, red "S".................... **65.00**
Playsets
Atomic Cape Canaveral............ **165.00**
Fort Apache.................... **95.00**
Johnny Lightning Fire Leap, orig box......................... **10.00**
Mr Potato Head, orig pcs and box, 1965........................ **5.00**
Weebles Haunted House, plastic furniture, glow in the dark Ghost Weeble, Witch Weeble, Boy and Girl Weebles..................... **10.00**
Pull Toy, Little Snoopy, 5″ × 9″ × 5″, Fisher Price, paper on wood, day–glow red vinyl wheels, spring tail, marked "693," 1965 copyright **20.00**
Space Toys
Flying Saucer, metal, Japan, 1950s.... **9.00**
Puzzle, Space 1999, orig box **12.00**
US Enterprise, Star Trek, seven 8″ action figures, Mego, 1975.............. **165.00**
Vehicles and Airplanes
Bus, Sun Rubber, 1935 .... **8.00**
Catapault Plane, 1950s **10.00**
Dump Truck, Wyandotte, 11″, red and green **35.00**

Ferrari, 6″, Japan, friction **75.00**
Grader, Doepke Adams............. **95.00**
Hoover Truck, Matchbox **8.00**
Mercedes Convertible, Matchbox, 1982........................ **3.00**
Tractor/Backhoe, battery-operated, Ford........................ **350.00**
Miscellaneous
Chicken, clucking, lays marbles, Baldwin......................... **35.00**
Marbles, ⅝″, slag, mixed colors including brown, gray, orange, tan, green, bag of 50.................... **30.00**
Mr Machine, Ideal, 1977............ **55.00**
Sand Pail, Ohio Art, litho tin, girl feeding chickens................... **28.00**

TRAINS, TOY

Toy train collectors and dealers exist in a world unto themselves. They have their own shows, trade publications, and price guides. The name that you need to know is Greenberg Publishing Company, 7566 Main Street, Sykesville, MD 21784. Their mail order catalog contains an exhaustive list of their own publications as well as those by others. If you get involved with toy trains, write for a copy.

The two most recognized names are American Flyer and Lionel and the two most popular gauges are S and O. Do not overlook other manufacturers and gauges.

The toy train market has gone through a number of crazes—first Lionel, then American Flyer. The current craze is boxed sets. Fortunately, the market is so broad that there will never be an end to subcategories to collect.

Clubs: Lionel Collector's Club, P. O. Box 11851, Lexington, KY 40578; The National Model Railroad Association, P. O. Box 2186, Indianapolis, IN 46206; The Toy Train Operating Society, Inc., 25 West Walnut Street, Suite 305, Pasadena, CA 91103; The Train Collector's Association, P. O. Box 248, Strasburg, PA 17579.

Note: The following prices are for equipment in good condition.

AMERICAN FLYER, S Gauge

295, locomotive, American Flyer, steam 4–6–2, black, white lettering, 1951 ... **30.00**
332DC, locomotive, Union Pacific, steam 4–8–4, black, white lettering, 1950 ... **100.00**
360, locomotive, Santa Fe, Alco PA unit,

Lionel, No. 233 "O" gauge set, #262 engine, #803 hopper, #902 gondola, #806 cattle car, #802 caboose, $250.00.

1950–1952, with 361 dummy, silver–painted finish **70.00**
613, boxcar, Great Northern, brown, white lettering, 1953 . . . . **6.00**
631, gondola, Texas & Pacific, red, 1946–1953 . . . . **25.00**
806, caboose, American Flyer, red, white lettering, 1956–57 . . . . **2.00**
936, depressed–center flat car with cable reel, Erie, gray, 1953–56 . . . . **6.00**
953, baggage and club car, American Flyer, red, 1953–56 . . . . **25.00**
24036, boxcar, New Haven, orange, black and white lettering, 1959 . . . . **10.00**
24309, tank car, Gulf, silver, orange logo, 1957–58 . . . . **6.00**

LIONEL, POSTWAR (1945–1969)

1130, locomotive, steam, 2–4–2, 1130T or 6066T tender, die–cast body, 1950 . . . . **20.00**
1885, coach, Western & Atlantic, blue, brown roof, 1959 . . . . **75.00**
2055, locomotive, steam, 4–6–4, diecast body, 1025W/2046W, 1954–1957 . . . . **80.00**
2330, locomotive, Pennsylvania, GG–1, green, gold stripes, 1950 . . . . **275.00**
2442, passenger car, Clifton, Vista Dome, aluminum paint, red stripe **20.00**
2472, caboose, Pennsylvania, metal, N5, red, white lettering, 1945–1947 . . . . . . **8.00**
3364, log dump car, 1965–1969 . . . . **15.00**
3413, Mercury capsule car, red, gray superstructure and capsule, 1962–1964 . . . . **40.00**

3462, automatic milk car, white, black lettering, 1947–48 . . . . **30.00**
4454, boxcar, Baby Ruth, PRR, electronic, orange, black lettering, 1946–1948 . . . **50.00**
X6004, boxcar, Baby Ruth, PRR, orange, blue lettering (O27) **2.00**
6176, hopper, Lehigh Valley, gray **3.00**
6411, flatcar with logs, gray, 1948–1950 . . . . **10.00**
6465, tank car, two–dome, Sunoco, silver, black lettering, 1948–1950 . . . . . . **3.00**
6560–25, crane, Bucyrus Erie, eight–wheel, red cab, 1956 . . . . **40.00**

MARX

99, locomotive, Rock Island, E–7 diesel, powered or dummy, plastic, black and red, 1958–1974 . . . . **15.00**
396, locomotive, Canadian Pacific, streamlined, sheet metal, electric motor, black cab, copper boiler, 2–4–2, 1941–1942 . . . . **25.00**
586, plastic caboose, Rock Island, deluxe eight–wheel, tuscan **7.00**
735, locomotive, stamped steel, windup motor, black, 1950–1952 . . . . **10.00**
2700, 3/16" metal flatcar, NYC & St. L, black **15.00**
3557, 3/16" metal passenger coach, New York Central, silver **40.00**
4571, plastic searchlight, WECX, deluxe eight–wheel, red, 1955–1965 . . . . **15.00**
17899, 3/16" metal gondola, T & P, light blue–gray **5.00**
95050, plastic caboose, Lehigh Valley, four–wheel, red body, 1974 . . . . **2.00**

TRAMP ART

Tramp art refers to items made by itinerant artists, most of whom are unknown, who made objects out of old cigar boxes or fruit and vegetable crates. Edges of pieces are often chip-carved and layered. When an object was completed, it was often stained. Tramp art received a boost when it was taken under the wing of the Folk Art groupies. You know what has happened to the Folk Art market. You make a bed, you lie in it.

Box, 5" × 6¼", dec sides **65.00**
Frame, 19½" × 17¼" **45.00**
Jewelry Box, 10½" × 10½" × 9", lift out int. tray, hidden drawer, brass trim . . . **55.00**
Magazine Rack, 15", hanging, dark finish, brass tacks **40.00**
Miniature Chest, 12" l, three drawers, old varnish finish **100.00**
Sewing Box, 9½" l, single drawer, pincushion top, orig finish **25.00**

Cross, 8¼" sq base, 15½" h, $60.00.

Wall Pocket, 11" × 16½", applied
strips **80.00**

TRAPS

When the animal rights activists of the
1960s surfaced, trap collectors crawled
back into their dens. You find trap collectors at flea markets, but they are quiet
types.

Avoid traps that show excessive wear
and pitting. In order to be collectible a trap
should be in good working order. Careful
when testing one. You may get trapped
yourself.

Mouse trap, wood and metal, 4½" d, $20.00.

Bear
Herters Kodiak.................... **285.00**
Kodiak #6, H in pan, teeth, setting
clamp......................... **275.00**
MacKenzie District Fur Co Ltd,

Fabrique 1886, HBC #15, double
spring, heavy 26" chain, 34" l, weighs
21 lbs **345.00**
Newhouse #15, Animal Trap Co...... **350.00**
Fish and Game, Gabriel, automatic set-
ting.......................... **85.00**
Gopher
JVJ, Crete, NE **30.00**
Renkens....................... **10.00**
Simplex, self–set **18.00**
Mole
Cinch......................... **15.00**
Nash, Kalamazoo, MI **15.00**
Mouse
Auto Scented–Rev–O–Noc, wood,
snap–type **8.00**
CM Coghill, attaches to fruit jar....... **15.00**
Evans, brass.................... **150.00**
Iron Cat, metal, choker–style, 1906 ... **20.00**
Schuler Folding Killer, metal........ **18.00**
Snappy, metal, thumb–set **10.00**
Streeter, iron, snap–type, pat 1897.... **90.00**
Up to Date, metal, traps at both ends ... **20.00**
Wiggington, glass **20.00**
WR Feemster, aluminum, Brooklyn,
MI **15.00**
Rat
Blizzard, wood, snap–type **10.00**
Little Jimmy, wood and tin, live trap ... **20.00**
Little Samson, iron, teeth........... **150.00**
Weasel, Official Weasel, wood,
snap–type, Animal Trap Co **8.00**

TRAYS

The tin lithographed advertising tray dates
back into the last quarter of the nineteenth
century. They were popular at any location
where beverages, alcoholic and nonalco-
holic were served.

Because they were used heavily, it is not
unusual to find dents and scratches. Check
carefully for rust. Once the lithographed
surface was broken, rust developed easily.

Smaller trays are generally tip trays.
Novice collectors often confuse them with
advertising coasters. Tip trays are rather
expensive. Ordinary examples sell in the
$50.00 to $75.00 range.

Advertising
American Brewing Co, 12" d, Jacob
Metzger, Indianapolis, IN, trademark
on star in center of flag **150.00**
Cascade Beer, San Francisco, illus of
Uncle Sam and five ethnic people ... **650.00**
Coca–Cola
1914, Betty, tip **65.00**
1950, Menu Girl **27.00**
Cottolene Shortening, 4½" d, litho tin,

Hornung Beer, gold horn, Jacob Hornung Brewing Co, Philadelphia, 12" d, $65.00.

multicolored illus on black ground,
  mfg by NK Fairbank Co, tip **40.00**
Falls City Brewing Co, 13" d, topless girl
  on horse **250.00**
Geo Ehret's Hellgate Brewery, NY, 13½"
  × 16¾", oval, tin **25.00**
Hebburn House Coal, 4" l, change, eagle
  in center, holding banner, wood grain
  ground **42.50**
Hopski Soda, litho, frog pouring
  drinks. **50.00**
Miller High Life, girl sitting on moon. . . **25.00**
Moxie Centennial, 1984 . . . . **35.00**
Old Reading Beer, red border, white
  lettering, blue ground **50.00**
Peerless Ice Cream **85.00**
Rockford watches, 3½" × 5", tin, girl in
  green dress **115.00**
Political
  McKinley and Roosevelt, aluminum,
    sepia portraits, inscribed "Nominated
    Philadelphia June 1900," millinery
    adv on reverse **25.00**
  Taft and Sherman, 4½" d, tip, litho tin,
    jugate portraits, rim caption "Grand
    Old Party/1856 To 1908," black and
    gold border. **125.00**
Souvenir and Commemorative
  American Line Ship, tip **100.00**
  Buffalo, 1901 Pan Am Expo, brass, han-
    dled **58.00**
  Chicago World's Fair, 1933, Century of
    Progress, 4¾" d, brass, emb, raised
    detailed exhibit buildings **25.00**
  Coronation, Queen Elizabeth II, June 2,
    1953, 4¾" d, pin tray, color coat of
    arms, gold trim, Paragon **31.00**
  New York World's Fair
    1939, 11½" × 17½", tin, litho, orange,
      blue, and white design **40.00**
    1964, 8" × 11", litho, Unisphere and

Avenue of Flags, eggshell white
  rim, gold inscription. **15.00**
Rochester, MN, 2½" × 6", ruby stained,
  gold trim **10.00**
Washington's Home, Mt Vernon, VA,
  7½" × 11", porcelain, portraits of
  George and Martha Washington and
  Mt Vernon, multicolored, sq corners,
  gold trim, marked "Germany" **75.00**
Other
  Floral Center, metal, hp, red, gold trim,
    Occupied Japan **10.00**
  Martini Center, card border, 11" d, red,
    black, and white. **50.00**
  Pinocchio and Gepetto, 8" × 10", tin,
    litho, 1940 copyright **20.00**

TROPHIES

There are trophies for virtually everything.
Ever wonder what happens to them when
the receiver grows up or dies? Most wind
up in landfills. It is time to do something
about this injustice.

Dad has begun collecting them. He is
focusing on shape and unusual nature of
the award. He has set a $5.00 limit, which
is not much of a handicap when it comes to
trophy collecting. In fact, most of his trophies have been donated by individuals
who no longer want them.

Always check the metal content of trophies. A number of turn-of-the-century
trophies are sterling silver. These obviously
have weight as well as historic value. Also
suspect sterling silver when the trophy is a
plate.

Tennis, Doubles Consolation, Muskogee, 1921, silver plated, 4⅞" h, $35.00.

TYPEWRITERS

E. Remington & Sons' 1874 Shoels & Gliden machine was the first commercially produced typewriter in America. The last quarter of the nineteenth century was spent largely in experimentation and attempting to make the typewriter part of every office environment, something that was achieved by 1910. Although there were early examples, the arrival of a universally acceptable electric typewriter dates from the 1950s.

The number of typewriter collectors is small, but growing. Machines made after 1915 have little value, largely because they do not interest collectors. Do not use the patent date on a machine to date its manufacture. Many models were produced for decades. Do not overlook typewriter ephemera. Early catalogs are quite helpful in identifying and dating machines.

Newsletters: *Typewriter Times,* 1216 Garden Street, Hoboken, NJ 07030; *The Typewriter Exchange,* 2125 Mt. Vernon Street, Philadelphia, PA 19130.

Clubs: Internationales Forum Historishe Burowelt, Postfach 500 11 68, D–5000 Koln–50, Germany; Early Typewriter Collectors Association, 11433 Rochester Avenue, #303, Los Angeles, CA 90025.

Blickensderfer #5, Stamford, CT, orig case, $150.00.

Blickensderfer, No. 7, oak case	**125.00**
Corona, black, three-row keyboard, case	**30.00**
Fox, metal case	**85 00**
IBM, Selectric, interchangeable ball type face	**20.00**
O'Dell, No. 4, Chicago, 1885	**80.00**
Oliver	
No. 4, c1900	**35.00**
No. 9, wood cov, 1916 patent	**150.00**
Remington, portable, c1929	**25.00**
Royal, No. 5	**35.00**
Simplex, Model 1, index type, red, white, and blue, orig box	**45.00**
Underwood	
Portable, orig case, 1921	**50.00**
Standard, No. 5	**25.00**

UMBRELLAS

Umbrellas suffer a sorry fate. They are generally forgotten and discarded. Their handles are removed and collected as separate entities or attached to magnifying glasses. Given the protection they have provided, they deserve better.

Look for umbrellas that have advertising on the fabric. Political candidates often gave away umbrellas to win votes. Today baseball teams have umbrella days to win fans.

Seek out unusual umbrellas in terms of action or shape. A collection of folding umbrellas, especially those from the 1950s, is worth considering.

Umbrellas are generally priced low because sellers feel that they are going to have difficulty getting rid of them. They probably will. Buy them and put a silver lining on their rainy cloud.

URINALS

When you have to go, you have to go—any port in a storm. You have been in enough bathrooms to know that all plumbing fixtures are not equal.

The human mind has just begun to explore the recycling potential of hospital bed pans. Among the uses noted are flower planters, food serving utensils, and dispersal units at the bottom of down spouts. How have you used them? Send your ideas and pictures of them in action to the Bedpan Recycling Project, 5093 Vera Cruz Road, Emmaus, PA 18049.

VALENTINES

There is far too much emphasis on adult valentines from the nineteenth century through the 1930s. It's true they are lacy and loaded with romantic sentiment. But, are they fun? No!

Fun is in children's valentines, a much neglected segment of the valentine market. If you decide to collect them, focus on the 1920 through 1960 period penny valentines. The artwork is bold, vibrant, exciting, and a tad corny. This is what makes them fun.

There is another good reason to collect twentieth century children's valentines. They are affordable. Most sell for less than $2.00, with many good examples in the 50¢ range. They often show up at flea markets as a hoard. When you find them, make an offer for the whole lot. You won't regret it.

Club: National Valentine Collectors Association, P. O. Box 1404, Santa Ana, CA 92702.

Mechanical, 4" × 6⅛", $4.00.

Art Deco, folder, 1920s	
3" × 3", heart shape	**1.50**
6" × 9", layered, lacy	**7.50**
Art Nouveau, folder, 1900s	
3" × 5", oblong, Whitney	**3.50**
5" × 7", oblong, lacy	**7.50**
Cameo, Berlin and Jones, 5 × 7", 1860	**35.00**
Comic Sheet	
8" × 10", c1920	**5.00**

8" × 14", sgd "CJH"	**15.00**
Diecut, 4" × 4", cardboard, hearts, cupids, c1900	**4.00**
Easel Back, 6" × 9", fancy cutwork border, 1900	**10.00**
Embossed, hand made, c1865	
Large, fancy	**12.50**
Layered, lacy	**7.50**
Embossed, lacy, c1885	
Folder, small, simple	**5.00**
Layered, lacy	**7.50**
German, mechanical	
Fancy, four layered	**12.50**
Large, train, 1914	**45.00**
Small, simple, pulldown	**4.00**
German, pullouts with honeycomb	
Fancy, pink umbrella	**35.00**
Large, pair of binoculars	**225.00**
Honeycomb, pullouts, 1920s	
Car, diecut, 10", black	**15.00**
Toad Stool, light red	**5.00**
Mechanical, R Tuck, large paper doll, 1900	**25.00**
Perforated Lacy, c1850	
5" × 7", Meek, hand written verse	**25.00**
Small, folder, sgd "H"	**20.00**
Standup Mantle Pieces, c1895	
5" × 5", hp	**12.50**
8" × 10", fancy, layered, fringed	**9.50**
Parchment, fancy center	**15.00**

VENDING MACHINES

Vending machines make great decorative accent pieces at home or in the office. Look for machines that operate for a penny or nickel.

Beware of repainting and marriages. Insist that any machine you buy have only correct period parts, retain the paint and other decoration with which it started life, and be in full operating condition. Unless you are a mechanical genius, you do not want to be faced with the task of trying to fix the mechanism of a broken vending machine.

Newsletter: *Coin Op Newsletter*, 909 26th Street, N.W., Washington, DC 20037.

Gum	
Columbus Model A, 1¢, replacement globe and padlock, restored, 1920s	**265.00**
Mansfield Automatic Clerk, etched front, clock wound mechanism, 1901	**325.00**
Masters Gum Machine, 1¢	**165.00**
National Self Service, 5¢, gum and mints, decal	**135.00**
Penny King, marked, 1930s	**90.00**

1¢ gumball machine, Columbus, green enamel, $140.00.

Silver Comet, 1¢, dispenses gum
  sticks 165.00
Match
  Advance Match Vendor. 395.00
  Diamond, 1¢, c1920 .... 300.00
Miscellaneous
  Four–In–One, dispenses four different
  products, Art Deco style, swivel
  base, four handles and coin entries,
  1930s 400.00
  Premier Baseball Card and Gumball dis-
  penser 265.00
  Reed's Aspirin Vendor, 10¢, graphics,
  orig aspirin packets 395.00
  Superior, peanut and gumball, round
  base and globe, 1920–1930. .... 175.00
Peanut
  Abbey, 5¢. 95.00
  Advance No 11, steel construction,
  chrome plated front 90.00
  Northwestern 33, porcelain finish, octagonal geometric base, cylinder
  globe, door marked "Northwestern,"
  1933. .... 100.00
  Regal Hot Nut Vendor, glass globe, light
  bulb, 1930s 100.00
  Pencil, Parker, 5¢, cast metal. 345.00

VIDEO GAMES

At the moment, most video games sold at a flea market are being purchased for reuse. There are a few collectors, but their number is small.

It might be interesting to speculate at this point on the long-term collecting potential of electronic children's games, especially since the Atari system has come and gone. The key to any toy is playability. A video game cartridge has little collecting value unless it can be put into a machine and played. As a result, the long-term value of video games will rest on collector's ability to keep the machines that use them in running order. Given today's tendency to scrap rather than repair a malfunctioning machine, one wonders if there will be any individuals in 2041 that will understand how video game machines work and, if so, be able to get the parts required to play them.

Next to playability, displayability is important to any collector. How do you display video games? Is the answer to leave the TV screen on 24 hours a day?

Video games are a fad waiting to be replaced by the next fad. There will always be a small cadre of players who will keep video games alive, just as there is a devoted group of adventure game players. But given the number of video game cartridges sold, they should be able to fill their collecting urges relatively easily.

What this means is that if you are going to buy video game cartridges at a flea market, buy them for reuse and do not pay more than a few dollars. The closer you try to buy a game to its release, the more you pay. Just wait. Once a few years have passed, the sellers will just be glad to get rid of them.

VIEW–MASTER

William Gruber invented and Sawyer's Inc., of Portland, Oregon, manufactured and marketed the first View–Master viewers and reels in 1939. The company survived the shortages of World War II by supplying training materials in the View–Master format to the army and navy.

Immediately following World War II a 1,000-dealer network taxed the capacity of the Sawyer plant. In 1946 the Model C, the most common of the viewers, was introduced. Sawyer was purchased by General Aniline & Film Corporation in 1966. After passing through other hands, View–Master wound up as part of Ideal Toys.

Do not settle for any viewer or reel in less

than near-mint condition. Original packaging, especially reel envelopes, is very important. The category is still in the process of defining which reels are valuable and which are not. Most older, pre–1975, reels sell in the 50¢ to $1.00 range.

Club: National Stereoscopic Association, P. O. Box 14801, Columbus, OH 43214.

Viewers
    Model C, 1946, black plastic, reel inserted in top 3.00
    Model D, lighted, focuses **35.00**
Reels, Single
    Hand lettered titles, white reel, blue and white envelope, No. 256, Mt. Lassen Volcanic National Park, California 2.00
    Gold and blue reel, hand lettered titles, blue and white envelope, No. 180, Phoenix, AZ 3.00
    White reels, printed titles, blue and white envelope
      81, Niagara Falls, NY, 1954 . . . .   1.50
      195, Beautiful Caverns of Luray, Virginia, 1946 . . . .   2.00
      506, Pyramids of Teotihuacan and Tenayuca, Mexico, 1944 . . . .   4.00
      820, Woody Woodpecker in the Pony Express Ride, 1951 . . . .   1.00
      2015, Making Swiss Cheese, Switzerland, 1948 . . . .   1.50
      CH–8, Bible Stories, The Wisemen Find Jesus, 1947, booklet 1.00
      FT-9, The Ugly Duckling, 1948, booklet 4.50
3–Reel Packets
    A–179, Disneyland, Tomorrowland, SAW 4.00
    A–671, New York World's Fair, 1964–65, General Tour, SAW **25.00**
    B-597, Emergency, GAF 4.00
    K-57, Star Trek, The Motion Picture, GAF, 1979 . . . . **12.50**

WADE CERAMICS

Dad has a Wade animal collection because he drinks quantities of Red Rose Tea. Red Rose has issued several series of small animals. Like many of his other collections, Dad is not happy until he has multiple sets. "Drink more tea" is the order of the year at his office. How much simpler it would be just to make a list of the missing Wades and pick them up at flea markets where they sell in the $.50 to $1.00 range.

Aquarium Figure
    Lighthouse, 3" h 2.50

Mermaid, 2½" h **2.00**
Ashtray
    Panda, black and white, yellow base . . .   **3.50**
    Starfish, figural **4.25**
Basket, yellow, basketweave ext. and handle **7.50**
Cigarette Box, cov, copper luster, pastel enameled flower dec **18.50**
Creamer and Sugar, Bramble ware, raspberry dec **20.00**
Key Chain, St Bernard, adv premium for St Bruno Tobacco **5.00**
Pipe Rest, green base, figural terrier dog **4.50**
Wall Pocket, pink tulips **10.00**

WASH DAY COLLECTIBLES

I keep telling my mother that women's liberation has taken all the fun out of washing and ironing. She quickly informs me that it was never fun to begin with. The large piles of unironed clothes she keeps around the house are ample proof of that.

Wash day material is a favorite of advertising collectors. Decorators have a habit of using it in bathroom decor. Is there a message here?

Bottle, Seabury Laundry Bluing, 4", light green **85.00**
Box
    Argo Starch, unopened, 1930s **10.00**
    Armour's Washing Powder **4.00**
    Gold Dust Twins Washing Powder, unopened **55.00**
Clothes Hanger, 17¾", turned wood **50.00**
Clothes Line Winder, hickory, hand hewn, 18th C **60.00**
Clothes Sprinkler, ceramic, elephant **25.00**
Drying Rack, 24" × 60", folding, poplar **200.00**
Iron
    Enterprise, straight back edge, removable handle **15.00**
    Ober, open handle holes, emb, marked "#12 Ober Pat Pend" **15.00**
Kettle, cast iron, wire bail, marked "Griswold, Erie, PA" **50.00**
Laundry Basket, Shaker, woven splint, bentwood rim handles **100.00**
Sock Stretcher, wood **30.00**
Trade Card
    Conqueror Clothes Wringer, fold up . . .   **12.00**
    Sapolio, Enoch Morgan & Sons, boy wearing fancy clothes **2.50**
Sign, Borax Dry Soap, metal, red and white **45.00**
Wash Board, double faced, tusk tenon mortising, cut nails **50.00**

WEDGWOOD

It is highly unlikely that you are going to find eighteenth–, nineteenth–, and even early twentieth–century Wedgwood at a flea market. However, you will find plenty of Wedgwood pieces made between 1920 and the present. The wonderful and confusing aspect is that many Wedgwood pieces are made the same way today as they were hundred of years ago.

Unfortunately, Wedgwood never developed a series of backstamps that helped to date when a piece was manufactured. As a result, the only safe assumption by which to buy is that the piece is relatively new. The next time you are shopping in a mall or jewelry store, check out modern Wedgwood prices. Pay 50 percent or less for a similar piece at a flea market.

Newsletter: *American Wedgwoodian*, 55 Vandam Street, New York, NY 10013. '

Clubs: The Wedgwood Society, 246 N. Bowman Avenue, Merion, PA 19066; The Wedgwood Society, The Roman Villa, Rockbourne, Fordingbridge, Hents., SP6 3PG, England.

Ashtray, 4½" d, spade shape, dark blue, white cupids, marked **30.00**
Box, cov, Bicentennial Commemorative, three color cameo of George Washington, sterling box, #458 of 500 . . . . **195.00**
Candy Dish, cov, jasper, green **40.00**
Cup and Saucer, jasper, green **40.00**
Hair Receiver, cov, jasper, heart shape, medium blue, white angel dec **250.00**
Pendant, oval, black basalt, lion chasing horse, beaded silver frame and chain **75.00**
Pin Dish, terra cotta, 4", oval, cupids playing **30.00**
Plate
  6" d, children's story, 1971/1972, MIB **20.00**
  8" l, leaf, green, glazed, majolica **35.00**
  9" d, emb strawberry dec, majolica, late 19th C **75.00**
  9¼" d, Capture of Vincennes, Paul Revere Chapter No. 317, DAR, Muncie, IN, deep blue transfer **30.00**
  9¾" d, Bennington Battle Monument, blue **35.00**
  10" d, Naval Academy, rose **20.00**
  10½" d, Newark, NJ, 1929, light blue . . . **20.00**
  12½", Cipriani **60.00**
Salt, 2¼", Dragon Luster, orange dog's head in bowl, blue ext **135.00**
Tile, calendar, 1910, Mayflower approaching land, brown and white **65.00**

Vase, 5⅛", Hummingbird Luster, gold outlined birds, mottled blue luster ground, mottled flame luster int **200.00**

WELLER POTTERY

Weller's origins date back to 1872 when Samuel Weller opened a factory in Fultonham, near Zanesville, Ohio. Eventually, he built a new pottery in Zanesville along the tracks of the Cincinnati and Muskingum Railway. Louwelsa, Weller's art pottery line, was begun in 1894. Among the famous art pottery designers employed by Weller are Charles Babcock Upjohn, Jacques Sicard, Frederick Rhead, and Gazo Fudji.

Weller survived on production of utilitarian wares, but always managed some art pottery production until cheap Japanese imports captured its market immediately following World War II. Operations at Weller ceased in 1948.

Vase, Atlas, script mark, 7 1/16" h, $40.00.

Ashtray, Roma, 2½" **25.00**
Basket, Melrose, 10" **100.00**
Bottle, Eocean, 11½" **225.00**
Bowl
  Blue Drapery, 5½", clusters of roses, vertical folded blue matte ground **20.00**
  Malvern, 10", matching flower frog **55.00**
  Pierre, 8", seafoam **20.00**
Candlesticks, pr, Blue Drapery, 9", double gourd form, clusters of roses **85.00**
Cigarette Stand, Coppertone, frog **150.00**
Compote, Bonito, 4"h **55.00**
Cornucopia, Softone, 10", light blue . . . **20.00**
Creamer and Sugar, Pierre, seafoam **35.00**
Ewer, Floretta, 6" **45.00**
Figure
  Canaries, two on branch, textured Brighton base **160.00**

Frog, Coppertone, 2"	75.00
Hanging Basket, Cameo	30.00

Jardiniere
Blueware, 8½" × 7"	150.00
Marvo, rust, 7½"	55.00
Mug, Louwelsa, blue, cherries dec	200.00
Oil Lamp Base, Dickensware I	125.00

Pitcher, Zona, 8", kingfisher, half kiln ink
stamp mark	175.00

Planter
Camel, sitting	40.00
Elephant, 4", blue-green	85.00
Powder Box, cov, Ivoris	35.00
Teapot, green, gold trim	35.00
Tobacco Jar, Louwelsa, brass lid	175.00
Umbrella Stand, Ivory, 20"	165.00

Vase
Alvin, bud	30.00
Ardsley, blue	75.00
Aurelian, 4", jug, floral	200.00
Baldwin, 7"	25.00
Barcelona, 6", green and tan	75.00
Blossomtime, 6½", green, double bud	36.00
Bonito, 10", Naomi Walch sgd	175.00
Burntwood, 5"	40.00
Clarmont, 8"	100.00
Cloud Burst, two handled	125.00
Forest, 8"	75.00

Glendale
5", bird on nest	185.00
6½"	200.00

Hudson
9½", square	195.00
10½", blue dec, bud	195.00
La Sa, 7½", gold, red, green, trees	225.00
Louwelsa, 6", floral	100.00
Luster, 6½", bud, cloudburst purple and gray	40.00
Turkis	65.00
Warwick, 10"	80.00
Woodcraft, 6½", bud	30.00

Wall Pocket
Blue Drapery, 9", clusters of roses, blue ground	50.00
Glendale	255.00
Woodcraft, azalea	95.00

WHISKEY BOTTLES, COLLECTOR'S EDITIONS

The Jim Beam Distillery began the limited edition whiskey bottle craze when it issued its first novelty bottle for the 1953 Christmas market. By the 1960s the craze was full blown. It was dying by the mid-1970s and was buried somewhere around 1982 or 1983. Oversaturation by manufacturers and speculation by non-collectors killed the market.

Limited edition whiskey bottles collecting now rests in the hands of serious collectors. Their Bible is H. F. Montague's *Montague's Modern Bottle Identification and Price Guide* (published by author, 1980). The book used to be revised frequently. Now five years or more pass between editions. The market is so stable that few prices change from one year to the next.

Before you buy or sell a full limited edition whiskey bottle, check state laws. Most states require a license to sell liquor and impose substantial penalties if you sell without one.

Clubs: International Association of Jim Beam Bottle & Specialties Club, 5120 Belmont Road, Suite D, Downers Grove, IL 60515; Michter's National Collectors Society, P. O. Box 481, Schaefferstown, PA 17088.

Ezra Brooks, ram, 1972, $17.50.

Jim Beam

Beam Club and Convention
Convention, Tenth, Norfolk, 1980	40.00
Five Seasons Club, 1980	12.00
Monterey Bay Club, 1977	15.00

Beam on Wheels
Circus Wagon, 1979	35.00
Stutz Bearcat, yellow, 1977	40.00
Casino Series, Harolds Club, VIP, 1967	55.00
Centennial Series, Statue of Liberty, 1975	12.00
Foreign Countries, Germany, Pied Piper, 1974	8.00

Political Series, Elephant, boxer,
1964. . . . . 18.00
States Series, Idaho, 1963 . . . . 55.00
Trophy Series, Pretty Perch, 1980 . . . . . 20.00
Ezra Brooks
Animal Series, Lion, African, 1980 . . . . 50.00
Bird Series, Owl, Scops #4, 1980 . . . . . 55.00
Heritage China Series, Liberty Bell,
1969. . . . . 8.00
People Series
Betsy Ross, 1975 . . . . 18.00
Oliver Hardy, 1976 . . . . 18.00
Sports Series, Bulldog–Georgia,
1971. . . . . 18.00
Cyrus Noble
Animal Series, Bear & Cubs, 1st Edition,
1978. . . . . .115.00
Carousel Series, Pipe Organ, 1980. . . . . 45.00
Mine Series, Music Man, 1977 . . . . 40.00
Sea Animals, Dolphin, 1979 . . . . 45.00
Grenadier
Bicentennial Series, 1976, 10th, 13
types, each. 15.00
Civil War Series, General Robert E
Lee, ½ gal, 1977 . . . . .145.00
Fire Chief, 1973 . . . . 85.00
Hoffman
Band Series, miniature, Accordion
Player, 1987. . . . . 15.00
Cheerleaders, Dallas, 1979 . . . . 25.00
Mr Lucky Series, music, Carolier,
1979. . . . . 45.00
School Series, Mississippi Bulldogs with
music, 1977 . . . . 55.00
Luxardo
Calypso Girl, 1962. . . . . 15.00
Hippo, miniature. 15.00
Polar Bear, miniature 25.00
McCormick
Bicentennial Series, miniature, John
Paul Jones, 1976 . . . . 18.00
Football Mascot, Indiana Hoosiers,
1974. . . . . 18.00
Great American Series, Robert E Peary,
1977. . . . . 30.00
Sports Series, Muhammad Ali, 1980. . . 50.00
Old Commonwealth
Coal Miners, #3, with shovel, 1977 . . . 40.00
Lumberjack, Old Time, 1979. . . . . 20.00
Pacesetter
Corvette, green, 1975 . . . . 35.00
Vokovich, #2, 1974 . . . . 30.00
Ski Country
Circus Series, elephant on drum,
1973. . . . . 45.00
Customer Specialties, submarine, min-
iature, 1976 . . . . 30.00
Indian Series, Dancer, ceremonial buf-
falo, 1975. .125.00
Wildlife Series
Jaguar, miniature 34.00
Otter, 1979. 65.00
Wild Turkey
Mack Truck 15.00

Series #1, 5, With Flags, 1975. . . . . 40.00
Turkey Lore Series
2, 1980. . . . . 38.00
4, 1982. . . . . 50.00

WHISKEY-RELATED

Whiskey and whiskey-related items are
centuries old. Normally, the words conjure
up images of the Western saloon and dance
hall. Since the taste of similar whiskeys
varies little, manufacturers relied on advertising and promotions to create customer
loyalty.

*Tray, Full Dress Maryland Rye, black and
white, 1907, 12″ d, $100.00*

Advertising Trade Card, Old Kentucky
Distillery, monkeys shortening cat's tail,
whiskey box chopping block, 1898. . . . 20.00
Ashtray, Suntory Whiskey, stoneware . . . 12.00
Bar Display, figural, camel, Paul Jones
Whiskey, orig miniature bottle 40.00
Display Bottle, 25″, Old Overholt 60.00
Mirror, Duffy's Malt Whiskey, pocket
type 45.00
Pitcher, G W Seven Star Whiskey, alumi-
num. 5.00
Shot Glass
Bottoms Up, cobalt 8.50
Sign
Calvert Whiskey, tin, litho. 28.00
Green River Whiskey, cardboard,
framed, 18″ × 22″ 140.00
Token, Green River Whiskey 65.00
Tray
Bailey's Whiskey, tip. 60.00
Fulton Whiskey, silver plate 30.00
Green River Whiskey, black man and
horse 75.00

WICKER

Wicker or rattan furniture enjoyed its first American craze during the late Victorian era. It was found on porches and summer cottages across America. It enjoyed a second period of popularity in the 1920s and 30s and a third period in the 1950s. In truth, wicker has been available continuously since the 1870s.

Early wicker has a lighter, more airy feel that its later counterparts. Look for unusual forms, e.g., corner chairs or sewing stands. Most wicker was sold unpainted. However, it was common practice to paint it in order to preserve it, especially if it was going to be kept outside. Too many layers of paint decreases the value of a piece.

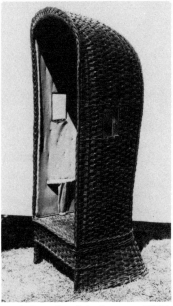

Porter's chair, painted dark green, 69¾" h, 28" deep, $550.00.

Book Case, 19½" × 14" × 42", fan back,
  turned finials, four shelves. **225.00**
Creel Basket, center lid hole, early
  1900. . . . . **55.00**
Lamp Stand, 16" d, 30½" h, scrolled supports, wood top, mid shelf **200.00**
Rocker, serpentine edges, braidwork,
  wood rockers, painted white, Wakefield
  Rattan Co. **225.00**
Side Chair, 39" h, shaped woven crest,
  vase shape splat, pressed seat. **170.00**
Smoking Stand, 28" h, brass tray. **60.00**
Stool, 13½" × 16½" × 12", painted
  white. **175.00**

Table, 20" × 27¼", round, repainted **150.00**
Towel Rack, 24" × 7" × 16", oval beveled
  mirror **80.00**

WILLOW WARE

The traditional willow pattern, developed by Josiah Spode in 1810, is the most universally recognized china pattern. A typical piece contains the following elements in its motif: willow tree, "apple" tree, two pagodas, fence, two birds, and three figures crossing a bridge.

Willow pattern china has been made in almost every country that produces ceramics. In the 1830s over 200 English companies offered Willow pattern china. Buffalo China was one of the first American companies to offer the pattern. Japanese production started about 1902, roughly the same date as Buffalo's first pieces.

Since the Willow pattern has been in continuous production, it is difficult to talk about reproductions. However, the Scio Pottery, Scio, Ohio, is currently producing an unmarked set that is being sold in variety stores. Because it lacks marks, some collectors have purchased it under the belief that it was made much earlier.

Newsletter: *American Willow Report*, P. O. Box 900, Oakridge, OR 97463.

Berry bowl, Allerton, 5¼" d, $10.00.

Bowl, 9¾" d, Ridgway **24.00**
Carafe, warmer base **140.00**
Cream Soup, Buffalo. **10.00**
Cup and Saucer, Allerton **25.00**
Demitasse Set, coffeepot, creamer, six
  cups and saucers, Occupied Japan **100.00**

Egg Cup, double	12.00
Miniature Lamp, blue, orig oil fittings	50.00
Mug, large	12.00
Pitcher, tall	80.00
Plate, 10" d, Johnson Bros	8.50
Platter	
Hexagon, large	75.00
Rectangle, 11" × 13½", Allerton, No. 7 mark	70.00
Table cloth, green, 54" × 72", unused	42.50
Teapot, Homer Laughlin	35.00
Vegetable Dish, cov, hexagon	95.00
Vegetable Dish, open, rectangular, 7⅛" × 9⅛", Allerton	45.00

WOOD

There is just something great about the grain, patina, and aging qualities of wood. This is a catch-all category for wooden objects that otherwise would not have appeared. The objects are utilitarian, yet classic for their type.

Bowl, 6", round	50.00
Butter Print, 3¾" d, swan, turned handle	125.00
Cheese Box, 15", round	30.00
Cookie Board, 4" × 7", carved urn of fruit	25.00
Dough Bowl, 9"	12.00
Food Mold, 3½" × 8½", cut turtle design, handle	50.00
Herb Drying Tray, wire nail construction	45.00
Lemon Squeezer	35.00
Potato Masher, leather strap	15.00
Pudding Stick, hewn handle, shaped blade	12.00
Raisin Seeder, plunger handle, wire grid, Everett	48.00
Rope Bed Tightener	25.00
Seed Box, 25" × 8", stave construction, int. divider	130.00
Towel Rack, 24½" × 32¼", pine, turned, worn finish	75.00

WORLD FAIRS

It says a lot about the status of world's fairs when Americans cannot stage a fair in 1993–1994 that is even one-quarter of the 1893 Columbian Exposition in Chicago. Was the last great world's fair held in New York in 1964? Judging from recent fairs, the answer is an unqualified yes.

Although it is important to stress three-dimensional objects for display purposes, do not overlook the wealth of paper that was given away to promote fairs and their participants.

Magazine: *World's Fair*, P. O. Box 339, Corte Madera, CA 94925.

Club: World's Fair Collectors' Society, Inc., P. O. Box 20806, Sarasota, FL 33583.

Stick Pin, Pan American, 1901, copper plated, $15.00.

1876, Philadelphia, Centennial Exposition

Cuff Links, 1⅛", tortoise shell, silver Art Gallery scene and title, pr	115.00
Liberty Bell, brass, wood handle, inscribed "Proclaim Liberty, 1776, 1876"	85.00
Watch Fob, hatchet shape	50.00

1893, Chicago, The Columbian Exposition

Atlas	30.00
Medal, white metal, bust portrait and inscriptions, 2" d	20.00
Paperweight, ferris wheel	90.00
Spoons, set of 6, orig box	125.00

1898, Omaha, Trans–Mississippi Exposition

Handkerchief, silk, tattered edge	10.00
Napkin Ring, engraved	10.00

1901, Buffalo, Pan–Am Expo

Letter Opener, brass, figural, buffalo	35.00
Pin, mechanical, bright brass, 1½" w hanger bar, 1½" brass mechanical skillet	50.00
Pinback Button, 1¼" d, "Official Button," multicolored, continental ladies shaking hands	20.00

1904, St Louis, Louisiana Purchase Exposition

Cup, Palace of Manufacturers decal, Germany	25.00

Egg, tin. **65.00**
Inkwell, porcelain **45.00**
Key Chain, 1¼" emb aluminum, Festival
  Hall and Cascades, blank back **12.00**
1915, San Francisco, Panama–Pacific International Exposition
Coin Purse, suede, silvered brass closure, 2½" × 3½" **25.00**
Souvenir Book. **30.00**
1933–34, Chicago, Century of Progress
Booklet, Alton RR **8.00**
Bottle, 6½" **20.00**
Butter Knife, sterling, 7" **15.00**
Compact **35.00**
Contest Ticket, A & P **10.00**
Needle Case **12.00**
Pinback Button, "I'm From New York–Visitor–A Century of Progress" **25.00**
Poker Chip. **15.00**
Postcard. **15.00**
1939, New York, New York World's Fair
Booklet, Tony Sarg, 15 pgs, maps **22.00**
Plate, Homer Laughlin China **65.00**
Playing Cards, one regular deck, one trick deck **35.00**
Salt and Pepper Shaker, pr, orig box . . . **45.00**
1962, Seattle, Century 21 Exposition
Cigarette Lighter, 9¼" h, chromed metal, tower shape, "Seattle USA Space Needle," unused **55.00**
Tumbler, glass, gold trim, Space Needle, set of 4 . . . . **20.00**
View Master Reels, various outdoor scenes, set of 5 . . . . **15.00**
1964, New York, New York World's Fair
Key Chain, license plate shape **10.00**
Milk Bottle Cap **5.00**
Nodder, 3½" d, Unisphere, dark blue composition base, 1961 copyright. . . **25.00**
Tray, 8" × 11", litho tin, Unisphere and Avenue of Flags, gold inscription. . . . **15.00**

WORLD WARS

World War I soldiers are a dying breed, and World War II veterans are not far behind. Although some World War I and World War II material was included in the militaria category, so much is available that a separate category is also warranted.

Magazine: *Military Collectors News*, P. O. Box 702073, Tulsa, OK 74170.

Clubs: American Society of Military Insignia Collectors, 1331 Bradley Avenue, Hummelstown, PA 17036; Association of American Military Uniform Collectors, 446 Berkshire Road, Elyria, OH 44035.

World War II, Recognition Pictorial Manual, *Bureau of Aeronautics, Navy Dept, Washington DC, June 1943, 80 pgs, black and white, $25.00.*

WORLD WAR I

Badge, Tank Corps, British cap, 8th Churka. **15.00**
Bayonet, 20½" l, sawtooth, German **65.00**
Belt, web **8.00**
Canteen, Army **10.00**
Cigarette Lighter, trench, German **30.00**
Flip Book, 2" × 2½" × ¼", soldier, sailor, and Uncle Sam presenting the colors, pledge of Allegiance, Liberty Bond promotion, 1917 copyright. **25.00**
Handkerchief, 11" sq, "Remember Me," soldier and girl in center, red, white, and blue edge **12.00**
Helmet, US, 3rd Army insignia **45.00**
Key chain, Victory Liberty Loan Award, 1¼", silvered brass, eagle and US Treasury Building on front, "Made from Captured German Cannon" and Treasury Dept message on reverse **20.00**
Leggings, motorcycle, leather **30.00**
Pillow Cover, 16" × 17½", full color printed soldier portrait surrounded by flags and American eagle, gold lettering "Forget Me Not," full color Miss Liberty holding stone tablet reads "World War Service". **35.00**
Pinback Button
  7/8", "I Care," black and white photo, soldier, red, white, and blue ground **20.00**
  1", multicolored, farmer behind horse–drawn plow, flag, field marked "Food Crops," balloon caption "For America and Liberty!", "Nail a Flag to Your Plow/Work For Your Country As You'd Fight For Her" rim inscription. **80.00**
  1¼", Liberty Bonds, celluloid, blue lettering, red, white, and blue flag, white ground, issued by Federal Reserve Bank District #10, c1917–1918 . . . . **22.50**

1½", black and white photo, cannon and operation base illus **18.00**

Pocket Mirror, 2¾", oval, "Leaders of the World War For Democracy," world leaders and flags **25.00**

Poster
"I Am Telling You," red, white, and blue, Uncle Sam with hands on hips illus, black lettering, James Montgomery Flagg **30.00**
"US Marines/First To Fight in France For Freedom," 30 × 40", multicolored, marines charging **125.00**

Ribbon, 2" × 5", "Welcome Home 26th Division" **12.00**

Stickpin, porcelain, wounded German soldier, 1914–1918 . . . . **25.00**

Toy, machine gun, wood and tin, magazine on top holds wood bullets, turn crank to fire **50.00**

Watch Fob, flag on pole, USA, beaded, blue **20.00**

WORLD WAR II

Activity Book, 10½" × 13", cut and stick, Merrill Publishing, #4835, 1942 . . . . . . **25.00**

Badge, Infantry, German **25.00**

Beanie, felt, multicolored, "Remember Pearl Harbor–Keep Em Flying" **22.00**

Bookend, figural, Churchill, 7½" h, molded plaster, tan color, glossy, wood dowel cigar stub **45.00**

Doll, Pat Parachute/The Para–Trooper, 6½" h, felt, stuffed, painted wooden head, gray felt cap, paper goggles, blue felt parachute pack, khaki parachute, orig tag and box, c1942 . . . . **90.00**

Gas Mask, Japanese, head straps, attached canister **40.00**

Helmet, MI, olive drab sand finish, olive drab chin strap, orig liner, thin mesh helmet net **120.00**

Key chain, 1¼", brass, emb, USS Missouri surrender treaty souvenir, battleship depicted one side, text other side, Sept 2, 1945 . . . . **12.50**

Lamp, 5¼" h, plaster, figural, ivory color lamppost, 3 ½" h soldier in brown coat and garrison cap, uses nightlight bulb **35.00**

Letter Opener, brass, rifle diecut, "Compliments of Dreifus & Co" **25.00**

Magazine, *Sea Power*, 1945 . . . . **6.50**

Map, silk, AAF rayon escape map, Holland, Belgium, France, and Germany, 1944, orig carrying case, mint **35.00**

Matchbook Holder, 1" × 1½" × 2¼", celluloid, black and white photo portraits of Roosevelt, Churchill, and Stalin on blue, red, and gold ground, flags on reverse, inscribed "Defeating the Greatest Tyrant in History," c1945 . . . . **60.00**

Medal
European African Middle Eastern Campaign, 1¼", brass, emb, beachhead soldiers, ship prow in background on one side, eagle, "United States of America" and "1941–1945" other side, brass loop at top **20.00**
Good Conduct, 1¼", brass, eagle standing on sword, book, "Efficiency/Honor/Fidelity" rim inscription one side, '" For Good Conduct" on other, ' red and white fabric ribbon, c1940s **18.00**

Model Kit, Silhouette, #CM–111, cardboard sheets, black, punch out, issued Feb 22, 1943, unused, orig envelope . . . **55.00**

Newsletter, Pacific War Theatre, Vol 1, #11, "Hive Harold,' 8¼" × 10½", six pgs, black and white photos of members of 16th Naval Construction Battalion, cov photo of Roosevelt, MacArthur and Nimitz, Sept 1, 1944 . . . . **35.00**

Paint Set, American Rangers, ½" × 4½" × 6", cardboard, litho, beachhead scene on lid, orig paint brush and watercolor paint tablets, American Crayon Co, 1942 copyright **22.50**

Paperweight, 2½" × 4" × 3", wood, syroco, three military men riding in jeep scene **24.00**

Patch, Pilot's Wings, leather, AAF, emb, standard design, flying jacket attachment type **25.00**

Pencil Holder, 3½", plastic, red, white, and blue, "Victory," back lumber yard adv **10.00**

Pin
Sweetheart, 2½" × 2½", cedar wood, varnished, heart shape, decal, eagle on letter "V", inscribed "My Heart is in the Army" **15.00**
Sword through Swastika, Nazi **15.00**
Victory, 2¼" × 2¼", diecut, silvered brass, "V" shape, amber, blue, pink, and green rhinestones **25.00**

Pinback Button
7/8", celluloid, "Remember Pearl Harbor," "Pearl" in red lettering, rest in blue **30.00**
1½", "Moo Club US Defender," two children firing milk bottle cannon, black, red, white, and blue, mid 1940s **25.00**
2½", "Jap Hunting License," red lettering, blue rim **60.00**

Plaque, 6" d, litho paper portrait of General MacArthur, cardboard backing, clear plastic dome, early 1940s **60.00**

Playing Cards, full deck, Joker depicts Hitler being bombed, aces depict Statue of Liberty, Eiffel Tower, House of Parliament, and Kremlin Building, face cards are Roosevelt, Churchill, DeGaulle, Stalin, and multinational allied soldiers, made in Belgium, orig box. **85.00**

Postcard, Boeing Flying Fortress, one of series of 10, details about plane on back. **5.00**

Poster

"Give War Bonds for Christmas," 22" × 28", paper, red, green, and white, #0–555428, dated 1943. . . . . **35.00**

"United Nations Fight For Freedom," 28½" × 40", paper, black, white, and gray Statue of Liberty, full color flags of 30 Allied Nations, #0–498304, dated 1942. **20.00**

Puzzle

Hand Held, "Trap a Sap," 1" × 3½" × 4½", blue tin case, clear glass cov over brown and sepia battle scene illus, trap three magnetic plastic pellets in plastic cage. **30.00**

Jigsaw, "Fighters for Victory," 14" × 22", 300 pc, troops storming beach head, fighter planes, full color illus, Jaymar, orig box, mid–1940s. **20.00**

Ration Book Holder, books 1–4, 4¾ × 6½", cardboard, brown, pocket, c1943. . . . . **25.00**

Shovel, fox hole type. **8.00**

Stamp Album, 5 × 7¼", soft cov, nine pgs, two battle scene stamps each pg, illus of maps, medals, and decorations, General Mills premium, 1945. . . . . **45.00**

Stickpin, artillery shell, Nazi. **10.00**

Toy

Airplane, Hubley, P–40, diecast, 8¼" wing span, 7¾" l body, yellow wings, orange balance and propeller, rubber wheels. **35.00**

Tank, 1½" × 2½" × 1¼" h, litho tin, replica, "General Patton" in red lettering each side, friction wheels, camouflage pattern, whirring sound, made in Japan, late 1940s–early 1950s. **40.00**

Victory Garden Packet, child's, 12 pg illus sales catalog, sample packet of radish seeds, 16" × 18" red, green, and white poster, 6¼" × 9" orig mailing folder, mid–1940s. **18.00**

Weapon, Cattaraugus 225Q Fighting Knife, mint condition blade, dark leather grips, leather scabbard. **125.00**

Window Banner, "Welcome Home," 8" × 12", red, white, and blue, cloth brown eagle, gold fringe. **7.00**

Whistle, ¾" × ¾" × 2", plastic, ivory color, "V" symbol one side, "Made In Alert USA" other side. **10.00**

WRISTWATCHES

The pocket watch generations have been replaced by the wrist watch generations. This category became hot in the late 1980s and still is going strong. There is a great deal of speculation occurring, especially in the area of character and personality watches.

Since the category is relatively new as a collectible, no one is certain exactly how many watches have survived. Dad has almost a dozen that were handed down from his parents. If he is typical, the potential market supply is far greater than anyone realizes. Be care before paying big prices. Many wrist watches are going to be sold five years from now at far less than their 1991 price.

Club: National Association of Watch & Clock Collectors, P. O. Box 33, Columbia, PA 17512.

Gruen, tank, 14K yg fill, 17 j, $45.00.

Character and Personality

Autry, Gene. **125.00**

Cassidy, Hopalong. **150.00**

Donald Duck, rect face, c1940. . . . . **100.00**

Evans, Dale, with Buttermilk, orig straps, c1950. . . . . **50.00**

Goldberg, Whoopi. **50.00**

Lone Ranger, metal case, orig tan leather straps, c1940. . . . . **150.00**

Nixon, Richard. **75.00**

Ruth, Babe. **175.00**

Lady's

Girod, 14K yg case. **150.00**

Longines, 14K yg case, orig box. **250.00**

Nicolet, 17j, flexible band, cabochon crystal, small diamond on each side of square face **95.00**

Man's

Baylor, 14K yg, fancy rect cast, small diamond set in dial **200.00**

Hamilton, 17j, gold filled case, stem wind, leather band, orig box **150.00**

Jergensen, Jules, quartz, day and date, leather band **150.00**

YELLOW WARE

Yellow ware is a heavy utilitarian earthenware that shades in color from a rich pumpkin to lighter shades that are more tan than yellow. Some pieces contain white or blue strip decoration. Most forms were designed for use in the kitchen.

English manufacturers also made yellow ware. Many of these pieces have worked their way into the American market as a result of the container shipments of the 1970s and 1980s. American collectors prefer American made pieces. When you find an unknown form, think English. Better to pay a little and be pleasantly surprised that it is American than the other way around.

Bowl, 10¾" d, blue band, incised dec, $35.00.

Baking Dish, 8" × 10", 2½" h, rect, c1880 . . . . **60.00**

Batter Bowl, 10" d, 6" h, spout, emb floral dec, c1890 . . . . **65.00**

Bedpan, 19" l, 12" w, 6" deep, oval body, three incised rings on curved tubular spout, large oval opening, c1890 . . . . . . **35.00**

Bowl

9" d, brown bands **35.00**

14" d, green sponge design **95.00**

Cake Mold

4" h, 10" d, round, center cone, spiraling fluted channels, c1880 . . . . **70.00**

5" h, oval, tapered sides, emb ear of corn design inside base, c1900 . . . . **65.00**

Chamber Pot, 10" d, 6" h, cup shape, rounded sides, flared rim, applied ear shape handle, rimmed base, brown and white bands, 1890–1900 . . . . **85.00**

Custard Cup

3" d, 3" h, round, three cobalt blue bands, c1900 . . . . **6.00**

3" d, 3" h, octagonal, tapered, raised floral pattern, c1900 . . . . **12.00**

4" d, 2½" h, round, white interior, rolled rim, rimmed base, c1900 . . . . **5.00**

Colander

11" d, 4" h, rolled rim, two holes in side, holes in lower body and bottom, c1900 . . . . **180.00**

13" d, 6" h, collar, two holes in side, groups of seven holes around base and in bottom, rimmed base, white and blue bands, c1900 . . . . **230.00**

Crock

6" d, 10" h, one black and six white bands, two handles, c1900 . . . . **125.00**

8" d, 6" h, cov, white band surrounded by brown stripes, c1910 . . . . **85.00**

Deep Dish, 12" d, 4" h, c1890 . . . . **35.00**

Humidor, c1900 . . . . **135.00**

Milk Pan, 7" × 10", rect, c1870s **75.00**

Mixing Bowl, 10" d, 6" h, collar, cobalt blue bands, c1900 . . . . **55.00**

Mug

4" d, 3¼" h, rolled rim, emb ring above flared base, applied ear shape handle, black and white bands, c1900 . . . . . . **65.00**

4¾" h, blue bands **60.00**

Pie Plate, 12" d, c1880 . . . . **40.00**

Pipkin, 6" d, 7" h, bulbous, rounded shoulder, wide neck, flared collar, pinched spout, hollow, tubular handle, flat lid with knob handle, c1870 . . . . **175.00**

Pitcher

6" d, 8" h, bulbous body, short spout, ear shape handle, c1890 . . . . **55.00**

8½", white bands **75.00**

Preserve Jar, 5" d, 8" h, incised ring on rounded shoulder, flared rim, c1870 . . . **120.00**

Salt Box, 6¾" h, three white bands, "Salt" in black lettering **160.00**

Serving Bowl, 10" l, 3" h, oval, flared lip, c1890 . . . . **60.00**

Soap Dish, rect, c1890s **125.00**

Spittoon, 8" d, 4" h, octagonal, concave sides, squared rim and base, triangular drainage hole, recessed bottom, c1870 . . . . **75.00**

Sugar Bowl, 7" d, 4½" h, collar, white and brown bands, button knob in lid, c1890 . . . . **55.00**

ZOO COLLECTIBLES

Dad has been trying for years to find a "Z" category to end *Warman's Americana & Collectibles*. His trouble is he spent too much of his childhood at the circus and not enough at the zoo. It's tough to beat the old man. Gotcha Pop!

Ashtray, glass, decal center, Denver Zoo............................ **4.50**

Button, pinback
  Audubon Society, multicolored, red cardinal perched on dogwood branch, light green ground, c1920–30 .... **12.50**

Fink's Anti–Pain Humane Club, sepia photo portrait, white ground, light green rim, white lettering, early 1900s, $1\frac{1}{2}$"d.................... **30.00**

Junior Naturalist, black and white photo of Uncle John, early 1900s, $\frac{7}{8}$" **10.00**

Medal, Philadelphia Zoo, c1960, silver finish **10.00**

Pennant, San Francisco Zoo **5.00**

Popcorn Box, Cretors Westview Park, illus of kids eating popcorn, animals in background, 1929, never used **45.00**

Sign, City Zoo, white and yellow, door hanger type, Do Not Disturb on back... **1.00**

Flea Marketeer's Annotated Reference Library

YOU CANNOT TELL THE PLAYERS WITHOUT A SCORECARD

A typical flea market contains hundreds of thousands of objects. You cannot be expected to identify and know the correct price for everything off the top of your head. You need a good, basic reference library.

As a flea marketeer, there are two questions about every object that you want to know: What is it? and How much is it worth? A book that answers only the first question has little use in the field. The books relating to objects on the following list contain both types of information.

The basic reference library consists of fifty titles. I admit the number is arbitrary. However, some limit was necessary. Acquiring all the titles on the list will not be cheap. Expect to pay somewhere between $1,000.00 and $1,250.00.

The list contains a few books that are out of print. You will have to pursue their purchase through "used" book sources. Many antiques and collectibles book dealers conduct book searches and maintain want lists. It is not uncommon to find one or more of these specialized dealers set up at a flea market. Most advertise in the trade papers, especially *The Antique Trader Weekly*, P.O. Box 1050, Dubuque, Iowa 52001. One dealer that I have found particularly helpful in locating out-of-print books is Joslin Hall Rare Books, P.O. Box 516, Concord, MA 01742.

Many reference books are revised every year or every other year. The editions listed are those as of fall 1991. When you buy them, make certain that you get the most recent edition.

One final factor that I used in preparing this list was a desire to introduce you to the major publishers and imprints in the antiques and collectibles field. It is important that you become familiar with Antique Publications, Books Americana, Collector Books, Greenberg Publishing, House of Collectibles, Schiffer Publishing, Wallace-Homestead, and Warman.

GENERAL PRICE GUIDES

Husfloen, Kyle, ed. *The Antique Trader Antiques and Collectibles Price Guide*, 7th ed. Babka Publishing Co., 1991.

There are over a dozen general price guides to antiques and collectibles. Of course, I think my

Dad's are the best. However, when I want a second opinion or cannot find a specific item in Dad's guides, I use the *Trader*'s guide. The descriptions are great and prices are accurate. Most importantly, it is a price guide that focuses on the heartland of America.

Rinker, Harry L., ed. *Warman's Americana & Collectibles*, 5th ed. Radnor, PA: Wallace-Homestead Book Company, 1991.

It contains the stuff with which your parents, you, and your children grew up and played. More than any other modern price guide it is a record of what is found in the attics, closets, basements, garages, and sheds of America. It will make you regret everything you ever threw out. It has gone ten years without a rival, which says a great deal about the Warman format that Dad developed for it.

Rinker, Harry L., ed. *Warman's Antiques and Their Prices*, 25th ed. Radnor, PA: Wallace-Homestead Book Company, 1991.

This book is more than just a list of objects with prices. It is a user's guide. The introduction to each category contains a brief history, list of reference books, names and addresses of periodicals and collectors' clubs, museums to visit, and information on reproductions. It is the first place to start whenever you need information.

IDENTIFICATION OF REPRODUCTIONS AND FAKES

Hammond, Dorothy. *Confusing Collectibles: A Guide to the Identification of Contemporary Objects*, rev. ed. Radnor, PA: Wallace-Homestead Book Company, 1979. Out of print.

This book provides information about reproductions, copycats, fantasy items, contemporary crafts, and fakes from the late 1950s through the 1960s. Much of this material appears in today's flea markets. Some is collectible in its own right. The best defense against being taken is to know what was produced.

Hammond, Dorothy. *More Confusing Collectibles*, vol. II. Wichita, KA: C. B. P. Publishing Company, 1972. Out-of-print.

Confusing Collectibles took a broad approach to the market. *More Confusing Collectibles* focuses primarily on glass. It contains all new information, so you really do need both volumes.

Lee, Ruth Webb. *Antiques Fakes & Reproductions, Enlarged and Revised*. Published by author: 1938, 1950. Out of print. Note: This book went through seven editions. The later editions contain more information. A good rule is to buy only the 4th through the 7th edition.

Dorothy Hammond followed in Ruth Webb Lee's footsteps. Webb's book chronicles the reproductions, copycats, fantasy items, and fakes manufactured between 1920 and 1950. While heavily oriented toward glass, it contains an excellent chapter on metals, discussing and picturing in detail the products of Virginia Metalcrafters.

BOOKS ABOUT OBJECTS

American Manufactured Furniture [actually *Furniture Dealers' Reference Book, 1928–1929, Zone 3*]. West Chester, PA: Schiffer Publishing, 1988.

This reprint covers a wide range of furniture manufacturers whose advertisements often contain important company history. A wide range of styles and forms are illustrated. All illustrations are priced. Ten years ago the furniture pictured was found in second-hand furniture stores or given to the Salvation Army. Now it is in antiques shops.

Andacht, Sandra. *Oriental Antiques & Art: An Identification and Value Guide*. Radnor, PA: Wallace-Homestead, 1987.

This is the best book currently available on Orientalia. It tends to be high-end and does not explain how to distinguish period pieces from later reproductions and copycats, a major problem when dealing with Orientalia. In 1992 a new guide to Orientalia will be published as part of the Warman Encyclopedia of Antiques and Collectibles series. Andacht is well worth owning in the interim.

Barlow, Ronald S. *The Antique Tool Collector's Guide to Value*. Windmill Publishing Company, 1985, revised 1989.

This is *the* book for tools. Barlow has compiled auction and market prices from across the United States. Since this book is organized by tool type, you need to identify the type of tool

that you have before you can look it up. There are plenty of illustrations to help.

Bunis, Marty & Sue. *Collector's Guide to Antique Radios*. Paducah, KY: Collector Books, 1991.

There are a wealth of radio books in the market place. This one is tuned in across a wide band of radios. Organization is by manufacturer and model number. Although heavily illustrated, the book does not picture a majority of the models listed. The book also covers radio parts and accessories.

Carnevale, Diane. *Collectibles Market Guide & Price Index to Limited Edition Plates, Figurines, Bells, Graphics, Steins, and Dolls*, 9th ed. Collectors' Information Bureau, 1991.

The best thing about this book is that it covers a wide range of limited edition types, from bells to steins. It serves as a collector's checklist. The worst thing is that it is industry-driven. Important negatives and warning about the limited edition market are missing. Field-test the prices before paying them.

Cunningham, Jo. *The Collector's Encyclopedia of American Dinnerware*. Paducah, KY: Collector Books, 1982, price update.

This is a profusely illustrated guide to identifying twentieth century American dinnerware. In spite of the fact that many new companies and patterns have been discovered since Cunningham prepared her book, it remains a valuable identification tool, especially since its pricing is updated periodically.

Docks, L. R. *American Premium Record Guide: Identification and Value Guide to 1915–1965 78s, 45s, and LPs*, 3rd ed. Florence, AL: Books Americana, 1986.

Although its prices are badly in need of a revision, it is an excellent testament to the variety of record collecting interest in the market place. Although a number of new specialized guides, e.g., Neal Umphred's *Goldmine's Price Guide to Collectible Record Albums* (Krause Publications, 1989), have appeared within the past three years, Docks remains the best general record price guide in the market.

Duke, Harvey. *The Official Identification and Price Guide to Pottery & Porcelain*, 7th ed. Orlando, FL: House of Collectibles, 1989.

This is the perfect companion to Cunningham. Duke covers many of the companies and lines of which Cunningham was unaware when she first published her book in the early 1980s. Illustrations are minimal, making it necessary to know the name of your pattern before looking anything up. The book is well-balanced regionally. Many West Coast pottery manufacturers finally receive their due.

Dolan, Maryanne. *Vintage Clothing: 1880 to 1960: Identification and Value Guide,* 2nd ed. Florence, AL: Books Americana, 1987.

This book has been selected because it is the only clothing book to go into a second edition. The vintage clothing market outside the major metropolitan area has stabilized. Because the range of surviving examples is so large, this book is merely window dressing. It is the best of a mediocre lot.

Editors of Collector Books. *The Old Book Value Guide,* 2nd ed. Paducah, KY: Collector Books, 1990.

There are always piles of old books at any flea market. Most are valued in the twenty-five to fifty cent ranges. However, there are almost always sleepers in every pile. This book is a beginning. If you think that you have an expensive tome, check it out in the most recent editions of *American Book Prices Current,* published by Bancroft-Parkman.

Editors of Krause Publications, Sports. *Baseball Card Price Guide,* 4th ed. Iola, WI: Krause Publications, 1990.

This is the new kid on the block that has become a superstar. It is more comprehensive and accurate than its competition. James Beckett's *Sports Americana Baseball Card Price Guide,* published by Edgewater Books, has been relegated to a bench warmer.

Florence, Gene. *The Collector's Encyclopedia of Depression Glass,* 10th ed. Paducah, KY: Collector Books, 1991.

This is the Depression Glass collectors' bible. Among its important features are a full listing of pieces found in each pattern and an extensive section on reproductions, copycats, and fakes. One difficulty is that there are hundreds of glass patterns manufactured between 1920 and 1940 that are not found in this book because they do not have the Depression Glass label. Supplement the book with Gene Florence's *Kitchen Glassware of the Depression Years,* also published by Collector Books.

Foulke, Jan. *10th Blue Book Dolls & Values.* Cumberland, MD: Hobby House Press, Inc., 1991.

Foulke is the first place doll collectors turn for information. The book is high-end, turning its back on many of the post-World War II and contemporary dolls. Within the doll field, it sets prices more than it reports them. Cross-check Foulke's prices in Julie Collier's *The Official Identification and Price Guide to Antique*

& *Modern Dolls, Fourth Edition* (House of Collectibles, 1989) and R. Lane Herron's *Herron's Price Guide to Dolls* (Wallace-Homestead, 1990).

Franklin, Linda Campbell. *300 Years of Kitchen Collectibles, Third Edition.* Florence, AL: Books Americana, 1991.

The second edition of this book was well organized, had a readable format, and was easy to use. The recently released third edition provides ample proof that bigger is not necessarily better. The new format is incredibly awkward. The wealth of secondary material may be great for the researcher and specialized collector, but it is a pain to wade through for the generalist. Franklin joins the Coca-Cola Company as someone who failed to recognize that they had created a classic. For now this is better than nothing, but it is a real opportunity for a challenger.

Gibbs, P. J. *Black Collectibles Sold in America.* Paducah, KY: Collector Books, 1987.

Black collectibles have gone through a number of collecting cycles in the past fifteen years. Popular among both white and black collectors, black memorabilia is likely to cycle several more times in the years ahead. Because of this, prices in any black collectibles book have to be taken with a grain of salt.

Hagan, Tere. *Silverplated Flatware,* revised 4th ed. Paducah, KY: Collector Books, 1990.

You do not see a great deal of sterling silver at flea markets because most dealers sell it for weight. Silver-plated items are in abundance. This book concentrates only on flatware, the most commonly found form. You can find information on silver-plated holloware in Jeri Schwartz's *The Official Identification and Price Guide to Silver and Silverplate, Sixth Edition* (House of Collectibles, 1989).

Hake, Ted. *Hake's Guide to TV Collectibles: An Illustrated Price Guide.* Radnor, PA: Wallace-Homestead, 1990.

TV collectibles are hot. They are part of that sizzling topic—Post-World War II collectibles. The book, organized by show, utilizes a priced picture format and includes material that Hake sold in Hake's Americana Mail Auction during the past several years. The short history provided for each show is helpful in dating objects.

Hake, Ted. *The Encyclopedia of Political Buttons.* 1896–1972 (1974, 1985); Book II, 1920–1976 (1977); Book III, 1789–1916 (1978); 1991 Revised Prices (1990). York, PA: Hake's Americana & Collectibles Press.

Do not be confused by the title. These volumes are price guides to all forms of political memorabilia, not just political buttons. Hake is one of the pioneers in the field of political memorabilia. Over the past twenty-five years, he has owned and sold almost every major political item available in the market.

Heacock, William. *The Encyclopedia of Victorian Colored Pattern Glass.* 9 volumes. **Antique Publications.**

One of the major gaps in the antiques and collectibles literature is a general price guide for glass. On the surface, the subject appears overwhelming. Heacock's nine-volume set covers glass manufactured from the mid-19th through the early 20th century. Actually, some volumes extended deep into the twentieth century. Book I on toothpicks, Book II on opalescent glass, and Book 9 on cranberry opalescent are among the most helpful.

Kaplan, Arthur Guy. *The Official Identification and Price Guide to Antique Jewelry,* 6th ed. **Orlando, FL: House of Collectibles, 1990.**

Kaplan's antique jewelry is an excellent introduction into the world of antique and estate jewelry. Of all the objects sold at flea markets, more identification and pricing mistakes are made in the jewelry area than anywhere else. The easiest way to identify the junk is to learn to identify the good stuff.

Klug, Ray. *Antique Advertising Encyclopedia.* **Volume 1 (1978) and volume 2 (1985). West Chester, PA: Schiffer Publishing.**

Klug is a classic. It is organized by advertising type and follows a priced picture format. It is by no means as encyclopedic as its title suggests. However, it serves as a checklist for many collectors and dealers. Originally published by L-W Book Sales, it was taken over by Schiffer several years ago. Make certain that you get the most up-to-date price list.

Kovel, Ralph and Terry. *The Kovel's Bottle Price List,* 8th ed. **New York: Crown Publishers, Inc., 1987.**

This is another category where the best of the mundane wins the prize. The book is organized by bottle type and within each type alphabetically by manufacturer. The quality of pricing is spotty. Totally missing are bottles in the ten cent to $4.00 range. This is precisely the range of most bottles found at flea markets. Jim Megura, bottle consultant at Skinner, is taking over authorship of the House of Collectibles bottle guide. Do not look for low-end bottles to appear in this book either.

Mallerich, Dallas J., III. *Greenberg's American Toy Trains: From 1900 with Current Values.*

Sykesville, MD: Greenberg Publishing, 1990.

When it comes to toy trains, the name to know is Greenberg Publishing, 7566 Main Street, Sykesville, MD 21784. Write for the company's mail order catalog. In addition to their own publications, they also distribute books in the toy train, toy, and military areas from other publishers. Mallerich's book provides an overview that will satisfy most general collectors.

McNulty, Lyndi Stewart. *Wallace-Homestead Price Guide to Plastic Collectibles.* **Radnor, PA: Wallace-Homestead Book Company, 1987.**

The problem with things made of plastic is that they tend to be collected within specialized categories, e.g., kitchen collectibles, advertising, etc. Plastic as a category has never really caught on. McNulty's book shows the potential. Opportunity awaits.

O'Brien, Richard. *Collecting Toys: A Collectors Identification and Value Guide,* 5th ed. **Florence, AL: Books Americana, 1990.**

The reason that there are no specialized toy or game books on this list is that you will have no need for them if you own a copy of O'Brien. The book dominates the field. It is not without its weaknesses, especially in the area of post-World War II toys. However, each edition brings improvement. O'Brien has enlisted the help of specialists to price many of the sections, an approach that greatly strengthens the presentation.

Overstreet, Robert M. *The Official Overstreet Comic Book Price Guide, No. 21.* **Orlando, FL: House of Collectibles, 1991.**

Overstreet has dominated the comic book guide market for so long that he has become a legend. On the surface, the guide appears encyclopedic. However, missing are many ground level and underground comics, Pacific rim and other foreign titles, and fanzines. The book is heavily weighted toward golden age comics, an area that is becoming very expensive and outside the "nostalgia" level of many modern collectors.

Reno, Dawn E. *The Official Identification and Price Guide to American Country Collectibles.* **Orlando, FL: House of Collectibles, 1990.**

It was a close call between Reno and Don & Carol Raycraft's *Wallace-Homestead Price Guide to American Country Antiques,* 11th ed. (Wallace-Homestead, 1991), the book that currently dominates the market in this area. Reno won because she presents a wealth of textual information about collecting areas, totally missing from the Raycrafts, and because she uses price listings, rather than priced pictures, which increases the number of her listings manifold. It is time the Raycrafts had some competition.

Schiffer, Nancy N. *Costume Jewelry: The Fun of Collecting.* **West Chester, PA: Schiffer Publishing Ltd., 1988.**

Costume jewelry dominates flea market offerings. The amount of material is so large that it is virtually impossible for one book to do justice to the subject. Nancy Schiffer's book comes the closest. It uses a picture format, something that is essential since word descriptions for jewelry tend to be terribly imprecise.

Shugart, Cooksey, and Tom Engle. *The Official Price Guide to Watches,* **11th ed. Paducah, KY: Collector Books, 1991.**

Although this book has been published by three different publishers during the past five years, it has never failed to maintain its high quality. It is the best book available on pocket and wrist watches.

Swedberg, Robert W. and Harriett. *Victorian Furniture: Styles and Prices.* **3 volumes: Book I (1976, 1984), Book II (1983), and Book III (1985). Radnor, PA: Wallace-Homestead.**

The Swedbergs write about furniture. Wallace-Homestead published their series on Oak, Pine, Victorian, and Wicker. Collector Books has published their *Collector's Encyclopedia of American Furniture, Volume I—Hardwoods* (1990) and *Furniture of the Depression Era: Furniture & Accessories of the 1920's, 1930's, and 1940's* (1987). All books utilize a priced picture approach. Text information, including descriptions for individual pieces, is minimal. Sources are heavily Midwest. The plus factor is that the books feature pieces for sale in the field, not museum examples.

Tumbusch, T. N. *Space Adventure Collectibles.* **Radnor, PA: Wallace-Homestead, 1990.**

The TV and toy markets are becoming increasingly sophisticated, *Space Adventure Collectibles* is typical of the wide range of specialized books on toy types, e.g., action figures, individual cartoon characters, e.g., Dick Tracy, and manufacturers, e.g., Tootsietoy, that are entering the market. It also demonstrates a problem found in many of these books—the use of broad price ranges for individual objects that often verge on the meaningless.

White, Sue. *Psychedelic Collectibles of the 1960s and 1970s: An Illustrated Price Guide.* **Radnor, PA: Wallace-Homestead, 1990.**

Want to be on the cutting edge of future collecting? Forget the 1950s and start acquiring things from the 1960s and 1970s. Today's junk is tomorrow's collectibles. Tomorrow's collectibles are the antiques of the future. I am not certain this statement is going to help you sleep any better tonight.

GENERAL SOURCES

Editors of House of Collectibles. *The Official Directory to U.S. Flea Markets,* **2nd ed. Orlando, FL: House of Collectibles, 1988.**

My opinion of this book is clearly stated earlier. Nothing has changed in my mind since I wrote that section.

Hyman, H. A. *I'll Buy That!* **Treasure Hunt Publications, 1989.**

Tony Hyman is one of the most magnetic radio personalities that I have ever heard. He writes and compiles. Most importantly, he hustles what he has done. This is a list of people who buy things. One good contact pays for the cost of the book. It is also a great place to get your collecting interests listed.

Lehner, Lois. *Lehner's Encyclopedia of U.S. Marks on Pottery, Porcelain, & Clay.* **Paducah, KY: Collector Books, 1988.**

The best reference book for identifying the marks of United States pottery and porcelain manufacturers. It contains detailed company histories and all known marks and trade names used. Whenever possible, marks and trade names are dated.

Kovel, Ralph and Terry. *Kovels' Antiques & Collectibles Fix-It Source Book.* **New York: Crown Publishers, 1990.**

Many flea market treasures have not withstood the test of time well. While they should probably be passed by, they all too often wind up in the hands of a collector. This book provides the options available to have these objects fixed.

Manston, Peter B. *Manston's Flea Markets Antique Fairs and Auctions of Britain.* **Travel Keys (P.O. Box 160691, Sacramento, CA 95816).**

When you are hooked on flea markets, they become part of your blood. Some of the greatest flea markets are in Europe. Peter Manston has written three flea market guides, one each for France, Germany, and Great Britain. Do not go to Europe without them.

Maloney, David. *1992 Collectors' Information Clearinghouse Antiques and Collectibles Resource*

Directory. Radnor, PA: Wallace-Homestead, 1991.

This is the one reference source book to buy when you are only going to buy one. It is a comprehensive directory to the antiques and collectibles field containing approximately 6,000 entries (Name, addresses, telephone numbers, and a wealth of other information) in approximately 1,500 categories. It is fully cross-referenced. It covers buyers, sellers, appraisers, restorers, collectors' clubs, periodicals, museums and galleries, show promoters, shop and malls, and many other specialists.

Miner, Robert G. *The Flea Market Handbook.* Radnor, PA: Wallace-Homestead, 1990.

This book explains how to become a flea market dealer. Collectors should read it to understand the mind set of the flea market dealer. Understanding the dealer makes doing business easier.

Rainwater, Dorothy T. *Encyclopedia of American Silver Manufacturers,* 3rd ed. West Chester, PA: Schiffer Publishing, 1986.

This book focuses on handcrafted and mass-produced factory-manufactured silver and silver plate from the mid-nineteenth century to the present. It is organized alphabetically by company. Each detailed company history is accompanied by carefully drawn and dated marks. A glossary of trademarks is another welcome feature.

Rinker, Harry L. *Rinker on Collectibles.* Radnor, PA: Wallace-Homestead, 1989.

This book is a compilation of the first sixty text columns from Dad's weekly column, "Rinker on Collectibles." Many are now classics. The book allows you to delve into the mind-set of the collector. It deserves textbook status.

Wanted to Buy, 2nd ed. Paducah, KY: Collector Books, 1989.

This is another book listing individuals who want to buy things. If you are a serious collector, write to Collector Books and see if your name and interests can be included in subsequent editions. The book differs from *I'll Buy That!* because it contains several dozen listings and prices for most categories.

JUST FOR THE FUN OF IT

Gash, Jonathan. *The Sleepers of Erin.* New York: Viking Penguin, 1983.

If you are unfamiliar with Lovejoy the antiques dealer, it is time you make his acquaintance. You will not regret it. I had a hard time picking a favorite. I could just have easily chosen *The Judas Pair, Gold by Gemini, The Grail Tree, Spend Game, The Vatican Rip,* and *The Gondola Scam,* all in paperback from Viking Penguin. *The Tartan Sell, Moonspender,* and *Pearlhanger* are in hardcover from St. Martin's Press.

Rinker, Harry L. *The Joy of Collecting with Craven Moore.* Radnor, PA: Wallace-Homestead, 1985.

Try never to become so serious about your collecting or dealing that you forget to laugh and have fun. Find out if you are Craven or Anita Moore or Howie and Constance Lee Bys. You are in *The Joy of Collecting with Craven Moore.* I guarantee it.

WALLACE-HOMESTEAD COLLECTOR'S GUIDE SERIES

These books do not appear on the above list because they are not general reference or price-oriented books. However, if you decided to collect actively in any of these category areas, they are must-reads. My Dad is as proud of his role as series editor for these books as he is of developing the Warman format. Read a few titles. You will see why:

Anderson, Suzy. *Collector's Guide to Quilts* (1991).
Bagdade, Susan and Al. *Collector's Guide to Toy Trains* (1990).
Hegenberger, John. *Collector's Guide to Comic Books* (1990).
Hegenberger, John. *Collector's Guide to Treasures from the Silver Screen* (1991).
Kirk, Troy. *Collector's Guide to Baseball Cards* (1990).
Mace, O. Henry. *Collector's Guide to Early Photographs* (1990).
Mace, O. Henry. *Collector's Guide to Victoriana* (1991).
Rinker, Harry L. *Collector's Guide to Toys, Games, and Puzzles* (1991).
Sanders, George and Helen, and Ralph Roberts. *Collector's Guide to Autographs* (1991).

Antiques and Collectibles Trade Papers

NATIONAL

American Collector's Journal
P.O. Box 407
Kewanee, IL 61443
(309) 852-2602

Antique Monthly
2100 Powers Ferry Road
Atlanta, GA 30339
(404) 955-5656

The Antique Trader Weekly
P.O. Box 1050
Dubuque, IA 52004
(319) 588-2073

Antique Week (Central and Eastern Edition)
27 North Jefferson Street
P.O. Box 90
Knightstown, IN 46148
1-800-876-5133

Antiques & the Arts Weekly
Bee Publishing Company
5 Church Hill Road
Newtown, CT 06470
(203) 426-3141

Collector News
506 Second Street
Grundy Center, IA 50638
(319) 824-6981

Maine Antique Digest
P.O. Box 645
Waldoboro, ME 04572
(207) 832-4888 or 832-7341

REGIONAL

New England

Cape Cod Antiques & Arts
Register Newspaper
P.O. Box 400
Yarmouth Port, MA 02675
(508) 362-2111

MassBay Antiques
North Shores Weekly
9 Page Street
P.O. Box 293
Danvers, MA 01923
(508) 777-7070 or (617) 289-6961

New England Antiques Journal
4 Church Street
Ware, MA 01082
(413) 967-3505

Middle Atlantic States

Antiques & Auction News
P.O. Box 500
Mount Joy, PA 17552
(717) 653-9797

The Collector's Marketplace
P.O. Box 25
Stewartsville, NJ 08886
(201) 479-4614

Eastern Seaboard Antique Monthly
3611 Autumn Glen Circle
Burtonsville, MD 20866
(301) 890-0214

The New York Antique Almanac of Art, Antiques, Investments & Yesteryear
The N.Y. Eye Publishing Co.
P.O. Box 335
Lawrence, NY 11559
(516) 371-3300

New York-Pennsylvania Collector
Drawer C
Fishers, NY 14453
(716) 924-4040

Renninger's Antique Guide
P.O. Box 495
Lafayette Hill, PA 19444
(215) 828-4614 or 825-6392

Treasure Chest
253 West 72nd Street, #211A
New York, NY 10023
(212) 496-2234

South

The Antique Press
12403 North Florida Avenue
Tampa, FL 33612
(813) 935-7577

Antiques & Crafts Gazette
P.O. Box 181
Cumming, GA 30130
(404) 887-3563

Cotton & Quail Antique Trail
205 East Washington Street
P.O. Box 326
Monticello, FL 32344
(904) 997-6759

The MidAtlantic Antiques Magazine
Henderson Daily Dispatch Company
304 South Chestnut Street
P.O. Box 908
Henderson, NC 27536
(919) 492-4001

The Old News Is Good News Antiques Gazette
4928 Government Street
P.O. Box 65292
Baton Rouge, LA 70896
(504) 923-0575 or 923-0576

Southern Antiques
P.O. Drawer 1107
Decatur, GA 30031
(404) 289-0054

Midwest

The American Collector
P.O. Box 686
Southfield, MI 48037
(313) 351-9910

The Antique Collector and Auction Guide
Weekly Section of Farm and Dairy
P.O. Box 38
Salem, OH 44460
(216) 337-3419

Antique Gazette
6949 Charlotte Pike, Suite 106
Nashville, TN 37209
(615) 352-0941

Antique Review
12 East Stafford Street
P.O. Box 538
Worthington, OH 43085
(614) 885-9757

The Buckeye Marketeer
P.O. Box 954
Westerville, OH 43081
(614) 895-1663

Collectors Journal
1800 West D Street
P.O. Box 601
Vinton, IA 52349
(319) 472-4763

Collectors' Marketplace
P.O. Box 975
Rootstown, OH 44272
(216) 325-7892

Ohio Collectors' Magazine
P.O. Box 66
Mogadore, OH 44260
(216) 633-1865

Yesteryear
P.O. Box 2
Princeton, WI 54968
(414) 787-4808

Southwest

Antique & Collector's Guide
8510 Frazier Drive
Beaumont, TX 77707
(409) 866-7224

Arizona Antiques News and Southwest Antiques
    Journal
P.O. Box 26536
Phoenix, AZ 85068
(602) 943-9137

Rocky Mountain States

Mountain States Collector
P.O. Box 2525
Evergreen, CO 80439

West Coast

Antique & Collectibles
Californian Publishing Co.
1000 Pioneer Way
P.O. Box 1565
El Cajon, CA 92022
(619) 593-2925

Antiques Today
Kruse Publishing
16430 Creekside Drive
Sonora, CA 95370
(209) 532-8870

Antiques West
P.O. Box 2828
San Anselmo, CA 94960

West Coast Peddler
P.O. Box 5134
Whittier, CA 90607
(213) 698-1718

Index